LOCAL AUTHORITY BORROWING

LOCAL AUTHORITY BORROWING

PAST, PRESENT AND
──FUTURE──

SIR HARRY PAGE, MA(Admin.), IPFA

Formerly City Treasurer, Manchester
Past President of the Chartered Institute of
Public Finance and Accountancy

London
GEORGE ALLEN & UNWIN
Boston   Sydney

George Allen & Unwin (Publishers) Ltd,
40 Museum Street, London WC1A 1LU, UK

George Allen & Unwin (Publishers) Ltd,
Park Lane, Hemel Hempstead, Herts HP2 4TE, UK

Allen & Unwin, Inc.,
8 Winchester Place, Winchester, Mass. 01890, USA

George Allen & Unwin Australia Pty Ltd,
8 Napier Street, North Sydney, NSW 2060, Australia

First published in 1985

British Library Cataloguing in Publication Data

Page, *Sir* Harry
  Local authority borrowing: past, present and future
1. Local finance — Great Britain — History
2. Debts, Public — Great Britain — History
I. Title
336.3'431'41   HJ9431
ISBN 0-04-352218-1

Library of Congress Cataloging in Publication Data

Page, Harry, Sir, 1911-1985
  Local authority borrowing.
Bibliography: p.
Includes index
1. Debts, Public — Great Britain — History
2. Local finance — Great Britain — History. I. Title
HJ9421.P34 1985   336.3'431'41   85-18661
ISBN 0-04-352218-1 (alk. paper)

Set in 10 on 11½ point Sabon by Columns of Reading
and printed in Great Britain by
Mackays of Chatham

SIR HARRY PAGE

An appreciation by Noel Hepworth, Director, CIPFA

In this country we are all of us fortunate that the public service has attracted so many fine men and women. In this uncertain world the security of the integrity of the public services contributes much to a civilized society.

Sir Harry Page was one of the great men of local government. He was a determined innovator and he applied his considerable talents with dedication, energy and success.

His talents were not only recognized in Manchester where he became City Treasurer in 1957, but also nationally. He was appointed in 1962 as the senior financial adviser to the Association of Municipal Corporations. During his period as senior financial adviser, which lasted until 1970, central–local government co-operation reached its peak and yet he was never seduced by central government. However, he was always a realist about local government and saw that it had to change to survive.

When Sir Harry Page was appointed City Treasurer of Manchester, he became closely involved with capital finance and this, coupled with his concern for simplification and his creativity, led to the development of a major new borrowing instrument for local government – the bond. The bond emerged as a mechanism above all other borrowing mechanisms. Through its use local government could borrow the vast sums it needed at the lowest price and administrative cost, to finance the demanded growth in public services.

The bond established his already growing reputation in the City of London, and on his retirement from the post of City Treasurer he joined Long, Till & Colvin (subsequently Butler Till), London money brokers, as a director. He was also appointed by the then Chancellor of the Exchequer as the chairman of a committee to consider the future role and development of the national savings movement and the Trustee Savings Banks. The Page Report was a *tour de force* and his committee's recommendations led directly to the Trustee Savings Bank Act 1976, which created the Trustee Savings Banks as a major force in British banking.

Harry Page was elected an Associate of the Institute of Municipal Treasurers and Accountants in 1938. He became a Fellow in 1957. He was voted on to the Council of the Institute in 1960, and in 1968 he was elected President. He dominated the Council table by sheer professional stature and his pervading interest in local government finance. He was awarded a knighthood before he was elected President, something unique in the history of Presidents of this Institute.

He encouraged the development of the Institute and its services and he welcomed and supported the widening role reflected in its changed name as the Chartered Institute of Public Finance and Accountancy.

The culmination of Sir Harry's knowledge and experience was his preparation as an honorary Simon Research Fellow of Manchester University of this substantive authoritative review of local authority borrowing. This is an original and monumental work and Manchester University, in recognition of Sir Harry's outstanding contribution to public service and local government finance, had agreed to award him the degree of an honorary Doctor of Social Science. Sadly Sir Harry Page died on New Year's Day 1985.

Acknowledgement by CIPFA

A professional institute is a product of the energies, ambitions, talents and, perhaps, above all, integrity of its members. They create a public reputation and hence public recognition of the contribution that an institute can make to society, for a professional institute is there to serve society not itself.

Sir Harry Page was a most distinguished Past President of the Chartered Institute of Public Finance and Accountancy. He contributed greatly to its success. The Institute is delighted that he and the chairman and directors of Butler Till Ltd (a firm of great integrity and repute and of long standing in the service of local authority capital finance) have on the publication of this major work on local authority borrowing offered it as a tribute to the culmination of one hundred years of development by the Institute. The Institute welcomes the singular tribute to its centenary in the publication of this volume.

N. P. HEPWORTH

CONTENTS

To my Wife

PREFACE

When in 1971 I retired from the Manchester City Treasurership (after forty-two years in that one department), I had two strokes of good fortune: the first was to be offered the chairmanship of the Chancellor's Committee to Review National Savings (which reported two years later to considerable effect), the second was in being invited to join the local authority money-broking firm of Butler Till Ltd (previously Long, Till & Colvin). I remained with them for some ten years, a happy and rewarding experience. During that time I produced the handbook *Money Services for Local Authorities*, a work originally undertaken as a means of enabling me to improve my grasp of the minutiae of local authority borrowing, but which after three painfully evolved editions ultimately gained acceptance as a detailed and authoritative vade-mecum of the day-to-day operations and the current underlying statutory provisions of local authority borrowing. This became for some years the source of reference for local authority loans offices, relevant government departments and many London financial institutions of all sorts and degrees (including, we have been led to believe, the Bank of England).

The search for 'historic origins' in the National Savings' Review (which in one aspect – the Trustee Savings Banks – went back to the beginning of the nineteenth century), and my pursuit of the precise statutory authority for current local authority borrowing practices, were both experiences which gave me an insatiable curiosity about the remote origins of the local authority system of capital finance. Encouraged by an honorary Simon Fellowship at Manchester University, I therefore set out to make what I intended to be an exhaustive study of the history of the subject into which events had led me. After some ten years of intermittent labour, I concede that what I have produced, from vast areas of what was once *terra incognita* to me, can be regarded only as a broad survey and the most that I can claim for it is that I have probably opened doors into areas which others may now be encouraged to explore more fully.

I have also to admit to a 'missionary motive' in writing this book. During my later years in Manchester I had been involved in the rationalization of the ancient form of mortgage, the reintroduction of the money bill and the launching of the modern concept of the bond and its derivative, the negotiable bond (and, on the other side of the coin, the introduction of local authority pension funds to the equity market). As financial adviser to the Association of Municipal Corporations I had also taken an active part in the consultations which led to the acceptance of the 'permanent' nature of 'temporary' borrowing. When the Local Government Act 1972 saw the light of day, I felt that it failed adequately to encompass these changes. My attempts through *Money Services* to urge a further and more penetrating rethinking of the local authority borrowing code were largely unsuccessful. I have therefore used this book to restate my case, and to base this case more firmly on historical origins and to make sure that my personal version of these experiences are recorded with such objectivity as I can muster.

I have owed a great deal over the past dozen years to the friendships which I have established in the Butler Till office. I am now further indebted to Butler's for their sponsorship of this book on a subject which, though of considerable economic importance, is in a highly specialized field and likely to have a limited appeal. Butler's are undertaking this sponsorship because they have long operated a commendable policy of contributing some of their earnings to the better understanding of the markets in which they work, and because they wish to make some tangible expression of their felicitations to the Chartered Institute of Public Finance and Accountancy on the attainment of its hundredth anniversary. I am highly delighted by this happy coincidence of events. Both Butler Till and I myself take this opportunity of offering warmest congratulations to the Institute on its magnificent achievements over this long period.

Readers will find that, as is my practice, I do not plunge straight into the subject. I prefer to spend some time – perhaps too much – in setting the scene, moving gradually into the heart of the matter. My early chapters are therefore to some extent a history of emerging local government and particularly of the changing area structure. Nor have I hesitated to go outside the theme of borrowing where I feel that this aspect would be better understood against a broader background. Local authority borrowing practitioners have managed very well so far without a detailed historical understanding of their expertise; nevertheless, I feel that things would have been better in the past, and will be better in the future (if there is to be a future for local government), if the origins of what we do – and the mistakes which both we and central government have made – are better understood.

H. R. PAGE
Fallowfield, Manchester
December 1984

ACKNOWLEDGEMENTS

Very many people – treasurers and their staffs, local history librarians, city and county archivists and others – have aided me in this research by replying with understanding and patience to my various importunings. I hope that I have adequately acknowledged such help where the subject-matter occurs throughout the text, but there are some names which I must specifically record here, of people who have helped me in a more general but material way to such understanding as I have of municipal capital finance.

First, I must mention three colleagues from the Manchester Loans Office whose support to me on borrowing issues both before and after my retirement was most loyal and valuable; these are John Swift, Philip Rogers and Donald Foley. And I must add to these the name of a member of the Town Clerk's Department, Arthur Fellows, Assistant Town Clerk and parliamentary expert, for his enterprise and guidance in obtaining the various statutory powers on loan matters which we developed in Manchester and which eventually stimulated my determination to write this book.

The contemporary municipal treasurer who in my view best combines knowledge and understanding of the basic philosophy, history and current practices of local authority borrowing is Norman Sage, formerly treasurer of Bullingdon RDC. He has been unsparing in his help to me, latterly at a time of great personal stress; his store of information and appreciation of the past, and his willingness to share these, have placed me under a great debt. Moreover, his book *Local Authority Capital Finance* has been an important and constant source of reference.

My colleagues at Butler Till Ltd have not only taught me a great deal about the operations of the London capital market, but much encouraged me in pursuing this research. I must refer specifically to Peter Clayton, then chairman and managing director and now a close personal friend, who first took me aboard, and to John White and Robert Bell, both friends of long standing (and both of whom are now launched on their own account). For the sponsorship I am greatly indebted to the present management – Don Turner, Gerry Wilton and, in particular, Chas Dobson – with whom I have established a very happy relationship. There are many others on the 'dealing desk' whose friendship and confidence I am pleased to share.

The secretary to the PWLC, Peter Goodwin, another friend over a long period, and his colleagues, have given me much valuable information – on the unearthing of which they must have spent a good deal of time and effort. A lady to whom I would especially like to express my thanks for encouragement in my early days in the local authority borrowing field is

Miss Joan Kelly of HM Treasury. We did not always see eye to eye, but our shared Manchester origin was a great help.

I would like to acknowledge the considerable assistance I have derived from the facilities offered by the Manchester Central Reference Library and its staff, and in particular J. Horton, who gave me much valuable help in my trawl through the public statutes. I have also, of course, found invaluable the resources of the Manchester University John Rylands Library. There was very little of what I sought which could not be found in one or other (often both) of these repositories.

The book which, of all those I have used, was of the greatest help was *Loans of Local Authorities*, by J. R. Johnson, former City Treasurer of Birmingham. I wish he had been alive today to know of my appreciation. *Municipal Capital Finance*, by A. B. Griffiths, one-time treasurer of Sheffield, has also been a useful aid.

I must also acknowledge my indebtedness to the Vice-Chancellor of Manchester University and the members of the Simon Fellowship Committee for the access to university resources which the granting of an Honorary Fellowship gave me, and their patience in extending this privilege over so many years.

Finally, I am grateful to my younger son, Oliver Page, for his painstaking scrutiny of the typescript, for his comments as an economist on my somewhat pragmatic concept of interest and his delving on my behalf into early statutes in the House of Lords Record Office. (My elder son, Andrew Page, FCA, would have wished to be equally helpful, I know, had his health permitted it.) My appreciation of my wife's support I hope that I have indicated in the dedication. She has shared the burden and turmoil of this book with me over a period of years which, though filled with many new experiences, have at times also been fraught with quite considerable problems for us both.

H. R. PAGE

LIST OF ABBREVIATIONS

The following are the main abbreviations used in this book:

CBC   County Borough Council
CC   County Council
CLF   Consolidated Loans Fund
DOE   Department of the Environment
GLC   Greater London Council
IMTA Institute of Municipal Treasurers and Accountants
CIPFA Chartered Institute of Public Finance and Accountancy
LCC   London County Council
MBW Metropolitan Board of Works
NCB   Non-County Borough Council
PWLB } Public Works Loan Commission or Board
PWLC }
RDC   Rural District Council
UDC   Urban District Council

PART ONE

Preliminary Considerations

INTRODUCTION

The local government authorities in this country have been borrowers of money on the open market for at least three centuries; the point has long ago been reached at which the scale of this activity and the resultant debt have a material impact on the national economy. This book explores the history of the statutory powers granted by the central government authority – the sovereign in Parliament – to the administrators of the subordinate local government authorities, permitting such local authorities to finance defined (capital) portions of their expenditure initially from money borrowed at interest rather than directly from current revenue, and subject to amortization over specified periods. The origins and development of the techniques used in the process of longer-term finance are traced to the present day, and the ways are examined in which (and the constraints and stimulations under which) the local government authorities have exercised the facility to borrow. This examination concludes with suggestions for the rationalization of current practices derived from the experience of the past and against the background of current trends in national and international finance. In this book borrowing is not treated as an isolated independent theme or operation, but in its context as an integrated and evolving function of local government administration.

Local government of a kind was operative long before borrowing was officially resorted to as a method of finance. The areas, and even the names, on which local government was – and by and large still is – administered similarly long preceded the introduction of capital financing methods, and to some extent preceded even organized revenue taxation for local purposes.

For better or worse, the view is here taken that, for a proper understanding of the subject, the evolution of local government needs to be visualized as a coherent whole from which emerges at a specific date and for logical reasons, the acceptance of the principle of finance of certain types of expenditure by borrowing, and resulting in the spread of the cost over users during a period of years ahead. The book begins therefore with a brief description of the creation of an area structure for local government and the gradual devolution on to the local authorities of a growing volume of responsibilities; alas, this long-term trend has been followed in quite recent times by a withdrawal of major duties from the local administrations and an increase in the pressure of central government dominance of locally administered activities!

British local government authorities are clearly to be seen as bodies which the central authority – the Crown – has selected to carry out certain of its decisions. In the ultimate these local bodies are exercising not their own authority, but powers devolved from the centre, and may operate only within this area of devolution. Even though they are given degrees of discretion, the local bodies must work *intra vires* and cannot branch out into other activities at their own will except by an Act of the central government granting permission for the undertaking of such activities. Such responsibilities, when created, are exercised 'by permission' of the central government. But the essence of the system is that although the powers administered are those specified or approved by the central power, the people charged with their administration are local. Sometimes these local administrators are selected centrally, sometimes locally. Thus the ancient sheriff (shire reeve), a once-powerful local official vestiges of whom still remain in the judicial system, was a local resident but centrally appointed and fully accountable to the central authority. There is a parallel in the justices of the peace – influential local officials on whom powers of the Crown have been devolved, but who remain answerable to the Crown as an integral part of the system for the administration of justice (initially for far wider purposes). In due course the local government administrators came to be wholly appointed not by central nomination, but by local democratic election – mainly by stages from the 1830s and principally from the 1880s – but even from the start there was a distinctly democratic element in the system, in that the boroughs and parishes though working within functions defined by central government were administered by local people locally selected, on however rough-and-ready a basis.

Among inherent problems the definitions of what should properly be regarded as a local authority and of what constitutes capital expenditure have, by the application of a somewhat pragmatical approach, proved less difficult than expected. Any organized body locally administering services which in due course became the official responsibility of a duly elected and statutory local authority has been adopted herein from its beginnings as an embryo or quasi-local authority. The obvious example is the county, an area which although administered by non-elective magistrates from the thirteenth century until 1888, then became a wholly recognized and defined elective local authority, and remains so, of high status and responsibility. Charter boroughs, also of early origin, have their counterparts today, however shadowy these may now seem. Even the parish, though later re-designated administrative rather than ecclesiastical, was from early times a unit of administration (and with something of an elective basis) within the county, and continues both to retain an identity and constitute the building-blocks of the present structure. All of these are clearly entitled to recognition as having been local authorities for some five hundred years or more. A departure from this pragmatic approach which should perhaps at least be mentioned is that early charities for the care of children and the foundation of hospitals, which in the mid-twentieth century were functions transferred to the local authorities, have not been treated as embryo local authorities.

The turnpike trusts, which played an important role in the introduction of borrowing, are less clearly recognizable directly as local authorities.

Nevertheless, here they have been so considered because they came into being as non-profit-making bodies with the task of improving the quality of the work which should have been performed (under statute, however unrealistic) by the parishes; moreover, the work performed by the trusts later became a major local authority responsibility and ultimately, in considerable part, a direct responsibility of central government. River navigation and harbour authorities, many of which bear a striking resemblance to turnpike trusts, are also treated as local authorities in so far as they evolved – as they frequently did – in co-operation with more easily recognizable local authorities, notably the boroughs.

On the other hand, the canal companies (and of course the railway companies) which were in the main profit-directed are not here recognized as local authorities because their function was not one which ultimately descended on the later statutory authorities. The intermediate trading undertakings – for water, gas, electricity and transport and others – many of which were in due course taken over by the local authorities (though some remained until recent nationalizations in private hands), are regarded as local authorities only to the extent that this transference later took place. Recognition of this borderline status assists rather than confuses the study of early borrowing.

There were other bodies which clearly must be regarded as true, if primitive, local authorities. The early Poor Law incorporations were simply combinations of parishes for more effective operation (including borrowing), and the Poor Law unions which followed them equally so, and even more entitled to recognition as perhaps the first specifically created statutory local authorities on a national framework. The overseers, really an offshoot of the parishes, but later in some instances (in the larger cities) separate entitites, positioned between the local authorities and the Boards of Guardians, may be recognized as local authorities in their own right, though their impact on the history of borrowing is negligible. Improvement, police and other commissioners, and the various groupings of parishes into highway and local sanitary and health authorities, which in due course became the urban and rural district councils, and in due course again the present district councils, are equally clearly stages in the evolution of organized local government.

On the whole, the later concept of a local authority as a body financed by the levy of a local rate – or with power to levy a rate (either directly or by precept) – would suffice to cover the majority of the types of organization covered in this book. This broad definition would however, in the early period, be subject to the exception of the turnpike trusts and some harbour and navigation authorities; although trading undertakings were expected to rely on their revenues rather than on the rate levy (in so far as they are of interest here), they were organized by bodies which were rate dependent. The counties present a difficulty, in that in the pre-1888 period they were administered by the magistrates in quarter and petty sessions. While involved in the rate-making process, and financing some of their own responsibilities by dependence on a rate, the magistrates are very much on the fringe of this general definition, yet clearly bona fide local authorities in respect of their administrative as distinct from judicial function.

From the dawn of local government, as here recognized, until today three principles of an almost constitutional nature have applied to the financial aspect of the system:

(1) Because the right to levy taxes was the fiscal prerogative of the Crown, no compulsory local tax could be levied without statutory authority. (There were some modifications of this rule in the charter boroughs which for a time had curious local taxing powers partly derived from the remote past, and partly from the bargain through which they achieved their charter rights.) There were two aspects: the right to levy a local tax, and the amount of tax (or at least the upper limits) which might be levied. Thus the early Poor Law legislation gave a right to levy a rate, but the amount of this was, at least theoretically, subject to the approval of the centrally appointed magistrates. The control of rate impact by central government lapsed or was considerably modified in due course, but at present is being reimposed in the name of economic stability.

(2) Consequently, borrowing to finance expenditure, although it avoided the immediate levying of a rate, was a commitment to a future rate and was therefore also subject to approval by the central authority as to amount and purpose, and for most of the time provision for amortization.

(3) Borrowing for revenue purposes was never given approval until recent times, and then only within the financial year as a cash-flow measure.

The application of these principles might be expected to have required a definition of capital expenditure and a clear specification of the reasons which could justify the spread of part of the cost over future generations of ratepayers. In fact capital expenditure has never been precisely defined. The problem is considered more fully later, but the simple pragmatic solution for which there has been a surprising consensus of opinion over the centuries has been that borrowing might take place for such projects whose cost the appropriate minister of the Crown considered might with justice be spread over a number of years. Only in the latest (1980) interpretations of this approach have detailed lists been formulated of what central government considers to be expenditure of a capital nature. The point is that what was at issue until very recently was not whether expenditure was of a 'capital nature', but whether the local authority wished to borrow to finance it – and if so, whether the minister considered that this project was one the cost of which should be shared by future generations. Any expenditure – whatever its nature – financed directly from revenue was of little concern to the central authority so long as it was *intra vires*; at the present time central government has assumed a direct interest in the total volume of local authority capital investment for a number of reasons, irrespective of the mode of finance.

Various reasons for finance by borrowing emerge in later chapters, but the three principal justifications have been that:

(1) revenue to pay for a project could not reasonably be collected until the project had been completed – turnpikes are the obvious example of this, so that borrowing to carry out the substantial repair or restructuring of a road was bound to precede the levying of tolls;

(2) the cost of a project likely to be quickly completed but of a long-enduring nature simply would be too heavy to be met by the ratepayers of a single year, and should therefore be spread over a number of years by initial borrowing;

(3) as a corollary of this and irrespective of the avoidance of immediate burden, borrowing with deferred repayment has been considered to be justified for projects from which the ratepayers of more than one year, or more than one generation, will derive benefit; such future generations of users should share the cost of the assets the use of which they enjoy.

These three reasons for borrowing might perhaps be called the 'classic' argument, the 'practical' argument and the 'philosophic' justification. The third – the 'philosophic' – argument is the one generally assumed today in support of finance by borrowing but, reasonable though it may seem, it has limited validity where there is continuing expansion of demand for the provision of capital assets. There is evidence that this principle has been pushed too far, with central government approval, from a desire to stimulate the speedy introduction or development of a service with avoidance of immediate excessive cost. When borrowing for the 'reasonable life' of the asset stretches to sixty or even eighty years, regardless of technological development, future generations – who will have their own problems – may feel less than gratitude to their predecessors for this inheritance. Moreover, as will be shown, future generations can be left to bear what they may feel is an unreasonable share of the cost simply by the manipulation of methods of amortization weighted against early extinction of debt. Whether inflation really reduces the burden of debt is another issue. In fact the line between maintenance revenue expenditure and true capital expenditure is a fine one at the point of interface; the stage at which maintenance involves major improvement, which in turn rises to the status of new capital works, is not open to exact definition.

The inherent problems therefore of what is capital expenditure and what justifies the bearing of the cost from money borrowed at interest are also seen to have been solved pragmatically. That money borrowed was subject to interest is not so self-evident. Theoretically, prior to the reign of Henry VIII, usury – simply a charge for the use of money – had been forbidden since 1179 on religious grounds, arising from the so-called Deuteronomic Prohibition of Usury. In practice, usury was rampant, either overtly or covertly, by many ingenious devices (much as agile minds today seek methods of tax avoidance). In an attempt at compromise in 1545 – a date close to the birth of local government in the modern sense – Henry VIII,* while still condemning usury, authorized the charging of a maximum interest rate of 10 per cent per annum. In 1552 his successor, Edward VI, said that Henry's compromise 'be utterly abrogate void and repealed', interest charging thus again being forbidden. In 1571 Elizabeth sadly admitted, in reference to Edward's prohibition, 'which latter Act hath not done so much good as was hoped it should', and despite 'all usury being forbidden by the laws of God is sin and detestable', reinstated (but in a somewhat vacillating manner) her father's concession of 'X li. for the lone of C li. for a yere'. James I in 1623 reduced this to 8 per cent; in 1651 a Commonwealth Ordinance reduced the 8 per cent to 6 per cent, and in 1660 this was reluctantly confirmed by the Parliament of Charles II; in 1713 a final reduction to 5 per cent was introduced. This was not abolished (despite powerful arguments for abolition by such people as Jeremy Bentham in his *Defence of Usury*, 1778) until 1854. Hence the frequent references in statutes prior to this final date to borrowing and the charging of 'interest at legal or lesser rates'.[1]

A confusion in terms is to be seen throughout local authority borrowing legislation which has led to much unnecessary labour in loans administration and to delay in the rationalized treatment of borrowed funds. This is the confusion between the period for which the incurring of a debt is sanctioned, and over which provision must be made for its amortization, and the periods for which individual lenders lend their money to the local borrower. The two periods may coincide, and when the loan is repayable by equal annual instalments, this constitutes the simplest financial arrangement – money borrowed for the same period as that for which the debt has been sanctioned, and an equal portion of the liability charged annually against revenue and repaid each year directly to the lender along with interest on the declining balance. But usually the periods will not coincide and the number of years for which the money is borrowed from the lender will frequently be far shorter than the loan sanction period in which the annual amortization provision is being made from revenue for the ultimate discharge of the debt. Thus the initial borrowing will fall to be repaid and replaced by further borrowing – 'rolled over' – involving a succession of re-borrowings, though each for a slightly less amount in so far as some annual amortization will have been set aside from year one.

If a loan sanction for twenty/thirty/forty years is given, for which one twentieth/thirtieth/fortieth is set aside each year for its ultimate discharge (accumulations from the investment of sinking funds being ignored) and if the initial borrowing has, say, a five-year maturity period, whether repayable in annual instalments or at the end of the period, there is never available until the end of the full loan sanction period sufficient money set

---

* The statutory references for all Acts quoted are given chronologically at the conclusion of this book.

aside from revenue to discharge the debt entirely. The initial borrowing for a 20/30/40 loan sanction may be for a very few years – indeed in modern practice even 'overnight' at some stage of the transaction – in the expectation that fresh borrowing will be readily available to replace it at a new 'going rate' at each maturity or 'roll-over' date of the original borrowing: pious though such hope may be, this is the system which has worked satisfactorily for centuries without serious difficulty. If this difference and its implications had been clearly recognized from the start of borrowing, a much simpler and more rational system would have evolved sooner than it did. The failure in legislation to dissociate the lending period from the loan sanction period, and to recognize the consequences of this disassociation, has led to great complexity in loan administration and volumes of unnecessary work, the earmarking and reinvestment of sinking funds, and arguments about the validity of the re-use of sinking funds for new capital works (the ultimate acceptance of which principle was in fact an unrecognized acceptance of the lack of any real link between period borrowed and period of amortization). This confusion of thought was not finally resolved until as recently as 1972 when the device of the consolidated loans fund was at last given full statutory sanction. In this book therefore the period for which money is lent will be referred to as the lending or maturity period, and the period over which the debt may be amortized from revenue as the loan sanction, redemption, or amortization period.[2]

While in the course of this inquiry an extensive search of the statute-books has been made from earliest times for measures applicable to local government in which reference to borrowing might occur, a problem has been created by the great volume of statute law which is in private local Acts applicable only to individual local authorities. The quantity of these local Acts has been such (particularly since the beginning of the nineteenth century) that parliamentary decisions have been made to restrict their inclusion in the printed statute-books. Because of the volume of these special statutes and their consequential difficulty of access, even the Webbs in their monumental history, *English Local Government*, confessed their inability to make a completely exhaustive review.[3]

None of the early statutes giving general powers to parish, borough and county administrations conferred powers to finance capital expenditure by borrowing, yet during the same period there were many Acts of local application which did give such powers. Even when general statutes relating to borrowing became common, variations and innovations continued to find place in local Acts down to modern times. Indeed only since the passing of the Local Government Act 1972 (which can scarcely be accepted, for reasons which will be given, as the last word in local authority borrowing provisions) has the Department of the Environment sought to discourage local authorities from extending their financial powers by local legislation.[4] Experimentation in local Acts has been of the utmost importance in the development of local government in every sphere, and especially in capital finance.

Those local Acts with borrowing provisions which have been identified are examined in due course but the problem is to decide whether the early local Act borrowing powers examined hereafter are indeed the earliest or the most significant; the suspicion must persist that there may be other local Acts giving significant relevant powers which have not been brought to light. Some assurance may be derived from the relative simplicity of these early powers, which suggests their novelty; that is, there is no sudden adoption of complex powers which appear without evolutionary precedent. The same problem does not arise (or if it does only minimally) with early rating law, where the powers have always been given in the general law and significant local variations not permitted.

A practice developed in the later eighteenth and first half of the nineteenth centuries of concluding local Acts with the words 'This Act shall be deemed to be a public Act and be judicially noticed as such' (which still did not ensure printing along with the public general Acts) arose because in so far as local Act powers were additional to, or amended, general statutes, they were to that degree contrary to general law, so that judges were prone to require excessive proof of their validity if any point came before the courts. The inclusion of this clause did not wholly alleviate this judicial concern. From 1850 (Lord Brougham's Act) the more generous principle was adopted that every Act is a public Act unless the contrary is expressed in the Act; this principle was followed in the Interpretation Act 1889, and reaffirmed as recently as 1978 in the Interpretation Act of that year, but this still did not result in the inclusion of Acts of a local character in the general statutes.[5]

The Turnpike Acts provide a good example of private local Act procedure; although in the course of time there were a number of general Turnpike Acts, each of the many hundreds of turnpike trusts was created, amended and extended by private Act. Fortunately there was much copying of standard provisions (including financial) from one Act to another, a feature of all local legislation, though subtle and significant differences, easily overlooked, can occur from time to time.

Access to the statutes gives us of course far less than the full story; there is a need to know why statutory powers were sought and what use was made of them. What problems were encountered? Answers to such questions as these are difficult to obtain even for recent borrowing legislation and virtually impossible for ancient activities. There is undoubtedly much to be found by examination of council records and abstracts of account, but the availability of much of this has been made difficult by subsequent local government reorganizations and would in any event present an overwhelming task, except on a much-narrowed field. The obtaining by a local authority of financial powers does not necessarily mean that these powers were utilized. Why, for example, did the treasurer of Swansea launch a campaign in 1923 for the creation of a 'true consolidated loans fund' and yet – although his arguments were widely accepted – not seek such powers for his own borough until twenty years later? Why did Torquay obtain such powers in 1923 but delay putting

them into operation until after Leeds had done so with powers obtained
only in 1927? Why did the several authorities who had all the necessary
bond powers before Manchester in 1961 fail to see the opportunity for
issuing a negotiable bond? Much less important in practice, but no less
fascinating, what was the outcome of the various borrowings by tontine,
and why did several authorities who obtained such powers baulk at using
them? On a broader plane what internal struggles in government circles
led to the production of two Acts with such a different approach to
borrowing as the Local Loans Act and the Public Health Act both of
1875? How, despite the general view of its unworkability even from the
start, have the provisions of the Local Loans Act retained a place in
current local authority borrowing legislation? Most of these and many
other fascinating byways have not been followed through in this book,
though the answers no doubt lie buried in the archives.

One of the peculiarities of the world of borrowing, both in the
commercial and public sectors, is the general lack of statutory or otherwise
precise definitions of terms both for instruments and certain of the
techniques involved. This is possibly because of the considerable antiquity
of these processes. The bill of exchange and the promissory note are
known by every student of finance to be exactly defined in the Bills of
Exchange Act 1882 (though many varieties of bill have evolved within this
definition and much judicial clarification has been necessary). These are
virtually the only two borrowing instruments to be specified precisely in a
statute (except to the extent that pro forma documents to be used, 'or to
the like effect', are frequently given in schedules to the Acts). The
important word 'debenture', and the scarcely less important terms
'mortgage', 'bond' and 'stock', are not defined in statutory form (and most
certainly not in local government statutes by which they have nevertheless
been adopted), though their attributes and varieties are well established in
common and case law and general practice.

Probably the most misused term of all is 'annuity', which is used in a
general sense in application to an annual payment, and in various specific
senses, one of which (perpetual annuity) does not involve what is usually
regarded as the essence of an annuity – the annual repayment of a portion
of principal. While the method of setting aside or using for annual
repayment an equal part of principal is well known and commonly used,
this is variously referred to as the EIP (equal instalment of principal)
method, the fractional method and even the straight-line method (as this is
how this system would appear in graphical form). This method, annual
repayment with interest on the declining outstanding balance, is certainly a
variety of annuity payment. Yet if the repayment is of such varying portion
of principal as together with interest will give a flat rate of payment of the
two sums combined each year over the life of the loan, this commonly is
referred to specifically as the annuity method but also the equal annual
charge method when applied to systems of redemption. Problems also arise
by confusion of the terms 'negotiable', 'marketable' and 'quoted'
particularly in relation to the bond in local authority use. Even the term

'security' is used in two distinct senses (sometimes in a single section of a statute): first, as a generic name for borrowing instruments; and secondly, in reference to the underlying financial guarantee offered against loans, for example, the rates and revenues.

To be precise, the bill of exchange and its simpler companion are not the only instruments defined by statute. The Statute concerning the Jews 1233 (Henry III) states that:

> no loan may be contracted with Jews by tally, but by chirograph, whose other part the Jew shall have, with the seal of the Christian contracting the loan appended, and the other part let the Christian contracting the loan have. The third part that is called the foot, let that be placed in the chest to be safely held by the chirographers. Christian and Jew, and a chirograph whose foot shall not have been found in the chest shall not be valid.

> No Jew may lend anything by penalty but let him take interest at twopence per pound each week and no more [which amounts to 43% p.a. simple interest] so that nothing is put to hazard save the sum first loaned.

This reference to 'penalty' is relevant to later practices in the use of bonds. The chirograph as a borrowing instrument is therefore clearly defined as a three-part document, the sealed portion given to the lender, a copy retained by the borrower and the third lodged in the hands of the equivalent of the modern registrar. The essence of an efficient borrowing instrument was clearly understood from a very early date.

The above record also illustrates that the system of wooden tallies was in operation by this date. Fortunately tallies play no part in local government financial recording. There is also a record of a two-part chirograph dated 1201. Doubt is expressed among historians as to whether the introduction of a third registered copy was to develop a market in bonds, or to facilitate the collection of a levy by the sovereign on all transactions, the modern equivalent of which was reflected until recently in the stamp duty on borrowing instruments. The suggestion is made that the prohibition of wooden tallies in this process, in 1233, was part of the attempt to prevent avoidance of the sovereign's tax – tax evasion at an early date.[6]

Our study now continues with a brief outline of the emergence and evolution of the units of local government into what has been a strikingly stable system over half a millennium, and of the services which have been allotted among the constituent parts of this system. This description begins at a stage before borrowing (or for a time even before rating) had been contemplated. It leads naturally into the introduction of rating and the emergence of borrowing when rating was found to be an inadequate means for the initial financing of assets of a capital nature. The growing acceptance of borrowing is then followed through in historical sequence beginning with the introduction of turnpike roads.

The limitation of this 'continuous historical' method is that while the growth of the use of borrowing techniques is thus illustrated chronologically, a clear picture of each method of borrowing and the considerations involved in the introduction and growth of each cannot be clearly discerned. This historical sequence is therefore followed by separate examination of each form of instrument from its first appearance to the present day, bringing out more clearly the aspirations of those who introduced the methods and the advantages and shortcomings of each instrument. The structural problem involved may be well illustrated in relation to the Public Works Loan Commissioners (where the surprising discovery is made that the title now in common use – the Public Works Loan Board – has no official justification). The commission, set up in 1817, is referred to from time to time during our historical sequence but is dealt with separately and more coherently in the later section. Likewise while methods of amortization are naturally referred to from time to time in the chronological section, their detailed development into the consolidated loans fund (via mortgage pooling) is also re-examined as an entity separately. Borrowing by bonds, a method found to be in use in early times, requires essentially a reconsideration to show the impact of early usages on the adoption of this technique which occurred in modest fashion in the 1920s and to the point at which it has become the major instrument in the 1980s. Some degree of duplication has been inevitable in this approach.

Sadly but inescapably the impression which emerges from these two strands of historical development is not so much the lack of ideas about methods of local authority borrowing, but the slow, laborious and incoherent manner in which the ideas have been brought to fruition and the lack of a penetrating and fundamental analysis of principle at the various points of change. The delays in the full acceptance of new techniques even after their operation and proved efficiency in limited but adequate experimental areas can only be described as disappointing and disconcerting. This procrastination in the adoption of measures of rationalization, innovation and improvement is partly the result of central government's reluctance to allow freedom of action to local government and a distrust of the efficiency of small-scale administrations, coupled with their own adherence to ancient and outmoded principles, not rethought in the light of changing circumstances and developing markets. It is also in part and most regrettably the outcome of a certain lack of enterprise by local authorities, perhaps partially justifying central government's reluctance to give local authorities greater freedom. However, such lack of enterprise by no means can be attributed to the preponderance of smaller authorities within the system as much of such enterprise as is shown emanates from the smaller authorities.

To take again two subjects mentioned above: the Public Works Loan Commission (PWLC) – not in any way a complex conception – took 150 years to develop to the point at which the commissioners at last seem to feel confidence in local authority capabilities and integrity, despite the *raison d'être* of the commission being to assist local authorities to carry out tasks allotted to them by central government. The consolidated loans fund, another effective but basically simple device, took astonishingly a century to reach full flower from its first tentative appearance, and even half a century from the time when its advantages were fully recognized and its operational techniques comprehended. In consequence, substantial numbers of local Act clauses, with all the expense and labour involved, were needed to give acceptable powers to those local authorities which chose to seek them before the provisions found their way into general legislation. But sometimes even when modernized provisions were available, many treasurers can be seen to have adhered stubbornly to outmoded practices. The value of experimentation can be held to justify some degree of use to local Act procedures, but in no way to the extent which events illustrate. Modern borrowing techniques are still hampered by central government, and in particular Treasury and Bank of England concepts formulated nearly a century ago, some of which have long been seen as anachronistic, and by retention of the vestigial remains of abandoned technique. This lack of dynamism in both central and local government is not confined to the financial issues in local government. Long adherence to the 'sealing' of borrowing instruments, despite the devices used to evade this requirement, and reluctance to recognize the change in the nature of the so-called 'temporary' loan and continued confusion between the mortgage and the bond – matters on which the 'market', which cheerfully continues to call a five-year bond a 'yearling', is not free from responsibility – are all indications of the turgid approach to the subject by some of the professionals. However, if the halting and reluctant nature of their approach to change by all parties involved can be demonstrated, perhaps the outcome may be a more vigorous acceptance of change in the future. (The lines along which the scope for future developments might be considered, together with questions about the propriety of the continuation of borrowing as a technique of local government finance and the validity of the basic principles of redemption, are dealt with in Part 4 of this book.)

NOTES: INTRODUCTION

1   For a fuller examination of the history of restrictions on the admissible rate of interest see my *In Restraint of Usury* (CIPFA, 1985).
2   For comments on this exasperating confusion of thought see, for example, Johnson's *Loans of Local Authorities* (1925), p. 96: 'An important difference exists between the redemption and the repayment of loans, the former consisting of the provision made to extinguish the amount sanctioned for borrowing within the period allowed, whereas repayment consists of the return to the investor of the amount of his investment.' See also A. B. Griffiths, *Municipal Capital Finance* (1936), p. 24: 'the periods for which loans are borrowed do not usually bear any relationship to the periods of the loan sanction . . . repayment and reborrowing in respect of the same sanction may take place on numerous

occasions during the life of the loan sanction.' And see A. Carson Roberts (District Auditor), *Local Administration, Finance and Accounts* (1930), ch. XI, and more particularly his comments on the paper on consolidated loan funds given by R. A. Wetherall (Swansea), 1923, p. 226 of the IMTA Conference Proceedings, 1923: 'The delay in this development [of the CLF] has been attributed to confusion of thought in connection with raising and repaying loans, on the one hand, and spreading capital charges by the help of borrowing powers on the other. The distinction between the obligation to the mortgagees and the obligation to the ratepayers is ... of primary importance ... Unfortunately the expressions which our language provides – "loans", "borrowing" – apply equally to both and that is why the statutory provisions are ambiguous even when it is clear that the distinction was present in the minds of those who framed them.'

3 Sidney and Beatrice Webb, *English Local Government from the Revolution to the Municipal Corporation Act* (9 vols, 1906–29), a monumental work but strangely lacking in references to borrowing.

4 For example: very many local authorities obtained powers by local Act from 1877 onwards to raise money bills (see later). However, general powers for the issue of such bills was not given until 1972. The Local Authorities, etc. (Miscellaneous Provisions) (No. 2) Order 1974 (SI 595) rescinded all these local Act powers on the ground that uniform powers were more appropriate. Authorities have been led to believe that variations of these standard powers will not be welcomed. The Order however permits local authorities to frame their own regulations on the detailed handling of money bills. On the other hand, general powers to establish capital funds leave the many local authorities which have local Act powers for this purpose to operate under those provisions – and presumably to seek amendments to them if they so wish.

5 This practice is examined in Sir P. B. Maxwell's *Interpretation of the Statutes*, 12th edn (London: Sweet & Maxwell, 1969) ed. P. St J. Langan. I am also indebted to W. Wentworth Pritchard, of Sharpe Pritchard & Co., Parliamentary Agents, for guidance on this point.

6 The discovery of the chirograph and the recognition of its striking relevance to modern borrowing was one of the several examples of serendipity occurring during the course of writing this book. The sources are: *English Historical Documents,* vol. 1, pp. 147, 350 (London: Eyre & Spottiswoode,1955) and H. G. Richardson, *English Jewry under the (Angevin Kings* (London: Methuen, 1960), p. 264. An illustration of a chirograph (which simply means a 'handwriting' or a deed) is to be found in W. H. Galbraith, *The Historian at work* (BBC, 1962), taken from the Public Record Office. This (relating to a land rather than a borrowing transaction) shows a sheet of parchment, divided by a horizontal line about one-third of the distance from its foot, with a vertical line dividing the upper portion. The text is written three times in these spaces, and the word 'chyrographum' is inscribed along each of the dividing lines, along which and through the word, the portions are then severed by indentured cuts.

Chapter 1

LOCAL GOVERNMENT AREAS IN ENGLAND AND WALES — A NOTE ON THEIR ORIGINS AND DEVELOPMENT

In 1871 Mr Goschen, in introducing to Parliament proposals on local government areas generally and rating in particular, said in a memorable and oft-quoted rhetorical outburst:[1]

> We have a chaos as regards authorities, a chaos as regards rates and a worse chaos as regards areas . . . every different form of election which it is possible to conceive is applied to the various local authorities who administer the various rates in the various areas.

He might well also have made reference to a confusion of borrowing practices, but his criticism does less than justice to the stability of the framework of local government organization over the centuries. (He might also have acknowledged the long-term stability of the source of finance – the rating system.) The local administration organizational chaos of the mid-nineteenth century, from 1835 to 1888, arose patently because Parliament failed to recognize the great burgeoning of interest in local government which was already under way, and could not be persuaded to continue the rationalization introduced under the Poor Law Amendment Act 1834 and Municipal Corporations Act 1835, themselves the result of the fervour which produced the Reform Act of 1832. The reluctance of the magistrates to relinquish their control of county administration (and to concentrate on their main business of the administration of justice) may well have been the root cause of procrastination on the part of Parliament.[2]

Though greatly confused in detail (not least by variant regional designations), the broad lines are reasonably clear on which present-day local authorities whose titles, territorial demarcations, functions and other features are now so clearly defined by statute, have emerged from the mist of history. From earliest recorded times the units into which the country has been subdivided for judicial, fiscal and embryonic administrative purposes have been the county (initially called the shire) and the borough, with the hundred as a further subdivision of the county and itself further subdivided into hides. Both the hundred and the hide have had other designations, in particular the wapentake as the equivalent of the hundred in those northern areas influenced by the Danish invasion.

Alongside this secular administrative structure was the ecclesiastical system of administration based on the diocese and the parish. The manorial system also persisted for several centuries alongside these systems but seems to have made surprisingly little impact on their history and development, or their evolution into the administrative system of today, except that the area of the manor and the parish may often have roughly coincided. The major change was the gradual usurpation of the administrative status of the hundred by the ecclesiastical parish from the mid-sixteenth century.

Even though the county structure was not fully demarcated until the reign of Henry VIII, the Anglo-Saxon shire, later to be renamed by the Normans as the county, has been the premier territorial division of England and Wales since time immemorial. Boroughs, with various degrees of independence of the county, have also an ancient history deriving from the Anglo-Saxon groups of population in 'fortified places', some of them later receiving a degree of self-government by royal charter. The confusion of minor, special-purpose areas which evolved in the mid-nineteenth century were in the main composed either of single parishes or groups of parishes which ultimately became the urban and rural district councils, consolidated in 1972 into district councils. The boroughs continued, some as county districts little different from the urban and rural districts and others as county boroughs independent of and with a wider range of responsibilities than the counties, until these too were demoted to district council status in 1972. Only the Poor Law unions had a somewhat different structure, but again based on the grouping of parishes from 1834 until their absorption into the 'mainframe' system in 1928. These groupings of parishes for Poor Law purposes, based it seems on groups of parishes adjacent to market towns, actually cut across county boundaries in some instances, a circumstance which led to later problems.

The rating system, despite the complexities which arose from the technical attachment of different rates to different services right down to 1925, was and has remained the basic source of local government revenue since before 1601 (usually considered, with a degree of inexactitude, to be the starting-point for rating). Within most recent times the rating system though under heavy criticism and threatened with abolition has nevertheless been reaffirmed by the present government (1983) as the most appropriate, or at least practicable, system for raising local revenue (certainly against the background of all other forms of taxation utilized by central government). There are ample grounds for the contention that the decade 1928–38 was the Golden Age of local government; if this period did represent the apotheosis of the system, its decline thereafter has been sharp and rapid. Nevertheless, by this period the great consolidation of services had taken place by the absorption into the main system of the rating authorities and the Poor Law unions (which included substantial hospital and child-care services). Local authorities were in the main responsible for the major trading services of gas, electricity, water, transport and others. The all-purpose county borough – surely the most successful unit of local administration ever to operate in this realm – was flourishing, and the government grant system was put on to what was then regarded as a highly logical and equitable basis. Uniformity of the administrative system and a moderately satisfactory borrowing system was introduced in a single code in 1933. Local government was highly respected and full of confidence in its future and, on the whole, in most authorities party politics played only a minor role. Perhaps it is mere nostalgia, but those who grew up in it (including the present author) will have no difficulty in confirming the concept of the Golden Age. The drift downwards began with the (necessary) nationalization of poor relief, but the advent of the Second World War certainly brought that age, among so many others, to an end. Of course the increase in communications, the desire for larger-scale areas for trading activities and a general increase in demand for standardization of services played a powerful part in the decline of local administration. Perhaps a bolder reorganization in 1933 – which on the whole simply consolidated a system already nearly fifty years old – might have made a difference.[3]

The subdivision of the country into counties, largely achieved by the thirteenth century, but not completed until the reign of Henry VIII, had its origins in the Anglo-Saxon shires.[4] These emerged from remote sources – ancient kingdoms, sometimes divided for the benefit of a king's family, tribal areas, areas occupied by invaders, artificial creations by Alfred around major towns from which they took their names and, finally, those created by Henry to facilitate the subjugation of Wales. At this stage, according to the Webbs, the number of fifty-two geographical counties was established.

The origin of the Anglo-Saxon term 'shire' is obscure. The *Oxford Dictionary* gives the derivation from the Old English 'scir', meaning 'care, an official charge', while Irene Gladwin in *The Sheriff* relates it to the Anglo-Saxon word 'scir' as meaning 'a piece shorn off'. The *New English Dictionary* more cautiously states that the etymology is doubtful, but denies its relation with 'shear, cut off'. However, all derivations are consistent with the idea of a subdivision of a larger kingdom under the care of an official appointed by the sovereign. Shires as administrative units are mentioned in legal documents under the laws of King Ine (late seventh century) which refer to the earlderman and scirman as officials responsible upwards to the king and downwards to the individual inhabitants of the area.

The shire reeve – a name believed to derive from the Anglo-Saxon 'gerif' (guardian) – was the officer for the local administration for centuries, originally under the shire moot. As the influence of the shire/county moot dwindled following the creation of the justices of the peace in quarter sessions in the fourteenth century, the influence of the Lord Lieutenant (the earlier earlderman) and the sheriff also declined.

The Norman-French term 'county', coming into use in this country after 1066, derives from *conte* – the area presided over by a count – the earlier designation being the Latin *comitatus*, the office of a territorial lord (although rather surprisingly the title 'count' was not adopted here).[5]

The boundaries of the geographical counties have not altered materially over the centuries, although some were subdivided for administrative purposes in 1888. In 1972 more drastic changes were made, by combinations of counties and by 'heroic' surgery. Whatever the means by which the physical boundaries were first delineated, they are now, under the 1972 Act, to be as 'merged by the Ordnance Survey'. In the 1972 changes two classes of county were created – the metropolitan counties in the highly urbanized and industrialized areas, and the remainder which because of their cumbersome and negative statutory title of non-metropolitan counties are colloquially known by the tautology, the shire counties.

The county administrations remained essentially organs of central power, operated by local people centrally appointed, from the fourteenth century until 1888, when the Local Government Act transferred the administrative functions from the non-elective justices to the new democratically elected units of local government, the county councils. The justices retained their judicial functions and their direct responsibility to the Crown.

Lipman in *Local Government Areas 1834–1945* painstakingly examines the problem of identifying precisely what constituted an administrative county in the pre-1888 period of the nineteenth century; this issue does not particularly affect us here, but the justices have played so important a part in early local government, together with their initiation of finance by borrowing for the construction of the turnpike roads, that a note on the origins of this continuing influential body is surely called for.

For 200 years before the statutory recognition of local government functions the justices of the peace provided a judicial service in the counties, and for a further three centuries after the first local government legislation they were also the administrative as well as judicial arm of county government. When in 1888 they parted with their administrative functions to the newly created elective county councils, they continued in strength in their judicial capacity. Thus although the office is now almost exclusively concerned with the administration of justice (except for certain licensing functions and in association with the Watch Committees in police administration – both quasi-judicial functions), the justices have from the fourteenth century played a prominent role in local judicial and civil administration and taxation.

The principle behind the magisterial system is clear. The justices are representatives of the Crown, centrally appointed from among the local people to supervise the effective application of laws laid down by the central government. But because these appointments are made from local inhabitants, familiar with local conditions and readily available at grassroots level, the magistrates – as they are also called – though representing the Crown, are able to convey back to the central authorities the views, problems and complaints of the inhabitants of the locality. That is to say, although they are central government appointees and representatives, the roots which the magistrates have in their localities enable them to effect a two-way exchange of ideas and reactions. Redlich and Hirst in their *History of Local Government in England* suggest that although appointed by the king, the justices of the peace 'are a significant landmark in the struggle against the centralising tendencies of government'; whether this was the original intention may be unlikely, but in practice the system established was in fact an eminently practical solution to the problem of central and local relationships. As Redlich also says, 'This system was a compromise between the two extremes – the centralising tendencies of the Norman tradition, and the obstinate provincialism of the Anglo-Saxon'.

The ancient principal function of the Anglo-Saxon shire administrators through the hundred moot was the establishment of justice and the keeping of the peace among neighbours (as well as the provision of fighting men when needed for national defence) and, in a way rather oddly, the upkeep of bridges. A more rational and national system emerged in 1195 when the Chief Justice, Archbishop Hubert, selected knights who were called upon to swear an oath to maintain the peace – an early step towards the central appointment of local officers.

At that date knighthood was not the acceptance of an honour bestowed by the sovereign, but rather a rank of responsibility to be assumed by landholders above a certain level of affluence who were expected to pay a fee for their elevation. This was apparently felt to be an onerous and unwelcome responsibility but appears to have been based on the belief that people with a personal stake in the nation's economy would be more inclined to uphold the existing system (a 'property-owning democracy' in current phraseology). Under Edward I, in 1278, a Writ of Distraint of Knighthood was issued to all sheriffs requiring them to see that all who were qualified to become knights – 'all in your bailiwick who have lands worth £20 a year . . . and ought to be knights but are not' – assumed this position. A roll was to be formed in each county by two law-worthy knights and presented to the Crown without delay. The writ ends with the threat: 'And we wish you to know that we shall make careful enquiry into your conduct in carrying out this order of ours and have a suitable remedy ready provided for it forthwith', a threat not dissimilar to that used today in regard to 'ratecapping'.

The knights appointed after 1195 under the edict of Archbishop Hubert were known as 'conservators of the peace' – *custodes pacis*. In 1285 the Statute of Winchester, concerned with watch and ward, required the inhabitants of areas where felonies occurred to produce the culprits. Under Hubert's system the powers of the shire moot gradually dwindled, but the step which was to have such long-term results was taken in 1361 when Edward III superseded the conservators of the peace by the more thoroughly organized system of justices of the peace; this designation was used in the title of the Act and in a side-note, but not in the body of the text. The statute stated: 'in every County of England there shall be assigned for the keeping of the Peace one Lord and with him three or four others of the most worthy of the county together with some learned in the law.' These persons were given powers, at some length, to arrest and chastise offenders according to the law and custom of the realm. Also in 1361 the first of what may be identified as combined judicial–administrative local functions were given to those 'which shall be assigned to keep the peace', who were required to 'enquire of Measures and also Weights' according to the terms of earlier statutes. The same problem was also dealt with in the next Act, which stated: 'All measures shall be according to the King's standard' and that 'Justices of the Peace shall enquire of all defaults'. Thus the new officers were finally referred to, in the body of an Act, by the title which they now bear.

Shortly afterwards a further statute of Edward III, in 1362, ordered the Commissions of Justices of the Peace to meet four times a year (hence the quarter sessions). The petty sessions (often based on hundred divisions) evolved as a means of handling minor and special matters expeditiously and with less effort to all concerned than required by full quarter sessions. The commission from the sovereign to each justice of the peace has remained practically unchanged since inception – to inquire into, to hear, determine and punish crimes and offences. The powers were confirmed, though with some restrictions, in 1495 under Henry VII when the justices were empowered to try all offences except treason, murder and felony. There have been many variations in the scope of the judicial functions over the centuries.

With the emergence of local government proper in the mid-sixteenth century, the county justices were well able to extend their judicial interests into the administrative field. They were given a statutory responsibility for the supervision of roads (which ultimately involved them in turnpike trusts) and more significantly in the administration of the Poor Law and of the rating system which went along with it (although the parish remained the rating authority). The justices retained an administrative function – partly executive and partly supervisory – until that great turning-point, the Local Government Act 1888. By this Act, sixty-two administrative counties were created on the basis of the geographical counties, subdivided in some instances. Although the justices were relieved of their administrative functions, they were required to co-operate with the newly elected county councils in police administration. The Act indicated *in extenso* the administrative functions which the new councils were to assume. Although the infrastructure of the county was not reorganized until 1894, a substantial development of borough administration also took place in 1888, in that boroughs of not less than 50,000 population were designated county boroughs. These new county boroughs were not merely counties within counties, but with the added feature that they were all-purpose authorities, unlike the real counties who continued to share their responsibilities with their subordinate units in a two-tier structure.

This situation resulted in constant conflict between the counties and the county boroughs, as well as with the non-county boroughs seeking promotion to county borough status, until the struggle was resolved in favour of the counties in 1972. The lower tier in the counties – the parishes, smaller boroughs and the conglomeration of *ad hoc* districts for various functions, mainly sanitary and highway duties – were shaken into pattern by the Local Government Act 1894, usually referred to as the Parish Councils Act but of wider significance. The resultant structure of county districts – parishes, urban and rural districts, and non-county boroughs – necessitated boundary changes to bring some of the ecclesiastical parishes within the exact county boundaries as administrative parishes. Only the Poor Law Boards of Guardians retained their independent status, though even they were still dependent on parish structures for rating and questions of pauper settlement.

The end of the nineteenth century was therefore reached with a reasonably rationalized system of areas for local administration – counties with county districts, consisting of rural and urban districts and subordinate rural parishes, and non-county boroughs, with all-purpose county boroughs as islands of independence dotted sporadically within the county areas.

The 1888–94 structure endured for almost eighty years, through a period of tremendous social and economic change and two world wars. It was therefore ripe for review, and many alternative schemes were put forward (of which the most logical and sustained was probably the Report of the Royal Commission on Local Government under Lord Redcliffe-Maud, issued in 1969, which favoured unitary authorities). All these proposals were ruthlessly overridden by the Conservative government of the late 1960s and a system was imposed which was based on the abolition of the all-purpose county borough and the supremacy of the county as the principal administrative unit, supported by district councils. (Boroughs and cities were allowed to retain these titles as a courtesy measure only.) The Local Government Act 1933, important though it was, had been mainly a consolidating Act which retained the county/district/county borough system, the overseers and the Poor Law unions having been absorbed by the counties and county boroughs in 1925 and 1928 respectively. The major reconstruction which took place around the early 1970s involved four Acts: the London Government Act 1963, which created the Greater London Council from the former London County Council, and the London boroughs from a larger number of metropolitan boroughs; the Local Government Act 1972, which created new counties and district councils (abolishing the county boroughs) in England and Wales; the Local Government (Scotland) Act 1973, which combined Scottish counties into six regions, with district councils, plus three Island Areas which because of their remoteness were given all-purpose status; and the Local Government Act 1972 (Northern Ireland), which abolished administrative counties and created weak district councils directly under central government supervision.

Under the 1972 Act the number of administrative counties in England and Wales was determined at fifty-three (excluding the GLC), six of which were designated metropolitan and the rest non-metropolitan, and their subordinate districts likewise. However ruthlessly the system was imposed, it must be seen as an attempt to recognize two organizational factors – the great difference in the problems of the highly populated industrialized conurbations as compared with the rest of the country, and the need, in any event, for wider areas of administration combining where possible towns with their surrounding rural areas, as a result of improved communications and the outward spread of populations. Thus the newly created metropolitan counties were based on the great cities; four of them formed a belt across industrial mid-England (Merseyside, Greater Manchester, West Yorkshire and South Yorkshire), plus one to the north of this belt, Tyne and Wear centred on Newcastle upon Tyne, and one somewhat south of the belt, West Midlands based on Birmingham.

What differentiates the metropolitan from the non-metropolitan counties and districts, in addition to their degree of urbanization, is that while districts of both types remain the rating authorities (a clear survival from the sixteenth-century parish as the rating authority), in the non-metropolitan counties the county has the major share of the duties and responsibilities, even where the districts were formerly important towns such as Bristol, Nottingham, and the like, whereas in the metropolitan highly urbanized areas the balance of executive responsibility lies with the district rather than the new county authorities. The metropolitan districts, for the most part former county boroughs deprived of their all-purpose status, have waged a constant battle for the abolition of the metropolitan county councils, and for a return to all-purpose status for themselves. They seem to be winning this battle, in that at the time of writing the present government, though Conservative like that which set up the metropolitan counties, has announced its intention of abolishing this (mainly Labour-controlled) tier in the great conurbations, despite the problems which will arise from unscrambling this omelette. Paradoxically the metropolitan boroughs now seem less than happy with the proposals; perhaps what is really needed is not abolition of the metro-counties, but a review of the allocation of duties in the light of ten years of experience.[6]

The hundred requires notice in this book because although as an administrative subdivision of the county it was gradually displaced by the ecclesiastical parish from the date of the introduction of recognizable local government, it nevertheless influenced the areas of petty sessional divisions. Petty sessions exercised some oversight, on behalf of quarter sessions, on parish activities and later, in some instances, provided the area for Poor Law incorporations (and hence later still Poor Law unions) – and subsequently the urban district councils (today's district councils) – thus giving a further indication of the long-term persistence of the local government area pattern. The hundred area survived in some parliamentary divisions (for instance, West Derby), and such peculiarities as the Salford Hundred Court of Record which dealt with, in the main, small debtors' claims until it was abolished some twenty-five years ago.

Despite its curiously precise title, this ancient Anglo-Saxon subdivision of the county ('wapentake' in northern areas) appears to lack a specific origin and significance. A possible origin is that it was a combination of

100 hides – a further subdivision of the county – but this takes the matter very little forward as the exact meaning of the hide is also obscure. A hide is thought to have been an area of land sufficient to maintain a single household, but this requirement must have varied substantially according to fluctuating size of families, the terrain and nature of the soil, and the enterprise of individuals. There is a view that the area of a hide varied between 40 and 130 acres ('Domesday Book' unit), as it might well, but even the acre was in early times an inexact measure. Moreover, while the evidence from the English Midlands supports this origin, further north the area designated by a hundred did not appear to contain any specific number of hides; presumably therefore while the term hundred may have begun as a theoretically exact subdivision in the minds of the early bureaucrats, it declined into a mere title of general use applied to more or less any natural grouping, as hides were inevitably combined, subdivided, or newly created over the course of time.

There is a manuscript of about AD 940 known as the 'Hundred Ordinance' (*English Historical Documents*, vol. 1, no. 39) in which the internal evidence fails to make clear whether the ordinance established the hundred or merely sought to clarify the responsibilities of already organized units. What is relatively clear is that those who administered the hundred did so almost entirely as a body of a judicial character concerned with the maintenance of law and order, and the apportionment of responsibility for that duty. This body appears to have been a court under a hundredman or reeve, which met monthly at places long established in the localities as centres of administration. For example, the first clause in this ordinance says: 'This is the ordinance of how the hundred shall be held. First, that they are to assemble every four weeks and each man is to do justice to another.' This code also referred to 'tithings' which are believed to represent small groups of inhabitants in a township or village, but might have been a group of ten hides within the hundred. Blackstone, in his *Commentaries on the English Law* (1765), says confidently that as ten families of freeholders made up a town or tithing, so ten tithings made up a superior division called a hundred, but this sounds like oversimplification or, at most, a theoretical basis which only worked out in practice in a much more rough-and-ready manner. However, superior groupings of hundreds did occur in some counties under such names as 'ridings' in Yorkshire, 'lathes' in Kent and 'rapes' in Sussex. 'Riding' may have been derived from a 'thriding', or third, and a 'rape' seems to have been a division of one-sixth.

The editorial comment accompanying the above-quoted document claims that there is evidence of assessments for taxes in round figures for 100, or multiples of 100, hides, but there is no earlier evidence than this ordinance to establish the origins of the hundred for judicial or administrative matters. There are a number of other ancient terms denoting areas, such as a 'carucate', possibly the term used in northern England for a hide, a 'vergate' and a 'bovate', and in cities the 'liberty' as an area of special privilege.

The parish, now under its administrative rather than its former ecclesiastical definition, is still, like the county and the borough, an active element in local government. The Local Government Act 1972 (s.9 *et seq.*) deals extensively with the constitution and powers of parish councils in their various forms according to their populations. Schedule 1 of that Act, which creates the new counties and districts, uses the parish as one of the basic building-blocks. For example, the newly created county of Avon (centred on Bath and Bristol) has listed among the existing areas combined into the new county 'in the rural district of Axbridge, the parishes of Banwell, Bleadon, Butcombe', and many others, plus parts of parishes divided to fit the boundaries of the new county. The same schedule creates new parishes as part of the tidying-up process required by the regrouping of the major ('principal') administrative areas.

The origins of the parish units which became so important an element in local government over so long a stretch of time and through to the present day are again obscure. The Webbs describe the parish in its administrative function by the useful phrase 'a unit of obligation', and say that 'The division of England into parishes was determined by no statute, and . . . by no royal decree or authoritative commission'; and they quote Bishop Stillingfleet as saying (1698):

> The settling of parochial rights or the bounds of parishes depends upon an ancient and immemorial custom. For they are not limited by an Act of Parliament, nor set forth by special commissioners, but as the circumstances of the times and places and persons did happen to make them greater or lesser.

But though at a significant point in the sixteenth century the parish began to take over from the hundred as the administrative subdivision of the county, to say that the civil administration took over an existing ecclesiastical unit is too facile. Certainly, the ecclesiastical authorities established the parish as the subunit of the deanery and the diocese, being the area served by a church and its incumbent – a 'cure for souls'. The *Everyman Encyclopedia* quotes Blackstone as describing a parish as 'that circuit of ground in which the souls under the care of one person do inhabit'. But the question is: what led to the siting of a church in the first place? Reason suggests that while people may have tended to live where there was access to a church, the more likely picture is of a church being built where there was already some reasonable grouping of people to be served, needing its facilities and prepared to maintain it. If some churches were provided by the lords of the manor for the use of themselves and their tenants, then these would by definition already be small centres of population. Certainly, if social, economic, or defence considerations brought a number of people to live together in an area, which might eventually attain a sufficient size to be called a vill or township, then the provision of a church would follow and the area become an ecclesiastical parish.

The term parish may even have a quasi-administrative origin. The *Oxford English Dictionary* gives the origin as the Old French *paroisse*, first introduced into England – like the county – in the Norman-French laws of William I, though the name does not appear in laws printed in English until the twelfth century. Thompson gives the origin as the Latin *parochia* (and that from the Greek, meaning 'a sojourner'), referring to groups of people not technically citizens of the Roman Empire who lived in enclosures in towns as racial minority groups, or in scattered villages. This term was later adopted by the Christian church as its unit of administration under a bishop, and extended over the whole of the Roman Empire by people who, originally at least, regarded themselves as minority groups. 'Diocese', according to Thompson, was also a Roman land division, adopted later by the church; in the same way, 'basilica', a Roman centre for community assembly, was adopted for the buildings used as ecclesiastical administrative centres.

Whatever and whenever its origins, the ecclesiastical parish was well established by the fifteenth century, although because of its casual origins there was no neat overall pattern conforming with county or borough boundaries and of standard size, and some unpopulated or remote parts of the country remained outside any parish for centuries. Later discussion of the Poor Law will show that parish 'bounds' were by no means coterminous with the county boundaries. As parishes were later combined into Poor Law unions and other groupings, this enshrined an administrative problem which had to be unravelled in the late-nineteenth-century establishment of a rationalized administrative structure and again in the twentieth century when the Poor Law was absorbed by the then general local authorities. However, as the parishes covered, by definition, groups of people who were in the habit of congregating in the church at least once in every week, they obviously formed a useful basis for any sort of social or administrative activity which needed the co-operation of the inhabitants, particularly if the parish priest could be relied upon to exercise a benevolent authority. The ancient offices of constable, taken over from the manorial system and the court leet but having even earlier origins, and churchwardens, an entirely historical emergence, were later added to by the surveyor and the overseers and guardians. All of these were on a 'voluntary' rotational basis, selected (sometimes by 'house-row') so that the parish earned its recognition administratively not as an elective democratic unit, but rather as the Webbs' 'unit of obligation', laboriously developed by the inhabitants, partly in their own interests and partly under pressure from the centre. That service in these offices was less than truly 'voluntary' is shown by the extensive provisions in various statutes for fines on refusal to accept office.

Lipman in his *Local Government Areas* points out that the Act of 1536 dissolving the monasteries put the duty of collecting voluntarily for the relief of the poor on to the churchwardens and two other responsible persons in every parish, and the head officers of the towns. Thus it was not Elizabeth I who introduced the embryonic Poor Law, although she may be considered to have initiated the Poor Law proper; all that has followed therefrom will be examined later, but one of the oldest local government services – the relief of the poor – certainly started with 'ecclesiastical exhortation' on a parish basis. The lack of success of exhortation led to the creation of a 'bureaucracy' for the purpose of an official rate levy.

Redlich and Hirst in their *History of Local Government in England* also take the view that 'The transition of poor relief from a religious to a civil function was one of the fruits of the Reformation'.[7] This is to suggest that severance of the relationship with Rome followed by the dissolution of the monasteries had, by removing the centres of voluntary assistance of the poor, thrust the duty on to the parish church, so that ultimately (more or less casually) the ecclesiastical unit became the civil unit of administration. In the event, the churches were unable to perform this duty adequately on a voluntary basis. Henry VIII therefore found that having suppressed the bodies which provided voluntary relief to the poor, he was faced with the necessity of providing an alternative; but he found that another purely voluntary system operated through the parish church could not adequately perform the task. Hence the necessity to import a legal responsibility backed by an official system of raising the necessary revenue. There arose also, as the conception evolved, the need to provide workhouses, for which borrowing became an essential means of providing finance.

Even the original democratic basis of the administration of poor relief through the parish ran into difficulties. While the original parish meeting held after church in the vestry had the elements of 'grassroots' democracy, in the course of time, particularly in the larger parishes, what came to be called the select (or close) vestry, consisting of selected or co-opted parishioners (presumably those who contributed most to the parish rate), seriously weakened the democratic basis of the open vestry. Moreover, what became one of the most serious and onerous duties, the collection of the rate, was performed by overseers who, although parish members, were the direct appointees of the justices of the peace. By 1600 the parish was the unit of obligation not only for the poor, but also for highways – and remained so for a very long time. The parish still today retains functions in relation to parish footpaths and lighting, but only in 1894 with the Parish Councils Act was the present democratic basis clearly established, with parish meetings in the areas of sparser population and elected parish councils elsewhere. As at that time the system of urban and rural district councils was also established, the parish as an operational unit was restricted to rural parts. The subsequent history of the parish as an administrative unit has already been indicated. After having been stabilized in 1894, its place was reaffirmed in 1933 and again retained in 1972 despite the trend to larger areas of administration.

The parish, despite its ubiquity and continuing survival, did not prove to be a particularly efficient or enterprising body, but hardly through any fault of its own. The problem was basically that the obligations placed on the parishes were from the start more than they were able or prepared to cope with. Parishes on the whole were either too small for effective administration or, if large, too sparsely populated, and the range of wealth between parishes was too great to ensure reasonable equality of burden. The obligation to maintain the road system within the parish boundaries and to maintain the poor of the parish, first, from voluntary contributions, and later from a parish rate, were too narrowly conceived, despite the optimistic provision that poor parishes could spread the cost to richer neighbours within the hundred area. In other words, the parishes were expected to cope with the problems and expense of what were even at that time emergent regional or national services.

These shortcomings led to the creation of the turnpike trusts and the Poor Law incorporations (which ultimately led to the fully fledged Boards of Guardians). Both of these more realistic institutions had powers to finance by borrowing.

What might perhaps be called the maverick unit of local government administration is the borough, a unit in one form or another probably as old as the shire, based on urban concentrations and having roots in Roman and Anglo-Saxon fortifications, some possibly stemming from Iron Age forts. These were areas which had evolved in a variety of places as directed by events without any particular pattern, and for different reasons, not forming a coherent overall national pattern. The essence of the borough within the English local government scene is that while there was for many centuries no standard type – each depended on a negotiated charter granted by the sovereign – there was an underlying general pattern of responsibilities and rights, although this did not become systematized until 1835. Thereafter this type of authority showed important developments and in one form, the county borough, played a vital role until 1972 – a role perhaps soon to be partially revived.

The standard pattern was that in exchange for an undertaking to pay central taxes and to take part in defence of the realm, the borough was granted varying degrees of internal self-government, generally under the control of a mayor, aldermen and burgesses, who might form a quite close-knit and relatively undemocratic body, linked with the trade guilds operating in the borough; this link is indicated by the occasional use of the term guild-hall for town hall. Their responsibility was to manage the town in such a way that reasonable living and good trading facilities were provided. Boroughs might be independent of county judicial control in varying degrees, and might in fact have the dual status of city and county, depending upon their status in the judicial system. This granting of county judicial status to some cities/boroughs is not to be confused with the later all-purpose county borough.

The early history of the borough like that of the county, hundred and parish is certainly obscure. While there were charter boroughs of a simple kind before 1066, the early fourteenth century was the beginning of the boom in the granting of charter powers. In 1373 Bristol was made what even then was called a county borough, giving it complete independence of the county; similarly, York in 1396, and there were others. Dr Martin Weinbaum in *The Incorporation of Boroughs* calls 1440 the 'classic age of incorporation'. By that time the basic characteristics of a properly incorporated town were clearly recognizable as those of a 'local government authority':

(1) perpetual succession;
(2) right to sue and be sued as a whole and in the name of the mayor;
(3) power to hold land;
(4) right to a common seal;
(5) power to issue by-laws for good government.

Later the assumption of particular duties began to be on confirmation by local as well as general Acts. One of the confusing features was that internal bodies of commissioners were established by local Acts independent of the borough council, for police, town improvements, and so on, and another was that the parish system also operated to an extent within the borough for Poor Law administration and through the overseers for rate collection, for instance. The main problem which boroughs present to us is that although they were not normally given specific powers to borrow money, many assumed this power by implication, in that they were bodies corporate and considered that they could do what a private person could do. There is adequate evidence, as described later, that for various functions and in various crises they did borrow from time to time – not as a general financing or statutorily authorized practice, but casually and on the security either of bonds given by private individuals (perhaps the mayor) or on the taxes which were levied on the citizens (householders and traders) or on tolls collected in markets, harbours, and the like. References are to be found to borrowing 'on the borough seal', that is, by a borrowing instrument authenticated by the common seal of the borough.

Ignoring for the moment the creation of the Poor Law unions from 1834, the borough can be credited as the first element in the local government system to be rationalized on a relatively democratic basis by the Municipal Corporations Act 1835; thereafter these units of local government waged a running battle for independence with the county areas. The 178 towns listed in the 1835 Act were added to as the century progressed. The modest borrowing powers associated with the early municipal corporations, as they were designated, will be examined in due course.

The borough structure was again overhauled, in 1882, in another Municipal Corporations Act; by this time sixty-two new boroughs had been incorporated and a further twenty-five were then added. Again in 1888 when the county councils were first placed on a democratic basis, the improved form of borough, the county borough, an all-purpose authority of great importance, was established – sixty-one in number. The struggle thereafter continued for boroughs to obtain the status of county borough, and for county boroughs to absorb within their boundaries portions of the surrounding county areas. This battle was thought to have been lost by the county boroughs in 1972 when all were demoted to the status of county districts, along with the non-county boroughs and the urban and rural district councils, but current political controversy indicates a possible return to something like county borough status in what are now called the metropolitan counties.

The Poor Law unions formed from 1834 onwards by amalgamations of parishes constituted a separate, *ad hoc* but elective system of local administration for a specific purpose, in parallel with the main system; this continued until the duty was transferred to the county and county borough councils in 1928 (but only a few years later largely nationalized). Therefore, before 1888, the main framework of local authorities consisted of the counties, subdivided into parishes, with semi-independent boroughs and from that date wholly independent county boroughs scattered throughout the system. Many of the parishes formed non-uniform groupings as sanitary and health authorities, highway authorities and from 1870 School Boards. In 1894 the parish was reorganized on a more standardized democratic basis of administration and the health authorities converted into a consolidated system of urban and rural district councils similar to, but of somewhat lower status than, the non-county boroughs; all three authorities were known generically as county districts. The School Boards continued until 1902 when, with widening concepts of education, the function was transferred to the mainframe local authorities at different levels of responsibility.

At around the turn of the century, then, the system was basically as follows:

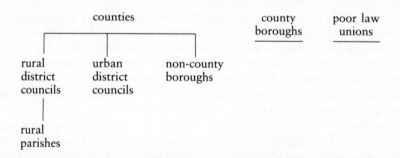

As already mentioned, the Poor Law separation was abandoned from 1928 and the parish overseers having already been absorbed into the county districts and county boroughs in 1925, the Local Government Act 1933 was able to confirm and consolidate the system as above. In 1972 the Local Government Act divided the counties into metropolitan and non-metropolitan counties, as described earlier, amalgamating all the other classes of authority into a second tier known as county districts (also of two classes) and involving the abolition of the county borough council. At this point the system showed the following simplified pattern:

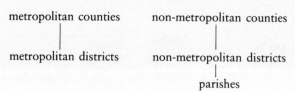

In Figure 1.1 overleaf an attempt is made to show the major stages in area development in historical sequence.

The shaping of the London metropolis began in 1855 with the creation of the Metropolitan Board of Works. In 1889 this became the London County Council with associated metropolitan boroughs. In 1963 the title was changed to the Greater London Council and various groupings of metropolitan boroughs were formed into the present London boroughs; throughout this time the Council of the City of London has retained a special status as a form of borough. The abolition of a county framework for the metropolis is threatened, along with the abolition of the metropolitan counties; why the seven areas of dense urban population should be denied an overall co-ordinating authority thought proper for the shire counties is far from clear to many.

In 1873 evidence to a Select Committee on Boundaries of Parishes, Unions and Counties contained a letter from the then Registrar-General (House of Commons Papers 308, appendix 4) in which he said, comparing the British system mainly with that established in France,

> The absence of symmetry and system which is a peculiar feature in our national organisation may be easily explained by a reference to the course of English history. At no point has there been attempted in this country a deliberate and scientific mapping out of the whole field of national activity, harmonising and co-ordinating the various parts under a comprehensive and well-balanced scheme.

This was certainly true at the time it was written. Since then there have been two systematic attempts to create a rationalized system – in the 1880s and 1890s, and again the 1970s. Do these invalidate the Registrar-General's view? Even the present system is seen to have strong roots in ancient county, parish and borough boundaries; whether it could have been otherwise must remain a matter for debate.

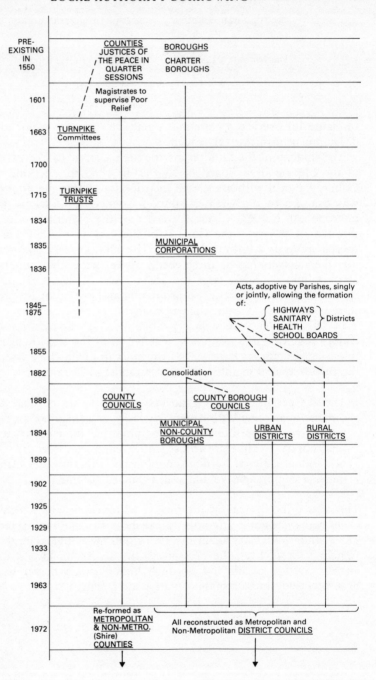

Figure 1.1   *The evolution and life span of the local government authorities in England and Wales*

PARISHES	RELEVANT MAJOR STATUTES	PURPOSES
ECCLESIASTICAL PARISHES		
Care of Poor: Overseers to collect Rate	Relief of the Poor 1601	Consolidation of earlier provisions for Poor Relief and Rating: Decline of ancient HUNDREDS
	An Act for Repairing the Highways etc. 1663	The first TOLL ROAD – Wadesmill – under a Committee of Magistrates
Start of Parish Poor Law Incorporations	Various	Incorporations beginning with London and Bristol: Development of Turnpike Committees
	Various	Advent of Turnpikes under Trusts, independent of Magistrates
POOR LAW UNIONS BOARDS OF GUARDIANS	Poor Law (Amendment) Act 1834	National system of locally elected *ad hoc* bodies
	Municipal Corporations Act 1835	First step in rationalisation of boroughs
REGISTRATION DISTRICTS	Act for the Registration of Births, Marriages and Deaths 1836	An extension of the Guardians' duties, though not strictly a Poor Relief function
	Various Acts, especially Public Health Act 1875	The era of 'chaos of areas'
	Elementary Education Act 1870	Period of decline of Turnpike Trusts
METROPOLITAN BOARD OF WORKS	Metropolis Management Act 1855	First of three major attempts to establish 'county type' structure for metropolis
	Municipal Corporations Act 1882	Consolidation in anticipation of forthcoming reforms
LONDON COUNTY COUNCIL	Local Government Act 1888	Elective County Councils – end of administration by Magistrates: Creation of all-purpose County Boroughs
Administrative (RURAL) Parishes	Local Government Act 1894	Elective County District system (UDC's, RDC's, and N–CB's) established
LONDON METROPOLITAN BOROUGHS	London Metropolitan Boroughs Act 1899	Creation of Metropolitan Boroughs
School Boards abolished	Education Act 1902	School Board duties transferred to local authorities
Overseers abolished	Rating and Valuation Act 1925	County Boroughs and County Districts created Rating Authorities
Guardians abolished	Local Government Act 1929	County Councils and County Boroughs made Poor Law Auths.
	Local Government Act 1933	Consolidation of system of Counties, County Boroughs, County Districts, Parishes
GREATER LONDON COUNCIL & LONDON BOROUGHS	London Government Act 1963	Material expansion and area re-organisation under GLC
Parishes retained	Local Government Act 1972	Drastic re-construction: Non-County and (All-purpose) County Boroughs abolished.

NOTES: CHAPTER 1

1   Parliamentary Debates, 3rd Series, Vol. 205. Quoted in V. D. Lipman, *Local Government Areas 1834–1945* (Oxford: Blackwell, 1949), and elsewhere.
2   A 'County Finance Boards Bill' put forward in 1836, which would have put the counties earlier on the road to the 1888 Act, was rejected by Parliament under pressure from the magistrates.
3   I am indebted for this Golden Age concept (and for so much else) to Fred Tolson, my deputy for some ten years and thereafter City Treasurer of Leeds. On this melancholy theme of decline see also my articles in the *Three Banks Review* 'Local government in decline', June 1971; and 'Local government – the final phase?', June 1975.
4   The sources used for the sections which follow, in addition to the statutes referred to, are: T. F. Tout, *An Advanced History of Great Britain* (London: Longmans, Green, 1920); V. D. Lipman, *Local Government Areas 1834–1945* (Oxford: Blackwell, 1949); I. Gladwin, *The Sheriff – The Man and his Office* (London: Gollancz, 1974); F. H. Spencer, *Municipal Origins* (1911); R. A. Brown, *Origins of English Feudalism* (London: Allen & Unwin, 1973); P.D. Thomson, *Parish and Parish Church – their Place and Influence in History* (Walton-on-Thames: Nelson, 1948); *English Historical Documents*, Vol. 1 (London: Eyre & Spottiswoode, 1955), and *English Local Government* series, *The Parish and the County* and *The Borough* (London: Longmans, Green, 1906–29); H. M. Jewell, *English Local Administration in the Middle Ages* (Newton Abbot: David & Charles, 1972); B. Keith-Lucas, *The Un-Reformed Local Government System* (London: Croom Helm, 1979); K. B. Smellie, *A History of Local Government* (London: Allen & Unwin, 1st edn 1946; 4th edn 1968); J. Redlich and F. W. Hirst, *The History of Local Government* (London: Macmillan, 1903; rev. edn 1970); and *Anglo-Saxon England* (London: BBC, 1957).
5   In passing, the term 'county' may be noted as being in common use in the United States, along with the title of sheriff; and also that the 'posse', so familiar in Westerns, derives from the ancient practice of the *posse comitatis* – the power of the English county sheriff to require all able-bodied men to join in a hunt for malefactors, the 'hue-and-cry'. The term 'county' continues in use in Canada and Australia as part of the administrative system.
6   A White Paper (Cmnd 9063) has been published on these proposals (October 1983) which contemplates joint boards for police and fire and possibly other services. A draft Bill has also been produced (November 1984).
7   The thought processes of the Reformation can also be shown to have influenced Henry VIII in relaxing the prohibition on usury: see my *In Restraint of Usury*, quoted above.

PART TWO

Historical Survey

First Period: 1530-1830:
The First Local Government Services
and the Emergence of Borrowing

Chapter 2

ROADS AND BRIDGES

The first service of a recognizably local government character to which attempts were made to apply a statutory national pattern was that for the maintenance of roads and their accompanying bridges. But what these mid-sixteenth-century statutes sought to introduce was the machinery not for creating a national system of roads and bridges, but for the upkeep of the already existing primitive system of communications, and a confirmation and continuation of responsibilities and processes established by usage and the common law 'from time out of mind', as the statutes were apt to say. What is remarkable is that these early statutes, elementary though their conception of communication needs was, and emerging from ancient common law as they appear to have done, continued to influence the pattern of highways administration until well into the nineteenth century. The explanation for the long survival of the limited concepts in this early legislation appears to be that so unfitted was the system optimistically introduced to cope with transportation needs outside the local parish requirements that this very inadequacy gave rise to the emergence of a separate, *ad hoc* system for the development of road communications. Had this spontaneous growth of a more rational system not emerged alongside the old, then surely some improved basic statutory system would have been undertaken long before it was.

The *ad hoc* system which developed as a result of the inadequacy of central statutory provision was the independent and fragmented system of toll-roads and toll-bridges known generically as turnpike trusts. Though the trusts were originally intended not for the construction of an adequate road network, but for the better maintenance of existing roads, and initially regarded as a stopgap method for correcting the shortcomings of the general statutory system, they quickly assumed the principal role, so that it was in the turnpike trusts – financed on a 'benefit received' principle, not established under general highways legislation – that borrowing was first introduced for a recognizable local government activity.

There are inherent problems in the characteristics of highways administration which persist to the present day. The root problem lies in the conflict between the local and national significance of a road network system. While the view that roads are in their origins essentially 'of the locality' is obviously true in a physical sense, it was not wholly true operationally even in mediaeval times. Indeed the first organized roads were a part of Roman military strategy. Though roads were naturally created and used by villagers in going about their husbandry and transporting their produce to the market towns, there were still the remains of the four great Roman roads, and the more ancient ways traversing large areas of the countryside. From earliest times there had been considerable military and other long-distance traffic; for example, traders, pilgrims and the king's justices, passing through the land. The growth of commerce and road standards are interlinked: commerce demands roads, better roads encourage more commerce. There is significance too in the fact that the first turnpike road established in primitive form in 1663 rose out of the inability of small, poor parishes to maintain their portion of what was even then a major through road – the Great North Road from London to Scotland. The inequity of expecting each parish to maintain what might be a lengthy portion of this road which lay fortuitously within its boundaries, irrespective of the parish's population or affluence, and regardless of the standard of road which would otherwise have satisfied parochial needs, was obvious – to the parishioners at least, if not travellers. The same problem is apparent today in the conflict between assessments of local and regional/national traffic.

A second conflict arises between users and those responsible for maintenance over the nature and quantity of traffic. Much legal effort was expended from the beginning of highways legislation in attempts to restrict the weight of traffic using the roads – that is, the size of wagons, width and character of wheels and number of draught-horses – much the same problem as arises today with juggernauts on a vastly different scale. A third area of conflict, when once some system of payment for upkeep in place of or along with statute labour service had been introduced, was whether the cost should be met from a local rate or by direct charges on the basis of ability to pay. In later times these problems were partly met by grants-in-aid from the central government and, finally, on the more important roads, by central government, or local authorities higher in the scale taking over the cost from the minor authorities. From the late sixteenth century until the nineteenth, and indeed in some respects even today (by toll-bridges), both systems have applied concurrently, initially through the introduction of the turnpike road toll systems. There are economists of course who argue that more of the locally provided services should be charged on the basis of benefit received rather than by general local or national taxation.

A fourth inherent characteristic of the road system is its suitability for initial finance by borrowed money, so that the work may be carried out expeditiously but with the cost spread over those who benefit from it directly, or indirectly over the course of time. The fact is that while minor road provision and maintenance was and is still financed from rates, the through-road provision – that carried out for 150 years by turnpike trusts – was financed from as early as 1663 from loans the servicing costs of which were met from tolls. The turnpike trusts thus lay claim to be the first quasi-local authorities to base their finances on borrowing.

From ancient times the legal concept of a highway was not as a strip of land in public ownership, alienated from adjacent land, but simply as a 'perpetual right of passage in the Sovereign for himself and his subjects over another's land' (see Webb and Webb, *The Story of the King's Highway*; Smellie, *History of Local Government*). Originally therefore a road or highway was simply those tracks worn by the passage of travellers and their vehicles, horses and livestock, not necessarily involving any structural much less engineering work in its creation and upkeep. On the other hand, a bridge, so essential a part of many highways, has an engineering character and clearly requires purposive construction and maintenance where roads must cross rivers and a ford or ferry is not available or inadequate. This is no doubt the reason that the first Statute of Bridges preceded that of roads by some twenty-five years. However, there was an important administrative distinction: roads began and long remained a parish responsibility, whereas bridge maintenance was from the beginning a county function.

BRIDGES   Reference occurs from early times to the problems of maintaining such bridges as had already been provided by a variety of means of a non-statutory nature, but what is astonishing considering the importance of the duty of providing new bridges and the automatic right to borrow for the purpose is that this was not granted to public authorities as a general power before the Local Government Act 1888. Yet the positive duty of assuring the proper maintenance of bridges was gradually imposed by statute on the justices of the peace in sessions from as early as 1530.

The origins of the early bridges are largely lost to us. They were certainly provided in a number of different ways; no doubt, some were Roman, many manorial on the basis that the lands of the manor could not be exploited without some means of crossing the rivers and streams upon them. Many of the smaller bridges were provided by individuals on their own land, some from hundred (and similar) resources, others by parishes as the latter superseded the hundred as the basic administrative unit; doubtless some were provided by monasteries, and certainly numbers were built by the early charter towns. The earliest legislation mentioning bridges assumes this pre-existence and is thus concerned not with their construction, but primarily with pinning the duty of maintenance on those who had originally provided them. Such legislation also discloses the efforts of those deemed responsible to shed the liability for maintenance or at least to share it. The Anglo-Saxon *trinoda necessitas* rule of the eighth century, a threefold obligation incumbent on every holder of land, embraced the 'buhr-bot' – the duty to assist in the upkeep of fortifications; the 'fyrd' – the duty to perform military service; and the 'brieg-bot' – the responsibility to repair bridges. The problem resurfaces in Magna Charta (1215), clause 23 of which declares: 'No vill or individual should be compelled to make bridges at river banks except those who from of old were legally bound to do so.'

The earliest positive statutory intervention, the Statute of Bridges 1530, was also directed to the maintenance of bridges and not to their construction. This may certainly be identified as the first general statute making provision for a service to be administered by a type of local authority over the nation as a whole. The three stages of action incorporated in this statute are significant.

It placed various responsibilities on the justices. The first of these was that where possible they must determine who was already regarded as liable to maintain any bridge. Persons who were inconvenienced by the poor state of a bridge could appeal to the justices by 'presentment' (broadly, submission of a complaint) and expect the justices to see that someone with an inherited duty took steps to effect repairs, that is, the justices were to take action 'against such as [ought] to be charged for the making and amending of such bridges . . . as it shall seem by their discretion to be necessary and convenient for the speedy amendment of such bridges'. The Act indicates that the putting of this duty of supervision on the justices was simply the transfer to them of duties previously carried out by a higher court under common law; in other words, justices of the peace must now carry out this responsibility for supervision 'as the King's Justices of his bench used commonly to do'.

The second level of provision in the Act was that 'where in many parts of this realm it cannot be known and proved what hundred, riding, wapentake, city, borough, town or parish, nor what person certain or body politic ought of right' to accept responsibility because the bridge had 'lain long without any amendment', then bridges in cities and towns must be repaired by the inhabitants, and elsewhere by the inhabitants of the shire or riding; if a bridge – as must have been common – linked two areas of administration, then the justices must divide the responsibility between the two bodies of inhabitants.

The third logical sequence in the Act was that where responsibility could not be established, then 'for the speedy reformation and amending of such bridges', the justices of the peace for the area were requested to assume a direct responsibility and could 'tax and set every inhabitant in the area to such reasonable aid and sum of money as they shall think . . . sufficient for the repairing, redefining and amendment of such bridges'.

This responsibility of the county justices for levying a rate for the repair of major bridges had a profound impact on the later development of bridge maintenance and, ultimately, construction, and also the recognition of what came to be called 'county bridges'.

And because a bridge no matter how skilfully repaired was 'of little or none avail' unless a reasonable highway gave immediate access to it, the justices were also granted power to insist that 'such part and portion of the highways as lie next adjoining to any ends of the bridges, distant from any one of the ends of such bridges 300 feet [CCC fote], be made, repaired and amended as often as need shall require' – a modest enough requirement, indicating a certain lack of enthusiasm for road maintenance in the population generally! The Act did not require or empower the justices to construct new bridges even where a public need could be seen to exist, but no doubt 're-edifying' could amount to what now would be regarded as a capital project, and this seems to have been at the back of the minds of the legislators – for instance, possible replacement of a wooden footbridge by a stone carriage bridge.

This early Act, then, gave power to impose a local tax/rate, on a county basis, for carrying out work of local benefit, well preceding the Statute of Elizabeth, in 1601, generally regarded as the first 'rating' Act. Although the Act of 1601 was on a parish basis, this did not much differentiate it from the rating by the county under the Statute of Bridges – as the county were to levy the rate by precept on the parishes, leaving the parish officers to collect it.

Logical as the three stages of the Statute of Bridges may have been, there is no doubt that problems would still have arisen in establishing precise responsibility, and what is certain is that the justices would at that early date be reluctant to levy rates. A wholly modern-sounding example of the exasperation of the central government with the intransigence of local authorities shines like a beacon through an Act of 1580, which provided for the 're-edifying of Cardiff Bridge in the County of Glamorgan'. Conflict about responsibility had clearly arisen between the county and town, which the justices had been unable to determine. The preamble to the Act complains 'more money was likely to be spent in the explaining and determining of [division of responsibility] than haply might have sufficed to have re-edified the said bridge' – the avoidance of a lawyers' field-day seems to have been uppermost in mind. This Act therefore determined that the cost of repairs and future upkeep should be shared between the county and the town on a five-sixths and one-sixth basis. The justices were empowered to assess and rate the county, with the several hundreds, and every town corporate, parish, and so on, to such reasonable sums in due and proportionate manner according as rates, taskes and tallages 'have before this time used to be rated and levied, or as near as they can'.

County bridges increasingly became the main positive duty of the justices when acting in their administrative capacity. Their other responsibilities, to the Poor Law, were mainly of a secondary supervisory character, and county buildings did not present much problem (county halls, houses of correction and prisons).

There is an unusual reference not only to bridge repair, but also to bridge-building in an Act of 1670 which was primarily a Highways Act. In providing for a rate levy where statute labour was likely to prove inadequate, the Act referred to: 'the common highways, causeys, and bridges within any parish, township or hamlet for the repair of which a rate may be levied.' Then a surprising provision appeared; the Act recited that:

there are many and sundry great and deep rivers in the Counties of Cheshire and Lancashire which cannot be passed over without hazard and loss of lives and goods for want of sufficient bridges . . . to build and erect which there is no law in force.

The justices are therefore authorized to 'cause to be erected and builded' such new bridges as they consider necessary and also 'to repair or rebuild such other bridges as were demolished in the late [Civil] war'. The respective counties or hundreds were to be charged with the cost and the money raised by a highways rate as under the original Act of Henry VIII. Why Lancashire and Cheshire should have been singled out in this way is not clear.

A second surprising addition to this Act allowed the justices for the County of Monmouth, for a period of ten years, to levy a charge on the inhabitants for the building of bridges over the Rivers Usk and Basalegg, but the sum is not to exceed £40 a year. The cost is to be collected by the levying of a rate for bridges as formerly settled for that county, which may imply some local Act powers. There was in fact an earlier Act concerning bridges in Monmouthshire, in 1597, introduced because of uncertainty about who should maintain bridges at Newport and Caerleon (taking into account the 'great poverty of the inhabitants of the said towns'). The duty was bestowed on the county authority, using a rate levy under the 1535 Act, and subject to fines on the magistrates of £10 each if they failed to effect the repairs.

The duty of maintaining bridges to support the highways of the county was extended 'administratively' in many parts to include widening, strengthening and even rebuilding bridges out of moneys provided through the county rate, there being no provision for borrowing for longer-term finance. The justices endeavoured however to confine their work to important bridges and to leave the maintenance of the smaller bridges to the parishes and the hundred. Naturally as trade and commerce grew the importance of communications, and thus of bridges, grew likewise, so that more bridges tended to become accepted by the county authorities. (Toll-roads also involved toll-bridges.)

Nevertheless, despite the obviously growing importance of bridges in the nation's economy, Parliament appears to have thought that the justices were showing themselves over-ready to spend county money and were stretching their powers, interpreting the term 'bridge repair' too widely. The County Rates Act 1738 (by which date the toll-road system was well established) provided that:

> No part of the money to be raised and collected in pursuance of this Act shall be applied to the repair of bridges [also gaols, houses of correction and prisons] until presentment be made at the respective Grand Juries, about the insufficiency inconvenience or want of reparation [of these structures].

This may indicate some uneasiness about the liberality of the justices with public money; but did it amount to a serious restriction on enterprising or energetic justices? No provision is made in the Act for borrowing for bridges (or other county purposes), but this is hardly surprising as even a general Highways Act as late as 1773 which attempted to consolidate the chaotic law of highways made no provision for finance by borrowing. The 1773 Act did however simplify the method of making presentment to the justices about bridges in disrepair, modifying the 1738 Act in so doing; the earlier Act had perhaps proved an effective brake on the expenditures of the justices.

According to the Webbs in *The Story of the King's Highway*, a momentous court decision on a relatively trifling case opened the floodgates for a substantial increase of responsibillity for bridge maintenance by the counties. In R v. *West Riding of Yorkshire (Glasbourne Bridge)* 1780, the county was held responsible for the maintenance of a bridge only recently erected by a township in replacement of one which the township had previously maintained. The Webbs quote the court's ruling: 'If a man build a bridge and it becomes useful to the County in general, the County shall repair it.' Consequent on this decision, attempts were made to control the private building of bridges which might later become a county maintenance responsibility, but the most that Parliament would accept (Lord Ellenborough's Act of 1803) was that the county justices had a right to approve the specifications of a bridge which they might later be expected to maintain. Thus the nineteenth century was entered upon with no public authority being empowered to build new bridges except possibly by private Act, and a somewhat confused allocation of responsibility for the maintenance of such bridges as were by one means or another provided.

The Webbs take the view that after the middle of the fifteenth century the practice of building new bridges ceased, with the explanation that this may have been the result of the impoverishment of the religious orders. The revival which took place in the seventeenth and eighteenth centuries was mainly the result of the introduction of turnpike trusts. Thus there were Acts, for example, authorizing the building of toll-bridges at Norwich (1725), Windsor (1735), London (1756, etc.), Manchester (1772) and many others. Some bridge-building was carried out under private Act by speculative builders.

ROADS Given the early common law concept of a road as merely a right of passage, the standards of road-making were equally primitive, so that statutes of quite late date were simply concerned with removing obstructions such as trees and shrubs which happened to have established themselves in the roadway, the digging of side drainage ditches and, more sinisterly, the wide clearance of verges in an effort to discourage footpads. As early as 1285 the Statute of Winchester called for work to be carried out on highways between market towns to clear them of bushes and dikes, so that no man could hide with evil intent within 200 feet of either side. Under common law the duty of maintaining the roads in passable condition with reasonable safety lay with the local inhabitants and was only defined statutorily in 1555, nearly twenty-five years after the statute which first took notice of bridges. This statute for the mending of highways 'being now both very noisesome and tedious to travel and dangerous to all passengers and carriages', laid down a system of statutory labour service which persisted for nearly 300 years, and applied to main roads, that is, at this time, those leading from each village to the nearest market town.

Under the supervison of the justices the constables and churchwardens of every parish were to meet during Easter Week with the inhabitants of the parish and together elect 'two honest persons of the parish' to be surveyors and orderers for one year. These surveyors were to inspect the roads and organize the work of maintenance to which every able-bodied male inhabitant was to contribute four days of effort each year, together with the appropriate tools and transport to keep these market roads in order. There were fines for refusal of office and for failing to contribute the necessary time; the income from such fines was to help pay for the work. An inhabitant could therefore avoid personal participation if he was prepared to pay a cash fine in lieu thereof.

This Act was introduced for a limited period but was re-enacted in 1562, with the four days' statutory labour increased to six. The significance of these two Acts may be judged by the fact that their provisions were incorporated into the Consolidating Act 1766 and that some provisions even persisted through to the Highways Act 1835.

In 1654 two ordinances of the Commonwealth were passed; although these introduced the power to levy a rate for highways maintenance purposes, this was in addition to and not in place of statute labour service, and the earlier Act of 1562 was not repealed. The opening words of the first Ordinance of 1654 indicate, not surprisingly, the lack of success of the system of unpaid statutory labour. However, the solution was not to abolish it, but rather to support it with a tentative power to levy a rate, presumably on the assumption that statutory service, though still required, would alone be inadequate: 'Whereas the several statutes now in force for mending highways are found by experience not to have produced such good reformation as was thereby intended', then to remedy this, two or more able and sufficient householders in the parish were to be elected Surveyors of Highways, and if this was not done, the Overseers of the Poor were to assume the responsibility. The surveyors were to estimate the cost of work required and levy a pound rate on the occupiers of houses, lands, and so on, 'according to the true yearly value'. This rate was subject to confirmation by the justices who could spread the cost of the work over a wider area than the single parish, if the cost was too high for the one. Rate defaulters were to pay double tax. Provisions of a like sort were also applied in towns, where pavements and streets were declared to be common highways. There were of course no borrowing provisions and the building of new highways does not seem to have been contemplated. However, there must have been the equivalent of new road construction when modest tracks assumed, through increased use and general development, the status of highways and began to form part of the surveyors' estimates. The second Ordinance of 1654 imposed a maximum rate of 12d a year on this function.

Restoration Parliaments made every effort to ignore what had been done under the Commonwealth interregnum. The Webbs, in their history, make a cogent comment on this attitude: 'We see, in one department of social life after another, the Parliaments of the whole of the ensuing generation picking up and hesitatingly re-enacting imperfect scraps of the bolder Cromwellian legislation.' In this instance an Act of 1662 went over the same general ground as though the ordinances had not been introduced, even paraphrasing the somewhat lugubrious preamble:

> Whereas the former laws and statutes for mending and repairing the common and public highways of this realm have not been found so effectual as desired . . . by reason of which the said highways are become very dangerous and almost unpassable . . .

Apart from the introduction of a reference to the width of roads, the main difference between the Act and the ordinances was that the maximum rate was brought back to 6d.

There was a time-limit to this statute. Its successor, in 1670, was directed to the 'better repairing and amending of highways now generally spoiled by the extraordinary and unreasonable lading of wagons and other carriages'. The significant feature was that the rate levy of 6d might only be made if the justices were satisfied that the normal statutory repair provisions would be inadequate to repair the highways effectively. This was the Act already referred to above under early bridge legislation, which made the surprising provisions about bridges in Lancashire and Cheshire and Monmouthshire. But what needs to be borne in mind is that 1663 was the year of the first Turnpike Act, which will later be described in detail, and the particular feature of which was that it contained a borrowing provision.

The rating provisions were again given only a limited life, so that by 1691 renewed power was needed. This Act took a noticeably more mature view of the importance of roads, referring to the assistance which good roads gave to commerce and in raising the value of land, but went on to confess that despite earlier laws many roads were still insufficiently maintained and almost impassable. Despite this better appreciation of the value of good roads, and although a time limit was no longer imposed on the power to levy a 6d rate, this could still only be levied where statutory labour proved inadequate. Inadequate it must have been because the reluctance of the villages to appoint surveyors led to the duty to make these appointments being transferred to the justices, to whom the surveyors were to report progress every four months.

By 1696 the point was reached where the road was clearly recognized as being something more than a mere right of passage over land; the Highways Act of that year (for Enlarging the Common Highways) provided for the purchase of land for road widening and established the compensation payable to owners.

The continuing unsatisfactory state of the roads and the inadequacy of the statutory labour system are obvious from the repetitive preambles to the various statutes without the need for reference to contemporary accounts of the hardships of travelling, so that the reluctance to abandon the archaic system and the caution in allowing the justices to levy a highway rate must cause surprise. How far does the advent of the toll-roads provide the answer?

Although the first toll-road had been authorized in 1663, the real advent of the toll-road system, with the creation of a system of initial financing from borrowed money, occurred from 1698 onwards. The sequence of events becomes clearer: Parliament continued to be reluctant to abolish statutory service – presumably on the ground that most roads, by mileage at least, are from their nature 'local' roads – and was also reluctant to switch from this casual system to a fully rate-borne system. The alternative of allowing independent bodies to improve through-roads of proven need, and to recover the cost from those who used them most, leaving local roads to local care, must have seemed a brilliant compromise. Whether this is the explanation or not, that is precisely what happened, and at this point the principle of borrowing for public services was introduced.

As will be shown shortly, each turnpike trust depended upon a private Act being obtained by interested parties, either as or in combination with justices, but at the same time as the turnpikes were expanding, general Highways Acts continued to be passed in an attempt to maintain and enforce the semi-voluntary statutory labour service system for the lesser and more local roads. For example, in 1715 'An Act for making the laws for repairing highways more effectual' was directed to emphasizing that the previous laws must be put into execution, and permitted a rate levy only as a last resort.

Even in 1766 'An Act to explain, amend and reduce to one Act of Parliament the several statutes for the amendment and preservation of the public highways of the Kingdom' made no change in the basic concept, except that with the approval of two-thirds of the parish, a skilled person appointed as surveyor could be paid. There is still no mention of construction of highways as such, though widening is provided for. The Act is prolific in detail – for instance, reference is made to wheels which were narrow or studded with 'rose-headed nails'.

An interesting indicator of the parallel development was that if inhabitants compounded in cash for their statute labour in an area in which there was also a turnpike road, the income must be equitably divided between the parish surveyors and the turnpike trustees. Although among the powers thus consolidated the power to buy land for road widening with compensation to the owner was included, this cost was still to be financed by a rate, even though borrowing was by now a widespread practice on the turnpikes.

In 1773 a further consolidating Act was necessary 'to explain and reduce to one Act of Parliament the highways law'; this went over much the same ground as the earlier Act, and in particular stressed the power of the justices to order the widening or diversion of roads which thereafter were declared to be public highways. The rate of 6d could be raised to 9d for special purposes. A startling array of 'appropriate forms' was added in a schedule to the Act, but borrowing was still not a recognized method of finance, although by this date – as we shall see – borrowing was now also a regular feature of local Acts for Poor Law purposes and was even being adopted for roadworks and other improvements in towns.

This book refers to Scotland only in respect of borrowing within the last 100 years; but an Act of 1778 which is included in the public statutes makes changes in highways law in the County of Wigtown, which were highly significant and not apparently at that time applicable in England for highways purposes, though to some extent they were for the Poor Law. This important Act states that:

> Whereas it hath generally been found that a reasonable composition in money in place of labour is more useful and effectual for the purpose of repairing the roads as well as more easy and convenient for the persons liable by law in statute service.

Such persons may then pay 'such a conversion in money or composition for the same as shall be fixed by the Trustees of each District'. Maximum charges were laid down; the sums were to be collected by the Collector of Land Tax who was to be allowed 5 per cent 'for his trouble'. In addition, a rate could be levied and 'applied towards building, making repairing and upholding bridges and repairing the roads in the said County'. This was however not the abandonment of statutory service, but the introduction of a right to compound for it.

But most important of all, the Act provided that:

> for the more speedy reparation of the said highroads within the said County . . . it shall be lawful for the Trustees of each District [on the request of 2/3rd of the parish] upon the credit of the conversions or sums by this Act appointed . . . to borrow any sum or sums of money that from time to time shall be deemed necessary for repairing the said highways (so as the same do not in all at any one time exceed three years' gross income of the duties arising from the parish for which the same is to be borrowed) and to assign the said conversions and sums so appointed to be paid . . . for such term of years as shall be necessary to repay the sum or sums that shall be so borrowed with interest for the same until repayment thereof.

Whether there were earlier Acts of this nature in Scotland has not been investigated, but this example of a power to borrow for highways purposes (as distinct from toll-roads only) was not paralleled at that time in England and Wales, although there were similar borrowing powers for Poor Law and individual toll-road purposes by this date. The security offered in Wigtown is of interest, in that it included not only a potential rate, but also the income from compounded statutory labour. The form of borrowing instrument is not specified, but clearly what was in mind was a form of 'assignment or mortgage' as in England, where by this date such a document was required to be 'under hand and seal on vellum or parchment'.

After 1773, the next significant Act was the consolidating measure of 1835 which made some attempt to rationalize the administration of the road system, still against the reluctance of the parishes to become seriously involved.

Chapter 3

TURNPIKE TRUSTS AND NAVIGATIONS –
THE FIRST STATUTORY
BORROWING PROVISIONS

The related developments of turnpike roads and inland navigation and harbour works contend for the distinction of producing the first statutory borrowing by what may be deemed a local government authority. Even without the single turnpike scheme which preceded the main body of turnpike legislation by thirty-five years, the turnpikes take first place as borrowers by a short head.[1]

The failure of the highways statutes to create a satisfactory system for the construction and maintenance of roads (particularly through-roads and those forming in effect part of a national trunk network) led to the creation of turnpike roads from 1663 onwards, first, under the magistrates, and thus a direct county function, and later under *ad hoc* bodies of trustees composed of interested persons. The view has already been expressed that the adoption and development of the turnpike system, which patently arose because of the inadequacy of the highways legislation, thus further delayed the introduction of effective highway administration until well into the nineteenth century.

By the same token, the inadequacy of the road system made inland waterways navigation systems of great importance. Indeed evidence will be produced in this book to show that the importance of the township of Ware at the head of the Lea Valley from whence access to London by water was convenient, brought about the pressure on the northern approach roads to that town leading to the creation of the first toll-road, and the borrowing associated with it.

Although the turnpike trusts were *ad hoc* organizations operating on selected stretches of roads, frequently overlapping parish and county boundaries, the work which they did was intended to have been under normal nationally applicable statute law, carried out by the parishes as the highway authorities. In practice, the Acts authorizing the setting up of turnpike trusts endeavoured with only limited success to incorporate the statute service of the old law with the work of the trusts.

The work undertaken by turnpike trusts was eventually taken over by the newly emerging democratic local authorities, and so remains today, with central government acceptance of responsibility for a national network of through-roads. Therefore, the trusts may fairly be accepted as *ad hoc* local authorities; the Webbs, in the volume of their history *The*

Story of the King's Highway, agree that the trusts 'became virtually permanent local authorities entirely unconnected with the counties and the boroughs'. This is not strictly true because of the uneasy partnership with the parishes implied in the statutes setting up the trusts. That the trustees were not democratically elected does not exclude them from local authority status: the members of the county administrations were not then elected, and the parish councils only to a limited extent.

This is not to say that the turnpikes, sensible though their establishment may have been in the light of the inadequacy of the statute law relating to highways, were an overwhelming success. There was much maladministration and neglect, encouraged by a system which gave more attention to safeguarding the investors than to the production of roads satisfactory to the payers of the tolls, and this led to much opposition, some of it (as later Acts show) violent. According to the Webbs, there were eventually 1,100 trusts, responsible for a debt of £7 million covering 23,000 miles of roads but on no overall pattern; on the other hand, Albert, who investigated the system more thoroughly, in *The Turnpike Road System in England*, believes that the pattern was more coherent (but fortuitously so) than the Webbs suggest, in that by 1750 all the main routes to London had been 'turn-piked'. The year 1750 was however notorious for turnpike abuses and consequential riots. As early as 1734 the penalty for breaking toll-gates was death without benefit of clergy.

A fundamental financial weakness with the concept of turnpike roads was that the amount which might be borrowed was never specified, and that the amount so acquired and expended does not seem to have been necessarily calculated in relation to the probable or possible income from the tolls to be levied; assurances from the promoters that the tolls would be likely to service the debt and to maintain the road were lacking. The general Turnpike Acts, like the general Highways Acts, concentrated on restricting the amount of heavy traffic using the roads which in the long run was a counterproductive exercise, in that the better the road, the more traffic it attracted. The administration of the turnpikes was not on the pattern of that of the canals and railways – that is, by formation of companies and the issue of shares – because the turnpikes were expected to be temporary measures only and, in any event, profits were not to be made from the use of the king's highway.

The logical justification of the trusts can, then, be seen to be that they were needed, and so called into being, to improve and maintain those roads which were patently of extra-parochial interest, to the standard called for by a wider regional or national demand. This approach is entirely in line with the current philosophy of highways responsibility, where districts, counties and central government share responsibility in accordance with demands on the roads by local, regional and national traffic. On this basis, however feeble the then general statute law may have been, there was logic in the attempt to draw support from the parish according to the degree of local need, and to call upon users – by tolls – to pay for the level of standard needed over and above parochial needs.

However, there were two flaws in this logic. The first was that despite having made some contribution either by work or rate levy to toll-road construction as part of their statutory service liabilities, the parishioners were also usually expected to pay as much as most other users for the local use of the road, and this they resented since for their own needs they did not require this upgraded standard. The second flaw was that, in the main, trusts were initially authorized to operate for a maximum of twenty-one years, on the theory that at the end of that time – or even earlier – the road would be in such condition that the parishioners could resume its maintenance, and that any debt incurred would in that period have been amortized. In fact the twenty-one-year periods were regularly extended by further private Acts on the ground that as the parish could not resume responsibility for the road at its upgraded standard, the road would therefore again deteriorate and money already spent would be wasted; also debt incurred had frequently not been fully amortized. The Acts allowed the cost of legislation to be a charge on borrowed moneys, and this alone proved a heavy burden (according to Albert) accounting for one-third of the debt.

Some light is thrown on this problem by an Act as late as 1812 (Kent), the third in a series of amending Acts relating to an original of 1730. In this third amendment the preamble included the sinister words:

> And whereas the trustees appointed under or by virtue of the said recited Acts have in pursuance of the power given thereby to them, borrowed a considerable sum of money on the credit of the tolls thereby granted, and the same is still due and owing and wholly unpaid.

Yet still the 'said roads are very much out of repair'. So in some instances at least the roads were neither properly maintained nor was the debt efficiently managed.

Despite their shortcomings, the trusts exhibit important financial principles. They are a clear example at an early stage in the history of local government of the operation of the principle of payment for the use of a service on the basis of benefit received rather than on ability to pay – that is, not by a rate levied on householders and others on the basis of the value of fixed property, but by a charge on those using the service in proportion to the degree of use. The idea sometimes canvassed today that the system of major and through-roads should be financed by a levy on petrol involves a similar concept. Not only are they the first service given statutory power to borrow, but also illustrate the soundest of reasons for capital borrowing – that money must be found and the work done before the raising of income becomes practicable. They demonstrate the basic simplicity of local authority borrowing, a pledge of payment of interest and ultimate repayment of debt against a simple document of acknowledge-ment secured on a statutory source of income. In the Turnpike Acts a borrowing code is gradually evolved which is closely reflected in current practices; in particular, they give lenders priority over all other creditors, presumably because the initial financial resources would not otherwise have been forthcoming.

The security base is significant throughout the history of local authority borrowing – the mortgaging or 'attachment' of income rather than asset value, particularly appropriate in this initial instance where roadworks offer no disposable value except in so far as an income may be derived from their use. Though at a later stage assets are included in the mortgage – toll-houses, gates and weighing machinery – this was simply so that any mortgagee taking over the tolls on default of interest or debt repayment could effectively collect income by the continued operation of the system. As we shall see, turnpike borrowing provisions involve the ambiguity earlier referred to in the use of the term 'security'.

If doubt is felt that the purposes for which the initial capital was borrowed was truly 'work of a capital nature', being variously described as 'repairing' and 'amending' or 'improving', there can be little doubt that as the original highways were in fact for the greater part casual creations over a long period of time, probably having never been positively 'constructed', what the trusts were doing was to construct such roads for the first time, or at least, so improve the standard that the work was the equivalent of a new road and eminently of a capital nature. Certainly, as there is no doubt that the funds required could not be collected from users until the road was in sufficient state to justify a charge, there was no alternative but to proceed on borrowed money.

The location of the first turnpike trust is without surprise – in a poor parish, near the southern end of 'the Great North Road from London to York and so into Scotland'. A considerable amount of traffic of no benefit to the parish converged on this road en route for Ware from which point there was access to London by water, a very much easier method of transport. No doubt, many of the parishes through which this great trunk-road passed suffered a burden, but the parish which showed both incapacity to meet the cost combined with sufficient enterprise to do something about shifting the burden was that of Standon in Hertfordshire.

In the first half of the seventeenth century this parish had on numerous occasions been taken before the justices on 'presentation' because of the failure of the parish officers to maintain the roads in its area satisfactorily. The justices, despite taking steps to increase the amount of statute labour required from the parish, appear to have had some sympathy with the burden placed on a sparsely populated parish because in 1631, and again in 1646, they petitioned Parliament (unsuccessfully) for financial help to be given to the parish in the shape of a power to tax heavy loads passing through. After further presentment in 1658, a third petition in 1660 was again dismissed presumably in the hope that the General Highways Act, passed in 1662, would lead to a solution. This was the Highways Act – which because of its rating provisions was given only a temporary life – which replaced the similar earlier Commonwealth Ordinance, and allowed a rate levy of 6d for parish highway purposes.

A Highways Act to permit a rate levy instead of, or in support of, statute labour was obviously of no help to a sparsely populated and impoverished parish, nor likely to provide adequate funds for such an important road. A final petition in which the county authorities of Hertfordshire were joined by those of Cambridgeshire and Huntingdonshire led to the passing of what was, despite its fairly trivial nature, a landmark not only in highways legislation, but in local government finance as a whole; that is, the Act of 1663, a private local Act entitled 'An Act for repairing the Highwayes within the Countyes of Hertford Cambridge and Huntington'. The preamble puts the case for the proposal but does not indicate why so important a principle should have been conceded in so limited an area. Many times since, local private Act powers have been conceded by Parliament as a prelude to more general legislation, but this Act is not in that category because general statutory powers, adoptive or otherwise, were never given, so that hundreds of local Acts were needed on the subject.[2]

A brief summary of the provisions of this significant statute clearly shows its evolutionary character. There is no mention in it of a turnpike as such. In essence, it provides for payment for the former 'voluntary' statute labour, and the raising of the funds to pay for the labour not by a rate, but by tolls, and pending the completion of the work and the institution of the tolls, the borrowing of the necessary capital moneys at interest. The preamble said that 'Whereas the ancient highway and post road leading from London to York and so into Scotland, and likewise from London into Lincolnshire, lyeth for many miles in the counties of Hertford, Cambridge and Huntington' and is in many places 'very ruinous and become almost impassable, [so] that it is become very dangerous to all His Majesty's liege people that pass that way', delay is caused to

> the many great loads and wagons that are weekly drawn through the said places, the great trade in barley and malt that cometh to Ware and so is conveyed by water to the City of London, and other carriages both from the North parts and also from the City of Norwich, St. Edmunds Bury, and the Town of Cambridge.

Then particularly 'the ordinary course appointed by the laws and statutes of this realm is not sufficient for the effectual repairing and amending of the same', and 'Neither are the inhabitants through which the said road doth lie of ability to repair without some other provision of money'.

Magistrates were therefore empowered by this Act to appoint surveyors who 'shall consider what reparations shall be needful', as well as a receiver of tolls (a treasurer) and toll-gatherers. The surveyors were to buy necessary materials, and to call upon those liable for statute labour to perform this (and supply transport) with the essential difference that now the statute labour was to be paid for at 'the usual rate for the country' (that is, countryside, the prevailing local rate of pay for this type of work). Instead of levying a rate to raise the money for this expenditure as the general Act of 1662 provides 'For the defraying and charge of such reparations', the surveyors were to use toll-gatherers 'to receive or take such sum or sums of money in the name of toll or custom' as are set out in the Act from users of the road. Many other details were also specified. The places at which they could be collected are given as Wades-Mill (Hertfordshire), Caxton (Cambridgeshire) and Stilton (Huntingdonshire) with a proviso that the justices might vary the Stilton selection. Although the Act does not specify the setting up of turnpikes, later amending legislation shows that 'gates' were in fact established. Then follows the borrowing provisions:

> And forasmuch as the moneys so to be collected by such receipt of the said toll will not at present raise a sufficient Stock or Sum of Money as may be sufficient for the speedy repairing of the premises . . . it is further hereby enacted and the said Surveyors are hereby enabled, by and with the consent of the said Justices . . . without further licence severally to engage the profits arising of the said Toll . . . in such sum or sums of money by them to be borrowed for that purpose and by Indenture under the hands and seals of the said respective Surveyors . . . to transfer the said profits of the said Toll and to grant and convey the same for any time or term not exceeding nine years, unto any person or persons that shall or will upon that security advance any present sum or sums of money for and towards the present repairing and amending of the said highways . . . for the repayment of such sum or sums of money so lent with interest for the same.

The use of the word 'Stock' meaning in this context 'cash balances or surpluses' should be noted for future reference.

The same paragraph contains another fascinating though short-lived provision. Realizing that there might be a shortage of lenders prepared to embark on a risk venture of this kind, the justices were authorized to raise the necessary capital by the levy of a rate subject to repayment out of the tolls – in other words, compulsory lending by the ratepayers if willing lenders were not forthcoming. The exact wording of this provision deserves to be quoted:

> or in case such sum or sums of money cannot be borrowed on the security aforesaid for the repair of the ways, that then it shall and may be lawful to and for the said Justices . . . when they see cause to make a rate not to extend to any other county but their own, nor to repair any other than the places aforesaid in that particular county where such rate is made, whereby they shall have power for their several counties to raise upon the parishes that lie in or near the said road (and so will benefit therefrom) such sum or sums of money as they shall see fit and convenient for the speedy effecting of the said repairs.

Provided always that it is enacted by the Authority aforesaid that the

said money advanced by the several towns in the said respective
counties shall again be repaid with interest by the several surveyors
. . . as it doth arise out of the said toll, every county paying for what is
so borrowed within its own county and no further.

The strange shift of terminology from 'parishes' in the rating paragraph to
'towns' in the repayment paragraph is perhaps a drafting slip.

Either from optimism or nervousness at their daring in instituting this
financial breakthrough, the promoters incorporated a further provision
that the tolls could be levied for eleven years only (two years longer than
the loan sanction period), or such shorter time as was required to put the
road into good repair, on the assumption that normal statute labour
would thereafter be sufficient. Any funds in hand on the cessation of tolls
were to be handed to the magistrates.

To recapitulate, what seems to have been the first statutory borrowing
power was for an unspecified sum but for a closely specified purpose, to be
borrowed at interest for a maximum of nine years on the security of tolls
at rates and places specified in the Act, on the road to be reconstructed;
the borrowing instrument was to be on the basis of an indenture under the
hands and seals of the surveyors, with a fall-back provision that a rate
could be levied (also subject to interest and repayment) to raise the
necessary capital if willing lenders were not forthcoming.

In 1818 a reprint of the statutes up to 1715 was published. In this copy
marginal headings not used in the originals have been added, one of which
says: 'Powers of Surveyors with consent of Justices to mortgage the Tolls'.
The word 'mortgage' does not occur in the statute – the power is simply
'to engage the tolls' as a pledge against debt and interest thereon.

As this is the first occurrence of the term 'indenture', later in common
use, the nature of such a document may be described (although some
reference to the practice has already been made in respect of the
chirograph in the Introduction). An indenture was simply an agreement
between two parties, not necessarily relating to money. The terms of the
agreement were written twice on a single sheet of parchment or vellum, the
two copies being then severed one from the other by the cutting of an
irregular wavy line – indented – so that the two parts could again be
matched if need be to establish their common identity. By this method, the
upper copy had the indenture at its foot, and the lower copy the indenture
at its head. In later times the term indenture is in regular use for
documents not in fact indented (for example, articles of apprenticeship).
By contrast, a 'deed poll', an example of which used as a borrowing
instrument will later be produced, is a document of a legal character in
which only one party makes a declaration; this document does not have a
counterpart and therefore does not bear any indentations – the edges being
simply 'polled', or cut. Traditionally an indenture begins with the words
'This Indenture . . .' and the date, while in a deed poll the opening words
are: 'Know all men by these presents. . .'.

The misgivings of the promoters about the availability of willing lenders for a novel enterprise seem to have been justified, unlike their expectation of the early reinstatement of the road and their reliance on its future maintenance under the old statutory system. Other problems also emerged.

In less than two years, in 1664, an amending Act was required 'for continuance of a former Act for repairing the Highways in the County of Hertford'. The preamble referred to the previous three toll locations, but there is no further reference in the body of the Act to that at Stilton. According to the Webbs in *The King's Highway* (p. 115), there was so much opposition to the Stilton toll-gate proposal that it was not proceeded with. All that this second Act says about the Caxton toll-gate is that 'it do prove useless and will not answer the end for which it was intended by reason of the place where the same was set'. The justices were empowered to shift the location to Arrington, where presumably evasion would be less simple, but thereafter no further mention of this gate occurs.

The toll-gate at Wades-Mill received extensive attention in this Act. While there is no further reference to the fall-back proposal for a rate levy for a 'loan', the Act admitted that 'Money could not be advanced by the toll in so speedy a manner as to repair the ruinous state of the road' and that 'none would lend their money on that security'. However, 'Divers gentlemen within the County of Hertford [who] have heartily set themselves to take care for the repair of the said ways . . . did upon their own credits borrow thirteen hundred pounds at interest to effect the work intended by the said Act'; as a consequence, 'they have made the same from a road impassable to be to the satisfaction of all that travel that way very passable and convenient'. However, the drawback was that the tolls were inadequate to repay 'the great sum expended and laid out and so borrowed' with interest in the nine years specified in the original Act. Another road of great importance in the area was also declared to be in an impassable condition. The period during which the toll could be maintained was therefore extended to twenty-one years, with no further mention of a limit on the borrowing period, and the income could now also be applied to the added length of road. A confusing addition was that the persons responsible under law for maintaining the highways (presumably under the normal statute service) should continue to be responsible and should pay a rate of 6d in the pound (as under the Highways Act 1662) such sum to be paid to the treasurer of the turnpike toll. Whether this meant that the 6d rate went to the turnpike income or the turnpike surveyors now assumed a general responsibility for all the local roads is not clear. (The first Act had said simply that the setting up of the toll did not relieve those already by law responsible for the upkeep of the highways.)

The provision occurs again that if the road is in a satisfactory condition and interest and debt cleared before the expiry of the twenty-one-year period, then the tolls should cease. Who the worthy gentlemen were who found the capital or personal bonds is not known. A letter from the Hertford County Archivist reports that early quarter sessions records make reference to the appointment of surveyors but do not disclose the public-spirited gentlemen, 'who may have been landowners along the route of the road and who therefore had an interest in its upkeep'.

A period of twenty-one years from 1664 would have taken the tolls to 1685. Albert, in *The Turnpike Road System in England*, claims that the tolls at Wades-Mill, Hertfordshire, were discontinued by 1680. This is broadly confirmed by an Act in 1692 which revived the two former Acts, 'both which said Acts are some years past expired'. The roads had again 'become dangerous and impassable'. The toll at Wades-Mill was 'to be revived, set up and taken again' for a period of fifteen years or such shorter period as should find the road in good shape again and debts cleared. All the detailed powers of the original Act were revived, presumably including power to borrow.

Fifteen years from 1692 carried the provisions to 1707; that borrowing had taken place is shown in another Act of 1706, which referred to the previous three Acts and noted that the 1692 Act was nearing its expiry date, but regretted that the roads were 'not yet so sufficiently repaired and amended' that the parishes would be able to assume responsibility. This Act also makes the points that 'the expenses already laid out will in great measure be lost [as well as] much money as was borrowed on the credit of the toll . . . which is not yet satisfied'. This indicates that the security had over the years switched, as was intended, from the personal creation of the 'divers gentlemen' to the tolls themselves. The continuation of the tolls was therefore authorized for a further maximum of fifteen years but at half-rate only ('the moiety of the said toll').

At this point the history of the toll fades into obscurity, though no doubt its further adventures are to be found in the appropriate archives. According to Albert, quoting the *Journal of the House of Commons*, at least three subsequent attempts to introduce toll-gates in other parts of the realm were defeated between 1663 and 1695, at which point the turnpike system burst into flower.

Later in this chapter reference is made to similar schemes to those used by the turnpike trusts for inland navigation and harbour improvement purposes. An event of startling relevance to the first turnpike trust emerges from this further line of inquiry. In 1571 an Act was passed to authorize works to bring the River Lea to the north of the City of London. This Act does not contain any financial provisions, but its significance to us is that the access to this river passage at its northern end was at Ware, the town specifically mentioned in the Wades-Mill Act as the target for the convergence of traffic to this point on the Great North Road. Thus the seeds of the 1663 turnpike are clearly shown to have been sown in 1571. A precisely similar situation can be imagined at whatever point on the south coast is chosen for the starting-point of a channel tunnel, should such an enterprise actually one day be undertaken. Incidentally the River Lea is not now a significant waterway, but forms an integral part of the system of London water supply.

The revival of the original 1663 Wades-Mill toll-gate in 1692 seems to have signalled Parliamentary willingness to accept at long last the general principle of toll-roads (and eventually toll-bridges) though, as mentioned above, never to the extent of passing general enabling legislation. What will presumably now never be known is why Parliament chose to take this course instead of rationalizing highways legislation generally, for example, by getting rid of service labour and making highways a county function not dependent on particular parishes. Perhaps Parliament considered that this was a limited problem (if so, how wrong they were) or that payment by use was a more equitable basis than by rateable value – in which case they might well have been right. At least the county authorities might have been given enabling power to institute turnpike trusts where necessary.

In 1695 the second toll-road scheme (London to Harwich) was given statutory authority and from then onwards the system flourished for a century and a half. Can this final acceptance of the toll-road device in any way be identified with the emergence of a spirit of public financial enterprise which brought about the creation of the National Debt on an organized basis in 1693, and the associated establishment of the Bank of England in 1694? Perhaps all these steps were seen as necessary preliminaries to the development of trade and commerce on a wider regional and national scale.

The theoretical basis of the turnpike system needs emphasis; in theory the turnpikes were not (as the Webbs suggest they were) intended either to replace or be entirely independent of the statutory labour system (though the difference between theory and practice might justify the Webbs' statement). The Turnpike Acts intended that those responsible for the upkeep of the roads, either by long-standing custom or the ruling statute law, should remain so. The turnpike trusts were intended to carry out work supplementary to, and not in substitution of, the normal service obligations where these had proved to be inadequate on particularly heavily used stretches of road with marked extra-parochial significance. And – initially at least – their work was regarded as of a temporary, merely remedial, nature only.

How the two responsibilities were to be co-ordinated was not clear from the early Acts. The Wades-Mill Act said that the nominated surveyors were to ascertain what work needed to be done on the specified length of road, to obtain materials and to organize those with a statutory duty to provide labour and transport. The difference was that the labour and transport was to be paid for at ruling local rates out of the tolls (or in the first instance, out of the borrowed money). This seems to mean that although statute labour was not to be abolished, it was to be paid for when it was carried out on a specified length of road to which tolls were to be applied. Some confusion is caused in this first Act when it also says that 'persons chargeable by law' for the repair of the road should remain so. This confusion is somewhat worse confounded in the first amending Act of 1664, in which all persons chargeable by law for the repair of the highways shall remain so, and pay 6d in the pound yearly according to the true value of their estates towards the repair of the highways, such money to be paid to the 'tresurer' appointed to receive the tolls.

When the second toll-gate was introduced in 1695, the surveyors were again authorized to call upon statute labour, and to pay for it according to the local rate for the job, but 'chargeable persons should still remain so chargeable' and 'do their respective work as before they used to do'. These directions were still ambiguous. However, in 1706 another Turnpike Act (Bedfordshire) made clear that the surveyors should pay for work if the persons were required to put in more time than their statutory liability required, or outside the limited area for which statute work could be demanded. The justices were to adjudicate in disputes about how much of the work should be voluntary and how much should be paid for. Possibly this is what had been intended from the start; possibly the problem had been overlooked initially. By 1759 townships and parishes could compound for that portion of the statute work owed to the turnpike road. Either the surveyors turned a blind eye, or many bitter disputes must have erupted.

The authorization to borrow is neatly worded:

The said Surveyors . . . are hereby enabled by Order of the said Justices . . . to engage the Profit arising by the said Toll for such sum or sums of money by them to be borrowed for that purpose and by Indenture under the Hands and Seals of the said Surveyors . . . to transfer the said profit and to grant and convey the same for any time or term not exceeding Fifteen Years unto any person or persons that shall or will upon that security advance any present sum . . . so lent with Interest for the same after the Rate of Six Pounds per cent per annum for every Hundred Pounds.

Turnpike Acts continued regularly from 1695 as the idea spread around the country. The reasons for the introduction of a toll-road were fairly standard in each Act (with occasional special reasons; for instance, damage to the roads caused by the carriage of heavy timbers and guns over roads leading to naval dockyards in Kent). Similarly, the logical and original reason for borrowing is repeated – the need for the work to be done before tolls could reasonably be demanded.

Interest is usually mentioned but not always specified; sometimes it is 'at such rate as the trustees shall agree'; or 'after the rate of 6%', which seems to mean at not more than 6 per cent, if the later added marginal note is to be relied on; or again the phrase was 'not exceeding 6%'; and, after 1713 (when the maximum statutory rate allowed by the usury laws was reduced), 'not exceedng 5%'. Yet another Act says that 'such legal or less interest as the trustees shall think proper', but this was in 1800, by which time this phrase was in general use with other borrowing activities of local authorities. With the maximum rate already laid down under the Usury Acts, there was no reason why the interest rate should have been specified in these early Acts; reliance might well have been placed on what would today be called 'market forces'. After the initial shorter period at Wades-Mill, Hertfordshire, the operating and borrowing periods varied between fifteen and twenty-one years. The amounts to be borrowed were never specified, certainly never related to prospective income, and not until much later was provision for redemption mentioned. For example, in 1761 the Act for a toll-road near Bolton, Lancashire, refers to assignment or mortgage of the tolls 'to secure repayment thereof with such interest', etc. In other words, as might be expected in the early stages of finance by resort to borrowing, the techniques utilized for such organized borrowing were somewhat primitive.

A material change in the original management structure underlying the toll-road system occurred at an early stage. Until 1706 the toll-roads were under the direct control of the magistrates who appointed and controlled the activities of the surveyors, but were not strictly speaking acting as legal 'trustees'. From 1706 bodies of trustees were named in each new Act. In 1697 however a variant occurred which foreshadowed the introduction of the trustee pattern, and also contained several features of special interest.

In this Act, for a road between Birdlip and Gloucester, the power to appoint surveyors who could erect a toll-gate and collect tolls was given to the magistrates as before, with borrowing permitted for a fifteen-year life against a life of the tolls of twenty years. Although all persons 'who by the law are chargeable towards repairing the said highway shall remain chargeable and shall do their respective work on the highway as before', another feature was introduced. So that passengers who would be paying the tolls should be assured that the road would in fact be 'put in sufficient repair' the turnpike could not be erected nor tolls collected until 'sufficient security shall be given by able and sufficient persons to the Justices . . . that the highway shall within five years be sufficiently repaired'. The reiteration of the word 'sufficient' no doubt led to some debate. And so that the persons giving the security shall be 'better enabled to repair and amend the said highway', they were given power and in fact were required to levy for twenty years a rate of 6d in the pound on all the parishes in which the highway or any part of it lay. They were also empowered to see that the parishioners performed the work required by law. However, by the general law this 6d levy should have been available towards all highways work in the parish. Then if the tolls together with the levy were not found to be sufficient to repair the road satisfactorily within the five years, these givers of security were also empowered to levy a rate of 2d in the pound on the hundred or hundreds in which the highway or any part of it lay. (The hundred was probably also the petty sessions area; this took the charge beyond the immediate parishes as a means of helping out poor parishes, but on the face of it the immediate parishes would have had to pay both levies.)

The unfortunate local inhabitants were thus confronted with liability to perform statute labour, to meet a 6d parish rate levy followed by a possible 2d hundred levy, yet were still required to pay tolls on the road when they used it. Worse followed since the Act provided that as many of the people who might be charged tolls for the use of this road would be residents not of the County of Gloucester, but of other counties, particularly Hereford, then these other road-users should not be liable to pay tolls unless the persons giving security for the speedy amendment of the road were also approved by the justices of the County of Hereford as well as of Gloucester. This was an extraordinary provision because the use of these roads by non-local people was the prime justification for the imposition of tolls in the first place. But, finally, to return to a borrowing context, money borrowed for the purpose should have the security not only of the tolls, but also of the parish levy (but not the hundred rate which might also be levied).

While applauding the determination of the framers of the statute to provide ample resources with which the road would be put into a state which justified the tolls, any financial administrator must be concerned at the practical problems with which such a system bristles. However, this appears to be the first statutory borrowing power given (if only partly) on the security of a rate as well as the revenue from tolls – in modern parlance 'on all the rates and revenues of the authority'. But the thought must occur that if statute labour plus the tolls and a parish rate were thought to be possibly inadequate (hence the provision for a hundred rate) for the maintenance of the road, the security of the lenders as to their interest and repayment must have been in some doubt. Perhaps after the initial five-year period to bring the road up to a 'sufficient' standard, the financial situation was expected to be easier.

Perhaps not surprisingly these onerous provisions do not appear to have been repeated in any other Turnpike Act, though in 1706 the Turnpike Act relating to Bedfordshire contains a 'modified 1697 Act' provision. In this Act there was no mention of a parish or hundred levy, nor reference to approval by any other county, but there was a similar embargo on the erection of a turnpike and the collection of tolls until 'sufficient security shall be given by able and sufficient persons . . . that the said way shall within three years be sufficiently repaired and amended'. (There are enough 'sufficients' in this clause to keep lawyers happy for a long time.) Because there was no provision for a levy, the security reverted to the tolls only. There was however another unusual provision that any person lending £300 or more should be appointed a surveyor.

This year 1706 is also the first in which trustees took the place of magistrates (Bedfordshire and Buckinghamshire Roads), and this became standard practice except for one Act of 1707 (Bath) which retained the former system of control by magistrates. The provisions of both of these Acts were otherwise normal except that the 1707 Act also included clauses related to lighting, cleansing and watching in the City of Bath, although the borrowing provisions covered the turnpike road only. By 1725 new Turnpike Acts were still following the standard form.* This means that for

---

* Passing reference has been made to toll-bridges in Chapter 2 on bridge legislation; what seems to have been one of the first statutory toll-bridges was authorized to be erected at Norwich in 1725. In this Act the mayor, sheriffs, citizens and commonalty were authorized to borrow for the purpose by writings under the Common Seal and to assign the tolls as security for such term of years as they thought proper at 'legall interest'.

over sixty years a very simple form of borrowing procedure had sufficed. Albert, in *The Turnpike Road System in England*, suggests that in some cases money could only be raised if personal bonds of trustees were offered in support (as in the original Wades-Mill scheme) but presumably by this time money gradually had become more easily borrowed. By 1760, at which date borrowing in other areas of local administration was becoming more common, not only was the management code of the Turnpike Acts substantially increased in complexity, but an almost complete borrowing code, on the lines of modern practice, had been established by a succession of local Acts. A good example of this stage of development is an Act (1759) relating to roads in Kent which includes a lengthy and reasonably comprehensive borrowing code.

The features necessitating the work authorized by this Act are summarized in its preamble to include 'the deepness of the soil', 'the many heavy carriages . . . loaded with timber and guns for naval ordnance service', the narrowness of the roads, their incommodious nature and generally dangerous state. A long list of trustees is given headed by the Earl of Middlesex, and high qualifications for trusteeships were required based on land ownership and personal property. The Act gave the trustees power to amend, repair, widen and keep in repair the designated road, a power which at first sight seems to fall short of major road construction. However, another clause allowed land to be purchased, so that the line of the road could be changed and the discarded land sold, and construction of causeways (that is, raised footpaths), bridges, watercourses and drains to prevent the road from 'being overflowed' were also allowed. The concept was therefore clearly of major reconstruction which by any standard would amount to work of a capital nature. But statute work was to continue to be due, and persons formerly 'by reason of custom or tenure' chargeable for repairing or amending the road were still to be liable. The justices and officers of the town of Maidstone were to settle how much statute work should be ascribed to the road. Parishes might compound in cash for this liability.

The trustees were permitted to reduce the tolls set out in the Act only when all interest had been paid and debt redeemed, unless with the consent of those to whom debt was still outstanding. The original justification for borrowing was still evoked; that is, because the money to be collected by the tolls and duties might not be sufficient for the speedy repair of the road, any fifteen trustees (this number varies erratically in different Acts) by any written instrument under their hands and seals might assign over or mortgage the tolls and duties to lenders for any term within the life of the authorization to collect tolls (in this case twenty-one years), as a security for the sums borrowed, with such interest not exceeding 5 per cent as the trustees 'shall think fit and agree to give'. After initial borrowing, any further sums required could only be borrowed after fourteen days' notice had been posted on all toll-gates and buildings.

Lenders or their executors or administrators could assign to any persons whatsoever the security (that is, the underlying guarantee of the toll income), benefits and interest, by endorsement of the security (that is, the document) or otherwise in writing, given before two witnesses, but such assignments must be reported to the clerk to the trustees within three months. Both the original mortgage and any assignments must be entered 'at length' in a book (in modern terms the register) and assignments were not valid until so registered. A fee for entry of subsequent assignments of 2 shillings was permitted.

Further assignments could be made *toties quoties* ('as occasion required'), and an assignment once made was binding. The tolls might be farmed out in three-year periods, the income from this to be used by the trustees for the purposes of the Act.

Thus the word 'mortgage' was now used directly in a Turnpike Act (presumably the legislators by writing 'assign over or mortgage' regarded these terms as synonymous), power to assign (give or sell the investment to another) is made clear, and a register of lenders established. The Act also introduced the ambiguity, which persists to the present day, about the use of the word 'security'.

The borrowing code, though now extensive, was not yet complete, but a further important development took place in 1765 (toll-road at Stockport). In this Act all lenders were given equal status irrespective of the date of lending:

> no preference shall be given to any person advancing or lending any sums on the credit of the tolls . . . in respect of priority or advancing or lending such sums . . . but that all persons to whom such mortgages or assignments shall be made . . . shall in proportion to the sum or sums therein mentioned, be creditors of equal degree one with another.

This point, which persists in modern borrowing legislation, is regarded by both sides as of great importance. (Incidentally many of the Acts say that all the documents shall be free of all stamp duty, but this referred to the tax on legal documents and not the later capital stamp duty.)

The detailed specification of the wording of a mortgage and an assignment to a later party (by this stage called simply a transfer) are given in a Bolton Act of 1800. This practice persists into current legislation, though the importance of it was (and still is) modified by the inclusion, after the words that the mortgage should be in the specified form, 'or such other form as the said trustees making the same shall think proper'. In specifying the form of transfer, the added phrase is 'or words to the like effect'. 'Or to the like effect' is the term used in the current Mortgage Regulations specifying the form of mortgage. It was an escape clause of this type which permitted the introduction of the simplified form of mortgage, first, by Manchester in 1960, and now in general use, despite the exact form specified in the regulations, of which more will be said later.

Another change in this Bolton Act was that the mortgage was not only of the tolls, but of all the buildings and appurtenances which a creditor would require to possess in order to collect tolls effectively in the event of default.

While earlier Acts had specified that mortgagees were of equal degree 'in proportion to the sum or sums lent', the mortgage now specified (in current use) that the sum assigned to the mortgagee was 'such proportion of the tolls . . . as the said sum shall bear to the whole of the sum due and the credit thereof'. Subsequent Turnpike Acts while specifying the form of mortgage sometimes do, and sometimes do not, indicate this basis of proportion. The borrowing code was taken a stage further in 1812, in relationship to roads in Kent, in an Act which said that interest should be paid quarterly, but this was not the general practice.

Finally, when the body which ultimately became the Public Works Loan Commission (PWLC) was set up in 1817, its authority extended to the making of loans to turnpike road trustees, and section 27 of the Act permitted a 50 per cent increase in authorized tolls to meet the cost of interest and repayment to the commission. The PWLC's hundredth Report records that in the first year of operation fifty-three applications were received for loans for roadworks, totalling £117,000, of which only £51,000 was advanced.

There were other transportational works which offer a parallel to the turnpike trusts: the railways, beginning in 1830, ultimately spelled the end of the turnpike road system, but long before this the canal system, beginning with the Bridgewater Canal in 1759, provided a competing means of transport, mainly for bulk items where rapid transit was not essential. Both the railways and the canals however, apart from arriving on the scene much later than the turnpike trusts, were different in character, in that they were commercially based with a profit motive, and are not therefore dealt with in this book.

There was however a further group of civil engineering projects which in character fall between the turnpike road system, on the one hand, and the canals and railways, on the other; these were harbour works and works to improve the navigability of rivers for the transport of goods, some of which were of a commercial character and others of which were on a trust basis and often directly associated with local authorities, particularly the boroughs.

While works of this class had been undertaken from earliest times, to a large extent because of the inadequacy of roads, the introduction of systematic improvement and the provision for this by borrowed money closely matched that of the turnpike systems. In a sense these works in so far as they were sponsored by local authorities or equivalent boards of trustees in the common interest, and without a profit motive, were, like the turnpike trusts themselves, an embryo form of municipal trading, financed usually not by a rate levy, but by the charging of dues on the principle of benefit received, or other forms of levy on the vessels using them or goods passing through them.

The Act of 1571 for bringing the River Lea to the north side of London which, although it lacked financial provisions, seems to have created the problems which led to the formation of the first turnpike trust has already been referred to. If the embryo turnpike trust date of 1663 is taken as the starting-point for local authority borrowing, then an Act of 1662 has relevance, giving authority for repairs to the harbour at Dover, being 'much decayed'. According to this Act, a considerable sum of money had already been provided by Charles II for the repair of the harbour, but more was required. Consequently, a duty was to be imposed on ships using the harbour, but when £22,000 had been raised the duty was to be discontinued. This work therefore was to be carried out without borrowing. In 1670 an Act for the repair of the harbour and piers at Great Yarmouth, Norfolk, was to be financed by a ten-year levy on coal and other goods passing through, also without any provision for borrowing. Nor did a similar Act of 1685 rely on initial borrowing. But in 1695, running neck and neck with the first of the main run of turnpike borrowing Acts, an Act was passed for making navigable the Rivers Wye and Lugg, near Hereford, and for maintaining them. Although this work was to be organized by trustees (appointed by the Bishop of Hereford), the finance was not to be provided by the levying of tolls, but by initial borrowing by the trustees supported by an annual charge on the County of Hereford, the City of Hereford and the borough of Leominster. The borrowing power extended to £16,000 at 4 per cent interest, but no further management details were given. While the borrowing was not actually by a local authority, three local authorities obviously shared the debt charges. The statutory reference to this Act is chapter 14 of 7 & 8 William & Mary, whereas the first Turnpike Act of the same year for the road from Harwich towards London is chapter 9, so that the turnpike trust led by a short head.

Repairs to the piers at Bridlington in 1696 were to be met by a levy on shipping without reliance on borrowing, but in the following parliamentary year, 1697, work was required for enlarging, repairing and preserving the bridge and harbour in the borough of Bridgewater which produced the first example of borrowing under statute by what was indisputably a local authority. The work was necessitated by 'the increase in ships, the overflowing of the tides and the violence of the fresh waters'. 'The Mayor, Aldermen, Burgesses and Commonalty of the said borough are in no wise able to bear any great sums of money' such as would be needed for these works. Consequently, increased duties were to be levied for a period of fourteen years on users of the port facilities. Collectors were to be appointed who were to pay over such income to the Receiver of the Issues and Profits of the Borough (now no doubt more readily recognizable as the borough treasurer). To ensure that the tolls collected were used as intended eight commissioners were to be appointed, four by the borough and four by quarter sessions (thus representing the county). Famliar words then follow:

And forasmuch as the moneys to be raised by the duties aforesaid will

not for a long time raise such a stock or sum of money as may be
sufficient for effecting the end and purpose of this Act be it therefore
enacted by the authority aforesaid that the Mayor Aldermen
Burgesses and Commonalty and their successors in Common Council
assembled or the major part of them are hereby impowered by
Indenture under their Common Seal to convey and assure the duties
granted by this Act or heretofor payable or any part or parts thereof
as a security for any sum or sums of money by them borrowed for the
end and purpose of this Act to any person or persons that have
already advanced or that shall advance any sum or sums of money
upon such security. All which money to be borrowed shall be
imployed for and towards the inlarging preserving and repairing the
said bridge or key of Bridgewater according to the true intent and
meaning of this Act.

These new duties (with a maximum of 12d) were to be inclusive of former
charges; the Act concludes with the direction that after the expiration of
the fourteen years allowed for the recovery of the costs of the harbour
works in this way, 'the ancient duties of keyage, pontage and cranage'
should continue as before.

This was closely followed by another Act of historical importance in the
same year of 1697 which uses the term 'mortgage' directly and throws
some light on the problems of fund-raising. This Act was for 'cleansing
and making manageable the channel from the Hythe at Colchester to
Wivenhow' (River Colne). Apparently work had been carried out earlier at
the expense of, or with the aid of, a non-statutory loan by William Hewer.
A toll now authorized to be levied on this stretch of river was to be used to
repay such sums of money with interest as were due to the executors of
William Hewer. Then as further money was needed to complete the work,
the Borough of Colchester might 'grant, mortgage or convey the [income]
from the tolls for a period not exceeding 21 years' to persons who would
lend the necessary sums on such security. With what proved to be
optimism as ill-founded as that shown with the early turnpikes, the tolls
were to cease if the work was completed and debt redeemed before the
twenty-one-year period had ended. The interest rate of 6 per cent was
specified, but the new borrowing was to rank second in preference to that
still owing to Hewer. In 1718 another Act was needed to extend the period
for a further twenty-one years and, in 1739, any time-limit was removed,
the preamble disclosing that £1,200 was still owing to the executors of
William Hewer, late of Clapham, Surrey (obviously not a 'local lender', at
least at the date of his death).

At the beginning of this scheme in 1699 the minutes of the borough
show that the two members of Parliament for the borough 'be desired to
discourse [sic] the Bank of England [only recently instituted] or any other
persons whom they think fit whether they will lend money under the
Channel Act at 6%'. The outcome of this 'discoursing' may be seen from
an order of the council made in September 1701 to seal an indenture of

assignment pledging the duties against a further £1,500 from William Hewer and John Crawley, who were presumably the executors of the former William Hewer. Either these two gentlemen had great faith in the prospects of the borough and the integrity of its officers or they must have felt that unless they kept the scheme afloat the earlier expenditure would be abortive and outstanding debts might founder. Despite the vicissitudes of this scheme, here is to be seen the first use of the term 'mortgage' in a local authority statute, in association with the term 'indenture of assignment'.

Over the next ten years there were a number of river and harbour schemes involving local authorities, some authorizing borrowing, others not. There were also 'trustees' schemes, but whether these can be regarded as quasi-local authorities, like the turnpike trustees, is a matter for doubt. Those Acts which allowed borrowing followed the turnpike principles closely, almost identical wording being used to cover the borrowing procedures. The repair of the harbour at Minehead in 1700 was to be carried out by trustees – this is six years before trustees had taken over turnpike management from the magistrates – and borrowing was by indenture under hands and seals, though the period and rate of interest were not mentioned. The preamble to an Act of 1702 for rebuilding and repairing the piers at Whitby is interesting in its reference to earlier history: Whitby 'hath had piers time out of mind which are now very much ruined and decayed for want of income' – another complaint with a familiar modern ring. The harbour was also described as choked and thus prejudicial to the town and neighbouring country and local shipping. The borrowing was for £6,000 at 6 per cent for a period of nine years only, which seems an optimistically short time. Also in 1702 a scheme to improve navigation of the River Cam, at Cambridge, was put in the hands of conservators appointed by the colleges, quarter sessions and the town council. Borrowing was limited to £2,000, and unusually a clause provided that the conservators should not be personally liable for the debt.

The significant Act of the period was that of 1705 for enlarging the pier and harbour at Parton, Cumberland. Trustees authorized to collect dues, were empowered to 'mortgage the profits' to support borrowing of £1,500 at 6 per cent. The use of the word 'mortgage' for the second time here, in relation to navigation schemes, is perhaps surprising when the Turnpike Acts confined themselves to indentures until many years later. The authorization is again to borrow 'such sums or stock of money' as would be needed.

Another historically interesting Act in 1709 was that for the building of a 'wet dock' at Liverpool – presumably what later was to become the Mersey Docks and Harbour Board. For this scheme the corporation, who gave the land, were to be the trustees, and were allowed to borrow up to £6,000 (interest rate not specified) on the security of the dues, by indentures under the Common Seal. After twenty-one years, provided the dock was then in good condition, one-quarter of the dues was to be paid to the city. The borrowing clause follows closely that used in the turnpikes. It comes as no surprise that a further Act was required in 1717 to extend the borrowing period and to allow further borrowing of £4,000.

Once the early date has thus been established for statutory borrowing by boroughs in this field, along with the use of the word mortgage, there seems little need to develop this side-issue, though no doubt over the course of time many coastal towns acquired powers to develop their maritime facilities. At a much later date – in the 1890s – Manchester was to produce an outstanding example in this area in the substantial loan which the city made to the Ship Canal Co., over a sixty-year period (followed by other loans and concessions) in order to make possible the completion of the inland waterway from Liverpool to Manchester enabling Manchester to establish itself as a great port.

Sad to say, a major portion of the canal and the whole of its associated Manchester Docks may shortly be closed, but two points emerge which illustrate the 'continuity' of the process of capital financing. When in the late 1950s the debt on the borrowing undertaken to lend-on to the Ship Canal was finally amortized, the income from the city's shareholding in the company of £160,000 continued, and a few years later was used by the city as part of its annual financing of the capital fund then established (described later). Moreover, the year in which the Ship Canal debt was finally amortized happened by coincidence to be the first year of major investment by the city council in Manchester International Airport.

NOTES: CHAPTER 3

1   The references utilized in this chapter are extensively the statutes quoted; William Albert's *The Turnpike Road System in England 1663–1840* (Cambridge University Press, 1972) has also proved to be a valuable source of information and reference. See also S. Webb and B. Webb, *The Story of the King's Highway* (London: Longmans, Green, 1913), a volume in their English Local Government series, together with information and copies of mortgages, kindly supplied by various county treasurers and county archivists, particularly in Hertfordshire and Kent. A personal visit of inspection to Wades-Mill, in Hertfordshire, found no indication of the first turnpike either by monument or in local folklore. The discovery of the significance of the work of 1571 on the River Lea Navigation (see later) is another example of serendipity, the importance of which might not have been recognized had the Lea Valley not been *en route* on frequent family visits.

2   The question arises as to why a general power to establish turnpikes was never given. The answer may be that, as after a brief initial period the trusts were established in an *ad hoc* way by groups of interested people, not necessarily magistrates, there were no appropriate administrative bodies on which such a power could have been devolved in general terms once the magistrates had officially withdrawn from the scene.

Chapter 4

THE COMING OF THE POOR LAW

The Poor Law has its origins in legislation for the suppression of begging and vagabondage. The first statutory hint that the care of the poor was recognized as a separate issue from the suppression of begging by idle and dissolute persons was an Act of Henry VIII in 1530, the title of which referred to 'Vagabonds and beggars and poor people'. The preamble of this Act quoted a series of earlier Acts back to 1350, which 'be acts made against vagabonds and beggars'. Thus while the suppression of vagabond-age and begging was an old and apparently intractable problem, Henry's Act allowed consideration of the genuine poor for the first time. From that point there has emerged, over 450 years, a stream of legislation leading in a direct line to the social security provisions of today – from the parish overseers, through the Guardians of the Poor Law Incorporations, the Boards of Guardians, the Public Assistance Committees, National Assistance and the Department of Health and Social Security. However, for a number of years the statutes continued to deal with the care of the poor and the suppression of idle begging as a combined problem.

The Poor Law was administered from early times first by the parishes, and then by *ad hoc* authorities; until quite recent times, that is, poor relief was fully accepted as a function appropriate to local administration. Although there were powers for assessing and levying local taxes before the poor rate was introduced (effectively from 1601), the poor rate became the core of the general rating system which subsequently developed as virtually the only form of local taxation. Ultimately there were three stages in the transfer from local to central authorities: the rationalization of the parish and local Act incorporations in a uniform system of unions in 1834; the transfer of the guardians and the work of Poor Law unions to the principal local authorities in 1930; and the further transfer to central government in 1948 (except for such locally retained services as institutional relief in old people's homes, and care for children and the handicapped) when Public Assistance became National Assistance. In contrast with the early development of rating for poor relief, active borrowing for Poor Law purposes was a relatively late introduction (in 1756).

Henry VIII's Vagabond Act of 1530 provided that justices of the peace in the shires and towns within England should make diligent search among their inhabitants for aged, poor and impotent persons who were compelled 'to live by alms of the charity of the people'. These persons were to be licensed to beg within defined areas with stern physical penalties for transgressions. Any person 'being whole and mighty in body and able to labour' who begged or could not explain how he gained his living was to be declared a vagrant, and could also be severely and even barbarously punished – ultimately, via branding and 'enslavement', to death without benefit of clergy. In 1536, 1547 and 1549 further attempts were made to emphasize the importance of the justices' duties.

In 1551 an Act directed more specifically towards helping the poor began with the words: 'To the intent that valient beggars, idle and loitering persons may be avoided, and impotent and lame provided for, which are poor of very deed.' Registers were to be prepared each Whitsuntide at which time the parson (or the chief officers in towns) 'shall gently ask and demand of every man and woman what they of their charity will give weekly towards relief of the poor'. Two or more able persons were to be appointed 'gatherers and collectors of charitable alms'. If gentle exhortation did not produce satisfactory results, then the aid of the bishop was to be enlisted and after that of the magistrates, who could assess any recalcitrant villagers and if need be commit them to prison for their obstinacy, 'without bail or mainprize [right to bail]'. Thus from the middle of the sixteenth century a recognizable system of poor relief was emerging which embraced registration of the poor, the establishment of settlement (that is, fixing responsibility on a specific parish), the setting of the able-bodied poor to work and the beginnings of a rate levy by the magistrates, and shortly afterwards, the identification of the responsibility of relatives of poor persons for their welfare, something which fore-shadowed the dreaded Family Means Test of the 1930s.

Elizabeth's first Act for relief of the poor – strengthening the earlier Acts – was in 1562, almost forty years before her famous 1601 Act. By 1572 the problem of an excessive number of idle persons was still prominent: 'Whereas all parts of this realm of England and Wales be presently with rogues and vagabonds and sturdy beggars exceedingly pestered, by means whereof daily happeneth . . . horrible murders [etc.]', then, all previous Acts were rescinded and a new code introduced against begging and in favour of organized poor relief. The justices were more closely implicated, in that they, instead of the church officials, were to set up the registers of the genuine poor and determine their places of settlement. The justices, rather than the parishioners, were to appoint the collectors and overseers for each parish. The term Guardians of the Poor – the administrators as distinct from the overseers who were the tax-collectors – was not used until 1696 in the Bristol incorporation.

The Poor Act of 1575 made the first provision for the setting up of stocks of materials on which the poor could be put to work. Although the provision of buildings was not mentioned, the necessity for workhouses was beginning to emerge. In this Act houses of correction were to be provided by the levy of a county rate for those who could, but would not, work. There seems to have been an assumption – later developed in relation to workhouses – that the work produced in these establishments would pay for their upkeep.

The Act of 1597 for the Relief of the Poor continued the orderly approach to the treatment of the subject on realistic lines. Its provisions were short term and were repealed in the major Poor Relief Act of 1601. Although the 1601 Act is that usually regarded as the beginning of the Poor Law, these earlier Acts clearly do more than merely prepare the ground – they establish the principles – and the 1601 Act was really the point of consolidation.

The scheme as produced by the 1601 Act, consolidating, amending and extending the earlier Acts, effectively launched the Poor Law on the principles which it maintained basically until 1834 and even right up to the date of nationalization. At Easter of each year the churchwardens and from two to four substantial householders were to be nominated by the justices as Overseers of the Poor. Their duties were:

(1) to set to work or put out to apprenticeships children whose parents could not maintain them;
(2) to set to work able-bodied persons who had no trade and could not maintain themselves;
(3) to provide stocks of materials with which such poor could be employed;
(4) to provide (with the consent of the lord of the manor) houses for the use of the poor on waste or common land.

To finance these activities the overseers were to raise by taxation of every inhabitant such competent sums as would enable them to fulfil their obligations. Under earlier law the tax was to fall on inhabitants and landowners, but in the 1601 Act this was specified in a more determined manner as 'every inhabitant, parson, vicar or other, and every occupier of lands, houses, tithes impropriate or propriations of tithes, coalmines and saleable underwoods'. (Cannon, in his *History of Local Rates*, recounts how the problems of who and what was to be rated were fought over by succeeding generations.) Sale of goods and distress could be levied for non-payment of tax or defaulters could be sent to the county gaol or house of correction. Provision was made for appeal to quarter sessions. Family liability was extended to embrace grandparents, parents, spouses and children. The officers of corporate towns were to have similar rights and responsibilities.

Provision was also made for a modest county rate (to be levied by precept on the parishes) for the maintenance of persons in county gaols, hospitals and almshouses; money and goods could be made available to those struck by natural catastrophes – fire, flood, and so on. If the parish was too poor to maintain its own paupers, the justices were empowered to spread the cost, first, over other parishes within the area of the hundred, and then if need be over the whole county. This mention of the hundred had a significance in relation to the development of the first borrowing by Poor Law incorporations.

Family liability and the responsibility of the parish for its own poor had far-reaching results. Paupers could not leave the parish, and if they did so could be returned to their area of 'settlement'. Definition and identification of 'settlement' continued to be a problem through to modern times.

Apart from workhouses, which later played a great part in the history of the Poor Law (and involved much borrowing), houses of correction (a county provision) effect a link between the provision for the suppression of vagabondage and the relief of the poor. The houses of correction could be used to discipline the poor who could but would not work, as well as those who would not bear their share of the cost of poor relief.

In the light of the vicious penalties in earlier times against rogues and vagabonds, from which the Poor Law code was hived off, an Act of 1609 has an ironic interest. It is entitled 'An Act for the due execution of laws and statutes heretofore made against rogues and vagabonds and sturdy beggars and other lewd and idle persons'. In its opening reference to earlier statutes the following words, which have about them an air of sad disillusionment, occur (and later recur in Poor Law as in highways legislation): 'which laws have not wrought so much good effect as was expected.' This was because the houses of correction had not been built as directed by earlier Acts and 'the said statutes have not been duly and severely put in execution'. Yet all this Act did was to reaffirm that the earlier Acts must now be resolutely applied.

So the care of the poor was instituted, like highways maintenance, as a parish function but with power given to the parish to levy a rate, in contrast with highways where the establishment of statute service was initially considered to make a rate levy unnecessary. Both services were under a degree of supervision by the county magistrates. Again the parish proved less than effective as a unit of administration overall, because of the variations in area, population and wealth. There was a double dilemma: the poorer the parish, the greater the proportion of destitute parishioners it would be likely to have, and the less its ability to maintain them; and the richer the parish, the less inclined it would be to share its neighbours' financial difficulties. The situation would be even more difficult where several adjacent parishes formed a borough without clearly defined internal boundaries. The fact is inescapable that both for highways and poor relief the parish was inadequate as the administrative unit on a national basis.

As a result of the impracticality of the parish as a functioning unit over the country as a whole, especially where the building of a workhouse and other accommodation was necessary, and in spite of the reluctance of parishes to share costs, a number of combinations of parishes were formed by the creation of corporations with the specific duty of the welfare of the poor and sick. These formed independent bodies of parish representatives, but where they occurred in the boroughs, the council of the borough was usually created as a separate Poor Law incorporation, sometimes with the addition of county representatives and clergy.

Not surprisingly, the first of the incorporations was in the City of London and its 'liberties' (which included, *inter alia*, the Inns of Court) where congestion and problems of lack of clear parish demarcations can be imagined as causing particularly serious problems. This first incorporation was created as early as 1647 under a Commonwealth ordinance. It was composed of members of the Council of the City of London but had the status of a separate body with the specific duty of relief and employment of the poor and the punishment of vagabonds and other disorderly persons. It was authorized to erect workhouses and houses of correction and to relieve the poor over all the wards of the city, financed by a rate levy against parish overseers, who did not become members of the corporation. The members of this special corporation were given the title of 'governors'. The ordinance was apparently soon found to be unsatisfactory as it was enlarged in 1649 by another ordinance in which problems of settlement were clarified, and the finance by a rate levy dealt with in more detail. These ordinances lapsed on the Restoration but the arrangements were to all intents and purposes confirmed, in 1662, in an Act in which concern was expressed that despite settlement provisions the poor tended to drift to the richer parishes.

There was no statutory provision for borrowing in the London scheme which was slow in getting under way, and further incorporations did not take place until the end of the century. The first of these, in 1695, provided for a Poor Law corporation in the City of Bristol by which nineteen parishes were merged for Poor Law purposes within the city. For the first time and thereafter the members of the corporation were described as 'Guardians of the Poor'. Again this corporation was not given statutory power to borrow (although this was the date of the breakthrough in turnpike trust borrowing) but the financial provisions are of some interest.

The corporaton was to estimate the cost of the necessary workhouses, hospitals and houses of correction, subject to a maximum of £5,000, which was to be financed by a levy on the parishes over not less than three years – a clear example of an early 'capital purposes' rate. As these establishments could have been provided in much less than this time, temporary borrowing must surely have been engaged in. This seems likely as there is evidence (discussed in Chapter 5 on borrowing by boroughs) that Bristol had undertaken a good deal of *ad hoc* non-statutory borrowing in earlier years for city purposes. The cost of maintenance had also to be estimated but was required to be financed within the poor rate, at a level levied in any of the three previous years. The money was to be collected by a precept on the churchwardens and overseers. These efforts to impose cash limits were obviously impracticable and increases had to be permitted in later Acts, but still without the introduction of a power to borrow. There is evidence in the Bristol records that revenue deficiencies occurred because of these rate restrictions, which had to be financed by short borrowing until the limits of the rate levy were raised. For instance, in an Act of 1713, Bristol obtained authority to increase the maximum

rate, because despite 'diligence and care and thrifty management' and the
receipt of sizeable charitable donations, the city had 'contracted several
great debts still growing heavy upon them by the daily increase of the poor
so that the said Corporation will unavoidably sink to the great detriment
both of the Rich and the Poor of the said City'.

The Bristol incorporation of 1695 was followed by a series of fourteen
incorporations in a variety of types of town from 1697 to 1711 after
which there was something of a pause. These Acts are generally in similar
form except for three which have surprising borrowing provisions. In 1697
the Act for the incorporation of parishes for Poor Law purposes for two
towns as far apart geographically as Exeter and Hereford have consecutive
chapter numbers – namely, 33 and 34 of 9 & 10 William III – and each
Act concludes with a clause after what is usually the concluding clause of
the other Acts in this series. This additional clause is in the following
terms:

> And be it further enacted by the Authority aforesaid, that it shall and
> may be lawful, from time to time, and at all times hereafter, for the
> Mayor, Aldermen and Citizens, of the said City of Exon [Hereford],
> and their Successors, by an Deed or Deeds, Writing or Writings, under
> their Common Seal, to grant, convey, and assure, for so long time as
> they shall think fit, to any person or persons whatever, all such Toll of
> the Market of the said City, that have at any time heretofore been
> collected or paid, as a Security for any sum or sums of Money that
> they shall think fit at any time to borrow, or take up, for setting to
> Work the Poor of the said City and County, and promoting the
> Publick Good hereby intended.

The exact repetition of these words in the two Acts certainly throws some
light on the practices of parliamentary draftsmanship even so long ago.
But why did each of these towns rely upon the market tolls as security
instead of on the poor rate? The answer is now lost in time, but there is a
possible explanation that there was adequate income from general sources
in these two boroughs – including the market tolls – to make unnecessary
at that time the levying of a poor rate; but this is no more than guesswork.

There is a further surprise – in 1711 the last Act in this short series for
parish incorporation at Norwich also gave power to borrow, specifically
for the provision of a workhouse and for setting the poor to work, but on
the security of 'all that parcel of land . . . known by the name of the Town
Close'. Land on which the bishop's palace stood was excluded from this
offer of security.

No similar borrowing powers appear in the incorporations at this time
even for such comparable cities as Kingston upon Hull, Gloucester,
Worcester and Plymouth. Unfortunately nothing further is known about
the exercise of these early powers to borrow, coinciding, as they do, with
early turnpike borrowing activities.

In 1722 a general provision known as Knatchbull's Act gave small parishes power to combine for poor relief purposes, but without mention of a power to borrow. Knatchbull's Act was, in any event, apparently found to be too limited in scope to produce much response. In 1727, in Canterbury, an extensive incorporation of the parishes was introduced similar to that in Bristol; this body took over several existing buildings such as the Poor Priests' Hospital originally given to the city by Elizabeth I. The Poor Law corporations consisted of the mayor, recorder, justices and twenty-eight other persons 'to be chosen out of the ablest and discretest inhabitants' at the rate of two from each parish, to be named the 'Guardians of the Poor'. This reference to the ability and discretion of guardians occurred frequently in Acts of this time. An important development historically was that this Act also included street-lighting provisions, also to be financed by the levy of a rate.[1]

Although the Act forming the Poor Law corporation at Bury St Edmunds in 1747 does not provide for borrowing, the forthrightness of its preamble is worth quoting:

> Whereas it is found by experience that the poor within the borough of Bury St. Edmunds do daily multiply, and idleness and debauchery amongst the meaner sort do greatly increase, for want of workhouses to set them to work, and a sufficient authority to compel them thereto, as well to the excessive charge on the inhabitants as the great distress of the poor themselves . . .

Just as the framers of the turnpike legislation took the optimistic view that once a toll-road had been restored statute labour would thereafter suffice for its maintenance, the builders of the early workhouses seemed to have believed that the work performed therein would produce income sufficient to reduce the poor rate materially. The provisions for the operation of the Poor Law corporation in Bury St Edmunds are extensive and similar to those at Bristol and Canterbury. While the corporation could 'purchase, buy, build, make or erect a workhouse', there was a cash limit on the rate levy of a mere £1,000. This Act also included powers for paving and the repair of streets. The omission of power to borrow is again surprising as there is evidence (see Chapter 5 on borough borrowing) that this town had a history of non-statutory borrowing.[2]

The year 1756 is the significant year on two counts; but before these are enlarged upon, mention perhaps might be made of an Act relating to the City of Chichester in 1753 for incorporation of the parishes into a single Poor Law authority (and for street lighting). Borrowing was not authorized, but the Act provided for the handing over of Cawley's Almshouses as a workhouse, together with two adjacent fields for the income they would yield, but they might alternatively be 'mortgaged or sold' to raise money for the purposes of the Act. (These fields remain today the property of the city.) Thus a 'transfer of assets' seems to have removed any need to borrow.[3]

The breakthrough came with an Act relating to Colneis and Carlford, in

Suffolk.[4] This Act marked the first seriously contemplated borrowing for Poor Law purposes (ignoring the peculiar 'flash in the pan' happenings at Exeter, Hereford and Norwich nearly sixty years earlier). In addition, it applied incorporation to a group of rural parishes rather than the parishes forming a borough, such parishes being within the overall confines of two former hundreds (probably then petty sessional divisions). Any parish which overlapped the boundary of the hundred could be considered as being within it for this purpose. Even taking the Exeter etc. cases into account, this Suffolk example was the first borrowing authorized on the levy of a rate as distinct from a toll. The preamble gives as the justification for borrowing 'that the poor are very numerous and supported at great expense' and that powers in the Act for the provision of a workhouse

> will tend to the more effectual assistance and relief of such as by age, infirmity, or diseases are rendered incapable of supporting themselves by their labour, to the better employment of the able and industrious, the correction and punishment of the profligate and idle, and to the education of poor children in religion and industry; and thereby the poor, instead of being wholly supported by the public may contribute to the support and relief mutually of each other, and be of some assistance to the community to which they have hitherto been a grievous burden.

The corporation was to be composed of all local clergy and richer property-owners who were to become 'Guardians of the Poor' (women property-owners could become guardians only by proxy). These guardians meeting quarterly were to elect a working body of twenty-four directors (still to be chosen from 'the most able and discreet of the Guardians') and thirty-six acting guardians, with necessary (paid) officers. Land could be purchased and buildings acquired or constructed for the purposes of a hospital, a workhouse, a house of correction and any other necessary premises. Purchase of such land and buildings was to be made from the money authorized to be borrowed, at not more than twenty years' purchase of the true annual value for land, and fourteen years for buildings.

Because of the historical importance of this borrowing clause, its terms are given here in full:

> And be it further enacted by the Authority aforesaid, That it shall and may be lawful for the said Guardians to borrow any sum or sums of money, not exceeding in the whole the sum of Six Thousand Pounds, at an interest not exceeding Four Pounds per Centum per Annum, and to assign over by writing under their Common Seal, all or any part of the Poors Rates, to be collected within the said Hundreds of Colneis and Carlford, as a security for repayment of the Principal and Interest of the money so to be borrowed; and such securities may be from time to time assigned and transferred; and such assignments and

transfers shall intitle the persons to whom the same shall be made, to all the principal and interest monies due and to grow due on such securities.

Despite the size of the working committee, control of borrowing and the budget was to remain in the hands of the full body of guardians. At each quarterly meeting 'for the better security of such sums of money as shall be borrowed' for the relief of the poor and other expenses, the guardians were to assess what sums were required from the parishes 'for paying interest on debt, defraying current expenses, and for and towards discharging the debt'. Income was to be raised by the issue of warrants (orders) against the parish overseers for their share, and this was to be allocated 'with as much equality and indifference as is possible'. The parish overseers were then responsible for collecting the money required. Irrespective of debt charges, cash limits were still to be observed; the sums to be levied on the parishes were not to exceed in any one year what had been assessed for the relief of the poor 'upon a medium' to be drawn from the preceding seven years. As despite the provision of land and buildings the rate charge was not to increase, there is no doubt that the expectation was that the proceeds of the activities of the workhouse would relieve the burden on the ratepayers. In fact the Act says as much:

> The profits of the work to be done by the said poor people in the said house or houses, deducting thereout such allowances and gratuities, as are herein before limited, shall be applied in aid of the said rates and assessments, towards the maintenance of the poor within the said two hundreds.

The justices were responsible for an annual audit. The Webbs, in their history, report that in this scheme an Admiral Vernon gave the land and loaned £1,000 at 3½ per cent. The Act is long and complex, containing an extensive code for the management of the workhouse and the welfare of the poor.

Several other Suffolk hundreds eventually adopted a similar plan. For example, two with identical preambles and general provisions were for the hundreds of Mutford and Lothingland (1764) and Loes and Wilford (1765). At Mutford, where borrowing of £8,000 was authorized, the guardians were to include county justices residing within the hundred. The amount which might be borrowed at Loes was £10,000 but with the curious proviso that no loan of less than £100 was to be accepted. A register of investors was called for and all lenders were to rank equally without priority, a very important principle for the future of local authority borrowing. A somewhat sinister note is struck in the Loes Act about the fee which might be charged for transfer entries in the register; this was to be 2s 6d: 'it being the intent and meaning hereof that the clerk shall have no more than 2s. 6d. for what is to be done by him touching every assignment to be made as aforesaid.'

Despite the acceptance of the principle of borrowing in these statutes, an Act setting up a Poor Law corporation in Chester, in 1762, did not include a borrowing provision, although Chester was undertaking *ad hoc* borrowing for general purposes at that very moment (one such purpose being the provision of a workhouse); this may again indicate that boroughs took the view that their status exempted them from the need for specific powers to borrow. However, an amending Chester Act of 1803 did give specific sanction to borrow, and Oxford in 1771 left the question beyond doubt. This Oxford Act was a very substantial measure for the welfare of the poor of Oxford, and introduced for the first time power to borrow by annuities for Poor Law purposes. (Annuities had been used in London for street-works in 1766, see p. 92.) By that date the four Poor Law functions had been clearly established – relief of the old and sick, better employment of those able-bodied but unfortunate, correction and punishment of the idle and disorderly, and education of orphans and pauper children.

A shortcoming of the Oxford Act, extensive though its contents were, was the lack of certainty that the borrowing was authorized for capital purposes only, and not to meet revenue expenses or to provide working balances. Land could be purchased and buildings and working stock provided, and many duties and responsibilities were imposed. Yet the powers to borrow by the issue of annuities or the mortgaging of the rate were widely separated in the Act and their purposes somewhat differently described – that is, they did not form a compact borrowing provision, specifically for the provision of capital assets. An overall maximum borrowing of £10,000 was imposed, the borrowing by annuities was 'in order to raise a proper fund to enable the Guardians to carry into execution the several trusts hereby imposed'; the alternative power to borrow on mortgage of the rate related to any sums (within the total of £10,000) 'necessary for the purposes of the Act'. Probably, in practice, while some borrowing might have been undertaken for cash-flow purposes, the major part would have been for the provision of capital assets. The situation is made somewhat doubtful because the central government at that time were not averse to borrowing by annuity 'in anticipation of revenue' – a questionable practice.

The nature of the Oxford annuities was specified in some detail. They were to be life annuities ('the full term of the natural life') on the life of the lender or his nominee, at a rate 'not exceeding 9%'. Confusion in modern minds is then caused by the following provision that they were to be sold 'to the best bidder for the same' after advertisement. The problems of the early use of annuities and the proper 'price' to be paid before the availability of efficient tables of life expectancy will be examined in due course, and examples produced of attempts to devise rough-and-ready formulae for coping with this issue. At this point all that can be said is that there were two possible variables: the rate which was not to exceed 9 per cent and which, in theory, could therefore be adjusted to suit each bidder; and the 'bids' which would depend on the age and sex of the lender or his nominee. If a single rate of return were fixed for all annuities on, say, a nominal value of £100, the value of the bid would vary with the age of the life covered. The reference to sale to the 'best bidder' suggests that the purchase price was the variable and not the rate of return attached to the nominal value. A successful applicant was to be given an interim receipt, later to be exchanged for 'an order on parchment or vellum' under the hands and seals of at least nine guardians. Payment was to be quarterly by warrant, that is, an order on the corporation's treasurer. The term 'warrant' as applied to the cheque on which local authority interest payments are made has persisted to modern times. Entitlement to annuity payments could be assigned, but of course would remain attached to the life originally nominated. An adequate register of annuitants was to be maintained to which any ratepayer could have reasonable access 'without fee or reward'. There is some possibility that the introduction of annuities was at least partially in an attempt to circumvent the usury laws, in that the 'true' rate of interest could be concealed in the composite annual payment.

The security for the annuity payments was 'the monies arising by the respective rates on the several parishes made by virtue of this Act' with the added and significant provision that upon receipt of the warrant ordering him to make payment the treasurer was to 'pay the same out of the first monies which shall be in his hands arising by the respective rates on the several parishes'. This sounds like the equivalent of the modern provision that interest and repayment of debt constitutes a first charge on rates and revenues.

By contrast with this relatively detailed treatment of annuity borrowing, the mortgage provisions some fifteen pages later in the statute, though concisely expressed, seem very much of an afterthought. The guardians were authorized

> to borrow and take up at interest any sum or sums of money which they should think necessary for the purposes of this Act and by writing under their hands and seals, to assign over the rates and assessments made by virtue of this Act . . . to the persons lending the same, for securing the repayment of any such sum or sums and interest thereon.

In default of interest or repayment the lenders were to have the 'same powers, rights and privileges for the recovery thereof as the annuitants are by this Act invested with for the recovery of their respective annuities'. There were no further administrative details relating to mortgages except the proviso that the raising of further annuities to repay the mortgages should be permitted outside the £10,000 limit – that is, a transitional arrangement and the only mention of provision for repayment of the mortgages.

The decade of the 1770s saw the introduction of a number of import- ant borrowing developments. Several areas, this time in Norfolk and presumably impressed by the success of earlier activities in Suffolk, set up incorporations on the bases of the hundred for Poor Law purposes of which that at East and West Flegg in 1775 is a representative example. In this case the emphasis was on mortgages. The directors and acting guardians from the combined parishes were empowered to assign not only the poor rate, but 'buildings, lands and premises' as security for borrowing £6,000, 'for the purposes of this Act'. Assignments were to be registered and could be further assigned by endorsement. All creditors were to rank equally. However, if the directors and acting guardians thought fit, up to £3,000 of the total sanctioned could be 'upon annuities for lives', on the same security. A recognition of the problem of the uncertain nature of life annuities is to be seen in the provision that no annuity was to be granted against the life of any person under the age of 50, nor for any sum exceeding £50 per annum. There was no reference to sale to the highest bidder, nor to the interest rate for either form of borrowing. This can hardly be suspected as a device to evade the control of usury.

In fact despite those provisions, according to Digby's *Pauper Palaces* (p. 38), this corporation raised a portion of its requirements by the speculative device of a tontine (East and West Flegg Minute Books, 1775–6), of twenty-five shares of £100 each. Similarly, the Hundred of Forehoe, in Norfolk, formed a Poor Law corporation in 1776. This Act simply gave the power 'to mortgage and assign over by writing under the Common Seal the buildings and poor rates as security for loans of up to £11,000'. Nevertheless, this corporation also borrowed £11,000 by means of a tontine of 110 shares of £100 each, some details of the progress of which are still known, in that while the initial rate was 5 per cent, by 1800 with only eighty-five survivors, it had risen to 6·20 per cent and by 1836 survivors were receiving 15·3 per cent.[5]

Tontines had been used by central government from time to time since the beginning of the century. They are a form of annuity, in which as holders die their annuity continues to be shared among survivors. Sometimes the participants are formed into groups on an age basis and the schemes are then described as 'subject to survival by classes'. The full and exciting history of the tontine has not yet been fully explored, but they are dealt with at some length as a form of borrowing later in this book, although their impact on money-raising by local authorities was negligible. Remarkable as they may seem as a form of public service borrowing, they are not dissimilar in underlying philosophy from the premium bond today and they are, of course, a form of lottery, a means of government finance in the past as it is moderately in local government today.

While the use of tontines marks a striking development of borrowing by a local authority, equally interesting attempts to break new ground in borrowing occurs in 1775 for the building of a workhouse at Marylebone. Here £10,000 was to be borrowed 'at the lowest rate of interest that the same can be procured' on the security of the rates. The money was to be borrowed 'upon bonds of £100 each'. This appears to be the first statutory use of the bond as an instrument for local authority borrowing, although it was common in all sorts of other ways, as the simplest undertaking of a contract. It had, for example, been frequently used in earlier legislation, in the sense that various officers – for instance, treasurers – were to give bonds as to due and honest performance of their duties, what would today be called a fidelity bond. It has also been used as already described in the earliest of the toll-gate schemes at Wades-Mill, Hertfordshire, where when money could not be raised initially on the security of the tolls, various gentlemen had given their personal bonds as security. Equally significant in this Marylebone Act, a more positive style of sinking fund was introduced; instead of relying as in an Isle of Wight Act in 1771 on a share of profits made from the operation of the workhouse, the Marylebone guardians could resolve at any of their quarterly meetings to 'pay off and discharge a sum not exceeding £500'. Equally interesting, the lenders who were to be repaid were to be selected by lot – by drawing numbered slips from 'a wheel or box'. Once a portion of debt had been repaid, reborrowing was permitted as necessary up to the total allowed in the Act of £10,000 overall. But most interesting of all – perhaps an indication of the City men behind this scheme – if the guardians found that money borrowed could be replaced at a lower rate of interest (not less than £500 at any one time), they were urged to repay and replace at the lower rate (or presumably negotiate a lower rate) – a form of what is now called a 'roll-over'. The intrusion of operational details of this kind into the Act which would today constitute normal day-to-day loan management is indicative of the way in which these early administrators were feeling their way into the emerging capital market. In contrast, in the same year 1775 almost simultaneously with the Marylebone scheme a workhouse at Clerkenwell was to be financed 'by annuities or upon bond or other security' (£300 maximum contribution for an annuity). But what is abundantly clear is that a considerable degree of sophistication was creeping into loan management just about 100 years after the first tentative borrowing at Wades-Mill.

Another scheme in the London area of this time had somewhat peculiar provisions. This Act of 1774 related to the care of the poor and also paving works in the Liberty of the Tower of London. The preference for annuities is shown in the section which says

forasmuch as the borrowing money upon annuities will be the most speedy and effectual method to accomplish the good ends and purposes intended by this Act with respect to purchasing, hiring, or erecting a workhouse and employing and maintaining the poor, and paving and regulating the streets . . .

Borrowing was permitted for both purposes by 9 per cent life annuities; a further provision for loans was made on assignment of the rate but this was confined to the paving functions of the Act. The Poor Law borrowing was to be supervised by the guardians, but the paving was the responsibility of commissioners.

Although the evidence is that tontines had, in practice, been used for Poor Law borrowing, neither the name nor the provision as such had been introduced into any Act. In 1776 a more positive approach to tontines appeared. There had already been an Act of Incorporation for the thirty parishes in the Isle of Wight, in 1771, but this had had no provision for annuities; money was to be borrowed by assignment of the rate, at 4 per cent interest. The optimistic provision had been included that one-half of the profit on the operation of the workhouse should be used in debt redemption (the other moiety for rate relief). The Isle of Wight Act of 1776 enlarging the scheme of the earlier Act, allowed two modes of borrowing – by mortgaging the rate income at 4 per cent interest or by a 'scheme of survivorship' – which although not so named meant a tontine. This clause described in some detail the operation of a tontine and is enlarged upon in this book when we deal with this method of borrowing (see pp. 234-9).

No contribution was to be of less than £100. Participants were to claim interest in person half-yearly, and if an investor failed to attend for this purpose within twenty days, he was to forgo the sum; however, if he (or other nominee) had died, thus dropping out of the scheme, the amount was to be included in the distribution to the others. If his failure to apply was mere oversight, he could reinstate himself by applying in person at the next interest-due date. Here too is to be found the introduction of the 'certificate of life', to be countersigned by a clergyman which every participant was required to produce from time to time to prove that he was still of this world. This life certificate is of course a common procedure today in superannuation schemes and insurance company annuity schemes. (It has sometimes been called a 'certificate of existence' but life certificate is the generally accepted term.)

There is reasonable evidence that the Act of 1774 (quoted above), authorizing the building of a workhouse and roadworks in the Liberty of the Tower of London, was the first Poor Law Act (and possibly any local authority Act) in which the form of the mortgage was specified in the Act, with the addition of the escape clause 'or any other words to the same or like effect'. The form was not specified in the major Oxford Act of 1771. In the form of mortgage the commissioners appointed under the Act 'do grant, bargain, sell and demise . . . such portion of the rates made for paving', etc. That is to say, that although the Act covered both Poor Law and paving, the borrowing for Poor Law works was to be by annuities and that for paving by mortgage, both on the security of the rates. The form of assignment of mortgages was also specified.

The form of annuity to be used first appears in an Act of 1781 relating to the welfare of the poor and also paving works at Plymouth Dock, where borrowing was authorized for the streetworks portion only by annuities not to exceed 5 per cent. What is recognizably a low rate for annuities is explained by the provision that these were perpetual annuities – that is, although known as annuities, no annual return of a portion of capital was to be made. The form specifies that the 'annuity or yearly sum shall be paid . . . in every year for ever'. The form of transfer was also specified –

as these were perpetual annuities and did not involve a nominated life, being in effect the equivalent of the much later 'undated stock', a market in them was to be expected.

Considerable attention is devoted today by major lenders to local authorities to the means available to them to recover debt, and reference will in due course be made in this book to the powers of such lenders to seek the appointment of a receiver in the event of default. This 1781 Act contains a reference to a power to recover an annuity on default of payment after one month; the annuitant is informed that he may proceed 'by Action of Debt, to be brought in any of His Majesty's Courts of Record' (broadly speaking, a system of courts for small debts).

In 1782 the first general statute (Gilbert's Act) was passed which authorized borrowing, but as this was part of a short series of Acts leading to the complete reorganization of the Poor Law administration in 1834, consideration of it is herein deferred until the examination of the development of local Act powers has been completed to that point. As will be shown, Gilbert's Act was very restrictive in the facilities which it offered, particularly for borrowing (see p. 214). Local Acts of some importance continued to be passed.

Some refinements of annuity provisions appear spasmodically from this time. In an Act of 1782 for the parish of St Luke's, Middlesex, power to borrow to replace a derelict workhouse was given by mortgage of the rates. As an alternative, life annuities could be issued; a praiseworthy but crude attempt was made to relate the value of the annuity to the age of the life nominated, that is, none on ages below 45, at 8 per cent on lives 45–49, 10 per cent on lives 50–59, 12 per cent on lives aged 60 and over. Thus in a rough-and-ready way annuities were linked for the first time in the actual statute to life expectancy; perhaps crude applications of this sort may have lain behind the requirements in earlier Acts that annuities should be sold to the best bidder. A year later the Birmingham Act reverted to 'highest bidder' annuities. However, there are several points of interest about this Birmingham Act. As an illustration of the area problem (and remembering that Bristol had merged nineteen parishes in its incorporation of 1696), the preamble of the Act says that 'Birmingham is a large and populous place, [but] though divided into two parishes, yet with respect to the maintenance of the poor it is considered one parish'. The guardians were authorized to borrow £15,000 in units of not less than £50 each, at the lowest rate obtainable. Although the application of the money was to be for building works, ambiguity was introduced by the added words 'and other purposes of this Act'. Every annuitant was also to be issued with a 'bond' to confirm his annuity, so that there were now both 'mortgage' bonds and 'annuity' bonds, perhaps indicating the simple nature of a bond as being the confirmation of an obligation.

These proposals for capital finance may be contrasted with those for building a new workhouse in the township of Manchester in 1790. Here the urban centre which bore the name of Manchester had been recognized 'time out of mind' as a semi-independent unit within the vast parish of

Manchester (which covered some 54 square miles and contained thirty townships). The churchwardens and overseers were authorized to borrow such sum as appeared necessary at a rate 'as low as can be procured', but while the sums borrowed could not be less than £50 each, they had also not to exceed £100. A form of assignment/mortgage was given, and all lenders were to rank equally. Life annuities were also to be made available at the rates of 9 per cent for ages 45 and over, 10 per cent 50 and over and 12 per cent 60 and over. The amortization provisions were more specific than in Birmingham. The form of borrowing instrument was specified, and the rate to be levied was to be sufficient to meet the current cost of relief of the poor, interest on money borrowed, annuity payments and the discharge of at least 5 per cent of the principal sum borrowed on mortgage, and at least 5 per cent was in fact to be discharged annually, the mortgages to be repaid being selected by lot (the 'wheel or box' again).

But while there was no nonsense about tontines in Birmingham or Manchester, the fen counties were still fascinated by this type of speculation, as is demonstrated in a well-constructed Act of 1785 for the creation of a Poor Law incorporation for the hundreds of Tunstead and Happing, in Norfolk. Borrowing of £15,000 was authorized by any of three methods. The first was by 'separate and specific sums not exceeding £100 each at legal or lower interest' in the form prescribed in the schedule to the Act, which is headed 'Form of Mortgage'. A period for repayment was not specified. Transfer by assignment was permitted but the clerk maintaining the register was to be paid for each transaction 'one shilling and no more'.

The second alternative offered was the use of annuities, without reference in the Act to ages. Annuities could be in one of three forms: life annuities; or 'for a term of years' (terminable annuities, the equivalent of a mortgage repayable on the 'annuity principle'); or 'to take place at the end of a certain number of years'. What this final offer meant is not clear, unless it meant some form of 'deferred annuity'; it cannot have intended a maturity repayment, for this would again have been equivalent to the mortgage. The draft form for securing the annuities is brief and does not clarify this point.

The third alternative borrowing method offered was a scheme of survivorship; this was to operate in the way already familiar but the specified form in the schedule to the Act was headed 'Form of Agreement and Mortgage by way of Tontine'. Thus although referred to in the body of the Act as a 'scheme of survival', it is also referred to in this schedule both as a tontine and a mortgage. In contrast, earlier Acts seem to associate tontines with annuities (for example, 28 Geo. III, c. 64, Paving at Cambridge '. . . by the granting of annuities for lives by way of Tontine or otherwise' – another attempt in the East Anglian area, which as it happens was not taken up). In fact the local authority tontine was not a mortgage or a true annuity because it made no provision for repayment of principal by the borrower, neither during the life of the annuity nor at maturity. Incidentally only the draft mortgage form makes provision for sealing. What the draft deed does emphasize is that a tontine in this form does not provide for return of principal (though a number of the lucky investors were intended to obtain the equivalent of this in enhanced interest rates) because the agreement says that after the death of the last survivor, 'the interest and principal sink into and become part of the stock of the said Directors and Acting Guardians' – another use of the word 'stock' as 'balances or reserves'.

Local Acts for the welfare of the poor continued with many variations; for example, Ellesmere in 1791 offered mortgages on buildings (and according to the marginal note, any tolls arising therefrom) as well as on rates. In this scheme life annuities are provided for anyone above the age of 20 years, at $7\frac{1}{2}$ per cent.

The conclusion is difficult to avoid that, impressive as the draftmanship of this early legislation is as a whole, the borrowing clauses leave much to be desired. They seem to lack consistency and incorporate variations which were not in line with the general evolution of borrowing at the various stages. There are many minor variations of wording, which are not particularly significant but which could have caused the courts problems if challenged simply because they were variants. A particular example is the Ellesmere Act, already quoted, which allowed loan creditors to 'enter upon . . . buildings, lands, hereditaments, and premises and receive rents, issues, and profits therefrom and for collecting the Poor's Rate and assessments', as near as can be to 'all the rates and revenues of the authority' (in the modern phrase). Yet the phrase which by then had become common, that all lenders ranked equally without priorities, is omitted, and there was no attempt there or elsewhere to make clear the equal ranking of mortgages, annuities and tontines. On the other hand, the subject of annuity and mortgage ranking was adequately dealt with in the Oxford 1771 Act. What is abundantly clear is that whatever the name given to the security (document) was not material as they could all borrow on the 'mortgaging of rates', and sometimes, erratically, the property also. The differences in practice were that assignments, mortgages and bonds paid interest and had for the most part obscure maturity provisions, whereas annuities, also secured by mortgaging the rates, had capital repayment incorporated, and tontines, in the few cases in which they were used, had no repayment of capital by the borrower.

While the developments in Poor Law borrowing were proceeding by private local Acts, there was from 1782 a series of general Acts designed to allow parishes to organize themselves more effectively without the need for local Act powers; the culmination of this was the complete reorganization of the Poor Law in 1834 on a basis which lasted for nearly a century. But the provisions of the 1782 and other intermediate Acts were disappointing and indicated a lack of central government confidence in the integrity and efficiency of the local Poor Law administrators. How strange therefore that at the same time as Parliament was exhibiting this nervous reluctance to trust the local authorities to levy rates and borrow reasonably, it was also giving imaginative experimental powers to even rural parishes such as Tunstead and Happing.

The Act of 1782, known as Gilbert's Act, has the distinction of being the first general local authority statute giving borrowing powers, however modest these may have been. Even so, it was not an Act of general application in the full sense, as it was subject to adoption, either by single parishes or groups of parishes, who thereby became corporate bodies. The management provisions of the Act are not relevant to this book except that the preamble lugubriously says that 'notwithstanding the many laws for the relief and employment of the poor, their sufferings and distress are nevertheless very grievous' largely because of 'the incapacity, negligence or misconduct of the overseers' and money frequently misapplied. Money was also alleged to have been wasted in defending 'litigations indiscretely and inadvisedly carried on' – all very much echoing the words to be found in bridges and highways legislation.

The borrowing provisions of Gilbert's Act were that when the expenses of providing land and buildings for a workhouse exceeded £100, this could be financed by money borrowed at interest, in sums not exceeding £50 'for greater ease in discharging the same'. The designated security document was called neither an assignment nor a mortgage, but simply the 'Form of Security for Money Borrowed' and 'a charge upon the Poor's Rate'; there was no reference to the equality of lenders or even a provision for registration or transfer, though both of these must have been assumed. Guardians were however required to 'keep down the interest of such money so to be borrowed', and if repayment was demanded, fresh loans could be taken up apparently by endorsement of the repaid document. Perhaps – except for the very low maximum loan, which could presumably be circumvented by the issue of several bonds to one lender, a clause as simple as this is really all that was, and still is, required.[6]

Subsequent clauses created difficulties for even this modest system of borrowing. The level of assessment ruling at the time when the workhouse was provided was to be maintained until debt and interest had been cleared, presumably again on the assumption that otherwise the 'profit' from the operation of the workhouse and the saving in outdoor relief would have permitted rate reduction. Furthermore, as soon as the savings on the Poor's Account were sufficient to pay off one of the £50 sums, the guardians were immediately to repay this and to continue to do so until all debt had been cleared.

Although not so named in the Act, these £50 loans became known as Gilbert's bonds in the Reports of Poor Law Commissioners. Almost all that can be said in their favour was that they were at least clearly designated as for capital purposes. Less than 100 Gilbert corporations were formed covering only a small proportion of the whole.

Unfortunately for Parliament, Britain was then running into the financial problems of the Napoleonic Wars, and by 1795 'the cash limits' on rate levies imposed by various Acts, including Gilbert's, were impossible to maintain. The Poor Relief Act of 1795 therefore recognized that the increasing numbers of poor, and the high cost of corn and other necessities, made the previous rate limits of various Acts impossible, particularly those depending on average rates levied in a previous series of years. Consequently, because rate levies so limited had failed to provide sufficient income to cover annual expenditure, not only had debts not been repaid, but fresh debts arising from revenue overspendings had been incurred extra-statutorily. This Act while, in effect, doubling the statutorily permitted rate levies made this extension subject to the overriding control of the amount by which the average price of wheat at the London Corn Market had exceeded the average price at the same market during those years on which average rate levies had been calculated. Modern critics of the complexity of the formula for the block grant or the uncertainties of the London inter-bank offer rate may sympathize with the problems of this 1795 method of cash control. These increases were to cover the cost of money borrowed for capital purposes and the revenue deficiencies covered by borrowings in the later years.

The 1795 Act had a general application to a number of earlier Acts, but two further short, peculiarly worded Acts were necessary to amend Gilbert's Act of 1782. The first was in 1802 which specifically lifted the provision that the rate levied should be maintained at that levied at the time the new premises were provided. The 1803 Act gave the guardians power to levy a sufficient rate to enable the repayment of at least one-twentieth of outstanding debt, without regard to other rate-restricting provisions; at least this was a positive attempt at an amortization policy, and indeed appears to be the first general provision of this kind.

The Public Works Loans Act of 1817, which provided for the setting up of the body which ultimately became the Public Works Loan Commission (PWLC), is of particular significance to the theme of local authority as well as Poor Law borrowing. In this initial instance, but without the use of this title, a body of commissioners was established, permitted to borrow £1½ million by Exchequer bills at a rate of 2½d per cent per diem, for the express purpose of lending money for the carrying out of public works and fisheries, and the employment of the poor in Great Britain (earlier schemes had been provided for commercial lending). This body was also authorized to lend money to turnpike trusts – turnpike loans being against tolls (additional levies of which were permitted to meet the costs of the debt), while the Poor Law loans were against the rates. A good deal more will need to be said about the activities of the PWLC in relation to local authority borrowing. At this point suffice it to say that the loans to the guardians could be either short-term (two to three years) or longer term (ten to twenty years). This will be seen to be a striking example of short-term borrowing by the government against longer-term loans to local authorities.

Limited though the scope of Gilbert's Act may have been, and subject to the relatively minor amendments described above, it endured for thirty years. Not until 1819 was a broader amending Poor Relief Act needed, and this was mainly to clarify and extend on the same basis the terms of the earlier Act. On the capital side the 1819 Act extended the powers to buy land (but not exceeding 20 acres) and to run farms as well as provide workhouses. An interesting provision was that not more than a rate of 1s in the pound should be expended (from revenue) on buildings and land, unless a substantial majority of the ratepayers should agree, and should they do so, the excess could be financed by borrowing either by loans or annuities, subject to the total borrowed not exceeding the proceeds of a 5s rate. The annuities could be life annuities, if the annuitants were not less than 50 years of age, or in the form of term annuities on a fifteen-year basis; the security for repayment of money borrowed was to be future rates made for the relief of the poor. There was an overall restriction that the future annual charge for borrowing should not exceed a 1s rate, unless two-thirds of the ratepayers agreed. The impression given is that there was an acceptance of the need to develop the service, and of the necessity for borrowing to do so, but a great reluctance to trust the persons involved in the financial decision-making. In the light of the admission of annuities into the scheme – a method already well accepted in local Act borrowing – the fact which must be realized here is that annuities are no more than a system of borrowing on the security of the rate, but with an in-built system of amortization of debt, year by year, instead of at maturity. It is the life annuity which involves an element of speculation (and of course the tontine), but this is still the basis of present-day life assurance and depends for its success on the reliability of the life tables used, and expectations of interest rate trends.

NOTES: CHAPTER 4

1   Information from Canterbury City Treasurer, S. W. Capon and M. Landon of that department, and the City Archivist, December 1979.
2   Information from William Serjeant, Suffolk County Archivist, assisted by M. Statham also of the Suffolk County Record Office, via City Treasurer of St Edmundsbury (as it is now called), L. G. Lockey, November 1979.
3   Information from Bernard Fieldhouse, West Sussex County Treasurer, and A. R. Eastland, Deputy County Treasurer, and the County Archivist – 'one of whose favourite statutes this is', September 1980.
4   Much valuable information again from William Serjeant, Suffolk County Archivist, and Dr Allen of the County Record Office, on Colneis and Carlford, Mutford and Lothingland, Loes and Wilford (and also on Stow, not used in text), September 1980.
5   Dr Anne Digby supplied valuable additional information by letter (May–June 1979) in enlargement of some of the financial matters discussed in her very useful book *Pauper Palaces*, particularly about East and West Flegg and Forehoe.
6   Gilbert's Act 1782 (22 Geo. III, c. 83). The borrowing clause of this first public general borrowing Act for local authorities merits recording; it reads:

> When any such buildings shall be agreed to be erected, repaired or fitted up at the expense of the parish township or place which shall adopt the provisions of this Act . . . the expenses thereof, and the purchase of the land necessary to be used for that purpose shall be paid by the Guardians of the Poor of such parish (etc.) and where they unite for those purposes, in the proportions settled and adjusted . . . in the manner directed by the Agreement to be made . . . and it . . . shall and may be lawful for the Visitor and Guardian of the Poor of any such parish (etc.), when such expenses or their proportion thereof shall amount to One hundred pounds or upwards, to borrow the same at interest, and secure such money, by a charge on the

poor's rate of such parish (etc.) in sums not exceeding Fifty Pounds each, for the greater ease in discharging the same, in the form contained in the said Schedule XI, or to that or the like effect; which charge shall continue upon the said rates until the money so borrowed, and all interest for the same, shall be fully paid and satisfied: And the said Guardians and their Successors shall, and they are hereby required duly to pay and keep down the Interest on such money so to be borrowed . . . when the Principal shall be called for, they may borrow from some other person or persons; and the same shall be secured to the Person advancing the same, by endorsement of such security indorsed on the back thereof . . . the Poor's Assessments shall continue at the same rate they were when such Poor House was first established under the authority of this Act, until the debt so contracted and the interest thereof be fully discharged . . . the said Visitor or Guardian, in order to expedite such payments, shall as soon as the savings in the Poor's Accounts shall amount to a sum sufficient to pay off and discharge one of the sums which shall have been borrowed, pay off and discharge such sum, and in the like manner as to all succeeding savings, until the whole debt so contracted and secured shall be discharged.

There is perhaps some confusion here, but the system seems to have been that where parishes combined for a workhouse, the parish representative on the joint body was responsible for organizing the borrowing, by his parish, of their share of the debt. Probably the datum line of £100 applied to each parish on a joint scheme.

Chapter 5

BORROWING IN THE BOROUGHS AND MAJOR PARISHES

The oldest still-surviving form of organization created specifically for local self-government is the borough; local government through the counties has been shown to be an offshoot of the judicial function of the magistrates and, in the parish, an extension of the ecclesiastial convenience that the inhabitants were a community unit which assembled regularly in the church. The borough set up by royal charter was effectively by definition a local unit for self-government, even though its democratic nature may have been limited. The borough was not only an administrative, but also a tax-gathering unit for both national and local purposes. Despite the antiquity of the boroughs, they were slow to seek statutory powers to borrow, although earlier chapters have shown that there were a few early cases – for example, Exeter for Poor Law purposes in 1697, and Bridlington for harbour works in 1696. Nevertheless, despite this late admission to statutory borrowing, there is evidence that the borough administrators believed that their coporate status gave them the facility to support their tax-raising by *ad hoc* borrowing as occasion required. Such *ad hoc* borrowing as took place does seem to have been quite casual, mainly as it were to help the borough council out of what might well be called cash-flow difficulties or to cover sudden revenue deficiencies. That borrowing was not a considered and organized function as a means of financing longer-term expenditure is shown in that early borough Acts where borrowing might have been a fully justified procedure did not include this power. For example, paving at Ipswich in 1571 was to be financed by a rental charge on frontages, and in 1580 paving and repair of streets in London 'without Aldgate' was similarly to be financed by frontage charges. Yet boroughs were borrowing by these dates as is illustrated by information about early borrowing in Bristol.[1]

Surviving records show that in 1574 money was borrowed by Bristol City Council to meet the cost of entertaining the Queen, and in 1579 to meet the 'new laying of the pipe' (probably of water rather than drainage). In 1586 money was borrowed to redeem the manor of Congresbury from debts. The sum was apparently £500, and to repay it an annuity of £40 was paid for thirty-one years from rents of lands owned by the mayor and commonalty. A sum of £600 was borrowed at about this time from the 'orphans' money' – money held in trust. A new quay was provided at a cost of £235 from borrowing. In 1642 £1,900 was borrowed at rates of 6 and 7 per cent. A list in the financial accounts for 1680 indicates that the corporation's debts were by then £12,428, about one-half of which was due to the orphans' fund. The bulk of the remainder was borrowed on what are described as 'City Seals' at 5 per cent, that is, deeds under the corporate seal. By 1685 the debt was £16,000, but by sales of land the city reduced this to £5,472 by 1700. Later in the century much more serious debts were incurred, substantially because the Poor Law authority for the city – the Corporation of the Poor – was subject to a rate limit and had to receive financial help from the city. The building of an exchange and a market and other capital projects followed, so that by 1785 the debt had risen to £77,000. This was borrowed largely on city seals, though between 1793 and 1795 a small amount of borrowing took place on promissory notes of £100. The details of this borrowing are no longer available, but this must have been essentially short-term finance, probably to meet a revenue deficiency.

However, at about this time *ad hoc* borrowing in Bristol began to give way to statutory borrowing in line with what was happening elsewhere (for example, at Oxford). For instance, in 1774 an Act for making commodious ways and passages and for enlarging a burial ground within the parish of St Stephen in Bristol permitted the borrowing of money, but only by annuities. A minimum age of 48 was specified on life annuities at a rate not to exceed 8 per cent. The linking of life annuities with the extension of a burial ground seems strangely appropriate. In 1835 when incorporation took place under the new legislation, the city council had a debt of £89,000, but the records do not show how much of this was from *ad hoc* and how much from statutory borrowing.

Even as late as 1747, an Act which dealt with Poor Law duties as well as 'the better repairing and paving of the highways' of Bury St Edmunds relied upon a rate levy and made no provision for borrowing. However, the Suffolk County Archivist[2] points out that:

The old corporation [of Bury St Edmunds] was in the habit of borrowing from its earliest days. Probably money was borrowed to meet the cost of incorporation in 1606 and certainly was necessary to help meet the cost of additional grants made by James I in 1608 and 1614. Money was also borrowed to buy-in the unexpired part of the lease of the market, fairs tithes and Almoner's House. Some of the sums borrowed seem quite substantial for the time, for example £2,000 borrowed in 1610.

Unfortunately this information is derived indirectly and details are not available. This again was clearly very much *ad hoc* borrowing.

The activities of the administrators in the City of Chester illustrate an attitude in which borrowing is not regarded as a special method of finance, but simply as something to be indulged in when circumstances made this necessary – a convenient extension of revenue finance.[3] Extensive local Act powers were obtained in 1762 for the care of the poor, watching, lighting and cleansing the streets, fire protection and even the regulation of hackney-carriages, but this Act did not authorize borrowing. It was not amended until 1803 when borrowing on the credit of the rate was then introduced, but even this power did not extend to the expenditure involved in the care of the poor (by which time however Gilbert's Act may have sufficed). Yet despite this lack of statutory borrowing power, the city council had in fact resolved in 1757 to set up a committee 'to consider methods of raising money to answer the City's exigencies'. On the recommendation of this committee the City Assembly resolved to raise £6,000 on life annuities, but on the basis that surviving annuitants would receive sharply increasing annuity payments – in other words, although the term does not appear in the minutes, by a form of tontine. Although tontines have already been referred to in Chapter 4 on early Poor Law borrowing, this Chester tontine is the earliest example discovered in the course of writing the present book. Details are given in Chapter 16.

Not surprisingly, the main preoccupation of borough administrations was with paving, lighting, cleansing and watching – and the greater the centre of population, the more pressing were these problems. The breakthrough into borrowing under statute for these purposes came in the mid-1770s; the experience of the City of London illustrates the succession of events.

A Commonwealth Ordinance of 1654 made provision for the appointment of Commissioners of Sewers to be responsible for highways, sewers and paving 'in and about the Cities of London and Westminster'. This arrangement was confirmed after the Restoration by the Act of 1662 covering street cleansing and improvements, scavenging and the regulation of hackney-carriages. Charges were to be made against frontages, and in particular scavenging was to be met from a rate 'according to the ancient custom'. This work was put on to a sounder basis 100 years later by Acts of 1766, 1768 and 1771.

Substantial borrowings were provided for in these later Acts for the execution of the work in the City of London and liberties thereof 'in the most expeditious manner'. The borrowings – of up to £100,000 – were to be on the credit of the rate, the instrument was to be a 'writing on parchment or vellum', at legal or lower interest paid half-yearly.

The 1766 London Act broke new ground by the introduction of life annuities, not used for Poor Law purposes until a few years later. Life annuities could be sold to persons not less than 45 years of age at a rate not exceeding 8 per cent paid quarterly, but by the later 1771 Act 10 per cent could be paid to anyone aged 60 or over. The price to be paid for these annuities was to be 'settled and adjusted by a public sale . . . to the best bidder', which again seems to indicate as suggested earlier that the price was to be negotiated on the age of the applicant. All lenders ranked equally and there were standard provisions for registration, transfer and inspection of records. As the Acts made provision for certain tolls on turnpike roads, part of the borrowing could be secured against these.

There were severe penalties against all kinds of frauds, still extending to death without benefit of clergy.

This seems to have been the first statutory power given to the City of London to borrow, but non-statutory borrowing had clearly preceded this. The Keeper of the Records for the City of London expresses the view[4] that there is evidence that the City was used by merchants almost as a bank (particularly before the establishment of the Bank of England at the end of the seventeenth century) and he quotes John Stow writing in 1698, 'The Chamber of London hath been accounted the safest and best security in and about London for monies paid therein to the use of the City'. Available records show for the period 1648–93 particulars of sums borrowed, names of lenders and interest paid, but not the purposes for which used. Possibly such deposits were accepted by the City to assist its cash flow but were not solicited loans. However, what is most peculiar is that at the very time when Stow was expressing this confidence in the City's financial stability an Act was before Parliament for measures required to save the City from its inability to meet its debts. This Act of 1694 was entitled 'An Act for the Relief of the Orphans and other Creditors of the City of London'; the preamble explained that the City

by reason of sundry accidents and public calamities have become indebted to the said Orphans and other Creditors of principal money and interest thereof, in a much greater sum of money than they are able to pay unless some assistance be given them.

A series of levies and taxes was authorized to enable the City to establish a fund from which to pay interest at 4 per cent in perpetuity on this debt; this arrangement was to be in full discharge. Presumably the instruments acknowledging this debt and perpetual interest could be sold and assigned, but this funding operation can have done little to reassure the public at this point about the City's creditworthiness.

The experience of the City of Westminster confirms the late arrival of statutory borrowing powers in the metropolis. Acts as late as 1751, 1753 and even 1762 made no provision for borrowing. These Acts related both to relief of the poor and streetworks in Westminster, this strange combination (shown also elsewhere) being in this instance because the Acts began with the amalgamation of three previously separate rates – poor relief, highways and cleansing – the combination of which 'would greatly tend to the advantage of the respective parishes'.

The Westminster Paving Commissioners were established in 1762 to work through committees for each parish or precinct, but power to borrow was not given until 1771, in borrowing provisions which bear the hallmarks of city financiers. The commissioners could borrow as necessary 'such sums as any person shall be willing to lend upon the credit of five-sixths' of the rate to be levied. A curious and rare typographical error then appeared in that the 'said *fifty*-sixths' were to be assigned as security against the borrowing, which was to be at legal or lesser interest, paid half-yearly. The remaining sixth part of the rate levy 'shall be deposited in the Bank of England as a sinking fund or for new-paving'. Thus appears an early, possibly the first, use of the term 'sinking fund' in local authority legislation. Lenders were to be entered in a register, which was to be open to inspection freely by any interested person. Each lender was to be 'a creditor of equal degree'. The repayment provisions are not as clear as a first reading suggests. Although one-sixth of the rate levied was to be set aside as a sinking fund or for new works, as the committee for the area thought fit, there appears to have been a secondary provision for repayment. If there was a surplus on the (five-sixths?) rate levy after paying interest, this could be used for repayment, if it amounted to £500 or one-eighth of the outstanding debt, and provided that all other necessary paving works had been carried out in the parish 'and not before', a reversal of the priority which applied to the one-sixth. Doubt is raised about the separate application of these two repayment provisions because the following clause provided that lenders must accept repayment out of the surplus rate or forgo further interest, but such a reservation is not made about repayments out of the original one-sixth allocation. However, repayment in some way was obviously a preoccupation of those concerned. The Westminster records show that this borrowing instrument was drawn up in the form of an indenture.

There were other variants of practice at about this time. In 1768 highway repairs and paving in the parish of St Leonards, Shoreditch, were to be financed by life annuities at 9 per cent without the alternative of mortgages. In 1769 paving at Gainsborough, in Lincolnshire, was to be financed from money borrowed on the security of a levy on all coal brought into the city (this revenue had previously been used for completion of the rebuilding of the parish church). Repayment was to be made from surplus duties. A further group of Acts in 1769 show the way in which the desire to improve the urban environment, by paving, cleansing and lighting measures, was taking hold but exhibit a lack of uniformity in methods of borrowing to do so. An Act for paving, lighting, cleansing and watching in New Windsor, in Berkshire, set up commissioners who could borrow by assignment of the rate at up to 5 per cent interest. A similar Act for St Martin's Le Grand, Westminster, allowed assignments and also the sale of life annuities to persons aged not less than 45 at 8 per cent, with no reference to 'sale to the highest bidder'. At St Botolph, Aldgate, borrowing was permitted only by life annuities at 9 per cent without reference to age; and in the parish of St Bartholomew (London) such street works could be financed by assignments at 5 per cent or life annuities at 8 per cent 'sold to the highest bidder'. In the same year in the parish of St Nicholas at Rochester, in Kent, streetworks and a turnpike were authorized to be financed simply by assignments of the rate and tolls. In 1772 paving in Christchurch, in Middlesex, could be financed by mortgages or annuities at 9 per cent, but as annuitants died fresh annuities could be sold, and the proceeds used to repay mortgages, a gradual transfer of all borrowing to the annuity basis with their automatic provision for annual repayment of principal. (A supplementary provision in a later Christchurch Act of 1788 shows that, by that date, the going rate for annuities was 10 per cent.) A somewhat similiar provision for the gradual replacement of mortgages by annuities appeared, in 1772, in application to the parish of St Sepulchre (Middlesex).

A rate of interest for the annuities was not given, though in an Act of the previous year relating to the Liberties of the Tower of London 9 per cent was quoted. In 1773 an Act permitted borrowing to finance works for lighting and watching at Kingston upon Thames ('in order that a sufficient sum may be forthwith raised', giving the rate levy as security) and included the draft instrument in the Act without referring to it as a mortgage. The interest rate was not to exceed 5 per cent. A variant occurred, in 1774, in allowing borrowing for paving and other works in Hereford, where the security offered was not the rate, but 'the credit of the said Commons or waste lands'. This seems to have been because this Act was principally promoted to authorize the enclosure of certain common lands.

Kingston upon Hull, which has had the anomalous distinction of being both a city and a county for legal jurisdiction, took powers in 1783 to erect a gaol (as a county) and to extend a burial ground (as a borough). These borrowings at not more than 5 per cent were wholly by assignment of the rate. Examples of bonds used to cover borrowings by the city council of Kingston upon Hull in 1640, 1696, 1698 and 1700 are in the city's records.[5]

An Act which demonstrates the problems of defining both local authority borrowing instruments as well as local authority areas was that of 1784 for a market and slaughterhouse at Sheffield. Here the power was not given to the town council, but to the Earl of Surrey, who was authorized to borrow £11,000 on 'deeds', on the security of the rents, tolls, and so on, which deeds are also referred to in the Act as 'mortgages'. The lenders were to be registered at the 'Register's Office' of the West Riding. This must probably be regarded as a commercial enterprise. An Act of 1785 for a package provision of a workhouse, paving works and a burial ground at Richmond, in Surrey, gave borrowing powers for £3,000 on bonds of £100 each, with a positive repayment provision by which not more than £500 provided from the rates was to be redeemed each year, the creditors to be repaid being selected by lot. In the same year at New Sarum, in Wiltshire, where the various public offices – county court, gaol, court of quarter sessions and guildhall – were 'both ancient and ruinous', replacements could be provided by borrowing – not as might be expected on the security of the rates, but of the 'market tolls, fees and perquisites' although a new market was not part of the provision; this security is specified in the draft 'Form of Assignment'. In 1787 borrowing for a new town hall at Grantham, in Lincolnshire, 'for the purpose of speedily raising a fund', was to be on mortgages from £50 to £100. These were on the security of the rates but the commissioners were to make provision from the rate, so that the debt would be repaid within twenty-six years, that is, not a specific mention of a sinking fund, but the official determination of a loan sanction period.

A Cambridge Act of 1788, mainly for paving, brings together many of the variations, but is still far from a complete code. The newly appointed 'Paving Commissioners' could 'mortgage, demise, grant or assign over' the rates, assessments, duties and tolls – a fairly comprehensive description of the modern term, 'all the rates and revenues of the authority'. They could also sell annuities at 10 per cent, and if they wished, these could be 'by the granting of lives by way of tontines'. The records show no evidence of a tontine having been used, though there are records of mortgages and ordinary annuities. This proposal is referred to again in Chapter 16.

The Cambridge Archivist has supplied copies of both assignments and annuities issued under the Act, which are of interest. A Dr Ewin was obviously eventually a satisfied customer. He first invested £1,000 on assignment at 4½ per cent, but a side-note in the register says 'See Order Book 31st March 1789 agreed to be made 5%'. Whereupon the doctor invested a further sum of £300 on 21 April 1789 and there is evidence of more later. Another copy annuity shows that £73 10s was to be paid annually through a trust on the joint lives of two spinster ladies. On the death of either the annuity was to fall to £50 10s, to be paid to the survivor for life. This annuity was purchased on behalf of the two recipients by two gentlemen in trust under a will. The consideration paid was £1,000, which clearly indicates that some attempt had been made to assess the life expectations of the two ladies at the making of the deal. The deed is laconically endorsed 'dead', without a date, but further documents show that this trust received approximately £1,700 between 1790 and 1819 at which point it terminated – a reasonable return. On the other hand, an annuity purchased by a widow in 1791 for a consideration of £100 produced total payments of only £60 before her death in 1797.

A puzzling statute relating to Liverpool was passed in 1793 by which the town was empowered to issue negotiable notes, payable to bearer, for short periods, to the substantial total of £300,000. The form of the notes as given in the Act shows these to have been promissory notes. Earlier in this chapter reference was made to borrowing by this means without statutory powers by Bristol at about the same time, but the outcome of this exercise by Liverpool is not now known, which is unfortunate as this was a development of great interest albeit that it seems to have been an isolated occurrence (further details of the notes are given in Chapter 19 dealing with money bills issued by local authorities).

We conclude this chapter on the note on which we began, that is, the tendency for boroughs to borrow without statutory sanction even as late as 1810. In that year the mayor and commonalty of Plymouth determined to meet the cost of land and buildings for a ballroom, theatre and hotel at £20,000 by

the grant of annuities to purchasers on the lives of persons to be named by them with benefit of survivorship and by way of tontine, or the obtaining of the said sum by any other ways and means that shall appear most advisable.

This tontine, which appears to have been most successful, is dealt with in Chapter 16 on this form of borrowing. Incidentally the instruments were referred to as 'tontine annuity bonds', a comprehensive terminology which shows little regard for exact definitions.

NOTES: CHAPTER 5

1 Information supplied by the City Archivist, Miss Mary E. Williams, partly based on unpublished research by Miss Livock, Livock MSS Bristol Record Office 36771.
2 Letter dated 4 December 1979.
3 Information from the City Record Office.
4 Letter dated 30 October 1979.
5 Mr Geoffrey W. Oxley, City Archivist of Kingston upon Hull, has supplied much valuable information about the use of bonds, annuities and a tontine in this city, which will be dealt with later in the appropriate chapters.

Chapter 6

BORROWING IN THE COUNTIES

Early provision for borrowing by the county administration might have been expected. For a long period of time the county administration through the quarter sessions had been directly responsible for important wider-ranging local services, and indirectly for the close supervision of other services through the parishes and to some extent the surviving hundreds, all of which functions had capital implications. However, power to borrow does not appear to have been given to county areas under private Acts until the end of the eighteenth century, or under general statutes until the beginning of the nineteenth. Until these dates the counties continued to finance both revenue and capital expenditure from the county rate, collected by precepts on the parishes.

The modern local authority financial administrator in the district areas might say cynically that this is entirely in line with the present pattern where the county, relying on precepts rather than on direct rating of the citizens, is often content to precept rather than borrow. Naturally the present county administrator will reply that a county charge for capital works spread over the whole area of the county in the form of a precept is frequently so trifling as not to be a serious burden and that the avoidance of debt is a commendable objective; and these may well be sound arguments.

For many years the Acts which placed responsibilities on the counties and authorized them to pass on the burden of cost were worded in a manner which was far from clear, and involved separate levies for separate purposes. For the cost of bridge repairs (Statute of Bridges 1530) the justices could 'rate every parish to such weekly sums as they shall think convenient'. For the cost of providing and repairing gaols the direction was that the justices should issue warrants 'by equal proportions to distribute and charge the sum or sums of money to be levied aforesaid upon the several hundreds, lathes, wapentakes, rapes, wards or other divisions of the said County'. For county Poor Law duties (under several Acts) the justices were 'to rate every parish to such weekly sum of money as they shall think convenient' but with a rate limitation. Other Acts contained other variants.

By the early years of the eighteenth century the county allocations of cost might relate to bridges, gaols, houses of correction, the upkeep of prisoners, conveyance of vagabonds and sturdy beggars, hospitals and almshouses and other minor responsibilities. In many instances the need to collect such a variety of contributions towards county costs involved such trifling sums that a statute of 1738 (the County Rates Act) provided for 'the more easy, assessing and collecting and levying of the county rates'. Although it stopped short of laying down a system of allocation, it was a workmanlike document listing the functions for which county rates could be collected, and admitting that the sums assessed were often so trifling that 'the expense of assessing and collecting [could amount] to more than the sum rated', as a result of which 'many doubts, difficulties and inconveniences have arisen in making and collecting . . . the said rates'. The amounts required at county level were therefore to be consolidated, so that the justices could

> make a general rate or assessment of such sum as they in their discretion shall think sufficient to answer all and every ends and purposes of the before recited Acts instead of and in lieu of the several separate and distinct rates directed thereby to be levied and raised.

In addition, 'And all and every such sums of money . . . shall be deemed and taken to be the public Stock' – the primitive county fund.

The justices were now able to determine a single consolidated rate for each parish, town, or place 'in such proportions as any rates heretomade in pursuance of the several Acts have usually been assessed'. This rather suggests a system of lump sum allocations rather than precepts based on totals of rateable value. Cannon, in his *History of Rating*, quotes an example from Norfolk in 1743 where the justices had a rule-of-thumb formula as to how much was to be collected from each parish in the case of 'a three hundred pound levy, a four hundred pound levy and a six hundred and fifty pound levy' over the whole county. The sums so assessed were to be 'collected by the High Constables of the respective Hundreds and Divisions in which any parish, town or place doth lie'. In fact not until the County Rates Act 1815 was the system of the county rate put completely on the same basis as the parish rate, and with a flat levy over the county as a whole of a 'pound rate on the full and fair annual value'.

However, the facts are clear that the county administration carried out through the justices had operational as well as supervisory responsibilities, and required income to enable them to carry these out. In addition, they had their main function of holding quarter and divisional sessions for the administration of justice; to carry out these functions they needed county buildings, though for centuries they seem to have used whatever convenient accommodation was available.

Reference should be made to another element in the local government structure, the significance of which had disappeared by the end of the eighteenth century but which played a part until then in the initiation of county expenditure. This was the grand jury, a body assembled by the sheriff, whose composition varied but usually consisted of magistrates and other eminent county personages. It had the function of selecting and placing before the magistrates various legal and criminal issues, but also of drawing attention to administrative shortcomings of the county by a system of what was called 'presentation'. The first turnpike activity had occurred as a result of 'presentments' about the unsatisfactory state of certain roads. According to the Webbs in their *Parish and County*, while the grand jury had a specific function in relation to roads and bridges, its involvement in county buildings was less clear, but that nevertheless it assumed such a responsibility and even on occasion acted as a sort of finance committee on behalf of the magistrates. Its function in relation to roads was spelled out in 1530 and, in 1738, this participation was endorsed in relation to bridges, gaols and houses of correction; and, finally, in 1769, in the Shires Halls Act to county halls.

COUNTY HALLS The county responsibility for which borrowing facilities might primarily have been expected to be needed was the provision of county halls in which the legal as well as administrative work of the county was conducted – the ancient days of the open-air meetings of the hundred, or of the wapentake, where decisions were ratified by the clashing of shields, being long past. However, the evidence is that statutory borrowing for county halls was a late development. This is confirmed by the general Act of 1769, referred to above, the purpose of which was simply to dispel doubts as to whether the justices had any lawful authority for *repairing* (much less building) shire halls and other buildings necessary for the conduct of their business. Money was obviously already being spent for this purpose; in 1698 the roof of the county hall in Derbyshire was repaired on 'presentation' and the grand jury acted as a Finance Committee for the magistrates on this occasion (see the Webbs' *The Parish and The County*). The provisions of the 1769 Act that such halls as were used for county purposes might properly be repaired at the expense of the county rate, with the reservation that any such halls as had 'time out of mind' been maintained by some other persons should continue to be so maintained, suggests that the idea that counties themselves might actually need to provide such halls had not occurred to anyone.

The lack of provision for borrowing for the building of county halls is further borne out by an Act of 1773 relating to the rebuilding of the Devonshire Shire Hall in Exeter. This Act described the old hall already in use for assizes and other public services in 1601 as being both 'ruinous and incommodious', but explained that 'no provision is made by the laws at present in being to authorise the raising of the money for the expense of taking down and rebuilding the said hall'. The provision of a new hall was therefore placed in the hands of a body of commissioners (consisting largely of the justices) who were to effect the replacement of the hall (including the provision of temporary accommodation) at the cost of the county rate both as to initial provision and future maintenance; by this date a borrowing facility might have been expected but was not provided. A similar procedure was adopted in 1783 for a combined county and guild-hall for the County of Salop and the town of Shrewsbury. The revenue basis of this provision was emphasized by the restriction that the rate was not to exceed 6d in the first two years and 4d in the third, and 1s 4d overall.

To take this matter further the first general Act which allowed the justices to provide themselves with county offices was in 1826, in the County Buildings Act, which widened the powers of the 1769 'repairing' Act to permit building, but the county rate was still the prime source of finance. However, if the cost of new provision was likely to exceed one-half of the county rate levied over the average of the last seven years, then the justices could borrow on mortgage of the rate sums of not less than £50 each (as compared with the Poor Law provision of Gilbert's Act which allowed borrowing in sums of not more than £50) on a fourteen-year loan sanction period (which was not increased to thirty years until 1872 in the County Buildings (Loans) Act, which is of no other significance). The originality of this provision for borrowing for the building of county halls is confirmed by the County Buildings Act of 1837 which was needed to clarify the situation where a town and county hall were combined.

OTHER COUNTY BUILDINGS Nor is any early provision for borrowing to be found for other county buildings. Houses of correction provided a difficult problem. The county was required to provide these for beggars and the re-calcitrant poor even as early as 1609. Because a single parish was unlikely to need such a building for its sole use, this provision was made a county requirement from the beginning. It was obviously not a popular function. The Vagabonds Act of 1609 said of the laws providing for these houses of correction, 'which laws have not wrought such good effect as was expected', and indicated that houses of correction had not been built as was required. The Act instructed 'all statutes and laws now in force made for the erecting and building of houses of correction . . . shall be put into operation' with a penalty on justices who did not make provision within two years. The cost was to be spread by a rate over the hundred area, but though some provision was made these establishments were not widely provided. The justices did not seem very clear about the lines to be drawn between workhouses, prisons and gaols, with houses of correction somewhere in the middle.

An Act 'concerning where and under what manner the Gaols within this Realm shall be edified and made' as early as 1531 created responsibility for the provision of gaols, putting the cost on a county tax (which, apart from anything else, shows that rating did not begin with Elizabeth I). Corporate towns with their own gaols were to be excused the county levy; any surplus was to be used for alms. But the first really positive Gaols Act was not until 1699; the preamble complained in strong terms about the inadequacy and ruinous state of county gaols, so that prisoners were 'left in distress', but the burden of provision remained a rate charge. The confusion of areas at this time was nicely illustrated, in that the justices were required 'by equal proportions . . . to distribute and charge the sums of money upon the several hundreds, lathes, wapentakes, rapes, wards, and other divisions' of the county.

A short and concise Act in 1735 providing for the purchase of land and the building of a county gaol in Maidstone, in the western division of Kent, made no provision for borrowing, but is highly illustrative of the conditions of the time and makes reference to significant financial and other procedures; the preamble explains that

> the Common Gaol at Maidstone is in great decay, too streight [restricted] for the safe keeping of prisoners and standing in the middle of the town is often from Distempers of the Prisoners, both offensive and dangerous to the inhabitants, and there being no prison for the confinement of Debtors ... for debts of very large sums of money.

'All of which Insufficiencies and Inconveniences of the Gaol aforesaid have been presented by the Grand Jury at the Assizes and General Gaol Delivery' – and because there were no powers for an extension or a new building and because the justices of the peace 'by the laws now in force, cannot raise a sufficient sum nor can they apply the Stock of the said County ... for this purpose', then to solve these dilemmas a body of named trustees was to be formed to buy land and build a prison with different wards, so that debtors and felons might be separated. This was to be declared a public and common gaol, and placed under the control of the sheriff, with the strange proviso that when he transferred the prisoners from the old to the new gaol, 'such removal shall not be deemed or taken to be an Escape'. The old gaol could then be demolished, the materials sold and the site revert to its previous owners.

In addition, an illuminating financial note was struck: 'And whereas there is a considerable Surplus of the County Stock now in the hands of the Treasurer', the justices might use some of this money for the approved purpose, and at the same time might raise 'such sufficient sums of money for and towards purchasing the ground and building the gaol and keeping it in repair from time to time by such Ways and Means as Money may be raised for the repairing of County Gaols'. This provision confirms that the powers existed to raise money for the repair of ancient gaols but not for the provision of new premises. Obviously the power to maintain the gaol in Maidstone had been sparingly used. The Act concludes – a very early example of this provision – with the declaration that: 'this Act shall be deemed, adjudged and taken to be a Public Act and shall be judicially taken notice of as such ... without specially pleading the same.' Even in 1775 a local Act for replacing the common gaol in the County of Hertford left the provision to be financed by a rate over four years, not to exceed 7d overall, or 3d in any one year.

In 1778 occurs what may well be the first borrowing for a county gaol – in this instance described as a 'jail'. It was to be at Bodmin, in Cornwall, and was to consist of a three-part structure – a jail for criminals, a prison for debtors and a house of correction for certain other offenders at a total cost not exceeding £6,000. This may in fact be the first statutory borrowing power for any county purpose, though there may be other county Acts with borrowing powers locked away in the statute-books; if there are, they are unlikely to be much earlier. The Cornwall jail was to be financed by a county rate levy on a wide sweep of areas within the county – every town, parish, hamlet or place, boroughs corporate, towns corporate and all other precincts and liberties. Hundreds find no mention, being absorbed in this range of other areas. But 'Forasmuch as the money to be raised . . . may not be thought proper to be collected so speedily as the same may be wanted', then to avoid 'inconveniences', the justices were empowered to raise money 'upon the best terms the same can be procured at interest'. Such money was to be repaid in due course 'out of the County Stock, which Stock is hereby declared at all times to be subject and liable thereto until full payment and satisfaction of the said principal money and interest'. So here was a loan secured not on the county rate, but on the county surpluses, created it must be supposed by the rate levy, in other words, what might now be called the county fund.

However, a modest general Act for the provision of gaols was soon to be forthcoming. In 1784 a general Gaols Act recognized in its preamble that building gaols as a direct rate charge was proving burdensome on the contributors to the county rate. When therefore the cost of the works was likely to exceed one-half of the annual county rate levy on a previous five-year average, the justices could borrow money on mortgage of the rates in a specified form, in sums of not less than £50 nor greater than £100, at legal or lesser interest. The county rate was to be charged with the interest and with not less than an equivalent sum 'in discharge of so many of the principal sums as such money will extend to discharge in each year' and, in any event, the whole debt was to be discharged within fourteen years. The selection of lenders for repayment 'shall be discharged by drawing lots, or otherwise . . . first discharging all such securities which shall bear the highest interest'. The form of mortgage was prescribed; another interesting feature of this Act was that it provided that the justices must employ a proper person to keep the accounts of any gaol project and that this person should keep proper books of account in which the borrowing transactions were to be kept quite separate and were to show accrued interest, so that 'it may easily be seen what interest is growing due and what principal money has been discharged and what remains due' – the first Borrowing Regulations?

What is puzzling is that no sooner had this general power been issued for the provision of gaols, than in the next year (1785) a local Act was felt to be necessary by the County of Gloucester. Perhaps there was an immediate realization that the general statute was overmodest in its format; the Gloucester Act was certainly substantially more complex. This time the provision was for a gaol, a penitentiary and houses of correction. Money could be borrowed for the work either by mortgages, at legal or lower interest by separate and specific sums not exceeding £100 each, or by life annuities for sums not exceeding £100 p.a., or term annuities for periods not exceeding twenty-five years, without maximum. These transactions were to be clear of costs to the lender, registered, and transferable. There was a fee of 1s 6d for registering transfers, at which cost the register was also open for inspection by any ratepayer.

In this instance the transfers could be made on a document under hand and seal or by endorsement 'as in the case of Promissory Notes', though there is not at this date any evidence of authority to use promissory notes. This simple endorsement system does not seem to mean that the securities were of the bearer type because transfers were not recognized until registered. As the annuities were transferable, the assumption must be, as mentioned earlier, that any life annuities transferred remained attached to the life of the original investor. All securities ranked equally with no priority as to time. As will be later demonstrated, term annuities are the equivalent of mortgages repayable on the so-called 'annuity basis'.

The basis for the issue of the annuities – some for life, others for terms of up to twenty-five years – is far from clear. The prices of the life annuities were to be arrived at 'by treating and agreeing' with the lenders, in public and after advertising, and 'the best bidder for every annuity shall be accepted as the purchaser thereof'. As to the term annuities, 'no annuity for twentyfive years shall be granted for less than 13 years purchase and so in proportion for any annuity for a lesser number of years'. This seems to suggest that the term annuities had also to be negotiated with each lender with a maximum interest rate of around 5¾ per cent. Nor does the schedule giving the 'Form of charge upon the County Rates for securing the Annuities' make the intention any clearer.

A curious sinking fund provision was introduced. Each year the justices were to provide that a county rate should be levied sufficient for normal purposes, but also to provide £2,000 for the servicing of this debt, so that after the covering of the initial costs of the Act and its implementation, any surplus on this £2,000 was to be used for meeting the annuities, and repaying mortgages, selected by lot. The selection by lot was to take place immediately the building work had been completed, the mortgages then numbered in the order drawn and redeemed according to this sequence. There are peculiarities in the reference to annuities. At two points reference is made to the 'growing annuities'. Annuities are either of a constant annual amount, which includes a gradually increasing proportion of repayment of capital and a diminishing amount of interest on the decreasing amount of outstanding capital, or they are of a fixed amount of capital with interest on the reducing balance and therefore they diminish annually, they do not grow. Nor was the Act clear about the way in which the £2,000 was to be utilized. The first use was to discharge the costs of obtaining the Act; the second was 'in keeping down the interest of the said Principal Sums to be borrowed'; then the surplus 'shall be applied in discharging the expenses of erecting, setting up and furnishing' the new premises (but surely this was what the sum borrowed was required for?); and finally, 'when such expenses shall be entirely discharged, then such Surplus shall be applied as a Sinking Fund for the gradual Discharge of the

Principal Sums borrowed'. There certainly seems to be a degree of confusion in these terms.

A consolidating Act for County Gaols was passed in 1823, in which the borrowing provisions of the 1784 Act were virtually repeated – borrowing permitted by mortgage of the rate when the cost was likely to exceed one-half of the county levy on the last seven-year (not as previously five-year) average; units of from £50 to £100 only; all borrowers to rank equally irrespective of date; fourteen-year repayment period; and the requirement that a proper person was to be appointed to maintain a record of accruing interest and outstanding debt.

This consolidation was soon deemed to be inadequate in certain respects. In 1825 an amending Act (the Mortgages of County Rates Act) made provision for early repayment and replacement of loans where this would bring about a reduction of the interest charge; the limit of £100 on each individual loan was withdrawn. Apart from its relevance to gaols, this Act and its predecessor have a special significance, in that their borrowing terms were picked up and incorporated in a Bridges Act of 1841 (see p. 130).

These provisions for confinement, either as paupers, vagrants, debtors, or criminals, led naturally to like provisions for pauper lunatics. Private Acts for the provision of asylums, with borrowing provisions, may have been passed but have not been discovered. However, in 1808 the first general Act for this purpose was passed. Whereas parishes had been deemed to be units of too small a size to have their own houses of correction, single counties were now deemed to be too small to need separate lunatic asylums. The preamble to this Act explains that as the confinement of lunatics to either workhouses, houses of correction or parish gaols was both unsatisfactory and dangerous, any two or more counties could combine to provide a pauper lunatic asylum. The borrowing provisions were similar to those already encountered in this area – wherever the cost was likely to exceed one-half of the normal rate levy for county purposes on a five-year average, borrowing by mortgage of the rate proceeds could be adopted for the provision of the necessary buildings. Incidentally the costs were to be divided between the participating counties in proportion to populations as ascertained in the first of the decennial Censuses which had taken place in 1801. This borrowing was to be undertaken when the cost became 'burdensome to the occupiers of land and other contributors to the county rate'. Loans were to be for sums of not less than £50, signed by the chairman and only two other justices, as compared with all other Acts where five, seven and sometimes more justices were required to sign every deed. These deeds were to be registered, they could be assigned and the lenders were to be of equal degree without regard to priority of lending. The county rate was to provide not only for interest, but for at least a similar sum to be used for repayment, the lenders so selected to be by lot. Again there is repetition of earlier detail about the keeping of proper books of account. Repayment of the whole was to be achieved in fourteen years.

Obviously the provision of asylums by the joint action of counties created difficulties; initially the power given should have been that any county could make this provision either alone or in combination, and not simply in combination. Twenty years later, in 1828, this situation was recognized in an Act practically identical in its borrowing provisions which allowed counties to make their separate provision for such asylums. However, even this later Act still confined borrowing to mortgages, whereas the amendment of Gilbert's Act had in 1818 extended borrowing techniques under general powers to include annuities.

CONCLUSIONS FOR THE PERIOD UP TO 1830

A case might be made that the 1830s represent the emergence of the first 'structured' local government system – the rationalization of the Poor Law on an *ad hoc* basis of unions, and the consolidation of the boroughs. But this would be an inexact statement; structured local government began in the 1500s when the parish was first selected as the convenient 'ready-to-hand' unit for local services, supervised by the county magistrates in quarter sessions. (Even at this date the system was dotted with semi-independent charter boroughs whose function was local administration.) Perhaps even the shire and the hundred may be so regarded. The difference between the movements of the 1500s and the 1830s is that at the earlier date the main elements in the framework had other primary functions – ecclesiastical administration and county judicial functions – to which local government functions were tacked on, whereas at the later date the units involved – the unions and the boroughs – were wholly dedicated to local government purposes.

Still, the developments between these dates were relatively modest – spasmodic rather than coherent. If government through the parish and the county is regarded as being firmly established, after earlier tentative essays, by 1601, and if in round terms the adoption of the principle of the finance of longer-term expenditure by borrowing is dated about 1700 (with apologies to the first turnpike in 1663), borrowing thus came about halfway through this first selected period. A coherent borrowing code cannot be said to have emerged – a really coherent code did not emerge for another century or so, if indeed a thoroughly rational code can be said to have developed yet – but at least the foregoing pages demonstrate that by 1800 legislation and practice had encompassed borrowing by assignment; mortgages; indentures; bonds; perpetual, life and term annuities; promissory notes; and even such curiosities as tontines.

Many of the constituent parts of a comprehensive borrowing code had also received mention by this date – possibly the most important being reliance on revenues rather than on physical assets as the underlying security, and the equal ranking of all lenders. The most obvious case of capital expenditure in which the physical asset could not satisfactorily constitute the security must surely be a turnpike road where the only value lay in the revenue which could be collected for its use. The other points of significance, later to form part of a complete code of borrowing, had also been recognized – a document of security signed and sealed, to be registered but assignable, and primitive references to loan periods and methods of redemption.

Second Period: 1830–1930:
The Evolution of Structured
Local Government and of the
Associated Borrowing Codes

Chapter 7

THE OPENING PHASE

Although a movement, which was recognizably local government, may have shown its first stirrings in the earlier half of the sixteenth century, the Act of Elizabeth of 1601, a codification and consolidation of earlier attempts at organizing poor relief though it was, merits acceptance as the principal landmark in early local government both organizationally and in finance. The first turnpike road in 1663, the developments of turnpikes generally after 1700 and the Poor Law incorporations of the middle of the century are all significant later stages. But the dates comparable in significance as landmarks in the history of local government to 1601 are 1834 and 1835, with the Poor Law Amendment Act and the Municipal Corporations Act of these years. These two statutes constituted the first comprehensive organizational steps in the rationalization of local government after the 1601 acceptance of the ecclesiastical parish as the unit of local administration. Clearly, they were carried by the fervour which produced the Reform Act of 1832, but unfortunately the wave of enthusiasm waned before the whole local government system had been reconstituted.

The approaches incorporated in the two Acts form a contrast. The Poor Law Act set in motion the formation of new authorities (by the grouping of parishes), which took almost twenty years to complete – the Unions of Poor Law Guardians, elective and with the *ad hoc* duty of administering to the care and relief of the poor, but under the firm guidance and control of a central government body, the Poor Law Commissioners. The Municipal Corporations Act reconstituted what had become an indeterminate number of corporate towns into 178 general-purpose municipal corporations of largely independent status. To an extent this system of independent boroughs provided a confirmation of the bulwark against central interference in local affairs, represented by the earlier charter towns, but in fact the powers initially allocated to the new boroughs were minimal, and as new responsibilities were gradually devolved on them central controls were introduced piecemeal. Under both systems the levying and collection of the rates remained a parish function.

The first task of the Poor Law Commissioners, and the assistant commissioners which they were empowered to appoint for work in the field, was to bring about groupings of parishes to form the new unions under the locally elected Boards of Guardians. The combinations of parishes selected were made without reference to county or town boundaries except where these fitted the commissioners' plan, which was said to be groupings within ten miles of market towns, though this must in practice have been an oversimplification. About 15,000 parishes were ultimately formed into about 700 unions. Although the unions were intended as 'single-purpose' authorities, a second duty was soon imposed on them – that of setting up and maintaining arrangements for the registration of births, marriages and deaths under the 1836 Registration Act, and this duty remained with them until their abolition in 1930. The duty of maintaining vital statistics, which was perhaps the logical sequence of the Census Act 1800, might more logically have gone to the county administration, but it seems to have found a home with the unions because both movements were instigated by the administrator Edwin Chadwick, who saw the compilation and analysis of mortality statistics as a first step in the improvement of the welfare of the poor and the introduction of public health measures generally (see Redlich and Hirst, *History of Local Government in England*). The allocation of this duty to the unions (with the patronage appointments involved) was also considered to be an incentive to the parishes to abandon their resistance to the creation of the independent Poor Law unions, and initially some unions were created which exercised only registration functions (see Smellie, *A History of Local Government*). Indeed the Act provided that where unions had not yet been established, the board could create temporary registration districts.

The borrowing provisions in this major Poor Law Act were disappointingly modest; they permitted the continued use of the restricted provisions of Gilbert's Act (1782) and its amendments (maximum loans of £50 each), but henceforth subject to the approval of the commissioners. However, a broader general power was also included allowing unions to borrow on the security of the poor rate, for the provision of workhouses, but the amount to be raised in any year was not to exceed the annual amount of poor rate raised on the average of the past three years. Loans were to be repaid by annual instalments over ten years. Access to the Exchequer Loan Commissioners, already available to parishes, was now extended to unions. These borrowing provisions are surprisingly sketchy, when so much progress in the evolution of a borrowing code had already been made generally. Obviously Edwin Chadwick had a greater enthusiasm for organization than finance. A surprising supplementary provision was that a rate or loan could be raised to defray the expenses of poor persons willing to emigrate; the total amount was not to exceed one-half of the previous three-year average rate levy, and any loans for this purpose were to be repaid within five years. This power was retained for many years.

On the question of terminology, although the rate was to provide the underlying security, no reference was made in the Act to the form of borrowing instrument, and the terms 'assignment' and 'mortgage' are absent. However, a clause clarifying the exemption of borrowing from stamp duty under earlier Acts refers to any 'bond or other security' entered into. The earlier Gilbert's Act, which specified the instrument, entitled it merely as a 'Form of Security for Money borrowed', and referred simply to such borrowings being a 'charge on the poor's rate', although, as already mentioned, in later years the commissioners' Annual Reports referred to 'Gilbert Act bonds'.

The ten-year repayment period for workhouse loans was immediately seen to be inadequate, for in 1836 an amending Act – the Poor Relief (Loans) Act – extended the repayment period to twenty years for loans from the Exchequer Commissioners and private persons. Unfortunately the parliamentary draftsman nodded in designing this provision, for in 1838 yet another amendment was required to explain that power to borrow from 'private persons' included the taking of loans from public companies.

This was followed by a further Poor Law Amendment Act of 1844 which allowed parishes and unions to create school districts and asylum districts, the one for the education of pauper children from infancy to age 16, and the other for the care of the sick poor (including those with infectious diseases) who could not be looked after in workhouses. Boards with the status of corporate bodies could be created for the administration of these districts with the power to borrow for the provision of school and hospital buildings as under the main Poor Law, subject to a rate limitation. These School Boards must not be confused with later boards created under the Education Acts from 1870.

The Poor Law Amendment Act 1851 introduced further organizational amendments among which was the specification of a form of borrowing instrument or 'as near thereto as the circumstances of the case will admit'. The form specified was designated as a 'deed' (and being a 'deed' was a document under seal), under which the borrowers 'do hereby charge the future poor rates to be raised in the several parishes ... with the repayment of the said sum'. This model was so drawn that it could be used by School and Asylum District Boards created under the 1844 Poor Law Act as well as by parishes and unions. The deed was based on yearly instalments for repayment, although interest could be paid half-yearly if desired and there was provision for premature repayment by agreement with the lender. There was no provision for maturity repayment. The document is rather oddly drawn and appears to provide for the listing of each of the dates, throughout the period, on which the repayment instalments were to be made. A further amending Act of 1869 – the Union Loans Act – is relevant. In it, repayment could now be made in thirty annual instalments with interest on the outstanding balance – the equal instalments of principal method – or by thirty equal payments of principal and interest combined, a 'true' annuity method. The form of security was redrafted to encompass the alternative methods of repayment. There was still no provision for maturity repayment.

To complete this succession of developments two further Acts must be noted. The first was the Poor Law Amendment Act 1867 which increased the amount that might be borrowed from the equivalent of one year's poor rate, on the average of the past three years, to two-thirds of the *aggregate* of the past three years – a substantial improvement, with a somewhat higher limit if the workhouse was in or near a municipal borough. The other significant statute was the Poor Law Loans Act 1871 which allowed earlier twenty-year loans to be extended to thirty years (with the lender's consent); several loans from the same lender could be consolidated. Yearly payments could be converted to half-yearly and, most important of all, a borrower's option could be included in future loans under which the borrower might seek an order from the Poor Law commissioners authorizing immediate repayment of a loan if a cheaper loan became available. Yet another important-sounding Act in 1872 – the Poor Law Loans Act – might have been expected to include a general consolidation, but its purpose was simply to tidy up certain points relating to the metropolis, and to make clear that the power to borrow for thirty years included power to borrow for lesser periods.

So that despite this positive movement to put the Poor Law on a rationalized basis and a succession of Acts relating to borrowing, a proper and comprehensive borrowing code was still lacking, although as will be shown, during this period extensive codes were introduced for general local government purposes. Obviously the Poor Law commissioners were determined to go their own *ad hoc* way. Perhaps the most significant feature of the Poor Law borrowing provisions is that they eschewed references to mortgaging or assigning the revenues, simply 'charging' the loans against the revenues. Why could not this simple concept – obviously adequate – have been adopted throughout the local government system?

Yet despite their independent attitude, the Poor Law commissioners seemed anxious to exercise a general influence on parish local government. In 1850 the Vestries Act described the holding of parish meetings in the vestry as 'productive of scandal to religion and other great inconveniences' and provided that the churchwarden and overseers with the approval of the Poor Law commissioners should provide alternative accommodation for parish meetings, and if necessary to that end 'borrow any sum of money which may be required for the purpose of this Act and charge the Poor Rate with the repayment of the sum and the interest thereon', such repayment to be by equal annual instalments over not more than ten years. They might also pay a vestry clerk at rates to be approved by the commission. A parish was defined as any place having separate Overseers of the Poor and maintaining its own poor.

THE MUNICIPAL CORPORATIONS ACT   The Report of the Royal Commission on the Boroughs (1835) said: 'The greater number of the governing charters of corporations was granted between Henry VIII and the Revolution.' Redlich and Hirst in their *History of Local Government in England* say bluntly: 'No statute ever defined a successful corporation. In 1833 you could hardly have found two municipal corporations of the same species.' Confusion was even worse confounded, in that in most boroughs the principal duties were carried out not by the municipality, but by separate bodies of commissioners created under local Acts.

From this confusion of charter boroughs with widely different powers, systems of election and accumulated duties, stripped in 1832 of their power to appoint members to Parliament, the 178 municipal boroughs recognized by the 1835 Act were created without regard to population or area. They were recognized as corporate bodies with councils democratically elected by a relatively wide franchise and were in two classes, those with and those without their own sessions. Those without still remained under county jurisdiction for the administration of justice. Their former charter powers were retained only in so far as they were not inconsistent with the terms of the new Act, although the powers given therein were very limited – the control of police through watch committees, lighting if there were not already improvement or other commissioners carrying out this duty, the granting of licences for the sale of drink, the making of good rule and government by-laws, and limited powers for the suppression of 'nuisances' (a first approach to public health functions). The common lands and the public stock (of money) were to be transferred to the new councils; a clerk and a treasurer were to be appointed and a 'Borough Fund' set up, into which were to be paid all the revenues of the authority,

> the rents and profits of all hereditaments and the interest dividends and annual proceeds of all monies, dues, chattels and valuable securities belonging or payable to the body corporate as well as all fees and penalties arising out of the Act.

If after crediting these revenues there was still a deficiency of income over expenditure, then a borough rate 'in the nature of a county rate' could be levied and collected through the parishes within the borough. This concept of the rate as a *residual* source of income to meet any deficiency which might arise after crediting central grants and miscellaneous incomes survives to modern times. The treasurer was responsible for moneys borrowed 'which have been already instituted or which may hereafter be instituted by way of mortgage or otherwise' as well as interest thereon. As no direct powers to borrow were conferred by the Act, but as past and future borrowing was thus tacitly recognized, the view expressed earlier that up to this point boroughs had an inherent right to borrow on their own security is confirmed. Where commissioners of one sort or another were operating under local Act in a borough, these continued their functions (which often included a power to borrow) unless they chose to hand over their powers to the borough. As new duties were devolved on the boroughs, shortly to be described, specific borrowing facilities were included, but the next general power to boroughs to borrow under certain conditions did not arise until 1860 in the Municipal Corporation Mortgages Act (at which chronological stage it will be dealt with in this book).

Apart from the organization of police administration, the main achievement of the Municipal Corporation Mortgages Act was to establish a type of administrative unit which could thereafter seek powers for itself through local Acts or, more important, be utilized for the devolution of responsibilities from the centre either on an adoptive or mandatory basis. But although the Act was a landmark in the development of the concept of

elective local government, its significance surprisingly in the field of
borrowing was negligible except that it appeared to confirm the practice of
ad hoc non-statutory borrowing which had been practised by charter
boroughs.

By presumably an oversight of parliamentary draftsmanship, while the
1835 Municipal Corporations Act authorized the levying of a borough and
a watch rate, or precept, it did not instruct or authorize the parish
overseers to take the subsequent action. A further Act – the Municipal
Rates Act – was therefore required in 1837 to authorize and require the
parish churchwardens and overseers within the borough to make and
collect a rate to meet the borough requirement; this Act also authorized
the borough to levy the rate itself, if the parish neglected its duties. That
this Act also had to make provision to cope with parishes only partly
within the borough, and with extra-parochial areas, indicates the
confusion of areas at this time.

THE CLAUSE ACT   In the mid-century Parliament adopted a series of
Clauses Acts which had a significant impact on the development of local
government activities, and two of which provided a comprehensive and
standardized code of borrowing practice applicable to local services (though
not, as will be shown, universally adopted). The two Acts of special
borrowing interest were the Companies Clauses Consolidation Act 1845
and the Commissioners Clauses Act 1847. There were other Clauses Acts
establishing administrative codes for land, markets and fairs, gasworks,
waterworks, harbours, docks and piers, cemeteries, police, town improvement and railways.

The function of the Clauses Acts was to standardize the terms and
reduce the cost of the substantial amount of private Bill legislation which
was being enacted during the middle part of the century, but these codes
were also adopted by reference in public general Acts. Local private Acts
dealing with the setting up of companies or of bodies for carrying out any
designated functions and appropriate general statutes could incorporate
selected provisions of the relevant Clauses Act by simple reference, thus
reducing the complexity and repetitiveness of the Acts, and assuring
themselves of acceptance of those elements in Parliament without dispute.
Other than the two Acts specially mentioned above, the Clauses Acts were
directed towards administrative and legal procedures only and did not
incorporate financial, and especially borrowing, provisions. Thus any local
or private Act for one of the particular purposes was obliged to adopt
selected provisions of one of the Clauses Acts for its main purposes, and
one of the two codes of the other two Acts for borrowing provisions.
Exceptionally the Towns Improvement Clauses Act itself embraced by
reference the borrowing code of the Commissioners Clauses Act, so that
any local Act incorporating the Towns Improvement Clauses also
automatically incorporated financial provisions at, as it were, a second
remove.

The parallel nature of these two codes of financial provisions is of
particular interest because they confirm the distinction already adopted in

this book between companies operating at a profit and public services not profit motivated. The distinction became somewhat blurred because many of the companies of a public utility character were later taken over by the public authorities; moreover, by a curious lack of understanding, the Companies Clauses Act provisions were on occasion written into public services statutes when those of the Commissioners Clauses Act would seem to have been more appropriate.

The borrowing codes incorporated in the Companies and Commissioners Clauses Acts, and by cross-reference in the Towns Improvement Clauses Act, were very similar and are summarized below. In the Companies Clauses Act the provisions related to borrowing on mortgages or by bonds of the conditional (penalty) type (enlarged upon in Part 3 of this book), over and above the initial share capital to which was related the amount which could then be borrowed but did not become part of share capital. Commissioners were to borrow only by mortgage or assignments. Because these Acts related to a wide variety of companies and bodies of commissioners, the underlying securities were expressed in general terms – in the Companies Clauses Act the 'tolls, sums and premises' and 'future calls payable by the shareholders', and in the Commissioners Clauses Act 'the rates and assessments or other property'. In each specific Act the precise security would of necessity need to be stated. The following is a general summary of the borrowing codes incorporated:

(1)   Every mortgage, assignation, or bond should be by deed, stamped, sealed and stating the consideration (amount of loan). This seems to mark the end of the exclusion of loans of this kind from stamp duty as given in so many earlier Acts.

(2)   Lenders were entitled to a proportionate share of the security (on default) without preference as to the dates on which the loans were made. (Extensive as these codes were, the point had not yet been reached where loans not only had equal priority, but had a first priority over other debts.)

(3)   The borrowing instruments were to be in the form prescribed 'or the like effect'. In the Commissioners Act the pro forma document is described as a 'form of mortgage' which granted and assigned the specified security. In the Companies Act two forms were provided – a mortgage which assigned the security, and a bond in which the signatories 'bound themselves' to meet the liability. In practice, as will be shortly shown, various later Acts appointing commissioners provided for bonds as well as mortgages. A striking point is that there is no specific mention of annuities in these Acts, though perhaps, with careful drafting, the granting of annuities, in so far as they were secured by a mortgage of income, might have been a practical possibility.

(4)   A register of loans containing details of the transactions was required, subject to inspection at all reasonable times by interested parties without fee.

(5) Lenders had the right to transfer the loan by stamped deed in the form specified, or the like effect – the same form for mortgages as for bonds – such transfers to be registered at a fee of 2s 6d under the Companies Act, and 5s under the Commissioners Act.

(6) Unless otherwise provided in the deed, interest was to be paid half-yearly.

(7) The deed might specify the period for repayment, and the office at which this would take place. Interest ceased if the lender failed to claim the repayment at the due date, but continued if the borrower failed to meet his liability for repayment of principal promptly. If a repayment date was not specified in the deed, then after one year either party had the right to give six months' notice of termination of the transaction. Today these are what would be called 'lenders and borrowers options'. However, the Commissioners Act had an additional 'roll-over' provision, in that even though a date for repayment had been specified in the deed, if at any time the Commissioners could borrow at a lower rate of interest than was being paid on an existing loan, they could – as is commonly done today with loans running at notice – reborrow and discharge the more highly rated debt (or presumably renegotiate the rate with the existing lender). There was no provision for the lender to take similar action if he could reinvest at a higher rate (except the six months' notice provision where there was no specified repayment date), nor was such a provision made in the Companies Clauses Act.

(8) Where a principal Act gave lenders power to apply for the appointment of a receiver on default of interest payment or principal repayment – but only if this point was specifically mentioned – both Acts set out the appropriate procedure – application to two magistrates, if there were arrears of thirty days in interest payment, or six months in the repayment of principal (without prejudice to the right to sue in a superior court). These provisions indicated that the principle of receivership was well established in the companies field before this date, but no earlier example has been discovered in a local government context. An implication may be read into this provision that there *were* such earlier references in local government private Bill legislation, but this does not necessarily follow and the provision in this Clauses Act may have been intended to relate to future Acts. The specific reference to a receiver provision in the Prisons Act (which will shortly follow) is some confirmation of this; as later references will show, acceptance of this provision was spasmodic. It is a strange provision because it is not known ever to have been called into operation in local government, yet its existence is still highly regarded by present-day institutional lenders to local government.

(9) The Commissioners Act alone makes provision for a sinking fund for the repayment of the debt, though the arithmetic is a little suspect. A sum was to be set aside to repay the loan in the prescribed term of years; if no term had been prescribed, then one-twentieth part of the

loan was to be set aside each year and invested in exchequer bills or
other government securities and thus accumulated at compound
interest until enough was available to pay off all or some of the debt,
the lenders to be repaid selected by lot. Because of the accumulation
at compound interest and premature repayment of some loans, the
real repayment period was obviously less than 20 years. The Towns
Improvement Clauses Act provided 30 years, and the system of
sinking funds is clarified in later Acts.

These two Clauses Acts, particularly that for bodies of commissioners
and incomplete though they still were, clearly were the the first positive
efforts to introduce a coherent borrowing code for local public services.
How unfortunate therefore that their adoption in practice left much to be
desired. The degree to which advantage was taken of these standard and
relatively complete codes is illustrated in the particular Acts for individual
services now to be examined, though some of the developments preceded
the Clauses Acts and therefore were obliged to provide their own
borrowing provisions.

Chapter 8

THE ACCRETION OF SERVICES AND THEIR ASSOCIATED BORROWING FACILITIES

By the year 1835, then, the local government structure consisted of the county administration conducted by the justices of the peace as an offshoot of their judicial function, with the ecclesiastical parish as the subordinate 'unit of obligation', and the municipal corporations randomly spread as largely independent islands within the counties. A framework of Poor Law unions with the additional duty of registration was in process of establishment nationwide (or shortly to be so), but although the unions were composed of groups of parishes, they were independent of the counties with whose boundaries their own did not necessarily coincide. The turnpike trusts were similarly *ad hoc* but on a less comprehensive, much more casual, organizational basis. There were also numerous bodies of commissioners, operating mainly in urban areas for a variety of purposes – improvements, lighting, cleansing, paving and drainage, water supply, police, harbours, and the like, with power also to use the parish as the rating authority, and usually also with power to borrow for their work.

Over the rest of the century, until the whole pattern of local government was put on a rational, consistent, democratic basis, many other duties were devolved on this patchwork system in a somewhat piecemeal manner. However, because the impulses which had led to the rationalization of the administration of the Poor Law and the municipal borough were lost, the problem was that these new duties had to be carried out on an unsatisfactory organizational base. Borrowing for capital finance also continued in a haphazard fashion until the final quarter of the century. These developments are now described.

LAND DRAINAGE   An Act passed in 1841 is of fringe interest in relation to borrowing. This was an important amendment to one of the first statutes of particular local application – the Statute of Sewers (land drainage) of 1531. This amending Sewers Act extended the power of Courts of Sewers to levy adequate taxes 'in proportion to the benefit and advantage received'. More significantly – and at this late date – because certain authorized expenses might have to be met before any general sewer rate could be recovered, the Courts of Sewers were authorized in 1841 to borrow at interest any necessary sums (by making a decree or ordinance) for a period not longer than seven years. This was to be on the security of the sewers rate, but the interesting detail is that the borrowing instrument was to be a 'certificate', setting out the amount, the rate of interest, the arrangements for instalment repayment, and promising the underlying security of the sewers rate, thus encapsulating a full and proper borrowing instrument under this plain title of certificate. The words of the form of security written into the Act include the assurance that the commissioners 'do hereby certify' that the rates to be levied should be the security. Another name for a standard borrowing instrument which, in effect, mortgages a rate income thus appears. The antiquity of land drainage measures is borne out in the words which say that nothing in the Act shall prevent any Court of Sewers from acting under earlier Acts or 'the Laws of Sewers of old time accustomed'.

POLICE   Two ancient and related duties are the appointment of police and the provision of prisons. Reference has already been made to the financial aspects (including borrowing) of early prison (gaol) legislation. The provision of police in one form or another has an equally long history, but the organized creation of police forces with proper financial backing came surprisingly late. The early history of the parish constable is said by the Webbs to be obscure; the office of constable was not strictly speaking a parish matter, but a manorial post under the court leet, and with roots in the early Anglo-Saxon 'tythingman', and proper statutory provision was lacking until the early nineteenth century. Counties and boroughs had used private Act or charter powers to institute some form of authority for law and order in parts or all of their area (for instance, Cheshire is considered to be the first in 1828). However, official statutory responsibility for providing a police force was not given until the Municipal Corporations Act 1835, which established watch committees and authorized a police rate. This Act was, as already described, short on borrowing arrangements. The first steps towards the provision of county police came in a permissive Act in 1839 allowing counties to appoint paid constables with government grant aid. This first attempt at county police was inadequate and necessitated a second Act in 1840 to authorize a county rate from which the force could be paid, and to provide station-houses and 'strong rooms', for the financing of which money might be borrowed on a twenty-year instalment repayment basis. Borrowing seems to have been resorted to earlier by parishes for this purpose, or at least debts incurred, as the old parish police rates were to be continued until the parish police debts were cleared. Possibly these debts arose from the parliamentary authority for a parish police rate in the nature of the poor rate as far back as 1662 but this seems to have been to meet the constable's expenses in relation to control of vagrancy.

Even as late as 1842 attempts were made to bring to life the obsolescent parish constable – every man between the ages of 25 and 65 rated at more than £4 a year was liable to be called upon to serve as constable – but the attempt proved a dead letter. The first positive and determined step was not taken until 1856 with the County and Boroughs Police Act in which these authorities were required to establish paid police forces, with government grant aid, subject to the maintenance of standards. Borrowing provisions were not mentioned, but in counties these would have been as under the 1840 Act.

The model for this national standard police administration was that established in the metropolis. The Metropolitan Police were created in 1829 under the Home Secretary, Sir Robert Peel (the 'peelers' or 'bobbies'). A further Act of 1839 extended the Metropolitan Police Area to cover an area of fifteen miles centred on Charing Cross; and yet another Act in 1856 reconstituted the Metropolitan Police under commissioners but still responsible directly to the Home Secretary, although the cost was shared with the local authorities.

PRISONS   As the main duty given to municipal boroughs in the 1815 Municipal Corporations Act was police administration, there is no cause for surprise that the first responsibility subsequently devolved on these new municipal authorities was the provision of prisons. Indeed the surprise must be that such a power was not included in the original Act. (There was a Prisons Act 1835, but this was an administrative measure only and had no reference to finance.) In 1842 the powers given to counties in 1823 to provide prisons were extended to municipal boroughs. This meant that counties were earlier than boroughs in having a national responsibility to provide prisons, but that boroughs were first in the field with powers to appoint paid police.

The 1842 Prisons Act authorized boroughs which had their own courts of sessions (group A in the Municipal Corporations Act) to provide prisons. Money could be borrowed for the purchase of land, and the building, rebuilding, repairing and enlarging of prisons, court-houses, or other buildings. A significant provision which indicates that boroughs had been borrowing under their old charter powers without statutory sanctions said that borrowing might be undertaken to repay money which had been borrowed for any of the approved purposes before the passing of the Act.

Borrowing could be either by the granting of bonds under the Common Seal or by mortgage of 'land tenements or hereditaments of the borough' or 'the issues, rents and profits' which by any law in force might be applied towards erecting or maintaining a gaol or house of correction. Although the Act indicates, as above, what assets were to be mortgaged, it continued by saying that any money borrowed was a charge on the borough fund or borough rates – without prejudice to any prior claims on the borough fund – or against a special gaol rate. A form of mortgage was given, 'or in any other suitable form', but not a form of bond. The gaol buildings for which the loan was being raised were to be specified in the mortgage. Repayment was to be on a thirty-year basis, or twenty years for advances from the Exchequer Loan Commissioners; interest was to be paid half-yearly. The repayment period for counties – previously fourteen years – was also extended in the same way.

These sketchy provisions were apparently soon found to be inadequate, for in 1848 a further Act was passed specifically to facilitate the raising of money for the building and repair of prisons. The Prisons Act of 1848 indicated that the terms of the earlier 1842 Act were too restrictive as to borrowing and replaced them with the wider powers of the Commissioners Clauses Act by then available. Because the receivership provisions of the Commissioners Clauses Act only applied if specifically adopted by the later principal Act, the 1848 Prisons Act provided that

> the mortgages and bondholders of the Corporation shall be empowered to enforce the arrears of interest or the arrears of principal and interest by appointment of a Receiver in the same manner as directed by the Commissioners Clauses Act 1847.

This appears to be the first public statute of a local government nature which specifically and categorically incorporated such receivership provisions. Although the Commissioners Clauses Act provided only for mortgages, the 1848 Prisons Act gave its commissioners power to use either mortgages or bonds (as in the Companies Clauses Act), and applied all its terms to both forms of instrument, which is perhaps another indication that the difference in borrowing instruments is in name only.

The Prisons Act rejected the Clauses Acts' one-twentieth provision for the formation of a sinking fund in favour of the alternative of the thirty-year provision given under the earlier 1842 Act. However, it included a strange provision that £6 10s per cent should be set aside each year and that such sum should be applied from time to time, *after payment thereout of interest*, as a sinking fund for the repayment of moneys borrowed, such sums being invested in government securities and accumulated at interest and used to repay debt from time to time as under the Commissioners Clauses Act. What this involved in real terms is difficult to disentangle, and depended of course on the annual charge for interest on which the borrowing had been undertaken.

FIRE PROTECTION   Passing reference is made to a function which bears a close relationship to police, that of fire protection, although this service has had no impact on borrowing techniques. Early mention is made of this duty in the statutes. In 1707 parishes were authorized to provide means 'for better preventing mishaps that may happen from fire'.[1] With the preamble to the Act referring to 'the many fires [which] have lately broke out in several places in and about the Cities of London and Westminster and other parishes and places within the weekly bills of mortality', parishes and their churchwardens were required to keep engines, provide pipes and stopcocks. Not altogether surprisingly, a further Act was almost immediately required in 1708 to enforce standardization of sizes of standpipes, to allow parishes to combine for this purpose and to permit the levying of a rate along with the poor rate. Even as late as 1867 in a Poor Law Amendment Act (which, *inter alia*, made the Poor Law Board permanent) provision was made that if no one else did so, the parish overseers themselves might provide a fire-engine. The incongruity of the Poor Law Commissioners concerning themselves with fire protection in parishes generally is another example of their general interest in the welfare of the parishes.

The main development of fire-fighting took place in the urban areas under the auspices, and at the expense of, the fire insurance companies (from as early as 1680 when the first of the companies, the Phenix, so spelt, was formed), and even when the Metropolitan Board of Works assumed the duty in the metropolis in 1866, substantial contributions continued to be made by the companies. By the time local authorities began to assume the responsibility (initially as part of the police function – firemen were sworn in as policemen) general borrowing facilities were available.

In fact a proper fire brigade Act was not passed until 1938, when the duties were confirmed as belonging to county boroughs and county districts. This was soon overlaid by the workings of the Air Raid Precautions Act 1937, and after the outbreak of the Second World War, nationalization of the fire service. When, somewhat to the surprise of the local authorities, the fire service was returned to them in 1948, the duty was imposed on the counties and county boroughs. Under the 1972 reorganization the duty remains with the counties.

MUSEUMS   If improved prisons can be seen as a natural consequence of the police powers of the 1835 Act, the advent of the next development, powers to provide museums of art and science, is more difficult to understand. Surely, the denser urban areas had more serious problems than the need to provide establishments 'for the instruction and amusement of the inhabitants'? Nevertheless, the Museums Act 1845 – a neat and unpretentious piece of legislative drafting – was directed to municipal boroughs of over 10,000 population. It was permissive only – 'if such council shall think fit to do so' – but the cost to fall on the borough fund was not to exceed a rate of ½d. Borrowing for the purchase of land and the construction of buildings was authorized with the approval of the Treasury, on the security of the borough rate, or a special rate if so levied. Despite the lack of a borrowing code in the Municipal Corporations Act 1835, this specific power to borrow was not set out in much detail, the Clauses Acts were of course not at that time yet available.

A point of principle needs to be made here. Whatever the arguments may be for 'pay-as-you-go' vs borrowing, this Act and others like it which impose a rate limit, virtually impose along with it a need to borrow. Was it otherwise supposed that during construction the work could be so organized that without undue delay the building could be provided on such a time-scale that not more than a ½d rate in any year would be required, and that after construction, the ½d rate would suffice for administration and the acquisition of new works? Or was it assumed that borrowing would be inevitable, but that the cost would have to be so calculated that the debt charges (and the period for repayment was not indicated), plus the running costs, could be contained within the limits? The early administrators of local government were faced with a severe philosophical problem – how much burden were they entitled to lay upon future citizens, and what problems of their own would these same citizens have without the burden of bequeathed debt? This issue will require later analysis.

A further curious feature of the original Museums Act was that it did not extend to public libraries, which might have been considered more important or at least more in demand than museums, so that a further Act was called for in 1850 to deal with public libraries as well as museums. This Act repealed the earlier Museums Act but was even sketchier on the subject of borrowing, and did not incorporate the Clauses Acts even though these were then available. A third attempt was needed; this took place in 1855 when what was simply called the Public Libraries Act, although it also dealt with museums, repealed the 1850 Act. This Act extended the option to boroughs of only 5,000 population, and included large parishes and areas covered by Improvement Acts. The rate limit was increased to 1d and bodies of commissioners were to be appointed to administer the Act except in boroughs where the duty naturally fell to the borough council. The Land Clauses Act was incorporated to cover the routine of site purchases and the Company Clauses Consolidation Act for borrowing matters (rather than the more obvious Commissioners Clauses Act), but without incorporation of the receivership provisions. Borrowing by mortgage or bond was specifically permitted, though these were the natural sequence of the adoption of the Clauses Act. Borrowing from the Exchequer Loan Commissioners was authorized. A further amending Act was passed in 1871 to apply the borrowing provisions of the Local Government Act 1858 (yet to be dealt with). Public libraries were also the subject of an Act of 1892 in which the borrowing power provisions were transferred to the terms of the Public Health Act 1875 (shortly to be dealt with).[2]

LUNATIC ASYLUMS Another addition to the duties of municipal corporations which occurred in 1845 was the extension (with amendments) of the Act of 1828, which had increased the powers of county councils to provide lunatic asylums. Although this Act had been preceded by the Company Clauses Consolidation Act, the borrowing provisions of that Act were not incorporated. Rather the borrowing provisions of the 1828 Act were somewhat dramatically revised, in that loans on mortgage of the rates instead of being required to be for not less than £50 each were now to be for not less than £500 each. Instead of the permission to borrow being linked to an estimated cost which exceeded one-half of the county rate on the average of the last five years, borrowing was now subject to the cost being in excess of a round sum of £5,000, or in smaller areas 'annexed to the county for this purpose' of £2,000. Interest was not to exceed 5 per cent p.a. (previously 'legal or lower interest' which was in fact 5 per cent at that date). A significant variation in the security to be offered was that this could either be a special rate levied for the purpose of the Act 'together with all other rates or funds, or any of them' – part of the move towards the concept of 'all the rates and revenues of the authority' of modern times. The usual provisions for form of mortgage, registration and transfer and equality of standing of lenders were included. The fourteen-year sinking fund and repayment provisions of the 1828 Act were extended to thirty years, with the setting aside of one-thirtieth of the amount of debt each year, in addition to the interest charge. A 'roll-over' provision was included, and there does not seem to have been any requirement for annual instalment repayment. Instead of selection of those to be repaid by lot, repayment was to be by agreement. Somewhat less officious rules were incorporated for the keeping of the books of account than in the 1828 Act. BATHS AND WASHHOUSES   In 1846 what can perhaps be seen as the first of the public health Acts was passed to encourage the establishment of public baths and washhouses, the baths in question being wash-baths (slipper baths) rather than swimming-pools (plunge baths), although the provision of open-air bathing places was also authorized. An interesting sign of the times and the evidence that wash-baths were intended was that the Act required that the number of baths provided in any one building for the labouring classes was to be at least twice the number provided for any other class. The Act was adoptive and could be taken up by any municipal corporation or – subject to the approval of the secretary of state – any parish where two-thirds of the ratepayers were so resolved. Though the Act was to be administered by the elected councils in the boroughs, separate bodies of commissioners were to be appointed in parishes, but with the status of a body corporate for this function. The expenses were to be met from the borough fund or the parish poor rate, but on this occasion a clear direction was given to the overseers that they must collect the rate called for. Borrowing was permitted subject to central Treasury approval, and access to the Exchequer Loan Commissioners was also authorized. Although this Act postdated the Commissioners Clauses Act, the borrowing code adopted was that of the Company Clauses Consolidation Act.

An interesting feature of this Act was that if after seven years' operation the borough or parish considered that the baths and washhouses were no longer required or were too expensive to maintain, they could be sold and the proceeds credited to the borough rate or parish poor rate; there was no specific requirement that the proceeds should be used to extinguish debt. BURIAL BOARDS   The Acts relating to provision for burial of the dead demonstrate the general slow and laborious pattern of development for the incorporation of a service within the scope of local government. Burials were of course taking place within the boundaries of churchyards, and private Acts had been used to establish commercial cemeteries, so much so that a Cemeteries Clauses Act had been needed in 1847. The pressure of population in the London area led to the Metropolitan Interments Act 1850, which set up the central General Board of Health as the executive authority for the provision of burial grounds in a defined metropolitan area consisting of the City of London and Westminster and a scheduled list of surrounding parishes. This Burial Board was permitted to borrow on the security of the mortgaging of the fees and payments receivable under the Act. There was to be no priority among lenders and the Public Works Loan Commission (PWLC) might provide funds. Debt could be repaid and reborrowed to keep down interest rates; a form of mortgage was prescribed along with provision for registration; and repayment was to be by agreement with lenders by instalments or otherwise without a specified period unless such was contained in the deed. If no date for repayment was included in the deed, lenders could give notice after 12 months. Interest was to be half-yearly, the books to be open to inspection and transfers permitted. A sinking fund could be set up for repayment, to be invested in government stocks on an accumulating basis. When fees and other payments were insufficient to meet expenses, a rate could be imposed on the constituent parishes, to be collected with the poor rate.

This Act had a short life in this form. In 1852 it was repealed and the duties transferred directly to the constituent parishes, except that the City of London was to assume the duty for all its parishes and liberties. The administrative provisions of the Cemeteries Clauses Act were incorporated. Thereafter, in the Burials Act 1853 similar powers were given to the remainder of the country's parishes outside the metropolis, and in 1854 the duty was extended to borough councils. In 1855 the powers of Boards of Guardians to bury paupers were extended to areas outside the parishes concerned.

The main development of significance to the history of borrowing took place in the Burials Act of 1857. Local Boards of Health could take up the duties of burial boards, and the Commissioners Clauses Act was invoked. Borrowing on mortgage with a five-year loan sanction period was permitted, but most significantly borrowing by annuities was introduced; these could be life annuities or term annuities for a maximum of thirty years. In 1860 Improvement Commissioners could adopt burial board responsibilities but a further Act was needed, in 1860, to make clear that the commissioners could borrow on the security of an improvement rate for burial-ground purposes and incorporate the terms of the Commissioners Clauses Act. Improvement Commissioners had for some time been taking upon themselves powers for burial provisions – for example, the Huddersfield Improvement Act 1848 gave the local commissioners powers to borrow up to £10,000 on mortgage of fees for the provision of burial facilities; repayment was on a thirty-year basis, by instalments or a sinking fund. As late as 1897 the power to establish joint boards under the Local Government Act 1894 was extended to burial functions. In retrospect the question is bound to arise as to why a complete and coherent pattern for the provision of burial facilities could not have been conceived at an earlier stage.

LODGING HOUSES AND DWELLINGS FOR THE LABOURING CLASSES   Two interrelated Acts of 1851 and 1866 introduced the first stages in the provision of housing accommodation by local authorities, initially for the 'working classes' but ultimately without this restriction, a duty which has by now overwhelmed the rest of their debt. This function began in the innocuous form of 'the provision of well-ordered lodging houses for the labouring classes' in the Lodging Houses Act 1851, an adoptive Act applying not only to boroughs, but to local boards of health, improvement boards and parishes generally. With the approval of the Treasury, any of these could borrow on the security of the appropriate rate; both the Land Clauses and the Companies Clauses Consolidation Acts were incorporated, but the receivership provisions of the latter were not adopted. Access was given to the Exchequer Loan Commissioners.

The shape of the 1866 Act was most peculiar. Although it was to be read as part of the 1851 Act and both were to be construed together, it was really a dramatic step forward. The provision of lodging-houses for the labouring classes was at a stroke extended to 'facilitating and encouraging the erection of dwellings for the labouring classes in populous places'; and although the short title was given as 'The Labouring Classes Dwellings Houses Act 1866', the long title described its function as being simply 'to enable the Public Works Loan Commission to make advances towards the erection of dwellings for the labouring classes'. In other words, the function of providing housing accommodation by local authorities was brought in not directly, but by an extension of the powers of the PWLC; in the words of the Act:

> Such advance on loan shall be made for the purpose of assisting in the purchase of land and buildings, or in the erection, alteration or adaptation of buildings to be used for dwellings for the labouring classes and in providing all conveniences which may be deemed proper in connection with such dwellings.

The remainder of the Act was occupied in elaborating the terms on which the PWLC could make advances. There was no direct statement in this Act that borrowing on the market was a permissible alternative, but as it was to be read as part of the earlier Act which took over the borrowing provisions of the Commissioners Clauses Act, a market borrowing facility must be implied. The earlier Act had given the PWLC power to lend for lodging-houses; presumably this wider function was regarded as requiring a positive extension of the PWLC powers, but the emphasis on the means of borrowing rather than the dramatic extension of function is certainly cause for surprise. However, the lending authority of the PWLC for this initial housing function also extended in this Act beyond local authorities.

The security to be offered was to be either the local rate or the land or dwellings on which the advance was made, or both. If the security offered was the land, then it had to be held on fee simple, or on an agreement with at least fifty years to run, and in that case the advance could not be for more than one-half of the value. An authority adopting this function automatically became a body corporate for the purpose. The terms of the Commissioners Clauses Act also applied. A period of forty years was allowed for PWLC advances, yet this does not seem to have been applicable to market loans, to which the twenty-year period of the Commissioners Clauses Act presumably applied. A 4 per cent maximum interest rate for the PWLC advances was provided. Indeed the impression is difficult to avoid that local authorities exercising this function were expected to do so only on PWLC loans.

Altogether this was a most peculiar Act; no doubt a better understanding of it would be possible on examination of the parliamentary debates. The main surge of housing development by local authorities did not in fact occur until the closing years of the century through the Small Dwellings Acquisition Act 1899, by which time the borrowing provisions were linked with the Municipal Corporations Act 1882 and the Local Government Act 1888.

HIGHWAYS AND BRIDGES   Between 1800 and 1835, as the Webbs point out in *The King's Highway*, 'parliament continued to render more complicated and incomprehensible a body of [highway] law which was already beyond the comprehension of any human being'. Finally, Parliament having been reformed in 1832 managed to put on to the statute-book the Highways Act 1835. This repealed the mass of existing legislation (except that relating to turnpikes) and revised and recodified the law in a substantial statute. However, while this was a positive improvement in the administration of the highways system, it still fell far short of what had been urged on Parliament by several commissions and was really quite inadequate to the needs of the time. Nevertheless, statute labour was finally abolished, provision was made for paid surveyors of highways and for the regular levy of a highway rate. There was no provision for borrowing. Highways Boards could be established but, in effect, this high-sounding title merely referred to the appointment of a committee of the vestry with a special responsibility for roads and the power was, in any event, confined to 'large and populous parishes', meaning those with more than 5,000 population at the last Census, though with power for parishes to combine (which they proved loath to do). The use of the county as the administrative unit was eschewed, partly on political grounds (Parliament was Whig and the counties mainly Tory) and partly from concern at the growing level of the non-democratic county rate.

Thus the smallness of the areas of highway administration, concentration on a rate levy with no power to borrow for longer-term works, and possibly the fact that major roads were under the jurisdiction of turnpike trusts, placed a severe limitation on the effectiveness of local road administration. Many abortive attempts were made during the next few years to improve this situation. In fact progress in urban areas, where the need was perhaps greatest, tended to be made under the public health and sanitary acts of this period.

Progress was made in Wales, where both the ordinary and the turnpike roads were put on to a county basis, but some sort of breakthrough in highways administration, in England, did not come until 1862 when an Act gave justices of the peace power to enforce combinations of parishes to form Highways Boards, but still with the limited revenue facilities. Many parishes avoided this form of reorganization by electing to become Sanitary Authorities under the Local Government Act 1858 (see p. 131), but this loophole was tightened by the 1863 Highways Act when the formation of such districts was limited to parishes of over 3,000 population. This confused and unsatisfactory situation remained until the 1870s, until when there was no effectively improved highways legislation and no provision for borrowing. Even by 1894 there were only 357 highways districts, but still over 5,000 separate highways parishes, electing their own surveyors according to the Webbs, and only the great Local Government Act of 1894 took positive steps to rationalize the approach to highways administration in something like modern terms. How extraordinary that roads, so essential a feature of social and commercial development, reaching back to the reign of Henry VIII and indeed beyond in their treatment by statute, should have lacked an effective financial base, including borrowing, until almost the year 1900! Attention to bridges was not a great deal more effective, but at least finance from borrowed money was contemplated, even if not for new bridges except by special Act. On questions of terminology the Highlands Roads and Bridges Act 1862 which transferred duties in relation to major highways, bridges and harbours from a commission to the appropriate county councils is of interest; this Act uses the phrase 'Interest accruing on the money so borrowed shall be regularly kept down and not allowed to accumulate'.

The first significant Act relating to bridges in this period, was the County Bridges Act 1841, but this was still confined to maintaining, altering, widening, repairing and improving bridges, with no mention of the building of new bridges which was still left to private Act procedures. However, this Act admitted that the cost of the permitted works was 'sometimes considerable' and that consequently 'it is expedient that money required for the purpose may be borrowed'; 'considerable' was defined as a cost which exceeded one-quarter of the county rate levy on the average of the last seven years. Sums borrowed were to be for not less than £50 each with repayment on a fourteen-year basis, annual repayment being selected by lot, yet still with the most expensive first to be repaid. Proper books of account were to be kept showing accruing interest. The terminology is slightly unusual; the loans were to be entered into by 'agreements' as a charge on the county rate, but the draft form appended was headed 'Mortgage and charge upon the county rate for recovery of the money borrowed'.

However, of particular interest is that the 1841 County Bridges Act refers back to an Act of 1825, itself amending the Gaols Act of 1823 – setting out general terms for borrowing for the provision of gaols. These borrowing provisions were in effect incorporated into county bridge borrowing by reference in the 1841 Act, mainly as to the facility to repay and renew loans, if thereby the interest charge could be reduced.

This County Bridges Act was followed by a Borough Bridges Act in 1850. This was in similar terms as to the degree of responsibility allowed, that is, it referred to making good or improving old bridges without giving a power to build new ones. Where the borough council found that the work proposed was likely to exceed the ludicrously small sum of £150, they could borrow on mortgage of the rate in a prescribed form in sums of not less than £50 each, subject to repayment over a fourteen-year period. Advantage was not taken of either of the Clauses Acts. Proper books of account were to be kept which had to show, among other things, 'what interest is growing due' and what principal moneys had been discharged and what remained due. These books were to be 'carefully inspected' by the council at its quarterly meetings. Provision was made for assignment, and all lenders were promised equal status. Again mortgages to be repaid were to be selected by lot, yet those with the highest interest rates to be taken first. These two Acts allowing borrowing for bridges or highways seem hardly to reflect the evolving codes of borrowing which had emerged during the previous seventy years or so.

PUBLIC HEALTH Between 1846 and 1872 there were numerous Acts dealing with public health in the widest context. These Acts appeared under various names – Nuisance Removal, Sewage Utilisation, Public Health, Sanitary and even Local Government. Together they were concerned with the development of services which were ultimately fully recognized as a proper part of the local government scene in the health and environmental sectors. Apart from problems of spelling out these new public service responsibilities, the framers of the legislation had also the considerable problem of bringing the services into being against a confused background of areas and authorities; the attempts in the preambles to define the authorities to whom they were applicable indicate in a nutshell the area problems of the time.

A considerable source of confusion in this subject is that the functions developed along two lines – the Sanitary Acts concerned particularly with the control of recognizable public nuisances, and the Public Health Acts covering the subject in a wider sense, including sewerage and sewage disposal, and water supply. For a time there were both Sanitary Authorities and Local Health Authorities. The Local Boards of Health covered the areas of boroughs, areas covered by Improvement Acts, and areas (mainly parishes) which had elected to assume the duties of Local Boards of Health. The sanitary authorities were the Local Boards of Health where these existed, and in rural areas where they did not exist, the Boards of Guardians operating through the unions. Gradually the two sets of functions were combined and the responsible areas became known as the Urban and Rural Sanitary Authorities; this somewhat casual formation of sanitary authorities led to problems when in later years they were virtually converted as they stood into urban and rural district councils.

Substantial arrangements for borrowing were made in the Public Health Acts of 1848, 1858 and 1872, but when the system was finally rationalized by the great consolidating and amending Public Health Act of 1875, the code contained in that Act, which for many years had a substantial influence on local authority borrowing, unfortunately clashed in material ways with the borrowing code embodied in the Local Loans Act of the same year. This situation will be dealt with in Chapter 9.

There had been earlier Acts of a public health character; as far back as 1603 steps had been taken in an attempt to diminish the spread of the plague, and early in Victoria's reign (1840) efforts had been made to encourage vaccination. There had also been numerous private Acts, some of which have already been noted, for setting up bodies of Improvement Commissioners in urban areas, whose duties of street cleansing, drainage and related work were public health functions within the context of the 1848 Act, and there was a minor Nuisances Removal Act in 1846. The 1848 Act was essentially the result of a report of the Poor Law Commissioners, urged on by Chadwick, arguing that poverty could not be controlled or reduced unless more attention was given to the establishment of sanitary conditions in both urban and rural areas. In consequence, the Poor Law unions might well have become (but did not) the 1848 Act health authorities and perhaps, ultimately, the future local authorities generally.

The Public Health Act 1848 embraced sewerage, drainage, water supply, streetworks, burial grounds and the regulation of offensive trades under the direction of a General Board of Health, a form of central control similar to that under the Poor Law and the distant forerunner of today's Department of the Environment. The Act could be adopted by boroughs or parishes, or imposed wherever the death rate was high. Local boards of health were to be set up; they were not given the status of corporate bodies (unless so already), but although the borrowing code of the Clauses Acts was not applied, nevertheless the Clauses Act codes obviously affected the 1848 Act's extensive provisions for borrowing. Subject to the approval of the General Board of Health, the local boards were empowered to borrow on mortgage at interest for 'works of a permanent nature' (which was at least some attempt to define capital purposes) on the credit of the various rates authorized to be levied under the Act (that is, special rate – the establishment of the general district rate was not made until 1861 by the Local Government Act of that year). The total borrowed was not to exceed the equivalent of the assessable value for one year of the premises assessable under the Act. This maximum, modified for sewerage and water supply, stood for many years. Lenders were as usual to rank equally irrespective of date. 'Roll-over' provisions were included but limited, in that a loan could not be repaid prematurely in order to reborrow more cheaply, without the consent of the lender (which presumably, if interest rates were falling, would not be easy to obtain). The mortgaging of the rate was to be represented by a sealed deed setting out the date, consideration, and time and place of interest payments and principal repayment; a register was to be maintained subject to inspection; and there was a power to assign, such assignments to be registered at a fee of 5s. Interest was to be paid half-yearly (unless otherwise provided in the deed) and selection for repayment was to be by lot. Local boards were given access to the Exchequer Loan Commissioners.

The Act also contained a workmanlike provision for an accumulating sinking fund in the following terms:

In order to pay off any monies borrowed and secured by any such mortgage, the Local Board of Health shall in every year, until the same be paid off, appropriate and set apart as a sinking fund such sums as together with the interest from time to time to accrue thereon, will in the period of thirty years amount to a sum sufficient to repay the monies borrowed and secured by any such mortgage, and shall from time to time cause such sinking fund and the interest thereon, to be invested in the purchase of Exchequer Bills or other Government securities, and to be increased by accumulation in the way of compound interest or otherwise.

Provision was also made for the possible appointment of a receiver; on default for six months of either principal or interest (not thirty days for interest as under the Clauses Acts) a lender (or two or more lenders together) to whom the amount owed was not less than £1,000 might apply to two magistrates for the appointment of a receiver to collect the rate in discharge of the debt 'without prejudice to any other mode of recovery'.

This was therefore, from a borrowing point of view at least, a competent piece of legislation, comparing very favourably with the thinking on highways and bridges finance at this time. A notable omission from the public health borrowing arrangements was any reference to annuities (widely used well before this date in private Acts), and of course borrowing by stock had not yet appeared on the scene.

The competent provisions were somewhat further stiffened by the so-called Local Government Act 1858, which was in fact a public health act required to be read with the 1848 Act. The General Board of Health, said never to have been popular, was abolished and the borrowing approvals required from that body were henceforth to come from 'One of Her Majesty's secretaries of state'. Hence the title Local Board of Health for the local bodies was reduced to Local Board presumably in recognition of the less specific title of this Act. The Act was extensive – part of the growing concept of local government – but the alteration of borrowing provisions though useful were minimal. The repayment provisions of the earlier Act were extended, in that they were repealed and replaced by a requirement that repayment should be either by equal annual instalments, or by an accumulating sinking fund to be used as the board decided. The limit on borrowing of one year's assessable value could be increased to two years' value for borrowing for sewerage and water supply expenditures and the borrowing period extended to fifty years, an early indication of the interrelationship of these two functions confirmed by today's concentration of them in the hands of the regional water boards. These two Acts had not invoked the Clauses Acts borrowing provisions, although they followed them closely. However, the provisions of the Land Clauses Act were incorporated in the 1858 Act.

In the minor Acts of a public health nature which followed, the only points of borrowing significance were that, under the Local Government (Amendment) Act of 1861, security for borrowing was transferred from special rates to general district rates, and that under the Sanitary Act 1866, the baths and washhouses and the burial boards Acts could be adopted by sanitary authorities. The Sanitary Loans Act 1869, though it sounds significant, merely gave the secretary of state certain borrowing powers in the event of a default by a local board.

Before reference is made to the Acts of 1872 and 1875, attention should be drawn to the formation of the Local Government Board in 1871 – virtually an admission that the abolition of the General Board of Health had been a mistake and a recognition that the subject was of such importance that a central controlling body was essential. This new body absorbed the duties of the Poor Law board, and those of the secretary of state to the extent that he had handled former duties of the General Board, together with certain minor responsibilities which had fallen to the Privy Council in this area of administration. This change was a landmark in the development of central control of local government.

The Public Health Act 1872 was a preliminary step towards the ultimate consolidations of the 1875 Act. The omnibus phrases 'sanitary authority' and 'sanitary districts' were used to override the earlier confusion of terms. 'Boroughs' were defined as the places within the Municipal Corporations Act as subsequently amended; 'metropolis', all places (mainly parishes) within the Metropolitan Board of Works area having power to levy a drainage rate; 'local government district', an area having a local board under earlier Acts; 'improvement district', any such area formed under a local Act; a 'parish', a place having, or entitled to have, a separate poor rate and overseer; and 'union' was a union of parishes for Poor Law purposes. While the lack of reference to counties is noticeable, the time was clearly ripe for rationalization of areas; another twenty years was to pass before this was achieved. This Act also brought about further refinements in borrowing provisions. 'Permanent works' as used in the 1858 Local Government Act as a subject for borrowing were defined as anything the cost of which the local government board considered should be spread over a term of years. The security to be offered was any rate or rates levied for Sanitary Act purposes. In place of the detailed borrowing provisions of earlier Acts, the Commissioners Clauses Act was now incorporated with the provision, as contained optionally in that Act, that the appointment of a receiver might be sought 'to enforce the payment of arrears of principal and interest'. But even this comprehensive provision was confused by an added clause which said that any sanitary authority or joint board 'possessed of any land, works, or other property in pursuance of or for the purposes of the Sewage Utilisation Act 1867' could borrow on mortgage on the credit of such assets as if the 'authority were the absolute owner both at law and in equity of' such assets. Perhaps because of the obscurity of this point and the switch to physical assets instead of a rate as the security, a provision was added, relating to this clause only, that the lender was not responsible for assuring himself about the proper application of such money. (This special treatment was repeated in the later 1875 Act.) Amounts borrowed for this purpose were limited to three-quarters of the value of the assets involved, but were in addition to amounts allowed to be borrowed under the Sanitary Acts generally.

Other clauses provided that previous borrowings made at a time when the deeds were exempt from stamp duty were still to be valid, and that local Act borrowing limits were no longer to apply to amounts borrowed by sanitary authorities for sanitary purposes. The PWLC could lend over thirty or fifty years as provided in earlier Acts, at 3½ per cent or such other sum as was necessary to avoid loss to the Exchequer. In making such advances the PWLC were to have regard to the 'probable duration and continuing utility of the works'. There were other minor provisions, but although this Act can be regarded as one of several which brought about an increasing coherence in borrowing legislation, the many and frequent changes must have proved confusing and frustrating to the operators involved. Furthermore, despite the valiant efforts of the central administrators to pull public health/sanitary provisions into a positive and coherent shape, the record indicates that little progress was made in the country as a whole because of reluctance to adopt the powers given and to risk increases in rate levels.

The Royal Sanitary Commission had met from 1868 to 1871 as a result of which many of the subsequent changes had been made. Its recommendation ultimately led to the Public Health Act 1875 which consolidated and amended over forty previous Acts and whose main structure endured well into the twentieth century.

As the Public Health Act 1875 exercised for so long such an important influence on borrowing methods (as well as on public health administration generally), and as its borrowing provisions had to compete with those of the Local Loans Act 1875, they ought perhaps to be set out reasonably fully here; they provided that:

(1) Any local authority might 'borrow, re-borrow and take up at interest' money required for Sanitary Act purposes, or for discharging earlier loans taken for these purposes; urban authorities might borrow on mortgage of any fund or rate involved in these Acts; and the security in a rural sanitary authority was to be 'the common fund out of which such expenses' were payable (which could in certain circumstances be a special rate or fund).

(2) Such a borrowing was subject to the requirements that
   (a) it was to be for permanent works the cost of which should in the opinion of the local government board be spread over a term of years;
   (b) it was not to exceed twice the assessable value of the district, and before it could exceed once the assessable value a local public inquiry must be held;
   (c) the maximum loan sanction period was sixty years, the debt to be paid off by one of three methods – equal annual instalments of principal or of principal and interest combined or by an accumulating sinking fund invested in government securities;
   (d) the sinking fund could be used to pay off debt at any time but, in this event, interest which would have been paid on the utilized sinking fund moneys must continue to be paid into the fund;
   (e) money reborrowed after a payment was to remain within the original loan sanction period.

(3) The curious special provisions about sewage disposal borrowing of the 1872 Public Health Act were repeated.

(4) The form of mortgage specified was to be used (or to the like effect); a register was to be maintained; and transfer facilities were to be provided.

(5) A receiver might be appointed after a delay of 6 months in interest or repayment, provided that the sum involved exceeded £1,000.

(6) The Public Works Loan Commission might make advances for periods of up to fifty years at $3\frac{1}{2}$ per cent or such higher rate as might be needed to avoid government loss; in deciding the lending period, the commission was to have regard to the probable duration and continuing utility of the assets to be provided.

Thus a quite extensive code was provided, yet it lacked a general excusal of the lenders from the responsibility to satisfy themselves that the borrowing was in order and no assurance that all loans ranked equally, or that the loans constituted a 'first charge'. Although the provision was for mortgaging, the repayment provisions included an alternative equivalent to term annuities. What is clearly evident is that the central department loan sanctioning system was firmly established. Many later Acts provided for borrowing under the terms of this statute.

EDUCATION A local government function which has been at least as significant as public health is education, a service which now accounts for approximately one-half of local authority revenue budgets. What is cause for much surprise is that while museums, art galleries and libraries had been provided in a series of Acts beginning in the middle of the century, the first elementary education Act did not appear in the statute-book until 1870 (apart from the provision of pauper schools mentioned earlier under the Poor Law). Before 1870, the provision of such schools as there were had been an ecclesiastical responsibility and this delicate interdependence of local government and the church authorities in this field has since been a feature of the education system in England and Wales. The Elementary Education Act 1870 was a substantial Act; its borrowing powers were simple though generally adequate. It applied to boroughs and, once again, to parishes, which were required to elect School Boards for the provision of elementary education to be paid for by a rate levied by the overseers.

The extensive service details of this important Act are not relevant here, but the borrowing provisions established that where a School Board incurred expense in providing or enlarging a school-house, the cost might, with the approval of the newly appointed central Education Department, be spread over 'several years not exceeding fifty' on the security of the school fund and the local rate. If the mortgagee agreed, repayment could be by equal annual instalments (presumably of principal with interest on the diminishing balance); otherwise a sinking fund of one-fiftieth of the debt should be set aside each year. The Act omitted to require the investment of this fund in government securities. The Commissioners Clauses Act 1847 was otherwise incorporated (except as to repayment period altered by this principal Act), although the receivership options were not taken up. The PWLC was authorized to lend for up to fifty years, at 3½ per cent. The London School Board could borrow from the Metropolitan Board of Works.

THE GROWTH OF BORROWING FACILITIES   From 1860 until the end of the century a number of important provisions relating to local authority borrowing were introduced. Some of these were in statutes concerned solely with borrowing, while others led up to and introduced the major reorganizations of the counties and their districts on a national network of democratic local authorities. In addition, there were private local Acts of profound significance in relation to borrowing. Unfortunately this series of statutes does not present by any means a clear evolutionary borrowing code; there was much confusion, amounting almost to contradiction and inexactitude of terms and a general lack of coherence. Some excellent opportunities seem to have been missed, so that the situation was not rationalized until 1933, and even then (and again in the further reorganization around 1970) inconsistencies and lack of definitive thinking persisted. The year 1875, in particular, then, was the year of loss of a golden opportunity for rationalization and simplification in the techniques of local government capital finance.

The implications of the Municipal Corporations Mortgages Act 1860 are somewhat obscure. It disclosed that municipal corporations were borrowing on the security of hereditaments owned by the corporation rather than on the rate levy. This Act appears to have sought to formalize this practice and to add to it a power to borrow on the security of the borough fund or rate, together with provisions for loan sanction periods and a statutory system of repayment under Treasury approval. The preamble to the Act declared that it was 'expedient to make further provision concerning mortgages and other dispositions of property belonging to Municipal Corporations'. 'Further provision' implies earlier provision, but there is no reference to the source of this. The presumption must be that the reference was to unspecified charter powers. Where the Treasury approved of any mortgage of any hereditament of the body corporate of any borough, they might 'as a condition of their approval' require that the money borrowed on the security of such mortgage should be repaid, with the interest thereon in thirty years or lesser period either by instalments or by means of a sinking fund, or both. The sums provided for repayment purposes were 'to become charged on the hereditaments comprised in such mortgage, or any other hereditaments or the Borough fund or Borough or other rates legally applicable' to the payment or discharge of the money borrowed.

Where money borrowed was directed to be paid out of a sinking fund, the council of the borough should 'out of the rents and profits of the hereditaments or out of the Borough fund or rates' invest such funds in government annuities. The dividends (interest payments) of such annuities were to be accumulated at compound interest with the sinking fund provisions. The implication here is that the investments were in normal government stocks and that the term 'annuities' was used in the general sense of annual transactions. This provision, in effect, emphasizes again that a rate levy was a residual means of finance which theoretically in a borough might or might not be necessary, depending upon the extent of the other wealth of the borough.

The Act then referred to certain borough mortgage debts which 'have been heretofore incurred for the payment and discharge of which no adequate legal provision now exists', in these circumstances the borough was to submit a 'scheme for the discharge of such debts by instalments or a sinking fund' but these repayments could extend 'over any term of years' without the application of the thirty-year maximum. When such scheme was approved by the Treasury, the provisions for discharge were to have the same security as other borrowings, that is, hereditaments, borough fund, or rate. This was an early example of what in later days came to be called 'scheme procedure' in which Acts introducing new responsibilities, or seeking the reorganization of old, called upon local authorities to prepare schemes intended to tackle the problem in a progressive manner over a period of time.

A further tidying-up provision permitted debts which had been incurred under Acts of Parliament with different repayment periods to be consolidated and fresh arrangements made for repayment, with the thirty-year maximum reinserted and with a charge on the borough fund or rate, with no mention of hereditaments. Yet another curious clause provided that where there was a surplus on the borough fund which had arisen from rents and profits receivable and not from a rate levy, such surplus could be used to repay debt incurred under the borough's duties as a local health board.

Another indirect reference to charter powers appears in the provision that boroughs which did not possess the power to purchase land and buildings and to hold land in mortmain, might now do so on terms and conditions to be approved by the Treasury, including borrowing for the purpose on mortgage. Provision was also made for the disposal of assets and the utilization of the proceeds for the general benefit of the borough.

This Act was to be construed with the Municipal Corporations Act 1835, a requirement which indicates that there were no significant intermediate developments. Another point to be noted as indicating the somewhat confused state of borrowing in the boroughs arises from the reference to Treasury approval 'of any mortgage of any hereditaments of the ... borough'. The need for any such Treasury approval was not called for by the 1835 Act – and such later service Acts as, for example, the Museums Act 1845 required Treasury approval for borrowing on the security of the rate. The reference to approval for borrowing against the value of hereditaments owned by the borough may have related to private local Acts, or possibly to a variety of provisions in various charters.

By any count, this was a curious piece of legislation worthy of further research. What is clear is that municipal boroughs were certainly acting in an independent *ad hoc* way in relation to borrowing. There is an implication that they were anxious to defend these independent practices but that the Treasury was taking a first step to pull them into line with the general trends in central supervision of local administration.

The Mortgage Debenture Act 1865 and the Mortgage Debenture (Amendment) Act 1870 related not to local authorities, but to companies under the Companies Act 1862 or special Acts; that they also applied to Commissioners of Sewers and Drainage indicates, as assumed in this book, that these were in the nature of companies rather than local government bodies. The Act permitted such companies to borrow money on debentures. The term 'debenture' is not defined as such, but the nature of a debenture is described as a 'deed under the common seal of the company, duly stamped, as a mortgage of the amount secured'. The draft form of mortgage debenture simply 'charges' all the registered securities of the company with the principal and interest due. The amending Act makes no changes significant to us here, but mention of these two Acts is made because the debenture as a form of borrowing instrument was shortly to be introduced into local government. The combination of the terms 'mortgage' and 'debenture' is also of interest; in the local government provisions 'debenture' was to be associated with 'stock'.

To retain the chronological sequence of events three local Acts must now be noted. The government of the metropolis began to take coherent shape in 1855 with the Metropolis Management Act. This Act established the strange-sounding Metropolitan Board of Works (MBW), later to become the London County Council (LCC) in 1888 and, ultimately, the Greater London Council (GLC) in 1963 – the latter at the date of this writing under threat of dissolution along with the metropolitan counties. This initial Act introduced detailed but straightforward mortgage borrowing provisions which were used quite extensively in a group of Acts relating to special metropolitan schemes over the next few years. The significant development of the period was the Metropolitan Board of Works (Loans) Act 1869, which was the first statute to give a local authority power to borrow by the issue of stock.[3]

The fundamental differences between borrowing on mortgage and by the issue of stock will be examined in the part of this book dealing with individual methods of borrowing (see pp. 209–98); the essential differences may be briefly summarized here. The fundamental difference is that while a loan on mortgage of the rate can be disposed of or sold by the lender and consequently assigned to a new owner, stock is created – against the same rate security – as an essentially marketable instrument for which positive provision is made through a stock market managed by the Stock Exchange for daily buying and selling at daily quoted prices, thus making it highly negotiable. This difference leads to material variations in the practices of management, that is, stock is 'issued' as a block on a single day, so that a market may immediately be brought into being, while mortgages are normally 'on tap', that is, available from the borrower from day to day until he has raised all that he needs. (The existence of so-called government 'tap-stocks' does not invalidate this distinction.) There are other differences in mechanics which will be dealt with elsewhere, but a significant difference which emerges in Acts shortly to be described is that while a mortgage is an instrument in the form of a deed, stock is in effect identified by an entry in a register maintained by the borrower, and is thus 'intangible' – although a certificate giving evidence of the entry in the books of the borrower may be (and is usually) issued, just as a marriage certificate is no more than a copy of an entry in an official register.

Yet in local government borrowing both forms (as well as others) have the same security and normally rank equally; neither is therefore 'better' or 'safer' than the other. Stock is more readily negotiable (having an organized market), and therefore tends to earn fractionally less than a mortgage but which form a lender prefers depends entirely on circumstances and what he is seeking.

The Metropolitan Board of Works (Loans) Act 1869 contained a number of important provisions. Consequent upon its introduction of borrowing by the issue of stock it made the first mention of a 'consolidated loans fund' (though this was not the comprehensive device later developed and now become a familiar tool of all local authority treasurers), and it provided for borrowing by annuities, so that taken with the 1855 Act it gave the board relatively complete borrowing facilities. Between these two Acts there had been a series of special metropolitan Acts mainly concerned with improvement and bridge schemes within the metropolis and these, because of their significance in the nation's capital, had been embarked upon with government guarantees of the loans involved. Conversion of these loans to stock was now facilitated but the guarantee was withdrawn. The board's debts had by this time reached £8 million, and a further sum of £2 million was needed. The board was to be permitted to issue 'capital stock to be called metropolitan consolidated stock'. The reference to capital stock appears to be the use of the older term stock as meaning 'stock of money' or 'cash balances' often referred to in older Acts as the 'county stock'. The stock/cash now to be raised was thus intended to be for capital purposes only. There seems to be no other explanation of this phrase. The stock was called 'consolidated' because one of its main purposes was the consolidation of large amounts of earlier separate borrowings, plus new money. By extension, this led to the use of the term 'consolidated loans fund' as being the fund which consolidated the handling of this new type of borrowing, rather than the wider implications of the modern consolidated loans fund the introduction of which was still far ahead.

This was to be a redeemable stock, issued at such times and under such conditions as to price and dividends as the Treasury approved. All stock was to rank equally and be 'charged indifferently on the whole of the lands, rents, and property belonging to the board . . . and on all moneys which can be raised by the board by rates under this Act'. However, the security for the stock was in this instance to be only a first charge after existing borrowings not brought into consolidation. An older improvement fund also formed part of the security. The PWLC was authorized to lend money on the consolidated stock, as also – the other side of the same coin

– were the Commissioners for the Reduction of the National Debt. Standard provisions were made for transfer. The point (as already made) emerges that the title to stock as distinct from that to other forms of lending was the entry in the register, but the board might 'if it thought fit' issue a certificate verifying the holding of stock which could be used by the investor as prima facie evidence of title in dealing. Another most important aspect of this Act was that it extended to this stock the facilities of the Stock Certificate Act 1863, which provided for the issue to holders of stock in the public funds of certificates payable to bearer and transferable by delivery. Because bearer stocks changed hands (by definition) without amendment of the register, every bearer certificate had initially to bear three times the stamp duty which would normally have been payable on a transfer. A provision in the 1863 Act that dividend coupons not presented within three years should lapse was excluded from the Board of Works stock. Except for this bearer stock facility, the provisions established were broadly those now in general use, though much more detail was later to be defined.

The consolidated loans fund might more properly have been called the 'consolidated stock fund'; though thus limited in conception to stock, it was nevertheless a step in the right direction. The purpose of this fund was given as the 'paying of dividends on and the redeeming of consolidated stock' though a later section went further than this. The moneys to be carried to it were: capital receipts arising from the disposal of land or property, the residue of the old improvement fund and the equivalent of 2 per cent on the total nominal amount of the consolidated stock – whether any of it had been cancelled or not – or such other sum as the Treasury accepted as necessary to pay the dividends on and redeem all the stock in sixty years from the creation thereof. The fund was to be invested in government securities, cumulatively, until applied. It was to be applied in the payment of dividends on the stock, and then in purchasing stock for redemption, but also in repayment of the principal of the securities granted before the passing of the Act. The consolidated loans fund therefore included redemption, but not the interest payment on earlier securities. Where the consolidated fund was used to pay off earlier securities for which a sinking fund had already been created, the equivalent amount was to be transferred from that sinking fund to the new consolidated loans fund account. Money could be borrowed by stock for the specific purpose of repaying earlier securities. A further provision allowed the Board of Works to borrow by this stock to lend on to the managers of the Metropolitan Asylum Board. Application could be made to the Court of Chancery by an investor for the appointment of a receiver after two months' delay in payment of dividends on the stock or interest on any other security. The Act is obscure about whether the receiver could repay outstanding amounts of principal. Investors were freed of responsibility for inquiring into the proper use of sums loaned.

Finally, the Act gave the board power to borrow by terminable annuities – Metropolitan Annuities – under terms approved by the Treasury and, *mutatis mutandis*, the terms of the Act applied to annuities as to stock. Recognition of consolidated stock as a trustee security and minor amendments of detail, with extensions of the services to which consolidated stock could be applied were made in further Acts of 1871 and 1875. Reading the Acts together, the board could borrow either by mortgages and stock – nominal or bearer – and annuities, a very useful spread of alternatives.

The Manchester Corporation Waterworks and Improvement Act 1872 is generally believed to be the second Act permitting a local authority to issue stock but in fact this Act is slightly preceded by the Swansea Local Board of Health Act of the same year. However, as the Manchester Act is closer in concept to the Metropolitan Act, it is here dealt with first. In passing reference should be made to the Bristol Waterworks Act 1872, in which the Companies Clauses Act was invoked to regulate borrowing.

The Manchester Act was one of a long series of Acts covering the creation of the vast and ambitious Manchester waterworks scheme, with its long pipelines from the Lakes to south-east Lancashire. Earlier Acts had given power for borrowing by perpetual annuities, mortgages and bonds. Unlike the metropolitan provisions, this Act introduced perpetual stock and there was no facility for bearer instruments. The concept of perpetual borrowing seems to be peculiar to waterworks undertakings, perhaps on the theory that this type of construction had an indefinite life – a reservoir having been created becoming part of the natural order. What does not seem to have been realized was that a perpetual debt puts an undertaking on to something of a company basis with permanent proprietors, but with the added disadvantage that the perpetual holders of stock in this instance were entitled to their dividends irrespective of the success of the undertaking, unlike company shareholders.

The Act therefore allowed the issue of consolidated stock the purpose of which was to consolidate previous debts or to enable previous debts to be repaid and replaced by stock. The wording here is significant because it illustrates the different conception of raising capital by stock. If holders of existing investments were not prepared to take the new stock, then they could be paid off and replaced by stock *instead of reborrowing*, almost as though a stock issue was not really a form of borrowing. Perhaps this was true, if it was accepted that stockholders were no longer lenders, but in fact proprietors. The same attitude is illustrated again in the same section. The money required for sanctions not yet exercised could be met by the 'issue of consolidated stock, instead of borrowing the same'. This stock was to be entitled to 'a fixed and perpetual yearly dividend or interest' not exceeding 4 per cent p.a. as a charge upon the city rate. The stock was to be without prejudice to holders of perpetual annuities or mortgages or bonds.

The stock was to be registered, and transferable by amendment of the register on production of a deed of transfer, but the register was to be 'evidence on all matters contained therein'. Although the register was the basic record, the corporation were to deliver on demand a certificate to every holder but were entitled to charge 2s 6d for this additional document – not merely for registering a transfer.

The City of Manchester still retained the power to issue perpetual annuities, and mortgages, but earlier mortgages retained priority. A sinking fund was to be established on a twenty-year basis for the mortgages only. While following so closely on the Metropolitan Act, this Act therefore differed in material ways, not least being that this stock was perpetual while the metropolitan stock was redeemable. However, while as the Manchester stock was 'perpetual' there were no requirements for a sinking fund, there can have been nothing to prevent the city from buying in stock for cancellation, as indeed happened.

Yet another pattern emerges in the Swansea Act of 1872 in which powers were given for the issue of annuities and debenture stock (though there is no indication as to how this differed from ordinary stock). These powers, although slightly preceding Manchester, do not seem to have been exercised until later. The claim cannot be made with certainty that Swansea was the first authority to acquire debenture stock powers but if as seems certain the Metropolitan Board of Works was indeed the first authority to obtain stock-issuing powers in 1869, then there are unlikely to be more than one or two authorities involved with stock between that date and the two instances in 1872.

The detailed and extensive preamble to the Swansea Act shows that borrowing had already been undertaken under the Public Health Act 1848 and an earlier Swansea Act of 1860, from which approximately £135,000 of debt was still outstanding. In 1865 the borrowing period had been extended by provisional order from thirty to fifty years. The 1872 Act repealed the earlier sinking fund provisions. The board might then pay or discharge immediately or in due course sums secured by mortgage or other securities, and 'redeem, satisfy, or discharge' annuities under the earlier provisions, by the exercise of new powers to grant fresh annuities for terms, or on lives, or in perpetuity, and by the issue of debenture stock.

The debenture stock was to have, as the Manchester ordinary stock, 'fixed and perpetual interest', payable half-yearly; there was no indication of any difference between debenture and 'ordinary' stock. There was no specific reference to a register, but the board was obliged to issue certificates to holders. However, as the want of such a certificate was not to prevent the holder from disposing of his stock, the concept of a register must be presumed to have lain behind the issue. Bearer stock was not mentioned. The holders of annuities and debenture stock were to have all the rights and powers of mortgagees. Access to a receiver on six months' delay of an annuity or interest on a debenture was allowed as under the Public Health Act 1848. As the half-yearly payments of annuities included an element of principal and the stock was perpetual, access to a receiver for arrears of principal was not called for.

Yet despite the perpetual nature of the stock, five years after the passing of the Act, a sinking fund of not less than 1 per cent was to be established and invested in government securities or the board's own securities and used to redeem 'debenture stock, or annuities or mortgages'. For obvious reasons reborrowing powers were not available for the replacement of debentures or annuities. The somewhat sketchy provisions of this Act as to stock were put into better shape by the Local Loans Act 1875; but before that Act is dealt with, a further reference to debenture powers is necessary.

This reference is the County Debentures Act 1873, a short-lived Act repealed by, and its terms consolidated and expanded in, the Local Loans Act 1875. It could therefore perhaps be ignored at this point, except that it introduced another general facility (though for counties only) in local authority borrowing, that is, the plain 'debenture' as distinct from the 'debenture stock', already described in reference to the Swansea Act 1872. As the Swansea Act was apparently the first use of the term in relation to stock, this Act appears to be the first use of the simpler term, without attachment to the concept of stock, in a local government context, though once again an earlier reference may be concealed in some forgotten local Act. The earlier reference made above to the Mortgage Debentures Act 1865 related to company borrowing only.

Under the Act of 1873 any county authority with power to borrow on the security of the county rate might now borrow by instruments with the nomenclature of debenture. The term is not defined in the Act except to the extent that 'Every debenture . . . shall be a security for a principal sum and interest to be charged on the county rate in the debenture specified'. This is very close to the concept of a debenture in modern company law, in which a debenture holder is generally one who has no other rights (unless particularly specified) than to receive payment of interest and ultimate repayment of principal, on the security of the company's land and undertakings. There does not in fact appear to be anywhere a strict legal or statutory definition of this type of security (unlike, for example, a bill of exchange which has a precise statutory definition).

These references do not in fact particularly differentiate a debenture from a mortgage or bond or similar instrument – or perhaps even a stock certificate which certainly acknowledges a debt. In fact this definition suggests that a debenture is a generic term for a group of borrowing instruments. In practice, the debentures introduced by this Act had this difference from mortgages – that they could be issued in either nominal or bearer form, the bearer certificates being transmissible by delivery, and the nominal certificates by normal deed of transfer, but this facility is by no means implicit in a debenture.

Whether in bearer or nominal form, coupons were to be attached to the debenture giving the bearer of the coupon a right to the periodic interest distributions. 'Coupon' is another term which has persisted until modern times, in that when a stock issue is made, stockbrokers are still apt to refer to the rate of interest as the 'coupon rate', even though no coupons are attached – in contradistinction to the 'discount rate' on a discounted issue. The use of coupons does of course still persist in commercial issues but is not used in local government where bearer issues are forbidden by the Treasury through the Control of Borrowing Order. County debentures under the 1873 Act were to be in units of £50, with a maximum of ten units, that is, £500. Forms for both types of debentures are given, or 'any form not inconsistent with this Act'. As is to be expected, these are in simple terms and are not materially distinguishable from a mortgage or even a simple 'assignment'. Careful referencing of debentures was prescribed because, against all early mortgage practice, each 'loan' (a group of debentures issued for a purpose at any one time) took priority according to the date of such 'loan', the first day of a debenture in one loan being the operative date. This might be suspected as being a transference from company debenture practice but in the Mortgage Debentures Act 1865 all issues ranked equally, irrespective of date of issue. In any event, in the 1873 Act the status of debentures was not clarified as against mortgages. Detailed transfer arrangements for nominal debentures were given, and lenders were excused from any responsibility for assuring themselves that the borrowings were necessary, authorized, or properly applied.

To protect lenders against non-payment of interest or principal, mandamus procedures were specified with the added safeguard that if the amount owed was £500 or more, application could be made to a Court of Equity for the appointment of a receiver empowered to levy a rate. Unless otherwise prescribed in a special Act, the county was required to 'pay off in every year of the period limited for repayment of the loan an equal portion thereof' with interest, and to provide for interest on outstanding loans. No provision was made for the selection of lenders for repayment. The new debentures could be used to replace earlier loans. This Act can therefore be seen as introducing a more flexible borrowing instrument – the debenture in bearer form – than hitherto available in the simple mortgage.

NOTES: CHAPTER 8

1   The party-walls between houses, extending 18 inches above roof level, still commonly seen in older parts of London, date from the requirements of the 1706 Act.
2   Johnson, in *Loans of Local Authorities* (1925), p. 17, makes the curious statement that under the Libraries Act 1855 loan repayment periods of up to 100 years were permitted and indeed so sanctioned, and that this was overridden by the 1871 Act which applied the Local Government Act 1858. There is certainly no reference to loan periods in any of these Acts, although the use of the Company Clauses Consolidation Acts leaves the period somewhat open. In this respect the Public Libraries (Scotland) Acts Amendment 1867 (30 & 31 Vict., c. 37) provided for 1d rate for libraries and borrowing on mortgage or bond to be repaid by yearly instalments over not more than thirty years and also invoked the Companies Consolidation Clauses Act for borrowing rather than the Commissioners Clauses Act.
3   This is confirmed by early Stock Exchange records as published in Burdett's *Official Intelligence* (1882); this record shows earlier issues of securities recognized by the Stock Exchange but these were described as annuities and bonds and not as stock.

Chapter 9

THE LOCAL LOANS ACT
1875

The Local Loans Act 1875 was a major Act of Parliament and the first to be devoted solely to general local authority borrowing. Coming at this stage, it might therefore be thought to have been of prime importance in the history of the capital finance of local authorities. It repealed the County Debentures Act, but reapplied the provisions to all types of local authority; it gave limited powers for borrowing by annuities; it set out the mechanics of stock issues (although this was applicable only to those authorities which had power under local Acts to borrow by the issue of stock); and it introduced 'bearer' and 'nominal' facilities generally.

Nevertheless, it was drafted in a cumbersome manner, and in several ways cut across the trends of borrowing practice which by then were beginning to emerge. It ignored the approach to borrowing embodied in the Public Health Act of a few months earlier (the statutory chapter number in 1875 of the Public Health Act was 55, that of the Local Loans Act, 83). The Public Health Act had emphasized the mortgage as the method of borrowing; mortgages find no place in the Local Loans Act which adopted something very similar but which it designated as 'debentures'; the Local Loans Act also referred to 'stock' as 'debenture stock' although there is no apparent significance in the added word. Johnson, in his *Loans of Local Authorities*, says: 'the Act was not favoured by the Local Government Board and probably for that reason was not much used'; and Griffiths's *Municipal Capital Finance* confirms that 'the provisions are rarely used'. The general histories of local government are silent about it (but so they are on most matters of local authority borrowing). On the other hand, the Local Government Acts of 1933 and 1972 repeat the powers to borrow by debentures and annuity certificates (but not debenture stock) 'under the Local Loans Act 1875' – and yet these methods still do not find favour in the world of local authority borrowing.

The range of authorities to which the Local Loans Act applied was comprehensive, the justices of any county and the council of any municipal borough, 'any authority whatsoever', having power to levy a rate (including the right to issue a precept dependent on the levying of a rate); 'also any prescribed authority'. The term 'prescribed' occurs frequently in this Act and is defined to mean 'prescribed (imposed or permitted) by any Act passed either before or after this Act authorising a local authority to borrow money'. The Act first dealt with debentures, again without precise definition except to the extent that a debenture was to be 'an instrument taking effect as a deed and charging the local rate or property with a principal sum and interest specified'. The significance of the term 'deed' is that in law it is 'an instrument comprehending the terms of a contract and the evidence of its due execution' (*New English Dictionary*). In other words, a deed is a confirmation of a contract; deeds are by tradition under seal. Though called a debenture, this instrument was to all intents and purposes a mortgage on the rates and properties of the authority concerned and might well have been so described. The only real difference was that unlike a mortgage either before or since the passing of this Act, these debentures were somewhat more flexible than a mortgage, in that they could be payable either to a nominated person or to bearer, bearer debentures being transmissible by delivery and nominal debentures by transfer in writing. In either event a document was to be issued, for which surprisingly a draft form was not provided in the statute. The issuing authority had the additional alternative of adding to the instrument coupons covering the periodic interest made payable either to a named person or to bearer. This certainly implied that interest would not be sent out to the holder – with bearer documents, could not be sent out, the current holder being unknown to the authority – but would only be paid on surrender of the coupon. The use of a bearer form does of course make an instrument much more readily marketable. A debenture under the Act was to be for not less than £20 or as otherwise prescribed. If the debenture was to be a charge on property as well as or instead of a rate, the property was to be specified in the deed.

The provisions for borrowing by debentures were then followed by requirements relating to the issue of debenture stock, but in this case available only to authorities having a specific power to borrow by this means. In other words, this Act did not give power to issue stock, but set out the mechanics of stock management for any authority which had acquired the power to issue under private Act – the forerunner of the Stock Regulations. An issue of debenture stock was to be of an amount not exceeding that authorized to be raised by stock in the appropriate local Act, which if the stock was to be issued at a discount would theoretically have produced somewhat less than was required for the scheme in mind. The stock was to be redeemable at par at the option of the authority on such terms and conditions as were announced at the time of issue. A point of particular interest in confirmation of earlier references in this book to the essentials of stock is that 'the title of any person to any share in debenture stock shall be evidenced by the entry in the register' with the further provision that the stock so entered 'should be a charge on the local rate or property in the same manner as if it were a principal sum and interest charged thereon by deed'. There was not even a provision for the ordinary holder to receive a stock certificate as of right, though he had to be issued with a 'printed copy of such conditions'. However if, to increase marketability, a holder requested the issue of a bearer certificate with coupons attached, the authority might grant this, in which case the instrument ceased to be dealt with through the register. Such bearer holdings could be reconverted to registered form.

The third type of security authorized by the Local Loans Act was the annuity certificate, which again was to be 'an instrument taking effect as a deed, and charging the local rate or property in such certificate specified with payment . . . of the annual sum therein specified'. Unless prescribed otherwise, the minimum sum was to be £3, implying indeed a modest amount of principal invested. The certificate could be in either nominal or bearer form; nominal certificates were transferable in writing and bearer certificates by delivery. There was no provision for registration, nor for the attachment of coupons, so that the annual sum was presumably to be paid to the person tendering the instrument, provided that with a nominal certificate that was the person named therein.

The Act does not specify the type of annuity. If bearer certificates were permissible, the annuity could not have been on a life or lives. The provision for repayment required that unless prescribed to the contrary the annuity certificates should be limited to expire within twenty years. Thus term annuities were obviously intended, though perpetual annuities would be feasible if so prescribed. Therefore, these were the equivalent of mortgages repayable annually by equal sums of principal and interest combined.

Provision was made for the form of register for all nominal-type securities, and for the handling of coupons to be attached to bearer certificates other than annuities. There was also an unusual provision that a borrowing authority might seek sanction to the issue of the loan from the local government board official, such sanction, when duly indicated, being sufficient to assure a lender that the loan was in order and in accordance with the Act. The lender could then also seek from the Local Government Board details of the rateable value on which the security was based, or if on property, the estimated value of the property, together with information as to the priority of the loan. Trustees having power to invest in debentures or debenture stock of railway companies, were also allowed to invest in the similarly named securities under this Act. The Public Works Loan Commission (PWLC) could also lend on any of the securities under the Act, including annuity certificates, which in that case would certainly have had to be term annuities.

The section of the Act governing priorities was very unsatisfactory. It provided that all borrowings raised by any securities under the Act 'in respect of the same loan' were to be without preference 'one over the other' by reason of date. This clearly assumes separate acts of 'loan-raising' for specifically identified projects. Where borrowing took place for different 'loans', priority was to be 'according to the date of such loan', but this date was to be such as the authority 'deemed most convenient' and not necessarily the date of issue of any security. Because power to borrow by debentures or annuities under this Act survived to the Local Government Act 1933 (and later to 1972), by which time all loans were of equal priority, this priority provision needed modification in the 1933 Act. For all instruments, lenders – described in the Act as 'persons advancing any money to a local authority and receiving in consideration of such advance any security under this Act' – were relieved of responsibility for inquiring into the application of money advanced. Even today institutional lenders are obsessed with the remedies provided for non-payment of interest or repayment of principal. This Act gave both 'mandamus' rights (for which any debt was to be a 'speciality debt') and receivership rights where the debt or debts amounted to not less than £500 and were overdue for 21 days, on application to the county courts. A somewhat embarrassing situation can be envisaged if a county authority – the magistrates – had failed to meet their commitments and found themselves faced with a demand to appoint a receiver to assume their local government responsibilities.

There is a general provision in this Act which is at first sight confusing. Section 31 allowed any authority, notwithstanding any provision in any other Act of Parliament passed before the passing of this Act, to 'borrow in manner provided by this Act any loan which it is authorised to borrow'. Yet the section of the Act authorizing borrowing by debenture stock allows this to authorities which already have such a power. This seems to mean that an authority such as the Swansea board (see p. 143) which had power to borrow by debenture stock could now use the terms of the Local Loans Act instead of those formerly given to it for borrowing by this stock. Earlier loans were also permitted to be discharged and replaced within the original borrowing period, by the Local Loans Act type of borrowing.

Unusually complex provisions were included for the discharge of Local Loans Act loans; indeed they were so complex as to be in some degree unworkable (which is one of the reasons why Johnson claims that the Act was unpopular). There was no problem about the annuity certificates as the annual sums to be paid would automatically be calculated on the recognized annuity basis, so that taking principal and interest together the debt would be cleared in the prescribed period (a provision which does not seem to have envisaged perpetual annuities). The alternatives for debentures and debenture stock were briefly as follows:

(1) By the issue of debentures payable in such manner that in each year such number of debentures will become repayable as will secure the repayment of the whole sum by equal annual instalments over the prescribed or a lesser period. If read literally, this would be a virtual impossibility, requiring borrowing instruments of equal amounts dated to range evenly from one to twenty years.

(2) By the annual appropriation of a fixed sum to discharge a certain portion of the loan.

(3) By a sinking fund, if prescribed in the special Act applicable.

(This requirement that a sinking fund must have been prescribed was repealed in a one-clause amending Act in 1885.) Method 2 was enlarged upon in a subsequent paragraph; it was intended that the fixed sum set aside each year should be an amount which would pay the interest and leave a balance for redemption, the proportion of repayment obviously increasing each year as the interest portion fell following progressive repayments. The difference between methods 1 and 2 appears to have been intended as a system of repayment by equal annual instalments of principal in method 1, but equal annual instalments of principal and interest combined by method 2. Where some lenders were to be selected for repayment each year, they were to be chosen by lot.

The sinking fund provisions were also complex, indeed almost unintelligible. The first stage was simple. Equal half-yearly sums were to be set aside which, accumulated at compound interest, would provide for the repayment of the loan in the due time, the rate of assumed accumulation to be as prescribed or agreed. These earmarked funds were to be invested as prescribed or as agreed with the Local Government Board or in trustee securities or in securities under the Act. The proceeds were to be used from time to time to discharge debt, as previously arranged, or by selection of lenders by lot. If this system produced a surplus, this could be transferred to some other appropriate sinking fund. Again there was the requirement that if the sinking fund was used to repay debt before full maturity, then a sum must continue to be paid in equivalent to the interest saved on the prematurely redeemed debt. Most curious of all, if the annual income of the sinking fund was not less than the annual interest payable on so much of the loan as was still outstanding, the equal annual sums required might be discontinued.

Municipal treasurers would indeed have had to be nimble-footed to cope with these repayment provisions. It cannot be that these methods of repayment, applying to debentures or annuities under this Act, can still be allowable under current legislation, as consolidated loans funds in the full sense now operate. Thus the extension of parts of the Local Loans Act to current borrowing legislation seems quite meaningless. The one local authority which is traditionally believed to have been an extensive user of the Local Loans Act is the City of London; possibly therefore the retention of reference to this obsolescent legislation may be accounted for by this explanation.

But for its complex and obscure not to say unworkable redemption provisions, the Local Loans Act can perhaps be seen not so much as a contradiction of the Public Health Act borrowing provisions, as has been suggested earlier, but as an extension of the very limited provisions of the Public Health Act, confined as it was to the mortgage. After all, in contrast with the simple mortgage of the Public Health Act, the Local Loans Act offered the flexibility of both bearer and nominal forms of instrument with a coupon system, together with term annuities, and set out the mechanics of stock issue. The debenture as introduced by the Local Loans Act might well have proved to be a more flexible instrument than the mortgage, if treasurers had felt able to adopt it. The understanding is that the Public

Health Act was introduced and piloted through Parliament by the Local Government Board and the Local Loans Act by the Treasury. (It has all the hallmarks of the Treasury mind.) How unfortunate that collaboration between the two departments did not produce at this time a coherent borrowing code. A great deal of pain and distress might have been saved in local finance departments (and in Whitehall) over the ensuing years, and perhaps by now a really comprehensive yet simple and coherent code might be in operation.

Chapter 10

THE DEMOCRATIZATION OF
LOCAL GOVERNMENT

The final steps in the creation of a structured and democratic system of local government took place over the years 1882 to 1894, a long time after the first tentative steps of 1834 and 1835. The resultant pattern was a workable one which endured, though not without stresses and strains, until the 1970s. Two unfortunate elements in the reorganized system were that the urban and rural districts which formed part of it were based on the haphazardly created urban and rural sanitary districts of the middle of the century, and that while rating was satisfactorily accommodated the finance of capital expenditure by borrowing was not at that stage dealt with in any systematic way.

A preliminary step towards the establishment of the reorganized system was a review of the municipal corporations, with consolidation and amendment of the 1835 and subsequent Acts (and, in particular, from the finance point of view the Municipal Corporations Mortgages Act 1860). This was effected in the Municipal Corporations Act 1882. In 1835 few services had been given to the newly created municipal corporations because of the reluctance of the various other bodies already involved (under private Acts) to co-operate. However, there had been provision for voluntary surrender of functions by improvement and other commissioners, and over the years new duties (see p. 160) had been devolved on the new municipal authorities, the most important relating to public health, education and municipal housing. In the meantime many boroughs had extended their boundaries and sixty-two new boroughs had been incorporated. The 1882 Act added a further twenty-five boroughs, but the day of the all-purpose county borough was still to come.

Part V of the Act dealt with 'Corporate Property and Liabilities' and was framed in the same spirit as the somewhat puzzling 1860 Municipal Mortgages Act (see p. 137). This part of the Act began by giving municipal corporations power to buy land 'not exceeding in the whole five acres' within or without the borough, and to build thereon a town hall and various premises for judicial administration 'or any other building necessary or proper for the purposes of the borough'. This final and somewhat ambiguous phrase probably did not imply quite the wide authority which can be read into it; in any event, it was probably in addition to the powers already given to purchase land under particular Acts for the provision of services such as libraries.

The borrowing provision for the expenditure involved in the provision of administrative buildings was somewhat clearer than that of the 1860 Act. With Treasury approval, the council might 'borrow at interest on the security of any corporate land . . . or on the borough fund or borough rate . . . for the purchase of land or the building of any building which the council are by this Act authorised to build'. The Land Clauses Acts were to be observed. This power to borrow was thus limited to the provision of administrative buildings, subject to the intended meaning of the reference to 'any other building', mentioned above. The Public Works Loan Commission (PWLC) were also authorized to lend to the borough for this purpose. There were extensive provisions for Treasury control on the alienation of land by a borough, and there was a section in particular dealing with the advance preparation of land for the provision of dwellings for working men, and the leasing of this to private developers. Another section incorporated the Borough Bridges Act provisions allowing the borough to 'maintain, alter, widen, repair, improve or rebuild bridges' for which they were responsible and to borrow on mortgage of the borough fund or rate for this purpose. The power to build new bridges was still omitted. The provisions of the 1860 Act calling upon boroughs to prepare schemes for the repayment over an unspecified period of debts contracted without previous 'adequate provision', and a further provision for the consolidation of authorized borrowing on a thirty-year basis, were also re-enacted.

As to provision for repayment of debt, the Treasury were to determine the period, with a maximum of thirty years, and whether the instalment system or a sinking fund, or both, were to be used. The underlying security was defined as the land comprised in the mortgage, or any other corporate land, or the borough fund or the borough or other rate. Where a sinking fund was directed, the amounts set aside from the rents and profits of the land, or the borough fund or rate, were to be invested in government annuities, with accumulation of dividends. Thus very little of substance was added to the powers of a municipal corporation to borrow; why the provisions of the Local Loans Act, the Public Health Act or even the Clauses Act were ignored can perhaps again be explained by the belief that in some way boroughs stood in an independent capacity. Yet there is no obscurity about the closeness of Treasury control on borrowing in this Act. The two fundamental Local Government Acts of 1888 and 1894 may for our purposes be taken together as, jointly with the 1882 Act, they finally established an overall national pattern of elected local government authorities. Unfortunately the pattern of borrowing facilities was not rationalized at the same time.

The 1888 Act made important structural changes. It established democratic local government in administrative counties by transferring the powers, other than judicial, from the magistrates to elected county councils, and it created from the major municipal boroughs a new class of local authority, the all-purpose county borough (sixty-one in number; eighty-three by 1933) – certainly, the most powerful and effective type of local authority ever produced in this country, but now abolished by the 1972 Act. The Metropolitan Board of Works was also given the newly created county status. Scottish administrative county councils were created in 1889.

The 1894 Act reorganized and regrouped the parishes – that persistent unit – on a more democratic basis according to size; converted urban sanitary authorities into urban district councils; and rural sanitary authorities – those parts of the poor law which were not within borough or other urban areas – into rural district councils. The urban and rural district councils, together with the residual boroughs not created county boroughs (the non-county boroughs), were known generically as the county districts; the function of the parish overseer for the collecton of the rate remained. The Poor Law unions also continued their independent existence, but the improvement and other commissioners were absorbed by the new authorities.

Under the 1888 Act the county councils, with the approval of the Local Government Board instead of the Treasury, could borrow on the security of the county fund or any revenues of the county, or both. Thus while county property as security was dropped, the security of the county fund (also later to be abandoned in these terms) was still linked with the county rate. Such borrowing was permitted for the consolidation of county debt, the purchase of land or buildings which the county were by any Act authorized to borrow, for any purpose which the quarter sessions had been authorized to borrow and any permanent works the cost of which should in the opinion of the Local Government Board be spread over a term of years. Loans could also be incurred for the encouragement of emigration and colonization.

Total debt after deduction of available sinking funds was not to exceed one-tenth of the annual rateable value of the county except with the approval of a provisional order of the Local Government Board and confirmed by Parliament. Borrowing without consent was authorized for 'roll-over' – reborrowing – loans, but all loans were to be repaid within the original sanction period, and no loan was to exceed thirty years or such shorter period as the county council, with the approval of the board, determined.

As to methods of borrowing, where a county council was authorized to borrow on loan, this could be raised as one loan or as several, and either by the issue of stock, as described under the Act, or debentures or annuity certificates under the Local Loans Act 1875 and its amendments; or if special reasons existed, by mortgage under the Public Health Act 1875. If stock was issued, mortgages had to be for periods not exceeding five years. These two restrictions on mortgages – 'special reasons' and 'five-year maximum when stock also issued' – are particularly odd, in that they did not apply to the debentures and annuities which the county could issue under the Local Loans Act; however, the restrictions were eventually lifted by the County Councils Mortgages Act 1909. The stock issued under the Act could be 'created, issued, transferred, dealt with and redeemed' only in accordance with regulations to be made by the Local Government Board and approved by Parliament. Such regulations could incorporate parts of the provisions of the Local Loans Acts and of the Acts relating to stock issued either by the Metropolitan Board of Works or by the corporation of any municipal borough, that is by private Act.

Repayment was permitted by equal yearly or half-yearly instalments of principal, or of interest and principal combined, or by means of a sinking fund as under the Local Loans Act (as amended). An admonitory section provided that where a loan was undertaken for a special county purpose, the council 'shall take care that the sums payable in respect of the loan are charged to the special account to which the expenditure for that purpose is chargeable'.

Unfortunately these borrowing provisions were not extended to the county boroughs created under the Act, whose borrowing remained under the same terms as for municipal corporations generally. However, by this time it was not a serious impediment, taking together the various borrowing powers of the municipal corporations; the main shortcoming was that boroughs could not borrow by stock except under local Act.

This deficiency was promptly corrected by the Public Health Acts Amendment Act 1890, part V of which extended to any urban authority, whether a municipal corporation, local board, or improvement commissioners, similar powers for the issue of stock to those given to the counties, but again under regulations of the Local Government Board. Thus rural areas were excluded from this method of borrowing and remained so for many years. Two sets of Stock Regulations were issued in 1891; these will later be examined in detail (see pp. 248–50).

The Local Government Act 1894 reorganized the parishes as administrative rather than ecclesiastical units with parish meetings for the smaller (under 300 population), and parish councils for the larger. The rural and urban sanitary authorities were renamed as rural and urban district councils and acquired the duties of the sanitary authorities and of various bodies of commissioners. No major changes of area were introduced, so that the new pattern – based on the original parish areas – continued to be somewhat haphazard and antique, but parish boundaries were varied sufficiently to bring them within the new districts, and the districts within the counties. All authorities were placed on the same democratic basis, and even in the Poor Law unions which remained inequalities of voting were abolished. So despite the somewhat arbitrary nature of the new boundaries (probably no more fortuitous than the original borough and county boundaries), at last there was a coherent democratic national pattern of local government administration; it had taken some seventy years to evolve, but it endured in this form for another seventy.

A parish council had an annual budget limit of a 6d rate but could borrow with the consent of its members, the county council and the Local Government Board. The purposes for which it could borrow were to acquire land and buildings where otherwise authorized, for duties under adoptive Acts (Lighting, Baths and Washhouses, Burial, Improvements,

Libraries) or for any permanent work or other thing the cost of which in the opinion of the county council and the Local Government Board ought to be spread over a term of years. The form of borrowing was to be as under the Public Health Acts, and the limit on the amount which might be borrowed was reduced from two years' assessable value to one-half of the assessable value. The county council might lend to a parish council. Borrowing by the newly named district councils remained under the Public Health Acts.

To complete the picture of the rationalizations of this period the Poor Law Act 1889 must be mentioned, in which it was

> considered expedient to simplify and include in one enactment the purposes and amount for and to which guardians of unions and managers of district schools and asylums have power to borrow, and otherwise to amend these powers.

All previous borrowing facilities were repealed and replaced by an extremely brief code. Guardians and managers could borrow with the approval of the Local Government Board to meet the cost of 'any permanent work or object, or any other thing the costs of which ought in the opinion of the Local Government Board to be spread over a term of years'. However, the total debt was not to exceed one-quarter of the rateable value of the union, with the proviso that this could be increased to one-half under a provisional order of the board. These meagre provisions were not enlarged upon until the Poor Law Act 1897. This established a maximum sanction period of sixty years as determined by the Local Government Board, and repayment by equal annual instalments of principal, or principal and interest combined, or a sinking fund. Any sinking fund was to be in the form required by the Local Loans Act 1875, with a prescribed accumulation rate of 3 per cent, but could not be invested in the Board of Guardians' own securities. Borrowing could be undertaken by the guardians without consent, to repay loans contracted before 1889. Why such a period of intensive and fruitful reorganization did not encompass an all-over rationalized borrowing code is difficult to understand.

Chapter 11

THE TURN OF THE CENTURY

In the period overlapping the measures for the establishment of local government on a democratic and (on the whole) logical national pattern, and extending into the first thirty years of the new century, there were a number of important service Acts as well as others of considerable financial significance. This transitional period took the First World War in its stride and concluded with further major steps of reorganization in the abolition of both the Poor Law unions and the overseers in preparation for the major consolidations and amendments of the Local Government Act 1933.

To begin with, another useful though not financially very significant method of borrowing became available to a number of the larger local authorities by private Act in the last years of the nineteenth century. This was the right to borrow limited sums by the issue of money bills – a very short-term marketable instrument more akin to the commercial promissory note than to the bill of exchange. The curious history of this development will be examined in detail, but despite its early introduction in 1877, the Metropolitan Board of Works, who first obtained these powers, did not operate them until 1897 – after which date other authorities immediately obtained similar powers, for instance, Leeds, Sheffield, Manchester, Birmingham and Liverpool (as well as certain Scottish authorities).

Two other events of borrowing interest at this time (which will require detailed analysis) were reports of Select Committees of the House of Commons, the first (House of Commons Paper 239, 1902) dealing with repayment periods for local authority loans; and the second (Cmd 103, 1909) on the re-use of sinking funds for new capital purposes. These were both subjects of much controversy which continued for some years. The conclusion of the first committee was in favour of the general extension of maximum borrowing periods from thirty to sixty years. The second gave a cautious and restricted approval to the re-use of sinking funds for new expenditure instead of requiring investment in government securities. Local Acts obtaining such powers had already been obtained by Liverpool as early as 1894, and by Leicester in 1897, whose clauses in this respect became the general model. In 1898 St Helens Corporation made a major breakthrough by obtaining powers for a common sinking fund for all its mortgage loans. This was the second required step towards the setting up of consolidated loans funds – the first being the Metropolitan Board of Works 'consolidated stock fund' – which nevertheless took another seventy years or so to become fully established. This problem is examined under the discharge of debt (see pp. 266–7).

During the period from about 1870 to the end of the century, and indeed up to the outbreak of the First World War, local government activities developed at an increasing pace, particularly after reorganization. A number of important service Acts – public and private – were placed on the statute-book, which instead of containing their own borrowing provisions now began to rely on the general provisions of earlier Acts but unfortunately still in an inconsistent not to say haphazard pattern.

For example, the Tramways Act 1870 permitted borrowing on a thirty-year period as approved by the Board of Trade, repayment to be by equal annual instalments or a sinking fund, subject to the conditions of the Commissioners Clauses Act, and despite this being a trading organization, the security was the rate. The Bristol Waterworks Act 1872 relied upon the Companies Clauses Consolidation Act. On the other hand, the Electric Lighting Act 1882, which also permitted borrowing on the security of the local rate, relied at that stage upon the Local Loans Act 1875 for its detailed provisions, with an added clause that authorities who had power to borrow by stock might do so for this new function. In the Lunacy Acts 1890 and 1891 counties and county boroughs might borrow for the provision of asylums under the Local Government Act 1888. The Municipal Corporations Act 1882 and the Private Street Works Act of 1892 relied upon the Public Health Act 1875. The Isolation Hospitals Act 1893, being a responsibility only of county councils, rested for its borrowing provisions on the Local Government Act 1888 despite the public health nature of the function. The Diseases of Animals Act 1894, applying both to counties and boroughs, fell back on the Local Loans Act, though there is some implication in this Act that borrowing for revenue purposes was in order if the cost of the Act was likely to impose a burden on the rate of more than 6d in any year. This may have meant a capital burden of this sum. Only a seven-year loan period was allowed, which is surprising at this date, if the expenditure referred to had been true capital expenditure. The loan period could be increased to fourteen years, if the rate charge was likely to exceed 9d.

The Small Holdings and Allotments Act 1908, a county function, still relied on the 1888 Local Government Act for borrowing, with a fifty-year period. The Children Act 1908 allowed borrowing by county authorities under the 1888 Act and municipal corporations under their 1882 Act, both for a maximum of sixty years. The Housing and Town Planning Act 1909, dealing with a district function, gave power to borrow by use of the Public Health Act 1875. The Mental Deficiency Act 1913 allowed counties to borrow for its provisions under the 1888 Act and boroughs under the Public Health Act 1875, for sixty years on the security of the rate.

Indeed because a reasonably rationalized borrowing code was not introduced until 1933, general Acts continued to be related to the borrowing provisions of the previous century. The Unemployment (Relief Works) Act 1902 was an excellent example of the variety of borrowing provisions. Counties could borrow to meet the provisions of this Act under the 1888 Act; metropolitan boroughs under the Metropolitan Management Acts 1855 to 1893; the City of London under the City of London Sewers Acts 1848 to 1897; and other councils under the Public Health Acts 1875 to 1908.

An Act of 1916 with an important-sounding title, but of such small effect that it has now disappeared without trace, was the Municipal Savings Bank (War Loan Investment) Act. This provided that for investment in securities issued for war-finance purposes a local authority might establish and maintain a savings bank. The Act applied to all municipal boroughs in England and burghs of over a quarter of a million population in Scotland. Deposits and interest were to be guaranteed on the rates but deposits could only be made by employers who would deduct the contributions from the wages of their employees, or otherwise collect, and deposit the savings. Even so, the total deposit from any one depositor was never to exceed £200, and to crown it all, the aggregate amount which a depositor could withdraw in any seven days was £1. The Treasury was to determine the rate of interest to be earned by deposits, all of which were to be invested with the National Debt Commissioners who were to reimburse a municipal bank with its outgoings. These banks were to be wound up three months after the termination of hostilities.

Another short Act in 1916 contrasts sharply with the Savings Bank provision both in significance and in the attitude of the central departments. This was the Public Authorities and Bodies (Loans) Act 1916. It consisted of one main clause, with four sub-paragraphs of which only two were significant, and both of which were subject to the 'duration only plus six months' limitation. The first of these was an enabling clause to allow counties, boroughs and urban districts, with the consent of the appropriate government department, to borrow on the security of the funds, property and revenues of the council, for the purposes of discharging any loan, replacing used sinking funds, or raising money for any new capital purpose. Just why such a clause was needed is not clear. The second sub-paragraph broke new ground. It allowed the same classes of authority to borrow by means of bearer bonds or other securities to bearer, whether within or without the United Kingdom, and if need be in a foreign currency. Such bonds or securities were to rank as the equivalent of a stock issue. So far as can be ascertained, these powers although their duration was later extended to 1933 came to nothing, but the strange story behind their introduction is told by Sir Harry Haward in *The London County Council from Within* (of which council he was at that time Comptroller).

In September 1916 the Metropolitan Water Board had issued 12-month bills for a sum of $6.4 million in New York, at 6⅛ discount (£6 10s 6d yield). The City of Paris had floated a large American loan and Dublin Corporation had made an issue of bonds of $2 million at 5 per cent for ten years at an issue price of £95. The Guarantee Trust Co. of New York (which had handled the Water Board bills) invited the LCC to consider a dollar loan. The British government supported the proposal for the curious reason that their own borrowing in the United States had almost reached the American legal limits (10 per cent of the borrowers' assets – though how the assets of the British government had been measured is not known), but there was apparently no objection to a loan being undertaken by the LCC and the money lent-on to the Exchequer. The LCC did not in fact need any capital moneys and had no legal power to borrow in a foreign currency. However the government undertook to cover the council against loss, and to pass 'instant legislation' to give the necessary powers. A loan of $100 million (only £20 million in those days) for fifteen years was planned. A parliamentary Bill was drafted towards the middle of December 1916 and passed into law in a single day. A prospectus was under preparation when the whole matter was suddenly aborted by America's declaration of war on the side of the Allies, as a result of which money then became readily available to Britain, and the strange LCC loan was no longer required. No such foreign loan is understood to have followed the granting of these powers to local authorities, although the provision which limited the powers to the duration of the war and six months thereafter was rescinded in the Housing (Additional Powers) Act 1919. Possibly this provision for the removal of the time-limit was incorporated into this Housing Act (along with the bond provisions about to be described) as one of the means for finding the vast sums for housing purposes thought to be necessary for this first real step in the saga of local authority provision of houses. This power, though apparently never used, was not repealed until the passing of the Local Government Act 1933. Even after 1933, the ghost of this peculiar interlude in local authority borrowing powers was still to exercise an influence when foreign borrowing again became a feature of local authority finance in the late 1960s. There were several Housing Acts during this period which were given their first consolidation in 1925. The borrowing powers made available were the 1888 Local Government Act; the London County Council (Finance Consolidation) Act 1912; in the City of London the Sewers Acts; in the London boroughs the Metropolitan Management Acts; and in the rest of the authorities the Public Health Acts.

In 1902 a major Education Act abolished the School Boards of the 1870 Act and made the county councils, county boroughs and the larger urban districts the education authorities. Borrowing by the counties was placed under the 1888 Act, but for the county boroughs, boroughs and districts the powers of the Public Health Acts were to be used. A provision which indirectly raised problems for other services was contained in the Education (Provision of Working Balances) Act 1903, which allowed borrowing for that specific revenue purpose. An Education (Administrative Provisions) Act 1907 extended the thirty-year repayment provisions of earlier Acts to sixty years for education purposes. The Education Act 1921 was mainly a consolidating Act, repeating these earlier borrowing references, with the addition that grants made by county councils to support district council education expenditure could form part of the borrowing security of the districts. Incidentally, while the Education Acts left borrowing provisions to earlier Acts, amounts borrowed for education purposes were not required to form part of any limits on total borrowing under the earlier Acts. There were other measures dealing with borrowing during the first thirty years of the century which require particular attention.

Another apparently modest Act of this period, but which had in the event most important long-term repercussions was the Local Authorities (Financial Provisions) Act 1921. This Act dealt first with certain minor points concerning the Metropolitan Poor Fund, but also provided two important borrowing concessions. Local authorities (defined as any county, county borough, borough, county district or Board of Guardians) were given power to borrow from time to time by means of 'temporary' loan or overdraft from any bank or otherwise 'for the purpose of providing temporarily for any current expenses that may be incurred by them in the execution or performance of their powers and duties' (including precept payments), such borrowings not to exceed in the aggregate such amount as might be sanctioned by the Minister of Health. Such borrowings were to be charged on the funds, properties, rates and revenues of the local authority and rank, *pari passu*, with all other mortgages, stock and other securities. The designation 'current expenses' must have meant 'borrowing in anticipation of revenue' similar to but not identical with the earlier power given to education authorities to borrow for working balances. Revenue borrowing was to be repaid before the end of the financial year in which the expenditure was incurred.

This provision for borrowing for current expenses does not seem to have envisaged borrowing in anticipation of longer-term (funded) expenditure, although such provision was made in due course and became a key part of local authority capital finance. Rather the provision was for very short-term borrowing, which although for revenue purposes, ranked equally with capital borrowing as to security. This gave it a status which temporary borrowing under the later 1933 Act did not have, but which was conceded again under the 1972 Act. Surprisingly however the Minister was empowered to extend the repayment period for up to ten years, if he thought fit. The Act first related to money borrowed before April 1923, in the nature of an emergency provision, but subsequent emergency Acts extended its operation until 1932, at which point the matter was taken over by the 1933 Act.

Apart from the permission to borrow temporarily, the specific reference to bank overdrafts was of great significance and dealt with a point which had for over a century been contentious. Cases had occurred in the courts as far back as 1824 which established that borrowing from a bank, without statutory authority, and not strictly by any of the means authorized by various Acts, was in fact illegal, though widely practised (see Johnson's *Loans of Local Authorities*). This is a reflection of the principle that as Parliament had in various Acts clearly specified the forms by which authorities could borrow for specified purposes, it was not in conformity with the expressed wishes of Parliament (although nowhere stated in categorical terms) to borrow by any other means. The basic theory, which underlies the rule that local authorities can only do what Parliament specifically authorizes them to do, as against the alternative that they might do anything they were not forbidden to do, can be expressed in the form that 'if Parliament had intended local authorities to borrow from the bank, it would have given them express powers to do so, and as it had not, the local authorities could not'. The well-known case of the *Attorney General* v. *De Winton* (4 LGR 549) in 1906 established that overdrafts were illegal, and interest paid on them was therefore illegal expenditure. The Education (Provision of Working Balances) Act 1903, already referred to, clarified the matter for education expenditure but not otherwise; in fact this could be held to reinforce the view that bank overdrafts were not authorized for other purposes.

The Local Authorities (Financial Provisions) Act 1921 did not clarify the matter for capital overdrafts; power to borrow had been given for various purposes but this led to the question – never resolved – of whether bank overdrafts on capital account were only in order if covered by a mortgage deed or other approved instrument. There was a further difficulty that if money was to be borrowed from the Public Works Loan Commission (PWLC), the fact that it had already been 'temporarily' borrowed from a bank meant that the PWLC application was in fact a 'reborrowing', to meet something that at that date was outside the powers of the PWLC. With the operation of a consolidated loans fund, the problem no longer arises; in any event, the PWLC are now no longer forbidden to lend to replace previous borrowing.

Another important clause in the 1921 Act related to capital works of a revenue-producing character. Sinking fund provisions could be suspended, subject to conditions, until the works became revenue producing, with a maximum of five years. This was a most useful provision for municipal trading undertakings and still operates. There were other provisions to facilitate borrowing for works designed to provide employment for unemployed persons, and to assist authorities which had had difficulties with sinking fund provisions arising from war conditions.

In the decade following the First World War important strides were made in the development of services, especially housing, and in the increased rationalization of the local government structure – the absorption of the Poor Law guardians and the overseers by the 'mainline' local authorities. In 1919 the Local Government Board was reconstituted as the Ministry of Health. There were also far-reaching financial developments: the institution of the system of central government block grants on a needs-basis formula, radical development of the bond as a borrowing instrument and the first statutory appearance of the fully-fledged consolidated loans fund. All of these changes provided the logical approach to the consolidating and amending Local Government Act 1933, with the final emergence of the 'all-purpose' county borough, the high status given to the county and a substantial degree of rationalization of borrowing provisions. Indeed the case has already been made that the decade 1928–38, that is, to the start of the Second World War, was the golden era of local government. The following decade, 1938–48, with war and its aftermath, led then to the decline in the status of local authorities, which despite the further reorganizations of the late 1960s and early 1970s still continues.

The general legislation of the post-1919 decade did not affect borrowing methods in any substantial way. The Housing Acts of 1919 to 1930 (and the many subsequent Acts) certainly led to the substantial growth of local authority debt, but generally speaking the borrowing provisions written into the 'service' Acts related to methods of financing the capital expenditure already set out in the earlier general Acts, as already described. The one exception to this generalization was the Housing (Additional Powers) Act 1919, and the 1925 Housing Act into which it was consolidated, relating to the powers for borrowing by local bonds. These are usually called colloquially 'housing bonds' to distinguish them from the general local authority bonds which were established in 1928 by Coventry, and over the course of years developed dramatically until they overtook the mortgage. Housing bonds were of a restricted character and the general bonds took many years before they developed into a significant rival to the mortgage, but at least they were introduced in this period. The curious history of the bond will be examined in due course.

The Rating and Valuation Act 1925 was the first of the restructuring measures of this era; it rationalized the organization of these functions extending back to the famous Act of Elizabeth I in 1601. Its provisions, given here in the merest outline as they related pre-eminently to the raising of revenue and not capital, provided for the absorption of the ancient office of Overseer of the Poor (the rate-collecting body) into the administration of the county boroughs and county districts; it abolished (with some limitations) the parish as the rating area, consolidated the poor rate with the other district rates, and reorganized the system of rating valuation (without altering the basis of valuation methods); and it imposed quinquennial valuations (a provision which has been sadly overridden in the subsequent years for various reasons, some good, some bad).

There was however a borrowing provision of considerable importance in the Act which finally cleared up the long-standing doubts about a local authority's right to rely on a bank overdraft. The 1925 Act said categorically that a local authority must levy a 'sufficient rate', that is, not more than needed to meet its residual budget fo. the year after taking into account all other revenues, and certainly not less than required, a situation which would have required borrowing temporarily or by overdraft to meet the subsequent and inevitable deficiency. Given this basic clarification of the adequacy of the rate levy, local authorities were then permitted to borrow short-term by bank overdraft or otherwise for both revenue cash-flow purposes and for capital purposes in anticipation of the raising of an approved loan. The wording of the section with its assumption that the 'treasurer' was some person distinct from the local authority, was archaic but clear in its intentions. However, the status and security for such borrowing was not made clear at that stage.

Section 12(2) of the Act said:

> The treasurer of a local authority may at any time advance to the authority any sum which the authority may temporarily require and which –
> (a) they are at that time authorised to raise by loan; or
> (b) they require for the purpose of defraying expenses pending the receipt of rates and revenue receivable by them in respect of the period of account in which those expenses are chargeable; and the authority may pay interest at a reasonable rate on any advance so made.

To limit revenue borrowing within the concept of a 'sufficient rate' section 12(3) said that if the overdraft arose out of 'wilful neglect' or 'default' in making and collecting 'such rates ... as are necessary', an interest payment became an illegal loss under the Poor Law Act 1844 and the Public Health Act 1875. The 1933 Act improved these provisions somewhat but failed to clear up the security and ranking problems. These were dealt with in the 1972 Act, though by that time the capital aspects of 'temporary' borrowing had lost most of their relevance, as will be shown later. There was also an extensive Public Health Act in 1925, which affected also baths and washhouses provision and dealt with 'matters for which provision is commonly made in local Acts'. It had no borrowing significance.

The Local Government Act 1929 brought about the next stage of reconstruction – the abolition of the Poor Law unions and the Boards of Guardians and the transfer of their duties to the counties and county boroughs. Although not widely recognized at the time, this break up of the old Poor Law was in fact a preliminary to the early nationalization of most of the duties of poor relief. The introduction of the first block grant formula – the General Exchequer Contribution – by this Act is not relevant to us here, but the reorganization of the Poor Law – that part of the 1929 Act most involving borrowing – was also a complex exercise and in fact took place in three stages. The first of these was the Poor Law Act 1927 which consolidated 'the enactments relating to the relief of the poor in England and Wales'; the second stage was the 1929 Act itself which then reorganized the administrative structure of poor relief by transferring the powers and duties of the Boards of Guardians to the two principal classes of local authority; and the third stage was the further consolidation of the codes contained in the 1927 and 1929 Acts in the Poor Law Act 1930. Whether the 1927 Act was an essential preliminary step is not now clearly obvious, but no doubt there was some virtue in drawing together the many and complex Poor Law provisions of the century since 1834, as a preliminary to the radical change in the authorities to whom the duty was delegated. Although the Poor Law borrowing provisions of the 1927

Act were superseded by the simpler provisions of the 1929 Act, which were themselves then incorporated in the 1930 Act, a summary of the 1927 Act borrowing clauses gives a useful recapitulation of the state of borrowing under the guardians to that point.

Sections 142–144 of the 1927 Act set out the following borrowing code:

(1) A Board of Guardians might borrow with the consent of the Minister of Health to raise money to meet expenses incurred or to be incurred for any permanent work or object the cost of which should in the Minister's opinion be spread over a number of years, such borrowing and interest thereon to be on the security of the common fund of the union.

(2) The total debt was not to exceed one-quarter of the total net rateable value of the union, subject to the power of the Minister to extend this limit to one-half.

(3) These provisions also applied to the managers of school districts subject to a maximum of one-sixteenth of the total net rateable value of the union.

(4) The maximum borrowing period was sixty years, debt being repayable by equal yearly or half-yearly instalments, or through a sinking fund as prescribed by the Local Loans Act 1875, with a prescribed rate of accumulation not exceeding 3 per cent p.a., and a prohibition of the investment of the fund in the board's own securities.

(5) Reborrowing was permitted to repay loans on an instalment basis within the overall original period.

(6) Securities were to be in the prescribed form or 'as near as the circumstances of the case will admit', and registers as prescribed were also to be maintained in prescribed form.

Provisions for transfer of loans and the lenders' rights on default by the borrowers were not included.

The Local Government Act 1929 was of epoch-making proportions. In the first circular issued by the Ministry of Health (LGA 17/4/29) concerning the Act the view was expressed that, with this Act, Mr Neville Chamberlain might in due course be seen 'to have affected the operation of local government more profoundly than the great Acts of 1834, 1835, 1875, 1888, and 1894' and with this opinion there is still little need to disagree, even if the Local Government Act 1933 were then to be added; perhaps the 1972 Act has been of equal significance.

In addition to the transfer of poor relief to counties and county boroughs, this Act transferred likewise the extraneous functions attached to the Poor Law – registration of births, marriages and deaths, vaccination and child protection; extended the county powers in the area of town planning and roads; introduced procedures for the review of county districts; made substantial alterations in rating and valuation – total relief of agriculture from rating and the partial de-rating of industrial and freight transport hereditaments; and probably most important of all introduced the General Exchequer Contribution, a formula system for the distribution of government grants on a 'needs' basis, in place of the great variety of then existing grants, mostly on a percentage basis. This formula system of central grant distribution, as drastically revised from time to time, continues to be a major source of contention not simply between central and local government, but between the classes of local authorities themselves. There were many consequential provisions in this major Act the main effect of which was to strengthen county and county borough powers and responsibilities. These two classes of local authorities acquired substantial capital assets in the way of Poor Law institutions and hospitals, and the associated debt. Because the former Poor Law union areas had been created without regard to the old borough and county boundaries, various schemes for revision of areas and the allocation of assets and liabilities were needed.

However, this vast and complex Act with the many circulars and orders needed to bring it into effect had little influence on statutory borrowing. Perhaps the most significant point affecting borrowing was section 74, surprisingly under the general heading of rating and valuation. This section belatedly recognized that the many and various restrictions on the aggregate borrowing totals permitted to various classes of authorities and for various responsibilities were outdated, mainly because of the many exemptions from the total which individual service Acts had introduced. These restrictions, the Ministry of Health said in a memorandum to the Act (LGA, 15 May 1929), 'have long since ceased to be of their original value', and also recognized that the calculations of those limits in relation to rateable value would henceforth be distorted by the de-rating provisions of the Act (the point which explains the inclusion of the clause under rating and valuation). The whole of the restrictions on aggregate borrowing were therefore removed.

As to outstanding debt and future borrowing, section 113 simply transferred all institutional and non-institutional assets and outstanding loans attaching thereto to the new authorities, while section 128 allowed counties and county boroughs to borrow for the purposes of the Act – the LCC were to borrow under the London County Council (Finance Consolidation) Act 1912 and subsequent amendments, county councils under the Local Government Act 1888, and county boroughs under the Public Health Acts 1875 to 1926. Section 114 made transitional provisions for temporary loans still outstanding under the Local Authorities (Financial Provisions) Act 1921. The Poor Law Act 1930 repeated precisely the borrowing provisions of the 1929 Act. All the preliminary steps had thus been taken to the 'new-look' consolidations of the Local Government Act 1933.

Third Period 1930–1984: Consolidation Evolution and Dissolution

Chapter 12

THE LOCAL GOVERNMENT ACT
1933

The absorption of the Board of Guardians and the Overseers of the Poor into the main framework of local government left the way clear for a consolidation and further rationalization of the administrative structures of the various classes of surviving authorities. This was achieved in the Local Government Act 1933, a product of the interim report of the Chelmsford Committee. An important part of the Act was the unification of borrowing provisions for all classes of authority, but important though this Act was in the history of local government it cannot be called revolutionary (as was, for example, the 1929 Act). The 1933 Act was largely a codification or standardization of what were considered to be the best elements of the past rather than an attempt to break new ground or establish an entirely new frame of reference for the enlarged and strengthened 'mainline' local authorities. Although the new borrowing provisions introduced a uniform code for all classes of authority and were reasonably comprehensive, yet they bear the hallmarks of an attempt to encompass a variety of previous arrangements, not altogether consistently, bringing in certain moribund provisions but neglecting other established methods of borrowing. Thus the provisions of the Local Loans Act 1875 were partly incorporated despite their neglect by both central and local government, but provision for the use of bills and bonds was not included and the approach to amortization was still in outmoded form. However, a number of important principles which had emerged over a long period of time were firmly established in this Act, so that the borrowing provisions, contained in part IX of the Act, merit detailed examination as they not only operated for another forty years, but influenced strongly the later code embodied in the Local Government Act 1972 at present operative.

Part IX of the Act still did not attempt to define capital expenditure, but as in earlier Acts set out the classes of expenditure which might be initially financed from borrowed money, subject to the consent of the sanctioning authority (and for parish councils, the additional consent of the county council). What this approach amounted to was that local authorities could borrow for any purpose which the Minister considered proper. The listed purposes were: acquisition of land and erection of buildings, execution of permanent works, provision of plant, and the doing of any other thing the cost of which the sanctioning authority agreed ought to be spread over a term of years; in other words, the list of approvals to borrowing which had been somewhat laboriously evolved in earlier legislation, but yet was effective in practical terms. However, words were also added that borrowing might be undertaken for any other purpose for which borrowing was authorized by statute or statutory order. To say that a local authority might borrow for purposes for which it was authorized to borrow by Parliament may seem somewhat unnecessary, but the true effect of these words was to indicate that even borrowing authorized under statute was subject to further approval by a sanctioning authority. A county council could borrow to on-lend to a parish council, provided that the parish council had the necessary loan sanctions. 'Sanctioning authority' meant generally the Minister of Health, although the Electricity Commissioners and the Minister of Transport were involved for purposes special to themselves.

This seems to have been a reasonably satisfactory and clear statement of the area to which finance by borrowing was appropriate: the modes of borrowing permitted by the Act were less all-embracing and logical. All authorities could borrow by mortgage. All authorities (including rural district councils but excluding parishes) could borrow by the issue of stock, subject to the consent of the Minister (thus the Minister had to consent both to the purpose of the borrowing and to the use of this method). All authorities might also borrow by the issue of debentures or annuity certificates under the Local Loans Act 1875. A further clause was considered to be necessary to declare that a debenture issued by a county council might be for any amount exceeding £5. There was no reference to borrowing by bills or bonds, both well-established methods. Perhaps a lack of reference to the Public Works Loan Commission (PWLC) should be noted; the logic of this omission seems to have been that borrowing from this important body was a source rather than a method of borrowing, mortgages of a special kind being used for PWLC loans. The arrangements under the Local Authorities (Financial Provisions) Act 1921 which permitted borrowing by bearer instruments and in foreign currencies were repealed, but the bearer facilities of the Local Loans Act continued to be available for the special purposes of that Act. Temporary borrowing was dealt with separately and is discussed below.

All money borrowed before or after the passing of the Act was to be charged indifferently on all the revenues of the authority, and all loans with the minor exceptions noted below were to rank equally and without priority. 'Revenues' were clearly defined as the county or general rate, and all other rates, Exchequer contributions and other revenues, whether arising from land or undertakings, or from any other source, receivable by the authority. These again were clear and logical statements. What is notable is that the security was confined to revenue and did not embrace the capital value of property as had been included with revenues in earlier Acts. Thus any mortgaging which took place was of income and not assets. The re-thinking behind the decision to omit reference to the assets of the authority as security may have stemmed from the realization that while the security might conceivably be called upon and facility for the appointment of a receiver invoked, there could be no question of winding up a local authority, or even of a service or part of a service, such as, for example, the closing of a school and the sale of the buildings to meet a loan debt because this might have been seen as a contravention of the statutory duty on councils to provide education. The utilization of revenues, even involving the levying of a larger or additional rate, was a more practical proposition had this grievous state of affairs – a debt default – ever arisen. The exclusions from the equal priority and ranking provisions were moneys borrowed by temporary loan or unsecured overdraft, and any rights of priority established before the passing of the Act. Thus any priority loans still extant under the Local Loans Act would retain that priority, but the local loans priority provisions were not to apply to any future loans, even those borrowed under the 'back-reference' to the Local Loans Act.

The provisions for the repayment of money borrowed continued, as in earlier Acts, the confusion between the period for which money was borrowed from the individual lender and the period over which capital outlay could be amortized. The sanction periods were to be determined by the sanctioning authority; the general maximum was sixty years. In practice, the maximum period was usually allowed for land-purchase loans (and early house-building); buildings were usually given a thirty/forty-year period; various works twenty years; and equipment, depending on its nature, as low as five years. A schedule to the Act introduced inconsistencies by allowing only thirty years for loans under the Tramways Act, but up to eighty years for land purchases for allotments and smallholdings and housing. Eighty years was sometimes allowed for major waterworks constructions under private Acts, but this long period was usually avoided. Two useful provisions were re-enacted: that on revenue-producing works repayment provisions could be deferred for up to five years and that lenders were relieved of responsibility for satisfying themselves that money borrowed by a local authority was legally borrowed and thereafter properly applied. The Act made only a brief mention of stock, in effect, to say that the subject would be covered by regulations to be issued. These were issued in 1934, as a further link in the chain of Stock Regulations issued since 1891 (see Chapter 17 on stock in Part 3 of this book).

Mortgages were dealt with somewhat more fully, but the form of mortgage previously set out in many special Acts was left to be covered by regulations and these too were issued in 1934 (see Chapter 15 on mortgages in Part 3). The use of a special form of mortgage by the Public Works Loan Commission (PWLC) was authorized. There was nothing new in the prescribed form, either for the mortgage deed itself or for the form of transfer, both of which were in simple terms. In fact the type of mortgage prescribed was repeated under the 1972 Act, despite the modernization of this instrument which, in practice, had been evolved by the local authorities in the meantime. The Act also provided for a register of mortgages and set out associated detailed requirements.

The mortgage provisions also included powers for a receiver to be appointed. This feature provides a good example of the lack of consistency which was allowed to persist in the Act but could easily have been removed. Thus the receivership powers in relation to mortgages were put directly into the Act; application could be made for the appointment of a receiver after two months' delay (for a sum of not less than £500 in aggregate) for either interest or repayment. The stock receivership provisions were left to the regulations, which provided for a receiver after two months' delay only in the payment of interest (redemption was presumably considered to be a special feature about which non-payment could hardly arise), without mention of an aggregate minimum sum. If any authority had used the powers to issue debentures or annuity certificates under the Local Loans Act 1875, the receivership provisions of that Act would presumably have applied; under these the aggregate minimum was also £500 but action could be taken after 21 days' default. For temporary borrowing no receivership provision was made, and this led to practical difficulties later. This was not the only problem created by the temporary borrowing provisions.

The provisions authorizing temporary borrowing, brought forward from earlier legislation, straightforward and innocuous though they seem, were already out of date in concept and did not provide adequately for the development of so-called 'temporary' borrowing which later became a serious issue, and indeed long before the passing of the 1972 Act brought about a major revolution in local authority borrowing practice.

Under section 215 of the 1933 Act a local authority was authorized to borrow without the consent of a sanctioning authority by way of temporary loan ('temporary' not defined), or unsecured overdraft from a bank or otherwise, for two purposes. The first was to defray expenditure (including meeting a precept), pending the receipt of revenues receivable by the authority for the period of account to which the expenditure related and taken into account in the framing of the estimates (budget) made by the authority for that period – a new and important point. This was a clear statement and a useful provision – a local authority might borrow at its own discretion to aid its cash flow (a term not then devised) on its established budget, with the implication that the forthcoming revenue would provide for the repayment of the borrowing.

The second provision in this section was that temporary loans could be taken up without sanction pending the raising of a longer-term loan (funding) to meet expenditure for which loan sanction had been given. Whatever the intention of this section, the net effect was that temporary capital borrowing could effectively be indulged in only for sanctioned expenditure. These provisions also seem to have embraced the old misconception that borrowings were still largely earmarked against capital projects, whereas by this date mortgage pools and consolidated loans funds were in widespread operation and based upon the separation of capital expenditure and borrowing. The time for amortization to begin to be charged to a borrowing account is from the date at which the expenditure takes place; the provision of capital funds by borrowing from lenders is a separate requirement and loans might well be 'turned-over' several times during the life of a sanction. At any one time the total borrowings and the total expenditures agree overall, but not in detail. Indeed this attitude of short borrowings and longer redemptions had been established since the beginning of borrowing but never thoroughly thought through, and nor was it seen clearly in the 1933 Act. In the state of the art at that time the only reason for temporary borrowing would have been to await more beneficial market conditions. Today the so-called 'temporary' borrowing is not in anticipation of funding, but as an element in the spread of a well-administered borrowing portfolio.

The full implications of this change of attitude will be explored later, but one point must be made here: section 197 of this Act, which said that all moneys borrowed were to be charged indifferently on all the revenues of the authority, without priority, specifically excluded temporary borrowing or unsecured bank overdrafts. This meant that banks who gave (often substantial) overdraft facilities were doing this generally without collateral as requests from banks that overdrafts should be covered by a mortgage were not usual. More important, this placed temporary borrowings generally in an inferior position to that of other loans, without recognizable security and bereft of receivership provisions. What security lenders of 'temporary' loans had was never clearly established, simply because the occurrence of the circumstances in which there might be a need to appoint a receiver was no more than a hypothetical possibility. Presumably, although never established in the courts, the security for such loans was that of any 'unsecured' creditor of a local authority, another issue which has rarely if ever been considered by a court of law. Moreover, this issue leads to another peculiarity of the 1933 borrowing provisions. Although the security and equal priority for borrowing was clearly established for funded loans, the presumption is that, as 'secured' debts, they would have had a priority over the 'unsecured' debts in the event of a financial catastrophe. The situation is conceivable that the 'unsecured' creditors would have had access to assets as well as revenues, a feature now denied to the 'secured' creditors. However, the hypothetical receivership provisions were 'without prejudice to any other remedy', so that lenders had in practice the fullest range of security if ever the need had arisen.

The 1933 Act provided that mortgages were to be repaid by equal yearly or half-yearly instalments of principal, or principal and interest combined; or through a sinking fund; or by a combination of methods. Annual returns were to be made to the Minister (as provided in earlier Acts) to enable him to satisfy himself that proper provision for amortization was being made. The provisions for sinking funds were generally in the form established in earlier Acts, that is, sinking funds had to consist of equal amounts of principal set aside (and not used for immediate repayment) as would repay the debt at the end of the required number of years (non-accumulating sinking funds), or such sums as set aside and accumulated at interest would provide the necessary final sum (accumulating sinking funds). Because of the impossibility of foreseeing the earning power of accumulating funds (unless they were in some way invested at fixed interest for the precise period of the repayment), the Minister was to establish the theoretical rate at which such funds should be presumed to accumulate. Such a system required that if the accumulation fell short, additional funds should be added and that excesses which might occur should be absorbed. This was provided by allowing the interest to be paid into the county or general rate fund, with a transfer to the sinking fund of the sum theoretically to be earned. Provision could be made for the use of excess funds arising from excess interest earned. Sinking fund provisions of this kind became increasingly notional in the light of local Act powers to deal otherwise, and the use of the pooling arrangements made in statutory orders relating to the accounts of those local authorities subject to district audit; the development of sinking fund provision is dealt with elsewhere (see p. 339).

The Scottish Act which was the equivalent of the English 1933 Act, in that it established a general administrative and borrowing code, was the Local Government (Scotland) Act 1947. The delay arose because the Act emerged from the considerations of a committee under the chairmanship of Sir John Jeffrey which did not report until 1938; due to the Second World War, the report was not published until 1943 and the Act did not reach the statute-book for another four years. This delay was not without advantage; generally speaking, the Scottish Act was based on a more penetrating analysis of the situation than the English Act.

The purposes for which borrowing might be undertaken in the Scottish Act were somewhat more clearly defined but still included the omnibus phrase 'the doing of any other thing' which might receive central sanction. What is rather surprising was that it imposed a general maximum borrowing period of thirty years, but then modified this in a schedule which gave various exclusions with periods ranging from twenty to eighty years. Quite the most important difference was that temporary borrowing and overdrafts were given the same ranking as other forms of borrowing as well as the security of 'the whole funds, rates and revenues of the Council and not otherwise'. The addition of the words 'and not otherwise' may have been a specific attempt to indicate that assets were no part of loan security. While temporary borrowing in anticipation of revenue was authorized as in the English Act, the temporary borrowing for capital purposes was not described as being in anticipation of longer-term borrowing, a significant concession. On the other hand, there was no authority to borrow by debentures and annuities, as given, for what it was worth, in the English Act. Another important distinction was that interest and dividends were specifically described as a 'first charge' on the revenues. That interest should in this specific way be given the status of a first charge seems to indicate three orders of precedence: interest, secured loans and 'other creditors'. The receivership provisions – under the Scottish term 'judicial factor' – were slightly more restrictive than in

England; the amount of debt unpaid after two months needed to be
£1,000 for any one lender, or £2,000 for a group of lenders – possibly no
more than the effect of inflation on the English amounts.

Yet another important difference – and the shape of things to come for
England – was that this Scottish Act made full provision for the operation
of a (consolidated) loans fund by local authorities at their option, and spelt
out in detail how such a fund was to be operated. The reference to
temporary loans in the Scottish Act also used the term 'deposit receipt' –
later picked up, in practice, though not in the statutes in England. The
suggestion has been made (in a letter from the City Chamberlain,
Glasgow, February 1983) that the use of this term as an alternative to
temporary loan receipt stems from Scottish banking practice. There is
considerable evidence that local authorities in Scotland borrowed (probably
extra-statutorily) by temporary loans from their bankers since late in the
nineteenth century, which gives credence to this explanation of the use of
the term deposit receipt. (Loans fund accounts for the City of Edinburgh in
1894 show substantial temporary loans – about 17 per cent of total debt.)

Chapter 13

THE 'SHORT-TERM'
REVOLUTION

During the years of the Second World War there was little local authority capital expenditure necessitating borrowing. The main activity was that on air raid precautions (Civil Defence), and although substantial sums were spent in that area on capital works (mainly air-raid shelters), the major part was met by government grants (much of it at 100 per cent), with the balance carried on rate revenue. Such borrowing as was required was mainly for repaying and renewing previous debt, and for this local authorities were left to their own devices without aid from the Public Works Loan Commission (PWLC). However, with the end of the war, and when rapid expansion was expected particularly in housing with inevitable competition from industrial borrowers, fears of confusion and overstrain on the market (an excuse not now as clearly evident as no doubt it was then) led to the passing of the Local Authorities Loans Act 1945. During the succeeding twenty years from this date a number of significant developments were introduced into local authority borrowing of which, without doubt, the evolution of the 'temporary' (ultra-short) borrowing market into a 'permanent–temporary' market was the most important. The adoption of so-called temporary borrowing by local authorities as a permanent feature of their borrowing portfolios did not happen overnight, but the Local Authorities Loans Act, despite its restrictive objective, can now be seen as the first of three stages in the precipitation of local authorities into the extensive adoption of the ultra-short borrowing facilities offered by the institutional money market.

That this should have been so is indeed curious as the Local Authorities Loans Act 1945 had the primary objective of taking the local authorities out of the borrowing markets, at least in a direct way, subject to a narrow exception. Section 1(i) of the Act said in a categoric manner: 'it shall not be lawful for a local authority, without the approval of the Treasury, to borrow money otherwise than from the Public Works Loan Commissioners.' The proviso to this categoric statement was that the Treasury might make regulations to allow minimal borrowing from sources other than the commissioners. The regulations (SR & O 1945/680) permitted direct borrowing by local authorities in the market for capital purposes on mortgage or non-marketable bonds, and by temporary borrowing, subject to the proviso that the borrowing by mortgages, bonds and temporary capital loans was not to bring the debt to a higher level than the debt on these instruments at any time between the end of the financial year 1938/9 and the date of operation of the Act. Temporary revenue borrowing was also allowed to continue, as well as capital borrowing from various special sources – for example, internal funds such as superannuation funds, local authority trusts and inter-authority loans.

Although evidence on this point is not readily available, the fact is that this limited escape from the complete closing of the door of access to the market is known to have been pressed upon the Treasury by the financial advisers to the local authority associations in the belief that local authorities should have a minimal opportunity of keeping their loans offices operational, and also of keeping the 'names' of local authorities in the minds of potential lenders.[1] Local authorities, particularly the larger ones, took full advantage of this concession, mainly in the 'small local lender' sector.

Other clauses of the 1945 Act were more progressive. Although the Act did not give a general power for local authorities to establish capital funds (something which at that date many local authorities had acquired by private Act, and yet to be dealt with here), it did authorize the use of such local Act funds by local authorities with the necessary powers for new capital purposes outside the restrictions – in effect, one of the 'internal funds' whose use was permitted. Another important and essential breakthrough in this Act was a clause permitting PWLC moneys to be carried to any loans pools or consolidated loans fund operated by a local authority, by then a widely established practice under local Acts.

The opening restrictive clause of this Act was intended to lapse after a five-year period, but in 1950 the operation of the restriction was extended for a further two years under the Expiring Laws Continuation Act, so that the provision finally and automatically lapsed in 1952; a rescinding statute was not required. At this point the local authorities were left to choose for themselves whether to continue to use the PWLC or to return to the open market. The PWLC is not aware of any letter or circular issued by it or the Treasury in 1952 drawing attention to the change in the situation. The lapsing of the 1945 Act meant that local authorities, having been in the market to only a limited degree during the war, and to an equally limited extent for seven years afterwards, were expected to begin to re-establish themselves as borrowers from 1952 onwards. This constituted the second stage in what ultimately became the rush to ultra-short borrowing.

The third stage in the progression occurred some three years later, in 1955. This was simply an announcement by the Chancellor of the Exchequer in his October Budget speech of that year that loans to local authorities by the PWLC would no longer be made except in a capacity as 'lender of last resort' where a local authority could establish that it was unable to find capital at reasonable rates on the open market. Extracts from this speech were conveyed in a circular letter to local authorities by the PWLC. A letter was also issued by the Treasury in November 1955 making no direct reference to the change, but enclosing a new type of application form which included inquiries about the applicant's ability to raise its requirements on the market. Although local authorities had complained to the PWLC about the original restriction in 1945, they were again disturbed by being 'thrown on the market' – a phrase much used at the time – in this somewhat abrupt fashion, being required to switch from virtually full dependence on the PWLC in 1952 to almost complete exclusion without warning in 1955. From this point onwards in their urgent attempts to fill the gap and gear themselves once again for large-scale open market borrowing at a time of what were then regarded as high long-term interest rates, the local authorities began to use the London short-term money market with rapidly increasing confidence and enthusiasm.

There were other interrelated factors at work. Interest rates for longer-term money, for which there was a considerable demand, were historically high because disturbed markets were less inclined to tie up money for long periods. Foreign banks were re-establishing themselves in London (to what has since become a very considerable number, in the region of 400) as a result of which much inter-bank (short-term) money was being generated. What had previously been a modest participation in local authority borrowing by money brokers was beginning to develop in the City (and has since become a cornerstone of the system). At first their role was to find medium-term mortgage money for local authorities (stockbrokers looking to the longer-term requirements), but as demand and supply began to interact it became to find short-term money, largely 7-day loans but with great flexibility in other short periods.

A history of local authority money broking would no doubt be of interest as part of the history of the City and of local authority capital finance. Suffice it to say that at this time at least two money brokers were active in this field. One of these was Short Loan & Mortgage Co. Ltd (founded by Norman Woolley) and the other Long, Till & Colvin Ltd (now Butler Till Ltd) (of whom the cloaked figure of Colonel Till is still within the recollection of many treasurers). Both firms began operations in 1933–4 and are still operating but now dependent for their success – as the many who followed them – on the inter-operation of local authority, inter-bank and commercial broking, international and foreign exchange dealings and the Eurobond, Eurodollar and financial futures markets. The local authority market would have great difficulty in operating on its present scale, and as expeditiously, without the services of these middlemen, who have also displayed much innovatory talent.[2]

Between 1955 and 1963 there was a considerable expansion of this short-term money market. Some treasurers were more adventurous than others. The problem lay in balancing the risks of borrowing for such excessively short periods to cover long-term capital outlay against the benefits to be derived from the comparatively low rates of interest for this short money. Even when short-term interest rates stimulated by demand rose above long-term rates, many treasurers preferred to borrow expensively for short periods in the expectation that longer-term rates would shortly fall, allowing lower-cost funding to take place. But some treasurers would have none of it, regarding temporary loans (as was clearly intended when the power was originally given) as available for temporary shortages of cash pending the receipt of revenue, or to meet some crisis, or as a capital holding operation while a long-term loan was negotiated. Others however, from this time onward, regarded this form of borrowing as a permanent feature – some of them as a predominant feature – in their borrowing portfolios. There were those who gradually built up their short borrowings until the total constituted as much as 60 per cent or more of total debt.

What constituted a 'temporary' loan had never (and has not yet) been defined, but by the time that Treasury intervention became inevitable the general understanding was that a temporary loan was one which had an initial borrowing period of less than a full year; indeed loans for precisely 364 days were part of the pattern. This working definition was aided by the income tax rule that tax must be deducted at source by the borrower on all payments of *annual* interest. Therefore, interest on 'less than a year' loans could be paid gross. Another factor, which perhaps should not have been significant but certainly was, was that temporary loan receipts (sometimes called deposit receipts) were hardly to be regarded as 'borrowing instruments' and thus could be charged stamp duty at only 2d (6d as 'agreements' when a promise was added that an official mortgage deed would be issued on request) instead of on the *ad valorem* scales of mortgages and other instruments. (The later abolition of all stamp duty on local authority borrowing removed this incentive.)

Temporary loans were therefore those from overnight (for which there was a surprisingly brisk market) to 364 days, with a wide range of variants between. Probably the most popular form was the loan for 7 days and thereafter at 7 days' notice ('7 plus 7' in market terminology). How far an authority could 'safely' go with this type of borrowing was a constant source of discussion among municipal treasurers at that time, but the truth of the matter probably is that while a few local authorities could expand their use of this market to considerable levels without excessive risk, if all authorities had followed that course, then a situation was created in which borrowers would have severe problems in coping with any sudden crisis in the money markets.

The situation did show every indication of developing to critical levels. At some stage, at a date which has not been identified, the use in England and Wales of the Scottish term 'short-term deposit' and 'deposit receipt' began to be used instead of the temporary loan and temporary loan receipt. This was in fact a stretching of the provision of the 1933 Act which allowed borrowing by mortgages or stock, plus unsecured borrowing temporarily (although the instrument of acknowledgement of temporary borrowing was never specified). This conversion of temporary borrowing to something more formal in the shape of a 'local authority deposit' verged on the introduction of a non-statutory addition to the 1933 Act provisions, and there can be little doubt that the use of this term was an attempt to gloss over the expansion which was taking place of the facility to borrow temporarily, with problematic security.

Leeds and Reading are two authorities, each with an earlier history of modest participation in this market, who developed its use extensively during this period, and from whom first-hand comments are available. A former City Treasurer of Leeds (J. Beer) has made an analysis (in a letter dated 21 April 1975), based on the examination of papers over a forty-year period, which shows the city using 7-day money as far back as 1937 at 1¾ per cent p.a. A few years later when 7-day money was obtainable at 2 per cent, money for 364 days was borrowed at 2½ per cent and by 1952 7-day money was still only costing 2½ per cent. In 1952 the short money formed only 6 per cent of total debt in Leeds, but thereafter there was a sharp rise. By 1956 it was 10 per cent of the total, rising dramatically year by year to 55 per cent in 1963, the date of the White Paper which heralded control. Despite the White Paper provisions, it continued to rise, reaching 64 per cent in 1966, at which point severe central government pressure was applied and the percentage fell rapidly, to 19 per cent in 1969.

The other exemplification of short-borrowing trends is contained in a paper emanating from the Borough Treasurer of Reading (G. C. Jones, 'Deposit loans', May 1962), another town known to be a high user – possibly the highest ever – of short borrowing. This paper examined a limited selection of local authorities, chosen because of their known interest in this market, and showing that 34 per cent of their total debt was for initial periods of less than 1 year (including bank overdrafts), a figure which the report says was approximately twice the national average. (The paper then claimed that this indicated that the treasurers of high-level authorities were thus shown to be 'experienced operators in that field'.) The White Paper on borrowing, published a few months after the Reading memorandum, said that between 1955 and 1963 local authority temporary borrowing had risen from 3¼ to about 15 per cent of total debt, a figure which bears out the Reading assertion. Also relevant to an appreciation of this situation are the following extracts from the report of the Radcliffe Committee on the Working of the Monetary System in 1959 (Cmnd 827):

> The local authorities are for many purposes autonomous bodies, but their borrowing powers are strictly controlled by law and by decisions at the centre . . . there is in practice no ultimate danger of default. The credit-worthiness of the local authorities is therefore virtually as high as that of the central Government; the yield differential against local authority securities . . . is accounted for by their inferior marketability.

Yet the practice of local authority short borrowing was 'clean contrary to the funding policy of the monetary authorities'.

In May 1962, as a result of these developments and the growing uneasiness about the extent of reliance on volatile loans of this kind, the Treasury set up a working party to examine the problem on to which were co-opted four treasurers of major authorities (who were honorary financial advisers to local authority associations).[3] While these local authority representatives were as uneasy in their minds as were the Treasury about the trend of events, they made the case (as outlined above) that having been 'thrown back on the market', and bearing in mind the levels of interest rates, municipal treasurers had sought to make optimum use of the facilities available to them. If they were now to be restricted in their operations in what was developing as a flexible and relatively cheap market in which, though risky, no unmanageable problems had in practice arisen, then there should be a *quid pro quo* in the shape of some reopening of access to the PWLC, and a widening of other borrowing facilities for local authorities. The case was also made that those authorities who had substantial proportions of short money in their portfolios could not be expected to fund this rapidly. On the other hand, the Treasury while conceding the force of these arguments made clear that sudden reopening of the PWLC to a substantial degree was not to be expected because of the pressure which this would put on government borrowing. A compromise was eventually reached in which both sides agreed that while local authority borrowing for less than one year should be restricted the funding imposed on those over the level of the new restriction should be gradual. Access to the PWLC was similarly to be provided in stages, with the two processes being given a transitional period of four years. The principal source of difficulty was at what level the restriction on temporary borrowing should be fixed.

As part of the recommendations of the Jeffrey's Committee, the Local Government (Scotland) Act 1947 had contained a provision that temporary borrowing in Scotland should be limited to 15 per cent of total debt. (The Jeffrey's Report actually proposed 10 per cent.) The Treasury proposed to apply the 15 per cent limit in England and Wales, while the local authority representatives sought a figure of 25 per cent. In the event the Treasury agreed to the compromise of a two-level ceiling of 20 per cent overall for borrowings for up to 364 days, of which three-quarters (15 per cent) could be for up to three months, with a promise that the Scottish figure would be amended to this level. These conclusions were incorporated in a White Paper (Cmnd 2162) in October 1963.

The White Paper set out the argument that local authority competition for short-term funds had on occasion forced interest rates to high levels, and created a large volume of short-term debt insensitive to interest rate policy; that it interfered with the government's policy of money management; and that it had implications for the balance of payments, in that high and fluctuating rates of interest offered by local authorities for this type of borrowing caused an undesirable ebb and flow of foreign funds (the so-called 'hot money'). A control of temporary borrowing was therefore to be imposed. The controls were those already mentioned; they are not very precisely expressed in the White Paper, but as already described, they meant that a local authority's debt outstanding at any one time which had had an initial borrowing period of not more than three months was not to exceed the higher of 15 per cent of outstanding loan debt or the authority's capital expenditure for the preceding 12 months; and that total temporary borrowing with an initial period of up to 12 months was not to exceed 20 per cent of total debt or one-and-one-third times its capital expenditure in the preceding 12 months. Borrowing in anticipation of revenue and internal borrowings were not included in these limits, and longer-term loans running into their last year before maturity were also excluded from the calculation. A special provision was required for what were at the time called 'escalator mortgages', which were a form of borrowing evolved by local authorities in which the lender could call for repayment after six or twelve months, but obtain a higher interest rate the longer the money remained with the authority.

The *quid pro quo* of this local authority 'acceptance' of restrictions was a re-opening of the PWLC to assist longer-term borrowing, and permission to reborrow from the board to assist funding and general debt management. Full access to the board was not to be given, but over a transitional period access was to be given up to 50 per cent of needs on a formula basis, at Exchequer borrowing rates plus a management charge. The starting figure of access was to be 20 per cent. To help smaller authorities it was to be permitted that all authorities take the first £50,000 of their needs from the board (later raised as promised to £100,000). The board was also to continue to act as 'lender of last resort' at market rates of interest. Another useful concession was that borrowings from the board were to be allowed on a maturity repayment instead of an annuity basis in order to assist the operation of the consolidated loans fund, although the minimum period of PWLC loans was to be raised to ten years (instead of seven) unless the loan sanction period of a project was less than ten years. The mechanics of access to the board were also to be simplified. Rather oddly, the restrictions were imposed by what was called a General Consent under the Control of Borrowing Order.

The ramifications of the Control of Borrowing Order need investigation, but before this examination is made, two comments must first be made on the vital breakthrough exhibited by this development of temporary borrowing. In the first place, these new arrangements constituted a *de facto* acceptance that temporary borrowing by a local authority was no longer a 'fall-back' device to be used from time to time as occasion demanded to help a local authority round a temporary cash-flow difficulty on its revenue account, or as an anticipatory step to some planned longer-term borrowing such as a stock issue. 'Temporary borrowing' was in effect now recognized as a legitimate utilization in any full-scale borrowing portfolio of the short end of the market, just as an issue of stock lay at the other end of the spectrum. From this moment such borrowing ceased to be properly designated as temporary – 'temporary' was no longer a proper synonym for 'short' in this context – and could be expected to be a regular and permanent feature of all local authority borrowing activities in the future. It became exactly similar to all other forms of statutory borrowing, subject to the flaw that historical chance had deprived it of the security and equal ranking of the other borrowing. Compensating advantages were that interest could be paid gross and that stamp duty was negligible. Despite this change in concept, both the local authorities and the Treasury continued to regard it as a separate type of borrowing. Even in 1972 when its status was further regularized to bring it into line with other forms of borrowing, 'temporary' borrowing continued to be referred to in the Act as though it had a separate identity.

The second comment to be made is that this important extension of local authority borrowing practices did not need any statutory change. The new concept was allowed as a re-interpretation of the 1933 Act temporary borrowing provisions, and the controls which were imposed to keep the figures within the agreed percentages were applied simply under the Control of Borrowing Order. The restriction of temporary borrowing in Scotland to 15 per cent of total debt which had been imposed under the Local Government (Scotland) Act 1947 (the Scottish equivalent of the English 1933 Act) was repealed in 1964, Parliament using as a convenience for this purpose the Public Works Loan Act of that year. Scottish control thereafter fell under the Control of Borrowing Order as for the rest of the United Kingdom.

The Borrowing (Control and Guarantees) Act 1946, still on the statute-book, has been of great significance in the exercise of Treasury control over local authority borrowing. As described in Chapter 19 on local authority bills, it has been used by the Treasury to override other powers given specifically by Parliament in local Acts and the 1972 Act. The preamble describes it as 'An Act to provide for the regulation of the borrowing and raising of money, the issue of securities', etc., and it begins with the categoric statement that 'The Treasury may make orders for regulating ... the borrowing of money in Great Britain' where the aggregate in a year exceeds £10,000, a provision not confined to but which naturally included local authorities. An order was made under the Act in 1947 and has been amended in minor ways since, the whole being consolidated in the Control of Borrowing Order 1958 (SI 1958/1208). The application of the order to local government was quite simple; local authorities could not borrow without Treasury consent, which was to be in addition to the appropriate sanctioning authority. Thus every new capital project intended to be financed by borrowing needed two central government approvals, one to the suitability of the scheme for financing by borrowing and the other to the actual borrowing. Borrowing in anticipation of revenue was excluded from the control, provided that the money was not used for capital purposes and it was repaid within one month of the end of the accounting period (later extended to three months), and the total outstanding at any one time was not more than one-half of the total revenues receivable. Despite the 1933 Act, 'local authority' was defined by reference to the Local Loans Act 1875, or to the Local Authorities Loans (Scotland) Act 1891.

Consequently, between 1946 and 1963 all loan sanctions received by local authorities were in two parts: one the approval of the sanctioning authority, and the other the approval of the Treasury. This laborious system was brought to an end under the 'deal' made in the discussion preceding the 1963 White Paper, with a Treasury promise to issue a 'General Consent'. The first version of the General Consent was subsequently issued to come into operation on 1 April 1964; it started well by saying:

> The Treasury, in the exercise of their powers under the Control of Borrowing Order, hereby give general consent for the purposes of that Order (subject to the exceptions and conditions hereinafter contained) to the borrowing of any money, or the issue of any securities, by a local authority, as defined in that Order.

The problem lay in the exceptions. By this date general powers for the issue of bonds had been given by the Local Government (Financial Provision) Act 1963 (see p. 193).

The General Consent excluded bonds issued at a discount exceeding ¼ per cent for each year of issue (the Bank of England had already imposed a similar restriction on stock issues requiring their approval), or bonds raised in a single operation of £1 million or more, unless the timing and terms of the issue had been approved by the Bank of England. (This was an early attempt to differentiate the 'quoted' bond.) Stock issues were similarly restricted by the Consent, together with borrowing (under private Act) by money bills (which the Treasury made clear would not in any event receive approval). Consent was then given to temporary borrowing, only if it came within the 15 and 20 per cent rules already described, such borrowing being defined as 'Borrowing for capital purposes of any money repayable in less than twelve calendar months'. The provision to facilitate the use of escalator mortgages was also included. Thus the Treasury were able to introduce a control over short-term borrowing without specific statutory action, and without indeed any reference to Parliament because the General Consent did not require to be laid before the House, except to the extent that it had been mentioned in the White Paper. The definitions made clear that the restriction on temporary money included bank overdrafts.

As will be shown, considerable problems of definition arose when unexpectedly the 'negotiable bond' was derived from the simpler local authority bond. An amended General Consent coming into operation on 1 February 1968 attempted to clarify this point, by referring to 'negotiable' bonds as those which the Stock Exchange or a discount house were to handle. The Consent also extended the transitional period for the reduction of temporary debt by those authorities in excess of the new maxima – a step towards simplification – and withdrew the need to obtain Treasury consent for borrowing for schemes under a local Act where departmental approval had been received. Internal funds were also excluded from the definition of temporary money. An interesting point was that the Consent also at this stage needed to make clear that the practice of some treasurers of issuing ordinary bonds, which did not need sanction, and later converting these to quoted bonds, thus bypassing the system, was unacceptable.

A third General Consent was issued to operate from 1 April 1974 to take account of the passing of the Local Government Act 1972. The main amendment was to make clear that local authority bills for which a general power was given in the 1972 Act were excluded from the General Consent just as the earlier Consent had excluded local Act bills. The information was also spread verbally that neither would specific consent be given, so that local authority bills were thought to be totally withdrawn. As we shall see, 'revenue' bills escaped the axe. Thus the powers given in the 1933 Act were restricted by these actions under the Control of Borrowing Order, and continue to be so restricted after the 1972 Act.

In the period after the war and up to 1972 several other useful, even important, developments in local authority borrowing law and practice occurred. The Local Government (Miscellaneous Provisions) Act 1953 not only dealt with such mundane subjects as the building of bus shelters and the improvement of arrangements for the emptying of dustbins, but had other important provisions allowing local authorities to establish certain special funds on the lines already obtained by many local authorities under local Acts. These were repairs and renewals funds, and more important for us, capital funds. Capital funds are dealt with more fully in Chapter 22, but briefly, a capital fund is a fund which a local authority may set up and into which it may pay certain surplus moneys or make regular contributions, and from which it can finance its own capital expenditure as 'free' advances to borrowing accounts, or on the basis that the borrowing account pays back the principal either with or without interest as for an ordinary advance from a consolidated loans fund. Although a capital fund can be somewhat burdensome to ratepayers, in that capital expenditure is financed in the first instance from money which could alternatively be used for the direct benefit of ratepayers, over the course of time a capital fund may accumulate to such an extent that outside borrowing is substantially reduced, and could theoretically be unnecessary. Capital funds have not been as widely developed as they might have been, partly because of other pressures on rate levies. Nevertheless, the provision was a useful recognition of the need to minimize open-market borrowing. Repairs and Renewals Funds, whose purpose is self-explanatory, have as an 'internal fund' also had some part to play in minimizing external borrowing.

A much more important event in this period was the Local Government (Financial Provisions) Act 1963. This was very much a collection of miscellaneous financial provisions, but for the purposes of this book, its principal achievement was the inclusion of a general and improved power for local authorities to borrow by means of the issue of bonds. This situation is developed more fully in Chapter 20 but the occurrence of this power, at this time, is of some significance. In the 1950s the Manchester Treasurer's Office had produced a new form of simplified mortgage with the variable data in a schedule at the foot instead of in the body of the document, a printed seal and signatures. During this process the idea of constructing an 'ideal borrowing instrument' was conceived. All existing forms of borrowing instrument (including private Act bonds) were analysed and compared and a new instrument (which was given the name of bond) was produced by selecting the 'best' provisions from the various other forms of instrument. Local Act powers were obtained for this instrument, although during the drafting of the clauses Treasury pressure removed several of the improvements, as later will be described. However, this possibility was raised by Manchester at the time when the White Paper on Control of Local Authority Borrowing was being drafted following the discussions of the joint Treasury and local finance officers group. Part of the understanding of the White Paper was that in exchange for accepting the controls of temporary borrowing some loosening up of local authority borrowing facilities would be encouraged. The introduction of the improved and simplified bond was just such a measure and was taken up with some enthusiasm by the Treasury, though in a more constricted form than was wished by the local authorities. Indeed so great was the Treasury's enthusiasm for this bond that in order to find room for the Bill in the legislative programme, a Member of Parliament was persuaded to adopt the proposal as a Private Member's Bill.

The revision of the concept of 'temporary' borrowing, and the coming of age of the bond in its general and quoted forms clearly can be seen to have been steps forward in local authority borrowing techniques of considerable significance. There is also no doubt that enthusiasm for these forms of borrowing at the short end of the maturity scale was greatly stimulated by the perceived high levels of interest rates ruling at this period, fluctuating between 10 and 15 per cent for almost any period of loan. Naturally treasurers sought to avoid long-term commitments at these levels, hence the enthusiasm for the under-one-year loans and the inevitable Treasury concern to restrict this dangerous and volatile area. The restrictions while accepted as reasonable by the majority of local authority treasurers, nevertheless simply had the effect of lifting the maturity periods over the one-year minimum but not excessively so. The result was that after the quota of temporary borrowing had been achieved, many treasurers sought to borrow in the one- to five-year area, and towards the shorter end of even this period. One of the effects of this was that at any one time there were substantial quantities of money borrowed at maturities just longer than those specified in the temporary loan restrictions, which with the efflux of time had reached a point less than one year from maturity. Gradually over the next decade this led to Treasury determination to institute further controls on the maturity periods above that applicable to temporary loans. The restrictions on temporary borrowing turned out to be only stage one in the Treasury's control of the maturity pattern of local authority borrowing. However, before stage two took place, a drastic reorganization of local authority areas was to be introduced, in measures which also included considerable improvements in the borrowing code.

STAMP DUTY   Yet another useful and indeed quite important development in this period was the abolition of stamp duty on local authority borrowing transactions. Local authorities were prior to 1967 entangled in a dual code of duty under the Stamp Acts and the Finance Acts (for loan capital duty).

Stamp duty is an ancient form of fiscal revenue upon documents of many kinds either at a flat rate or sometimes *ad valorem*. Its application to documents embraces various borrowing instruments including those of local authorities. The principal operative Act is the Stamp Act 1891, but there were many before this consolidating measure – for instance, the Stamp Act 1804, which even at this early date simply 'revised' the duties on 'stamped vellum, parchment and paper in Great Britain'. In the extensive schedules to both Acts, bonds, bills of exchange and promissory notes appear along with a great many non-financial documents.

Local authority loans were also dealt with rather more comprehensively under the Finance Act 1899 (section 8), which is thought to have been an attempt to cover instruments which might have squeezed their way past the Stamp Act. Incidentally, while a clause in this Act exempts those instruments which have already paid duty under the Stamp Act, there is no reciprocal provision. This was one of the problems created by the dual system, although the Inland Revenue have always taken a reasonable view, provided that duty of one sort or another has been paid. The rates of charge are similar, but not completely identical, under the two Acts. For example, the basic rate for both types of duty was 2s 6d% and this applied also under the Stamp Acts when a loan became due for repayment and was replaced. However, where local capital duty had been paid on a maturing stock issue, the duty on replacement borrowing was reduced to 6d, if this replacement could be proved specifically. The payment of stamp duty was usually acknowledged by an embossed stamp added to the document (by the Stamp Office of the Inland Revenue), whereas loan capital duty was normally payable (principally on stock) in a lump sum before the stock was issued.

Many problems arose in the course of time, the most extraordinary one coming from a court ruling known colloquially as the 'Dead Horse' case. While duty was paid on stock on issue, the duty on transfer (which by custom was paid by the local authority borrower) was paid either when the transfer arose or by 'compounding', whereby the local authority paid a much-reduced duty on the whole of the stock on issue at each half-year. Treasurers were forced to speculate as to which was the cheaper way. Stock being a marketable security was liable to change hands a good deal immediately after issue, but transfers tended to decline substantially thereafter until the stock neared its maturity date, at which stage it became a useful short-term investment in the money market. The problems of speculating as to which would be the cheaper way to bear duty were accentuated in the early 1950s by the repercussions arising from estate duty law of the 'Dead Horse' case. At that time gifts *inter vivos* were liable for estate duty, if the donor died within seven years of the bestowing of the gift. A case occurred in which a racehorse had been 'gifted' but died between the date of the gift and that of the death of the donor. On the death of the donor the courts held that the gift was not liable to estate duty because the asset had 'expired' (as well as the donor). By an extraordinary ruling this principle was applied to stock transferred by gift the maturity of which took place before the death of the donor and thus held to have 'expired'. Gifts in the form of short-dated stock therefore became popular as a means of avoiding estate duty, and the transfer duty involved (£1 per cent) cost local authorities a good deal of money. Their only alternative was to begin to buy-in their own stock, as it began to reach maturity date, to forestall late transfers.

Another practical stamp duty problem may be illustrated by reference to the issue of temporary loan receipts. In the 1960s and 1970s treasurers were unsure whether these should be stamped as 'receipts' at 2d or as agreements at 6d. The Inland Revenue, when asked by the Treasurers' Institute for a ruling on this point, suggested that the query should not be pressed because of the danger that the receipts might be found to be 'debentures' and liable for full *ad valorem* duty under the Stamp Act, although the 1899 Act excluded from loan capital duty a 'loan raised for a merely temporary purpose not exceeding 12 months'. Treasurers therefore adopted a rule-of-thumb that if in ordinary receipt form, these should bear 2d duty, but that if an undertaking was added to the receipt to exchange it for a mortgage at the request of the lender (as explained earlier), it became an 'agreement' on which a 6d stamp was appropriate. This was not invariably followed, and the Inland Revenue themselves never pressed the issue. However, there is now clear evidence that this point was established shortly after the Local Authorities (Financial Provisions) Act 1921 had first given local authorities tentative powers to borrow temporarily. Writing in 1924, J. H. Burton in his *Loans and Borrowing Powers of Local Authorities* describes this as the accepted principle – 6d stamp if a promise to issue a mortgage on request was incorporated in the receipt, 2d if not – though whether this understanding had official blessing at the time is not known. Burton also establishes that even at that date the term 'deposit loans' was in general use. These were of course relatively minor issues but illustrate some of the many practical problems which arose in this area (see my article examining the situation in *Local Government Finance*, September 1964, p. 314).

The difficulty was finally resolved in two stages. To eliminate the delay in the issue of mortgages by the necessity to submit them to the Stamp Office for the embossing of the duty stamp, under proposals pressed by the local authorities, the Finance Act 1963 provided that *ad valorem* stamps need not be embossed on the instruments, but that instead treasurers might account periodically to the Stamp Office by certificate for the volume of loans they had taken. A declaration was printed on the documents under this system to certify that stamp duty had been or would be paid. This much speeded the issue of loan instruments. This point is specifically mentioned in the 1963 White Paper as one of the means of simplifying local authority borrowing practice arising out of the discussions on the restriction of temporary borrowing. However, the major development was in 1967, when under the Finance Act of that year both *ad valorem* stamp duty and loan capital duty on local authority borrowings were abolished. Even then a minor misunderstanding arose. The exemption was thought by treasurers not to apply to temporary loan receipts as these were marginally not 'true' borrowing instruments. However, the Inland Revenue took the view that such receipts did indeed come within the exemption. Thus for the second time the Stamp Office evinced a helpful attitude towards local authorities and their temporary borrowing. The operation of the Stamp Acts was an extremely complicated (and expensive) matter, so that local authorities were delighted by this exemption.

NOTES: CHAPTER 13

1 Sir James Lythgoe, then City Treasurer of Manchester and financial adviser to the Association of Municipal Corporations, was largely instrumental in obtaining this concession.
2 Brokers, scriveners and drivers of bargains are referred to as early as 1571 in Elizabeth's Act Against Usury (13 Eliz. I, c. 8) and again, with the 'brocage' they may earn, in 1623 (21 Jac. I, c. 17) – 5s per cent for 1 year or 12d for renewing a bond or bill; this mention also indicates the early use of these instruments.
3 Holland (GLC), Chisholm (Cheshire County), Esslemont (Glasgow), and the author (Manchester).

Chapter 14

THE FURTHER REORGANIZATION

After several near-starts in the 1960s, the reorganization of local government in the United Kingdom on to the system at present (1984) operating finally took place in England and Wales under the Local Government Act 1972; in Scotland under the Local Government (Scotland) Act 1973; and in Northern Ireland under the Local Government Act 1972 (Northern Ireland). London's government had already been reconstituted under the London Government Act 1963. These statutes produced the present system of counties and districts (plus parish and community councils), regions and districts and three all-purpose Island Areas in Scotland, and districts directly under a central authority in Northern Ireland. London was organized under the Greater London Council (GLC) into a series of amalgamated London boroughs, and the City of London. In Scotland the reorganization of the financial base, including borrowing, did not take place until the passing of the Local Government (Scotland) Act 1975; there are grounds for the belief that the financial sections of the English Act were intended to be treated in a separate statute, but in the event the financial clauses were somewhat hastily included in the main Bill without full discussion.[1]

This last-minute change of intention may explain why the borrowing provisions of the 1972 Act, although they contain important developments and certainly make a brave attempt to set out a really comprehensive borrowing code, have certain disappointing features. Their shortcoming is that while they do bring together for the first time the many and varied earlier provisions, these have not been logically assimilated; they do not take into account the interaction of the evolutionary changes, and consequently do not altogether produce a modern or coherent pattern of the necessary facilities. In summary, the 1972 Act borrowing provisions show a lack of fundamental analysis of purpose in a present-day context.

The pattern began with section 172, which said that: 'Part 1 of Schedule 13 to this Act shall have effect with respect to the powers of local authorities to borrow and lend money and with respect to their funds.' This part of this schedule might therefore be thought to be the complete operative code for local authority borrowing. However, the facilities it contains were, and continue to be, sharply affected by subsequent regulations, by the Control of Borrowing Order and a number of administrative decisions made by the Treasury and the Bank of England.

The schedule begins with a curiously misleading section giving principal councils power to borrow in order to lend to other local authorities. This is immediately recognizable as the earlier power given to county councils to lend to district councils and parishes, which according to Ministry officials is the kind of facility still intended. However, this wording can be read more widely, and some few authorities (with good names) are known (through the London money market) to have used the power more broadly simply to borrow money for lending-on, when the treasurer of the authority considered that marginal profit could be made in this way – a somewhat risky attitude and hardly a proper function for a local authority.

The general power to borrow next given in the Act represents a substantial simplification and rewording of the 1933 Act. Excluding the GLC (which obtains its borrowing authority in an annual Money Bill), local authorities may 'borrow money for any purpose or class of purposes approved by the Secretary of State and in accordance with any conditions subject to which the approval is given'. This replaces the earlier list of functions, such as purchase of land, erection of buildings, and so on, of the 1933 Act. This is also less categoric, in that the 1933 Act referred more specifically to 'the consent of a sanctioning authority' before money could be borrowed for any of the listed activities. The new section is still taken to mean that sanctions for *schemes* were required, although the section actually says that it is *purposes*, in a general sense, which need approval. In fact shortly after the coming into operation of the Act, the Minister adopted a method of sanctioning borrowing less restrictive in detail, which will shortly be discussed.

The methods by which borrowing might take place were then listed. Naturally they included the use of mortgages, the issue of stock, and from the Public Works Loan Commission (PWLC). The issue of bonds and bills was now added to incorporate the bond provisions of the 1963 Act and, at last, the bill-issuing powers obtained by many authorities under private legislation. Power to borrow by the issue of debentures or annuity certificates under the Local Loans Act 1875 was repeated. While debentures and annuities are not at present used, presumably circumstances might arise where this power might be useful. However, there must surely have been a better way of covering this point than by reference back to a century-old statute which had never at any time been popular. The list also included 'any other approved means'. A local authority might also borrow by any of these means 'outside the United Kingdom and in a foreign currency', a useful provision which recognized that a number of large authorities had in recent years obtained this power by local Act. Later still in the schedule power is given to a local authority to 'issue bonds transferable by delivery (with or without endorsement) and other securities so transferable', with consent and subject to conditions. This again was a recognition of local Act powers (although bearer document powers also exist for debentures in the 1875 Act). The Treasury have since made clear that they have no intention at present of giving consent to the issue of bearer instruments by local authorities.

Much later in the schedule local authorities are given power to borrow 'by way of temporary loan or overdraft from a bank, or otherwise any sum which they may temporarily require' pending either the receipt of revenue or 'the raising of a loan which they are authorised to raise'. This continued misconception of the modern function of short-term capital borrowing is compounded by a paragraph which reminds authorities that amortization must start from the date of the temporary loan, even when it is replaced by a later loan.

The same approach appeared in the Northern Ireland Act, but there was no such outmoded misconception in the Scottish legislation. There temporary borrowing was authorized in anticipation of receivable revenue, or 'for the purpose of the raising of a loan in the exercise of any statutory borrowing power'. This, a repetition of the 1947 Act provisions, and which might have been a guide for the draftsmen of the English Act, was a proper recognition of the fact that, particularly against the background of consolidated loans funds, borrowing is nevertheless 'borrowing', whether it is for one week, one year or twenty years.

But while the Scottish Act may be thought to be superior to its English counterpart in this respect, it is subject to the criticism that having gone thus far, it fails to recognize that there was then no need to make any mention, in relation to capital expenditure, of temporary borrowing as this is no different, however short the period, from any other form of borrowing. The case will be argued here that particularly since the abolition of stamp duty, and the White Paper of 1963, there is no reason to suppose that a loan with an initial period of less than one year needs a special instrument. This simple concept has taken a long time to emerge and is far from having received general acceptance. The term 'deposit receipt' has now been dropped from the Scottish provisions but is still to be found in the Northern Ireland Act.

One undoubted improvement in the English law (already applicable in Scotland) was that temporary borrowing and overdrafts were now given the same security as other forms of borrowing, and with equal ranking. In future all borrowing was to be 'charged indifferently on all the revenues of the authority' and to 'rank equally without any priority'. The terms of the Scottish Act, deriving from the earlier statute, were even more categoric; in Scotland all money borrowed is 'secured upon the whole funds, rates and revenues of the authority and not otherwise' and has 'the same charge and security and shall rank *pari passu*'. Presumably both sets of expressions mean the same thing?

The Scottish Act again made interest and dividends a first charge on the same security as that on which the principal rests. There was no similar provision or indeed any reference to the security of interest in the English 1972 Act, but there a clause was inserted in the Local Government Finance Act 1982 to the effect that the references in the 1972 Act to money borrowed by a local authority being chargeable on all the revenues 'includes reference to the interest for the time being payable in respect of that money'. This certainly removes any doubt and gives 'interest' the same security as 'principal', but it is less dramatic than the 'first charge' given in Scotland.

Some restrictions on the basic borrowing provisions occur in schedule 13. In the first place, the use of mortgages, bonds and stock is subject to regulations (which have since been made and are examined in the sections dealing with those instruments); the use of 12 months' bills is also restricted to those authorities with a rate intake of not less than £3 million (a very low limit in modern times); and issues are in any event, whether for capital or revenue, restricted to one-fifth of retained rate income, that is, after parting with precepted amounts. A number of more severe controls are at present applied to borrowing under the Control of Borrowing Order and by administrative action by the Treasury and the Bank of England. These will be examined in detail in Chapter 25 dealing with a rationalized borrowing code.

A shortcoming of the English Act is that it makes no provision for the possible appointment of a receiver, while the Scottish Act does ('judicial factor'). Anecdotal evidence is that the receivership provisions were omitted from the 1972 Act as the Ministry officers at the time – with a good deal of justice – considered them to be of no significance. However, in response to pressure by money brokers who had first-hand experience of the responses – however irrational – of institutional lenders, the provision for a receiver was inserted in the subsequent regulations for mortgages and stocks and bonds. Thus while the provision applies in Scotland to all borrowing, it now only applies in England and Wales to methods of borrowing covered by regulations – which does not include bills or the important 'temporary' borrowing area.

Both Acts re-enacted the provisions permitting the establishment of capital and repairs and renewals funds. More important, the Scottish Act repeated the detailed requirement that all loans are to be handled through a loans fund. The English Act, while quietly dropping the provisions for repayment included in the 1933 Act (annuity or sinking fund methods), provided in a brief clause that a local authority might establish and operate a loans fund for defraying capital expenditure and the repayment or redemption of debt. Surprisingly, each local authority is left to design its own scheme for such a fund. Perhaps but for the haste in which this schedule was put together, a detailed scheme would also have been incorporated in the English Act. Nevertheless, the Stocks and Bonds Regulations *require* that any authority borrowing by these methods must establish a loans fund. This is without doubt a consequence of the old provision in local Acts that authorities given power to issue stock should use a 'consolidated loans fund', which was in fact consolidated only in so far as it incorporated all stock borrowings. The insistence on a loans fund does not appear in the mortgage regulations, but local authorities have now little excuse for not using a loans fund – not that, for the most part, they would wish to avoid this most useful technique.

The helpful provisions of the Local Government (Financial Provisions) Act 1963 that not only redemption provisions might be suspended for up to five years for revenue-producing undertakings, but that interest on these borrowings might be met from further borrowings for this type of loan, were extended by the 1972 Act. This later Act also gave the Minister a general power to specify any land which could be so included in this arrangement, and to increase the deferment to ten or even more years. This was to enable longer-term projects such as city centre redevelopments to be included. In fact the Community Land Act 1975, under which land was expected to be purchased for resale, gave power for the complete suspension of repayment provisions in the expectation that income from sales would ultimately discharge outgoings. This Act was completely repealed in 1980, but these powers were re-inserted in the Act of that year. Finally, the 1972 Act repeated the standard provision that a lender was excused from the need to satisfy himself that money was properly borrowed and applied.

The overriding impression created by the borrowing provisions of both the English and Scottish Acts, more particularly the former, is that the provisions were 'patched together' rather than having been re-thought out and restructured to meet the changing attitudes of an actively developing market. The concept yet to be examined here, in the context of suggestions for a rationalized borrowing code, is that since, for example, mortgages, bonds, temporary loan receipts and even the neglected debenture have the same security and ranking, they are in fact *the same thing* whatever name is attached to them, and that differences of title, significant in the commercial world where they would indicate different rights and an order of priority, in the local government context are meaningless. Certainly, the English Act borrowing provisions are constructed in a clumsy and meandering manner. The important provisions for the creation of a loans fund occupy five lines in the schedule, while the clauses relating to the deferment of amortization on revenue-producing schemes – not a provision which will be widely used – occupy almost two pages. The development of borrowing provisions is seen to have been painfully slow over almost two centuries; there is clearly a real need for a standard and rationalized code and one which in spite of nationality difficulties could apply equally in England and Wales and Scotland, where the purposes and objectives of the exercise are precisely the same. The spirit of standardization and rationalization which gave rise to the Clauses Acts and even the unlamented Local Loans Act needs to be revived.

Apart from the improved borrowing provisions of the Acts bringing about reorganization in the period between 1970 and 1984 – at which point this book ends – four significant 'movements' relating to local authority capital finance can be identified. These are: changes in the method of central control of capital expenditure, further pressures to lengthen the maturity pattern of debt portfolios, significant changes in market practice and the reintroduction of the Public Works Loan Commission (PWLC) as the major supplier of local authorities' capital funds. What can now be clearly recognized is that the changes in control of capital expenditure – loan sanctioning – had their roots in the White Paper discussions on the control of temporary borrowing and that the recently evolved 'maturity code' is in fact not a new concept, but simply a second stage in the central government's determination to lengthen the maturity pattern of local authority borrowing.

CAPITAL EXPENDITURE CONTROLS   The 1963 White Paper promised, as part of the *quid pro quo* for the acceptance by the local authorities of restrictions on temporary borrowing, that 'impediments to the adoption of modern lending and borrowing techniques should be removed'. One of the matters which the local authority representatives had pressed for during the discussions was the removal or at least the thoroughgoing simplification of the need for specific loan sanction for every proposal for capital expenditure. Part of the improvement promised in the White Paper was that PWLC loans should not henceforth be tied to loan approvals, and this change was later brought into effect. At the same time the White Paper argued that loan sanctions could not be completely abolished, but that their operation would be reconsidered and improvements introduced. Changes were indeed made after a considerable delay but were of a limited nature. It was not until 1980 that the system was radically amended and then in a way which moved substantially away from detailed control but increased overall control.

The problem with the loan sanction system was not only that it placed a restriction on the freedom of local authorities to determine the amount and direction of their capital investment, but that over the course of time the underlying functions of the sanctioning system had been extended in ways not originally envisaged when loan sanction procedure was first incorporated in statutes. The three purposes which Whitehall claimed for the loan sanctioning procedure were clearly set out in the first circular dealing with the revised system, which is described on p. 197. These three functions are given as 'regulating the total level of capital expenditure, ensuring that individual projects meet the standards set by the departments and monitoring the overall level of local authority borrowing on the market'. The first and third of these reasons must be unexceptional, as measures of national economic control, but the second purpose is open to question. Using the procedure as a tool of financial management is one thing; using it as a means of non-parliamentary departmental application of policy is another. A typical example of a decision which lay partly between policy and triviality (for which documentary evidence cannot now be produced) related to the use of turnstiles in ladies' conveniences, because of the problems caused thereby for pregnant women. The Ministry, partly in response to public pressure, adopted a policy of refusing loan sanction to any scheme for public convenience loan expenditure which incorporated turnstiles. This was no doubt a commendable decision, but the implementation of such a policy of social concern by manipulation of a financial loan sanction procedure was questionable. The larger authorities who built conveniences as a revenue charge could bypass this control.

A rather more understandable use of local sanction procedure was in control of overall costs through the institution of what came to be known as 'yardsticks'. Under this system loan sanctioning for schools would not be granted, if the estimated cost per place to be provided exceeded figures established by the central department (usually in consultation with local authority representatives). The area of playing-fields was also centrally determined on the basis of number of pupils at the school. Similarly, extensive use of yardsticks was made in the control of the heavy capital cost of house construction. Housing was another service where central department ideas of what was and what was not 'proper' provision in municipal housing determined what loan sanctions could be given. For example, in the early 1960s when substantial efforts were being made to hold down the rapidly increasing cost of house construction, a bitter conflict arose between the Ministry of Housing (as it then was) and the Manchester City Council on whether living rooms should be 8 ft high (as Manchester wished) or 7 ft 6 in high (according to a new Ministry policy). Loan sanctions were not forthcoming until Manchester had accepted the central decision. Clearly, a conflict of this kind falls midway between the imposition of a social standard and an effort to restrain expenditure on a costly service. The government was of course a substantial contributor to housing costs.

An older example of loan sanction conflict was the now legendary case of the reconstruction of Waterloo Bridge when Mr Herbert Morrison was leader of the London County Council (LCC). The Ministry of Transport on economic grounds refused loan sanctioning for this project; thereupon the LCC expressed a determination to proceed with the scheme as a rate charge, even though government grant would be lost by doing so. Eventually the Ministry agreed to give loan sanction and also paid substantial grant.

Another problem which arose out of loan sanctioning but which was never officially published was encountered by local authorities in their daily contacts with the departments. This concerned the annual internal Treasury decision as to the total amount of local authority capital investment to be authorized through loan sanctions. This sum was allocated by the Treasury among the government departments responsible for various aspects of the work of local government, and departmental loan sanctions were consequently restricted to these totals. This meant that decisions about the priority of needs of a particular local authority area were on numerous occasions taken from the hands of the local authority on the ground that the total of sanctions available in the year for, say, old people's homes, had been exhausted. Often at the same time the local authority might be informed that while sanction for an old people's home had been 'deferred', sanctions were available for, say, police stations, or – a common occurrence – for roadworks, if these could be started before the end of the financial year. This led to an imbalance of local authority investment as against the priority of needs which the local council saw for its current problems.

The point of view was sometimes advanced that Whitehall's nationwide experience was thus placed at the service of the local authorities. The local authority standard answer was that Whitehall did not appreciate the local problems and priorities which were the especial duty of local government, and that the mistakes which local authorities from time to time might make were no more serious than those made by Whitehall in its imposition of national solutions.

From the government's point of view there was another fundamental weakness in the loan sanction system, particularly in the light of its desire in recent years to control the money supply and the public sector borrowing requirement. This was that a sanction once given did not necessarily mean that all, or any, of the money would be spent in the financial year in which it was given. The expenditure under some large loan sanction schemes might well be spread over two, three, or more years. When Whitehall finally took a completely new look at the system, 'cash limits' had become the basis of much control of public service spending, and a system on this basis was statutorily applied under the Local Government Planning and Land Act 1980. However, the initial and interim scheme must first be described.

Although the White Paper made reference to the matter in 1963, the first step was not taken until 1970 (Department of Environment Circular 2/70, with a similar circular issued by the Welsh Office). Under this circular capital schemes were divided into three groups – key sector, locally determined schemes (LDSs) and an intermediate group covering land for education, principal roads and housing. No changes were made ('or envisaged') in the system of individual sanctioning of key sector schemes, which were also to some extent involved in three- or five-year 'rolling programmes' introduced to enable central departments and local authorities to operate a degree of forward planning. As the key sector services included were education, personal health and social services, child care, housing, water, sewerage and sewage disposal, principal roads, police, major transport infrastructure schemes, urban programmes and some minor items, they constituted, then, about 90 per cent of local authority capital development. The intermediate group covering land for education, roads and housing was treated separately and being for longer-term land purchase did not count against total allocations of available sanctions. The remainder, the minor locally determined schemes, were to be controlled on the basis of 'an annual block allocation of capital payments' – which in the event proved low and hence restrictive. This type of overall block sanctioning was, in effect, what the local authorities had been seeking for all capital expenditure in the belief, perhaps, that this could be simply administered. The problem was of course that the needs of different authorities were substantially different, depending upon their enthusiasm and the extent and nature of their local problems. However, some provision was made for transfer of surplus allocations between authorities in the same county, and there was overall a 'large projects' reserve kept in hand, in Whitehall, under which authorities could apply for a special allocation for any major 'one-off' scheme outside the normal scope of their annual capital outlay. Subsequent circulars clarified the many detailed points which could be expected to arise under such a change of system. It endured for some ten years and was replaced by the much more thoroughgoing system, with a completely new approach, introduced by the 1980 Act. However, the key services system, described above, already operating by the time the 1972 Act was passed, explains why that Act no longer referred to specific lists of activities – land, buildings, and so on – but dealt in general terms with 'purposes' which the Minister might approve. Thus the 1972 Act confirmed the wider approach which had already been instituted but was inadequate for the subsequent recasting of the system of central approval of local authority capital expenditure.

The more fundamental change in the system, in 1980, really went back in motivation to the views of the Plowden Committee of 1961 (Cmnd 1432) on the control of public expenditure, the consequent National Economic Development Council (NEDC) and the Public Expenditure Survey Committee (PESC). The Act introducing this change was the Local Government, Planning and Land Act 1980, a substantial measure covering a wide range of provisions, some trivial, others fundamental. The opening words of the preamble no doubt caused the local authorities some cynical amusement: 'An Act to relax controls over local and certain other authorities.' There is a sad but firmly held view among many senior local government officials that the words 'relaxation of control' usually mean no more than a shifting (accompanied by a tightening) of the grip. Certainly, there was a lengthy series of matters on which central control was withdrawn or relaxed, but these involved relatively trifling issues which had accumulated over the years, such as the need for central approval of various charges which local authorities might make, and the levels of interest which they might charge in certain circumstances – a very mixed collection indeed of matters on which the need for central approval in the first place was difficult to understand. The importance of these de-restrictions (while much welcomed) was far outweighed by the significance of the restructuring of financial controls.

The financial provisions of the Act are described in the preamble as 'to make further provision with respect to rates and to grants to local authorities and other persons and for controlling the expenditure of local authorities'. These include measures to control the operation of direct works departments; the abolition of the (theoretical) quinquennial re-valuations for rating; dates for revaluation to be in future on the Minister's decision; and an entirely new, wider approach to the control of expenditure on work of a capital nature *whether met from borrowed money or otherwise*. A circular from the Department of Health and Social Security issued while the Act was still going forward as a Bill (LASSL (80)5; several departments issued similar 'guides') said that 'The bill seeks to strengthen the overall control of local authority capital expenditure while giving local authorities greater freedom to determine their own priorities' – an acceptable objective in its simple terms, but one for which the detail proved very complex.

The new capital controls were an extension of the movement already under way towards the imposition of annual cash limits for local government revenue spending, linked with the amounts which the government intended to contribute in grants. Some steps had also been taken in earlier years to impose cash limits for housing and transport capital expenditure. Under the new system the Minister was given power to fix allocations for each local authority not of total annual loan sanction, but of cash disbursements on work of a defined capital nature whether met from borrowed money, internal funds, or revenue. The statute is too recent for a considered assessment of its likelihood of success to be made, but the intentions of the Act can be summarized, and there is sufficient data to indicate the way in which the central departments are bringing the new controls into effect.

The Minister is now required to inform local authorities each year of what they may spend in the way of 'prescribed expenditure', that is, in capital investment on types of work broadly similar to those previously listed in earlier Acts as requiring loan sanction, if financed from borrowed money – purchase of land, erection of buildings, plant, equipment, and so on. These allocations are, in practice, based on 'bids' by each local authority. Local authorities are expected to keep their expenditure within the limits then prescribed for this work, subject to a 10 per cent margin, which if used is to be deducted from the approved expenditure for the next year. Spending beyond these limits is virtually declared to be *ultra vires*, even though the purpose of the expenditure has been approved by statute. In practice, many local authorities meet a good deal of expenditure of a capital, or marginally capital, nature from revenue, capital funds, or capital receipts (disposal of capital assets). All expenditure from such moneys is now brought within the annual allocation, with the exception of capital items costing less than £5,000. Provision is made for major works of a national or regional significance, or of a sufficiently exceptional scale, to be dealt with outside the allocation with the Minister's approval. There is also some provision for the use of surpluses from trading activities to be utilized for capital purposes outside the allocation. The complete definition of included and excluded expenditure is quite complex, particularly during the transitional period.

Timing and control of capital works to within 10 per cent of anticipated annual expenditure, particularly when decisions have to be made several months before the beginning of the financial year, is bound to be difficult when weather, availability of materials, labour and other problems, unexpected ground conditions, and so on, may cause complete disruption of programmes.

Department of the Environment Circular 14/81 disclosed that the former system of key/intermediate/locally determined schemes was completely withdrawn and that the new allocations were to be given under five headings: housing, education, transport, personal social services and 'other'. Home Office controlled expenditure on police, probation service and after-care, and magistrates courts was excluded from the new system and will remain under separate sanction procedures.

Local authority treasurers (in a memorandum issued by the Chartered Institute of Public Finance and Accountancy) were willing with some misgivings to accept the new basis of annual cash limits, but emphasized the need for an understanding by Whitehall of the problems involved. They would also have preferred a single allocation rather than five, even though virement may be permitted. What treasurers find particularly difficult to accept is the necessity to include capital ex-revenue expenditure within the allocation, particularly as the government is also imposing strict limits on revenue expenditure.

Because of the stern words issued against the overspending of capital allocations, local authorities have so far tended to err on the side of caution, and first results indicate quite appreciable underspending of the allocations, with the result that the Minister has already criticized them for adding to the nation's economic difficulties by a shortfall in their capital investment. But the shortfall has also been caused by the awareness of local treasurers of the old adage that 'the capital expenditure of today is the revenue expenditure of tomorrow', and as they are being pressed very heavily indeed to reduce revenue expenditure, they are loath to add to their own problems by overenthusiastic capital expenditure, from which the revenue consequences will speedily ensue. The Minister seems to hold the view that local authorities should spend their full capital allocations by selecting types of expenditure which have minimal repercussions on later revenue costs whether or not any such schemes which may be devised locally have any right to priority.

Local authorities have certainly been given what they were seeking a decade or more earlier – overall capital approvals leaving them with wide internal discretion – but the giving of these in the form of rigid annual cash limits and the tying-in of revenue expenditure on work of a capital nature is something they did not bargain for. The next few years will no doubt require a good deal of give and take on both sides, if the new system is to be made to work.

MATURITY CONTROL   The restrictions on borrowing introduced in 1963, with an initial maturity period of less than one year, and which were intended to be brought into operation over a four-year period, took somewhat longer. This was partly because of the reluctance of treasurers to borrow for lengthy periods at the prevailing high interest rates, and partly because the government was not anxious at that time to progress too rapidly with the reopening of the PWLC to the local authorities. Several other factors were at work. First, those highly prudent local authorities, who had always kept their temporary borrowings at a low level, now regarded the new agreement as some sort of official sanction that a 20 per cent level was not unreasonable or risky and began to increase their temporary borrowing towards the limit, though usually still leaving themselves a margin for emergencies. The second factor was that the sources of supply, particularly banks, and more particularly still, foreign banks in London, which had responded to the demand by local authorities for very short loans were often not in the business of lending for longer periods, even with the attraction of high interest rates.

The high interest rates and the reluctance of lenders to 'go long' had the result that, while local authorities gradually accepted and adhered to the 'temporary' borrowing restrictions, their borrowings outside the area of control were only marginally on the right side of the one-year dividing-line. The reopening of the PWLC to the local authorities was with a ten-year minimum period, so that local authorities continued to judge it wise to offset these long-term and fairly expensive loans with loans as short as they could obtain without contravening the restrictions. One-, two- and three-year loans therefore became popular. In particular, such devices as became known as 'eleven plus one' – that is, loans for eleven months and thereafter running subject to one month's notice, a minimum of exactly one year – were attractive to both sides. Obviously on the day after they were taken out such loans immediately assumed a maturity period of less than one year, although they did not count as 'temporary' loans under the formula because their initial borrowing period had been for a minimum of a full year. Also the greater part of PWLC borrowing was subject to repayment on the annuity principle – that is, an instalment each year – so that even a ten-year PWLC loan necessitated some repayment each year.

Another feature was that the new bond, in its negotiable form, was considered by the market to be desirable one-year 'negotiable paper', and indeed the market adopted the name of 'yearling bond' for it (still used later even for bonds covering longer periods). Although the Bank of England firmly held down the volume of negotiable bonds which a local authority could issue, their use added to the quantity of very short maturities technically outside the 'temporary' restrictions.

The Treasury and the Bank of England became increasingly concerned at the amount of money which at any one time, despite the formula, fell for repayment within a year or in the relatively near future. The central authorities showed a good deal of patience about the development of this situation, despite the large volume of money involved, but as the need to control borrowing in the public sector became increasingly important in national monetary policy some further intervention was inevitable. In an address to the Society of County Treasurers in 1975 the Governor of the Bank of England expressed concern that some 40 per cent of local authority loans of all kinds were due to mature within the next 12 months. Even though this included the accepted proportion of debt in the 'temporary' sector, and annual repayments to the PWLC, it nevertheless was clearly a dangerously high proportion of total debt.

Whitehall's first response was to propose another code of restrictions on local authority debt through the Control of Borrowing Order, aimed at extending the pattern of borrowing maturities. The local authority associations' financial advisers resisted this, although they recognized that something needed to be done, and was in fact going to be done whether they agreed or not. Surprisingly, they were able to convince the Treasury of their good intentions and succeeded in persuading Whitehall to allow the local authorities to devise a 'voluntary' code of borrowing aimed at lengthening maturities. Such a code was finally agreed and published in June 1977[2] and came into operation without statutory sanction or even the use of the Control of Borrowing Order and the General Consent. This publication was given the misleading title *A General Code for the Regulation of the Borrowing of Local Authorities in England, Scotland and Wales*, misleading because its sole objective was the regulation of maturity periods by lengthening; it was far from a general code of practice. The new code was directed to the control of the maturity periods of *new* borrowing, and ignored existing borrowing portfolio profiles. Because of the differing circumstances of many authorities the code became somewhat involved.

The basic requirement of the code was that over the four years 1978–81 the *average maturity periods of all loans raised*, but excluding borrowings under the temporary loan restrictions, should increase step by step from four to seven years, and thereafter continue at the seven-year level unless varied by agreement. But so that very short one-, two- and three-year loans could not be used to excess and be offset by a few long-term PWLC loans, there was an additional requirement that not more than 15 per cent of loans raised should 'fall to be repaid' in any one of the three financial years immediately following. In the first year of the new code it was to be 20 per cent. Negotiable yearling bonds were seen to present a particular problem, so that a further clause was added that the two percentages did not need to include money borrowed by negotiable bonds, but in that instance the two alternative percentages were to be reduced by 2½ in the year in which the negotiable bonds fell due for renewal. The code was subject to review in the light of circumstances and, in any event, not later than June 1979. When that review took place, all that was found to be required was that the maturities agreed for the last two years of the four-year period were each reduced by a year, so that the seven-year average did not come into effect until a year later (1981–2) than originally intended. (This modification was announced in a circular, in 1980, issued jointly by the Associations of Local Authorities.) That so little needed to be done, and that nothing else has since been altered, is some indication that complex though it seemed the code was indeed a practicality.

In 1981–2 when the required average maturity period reached seven years, the PWLC quota was raised to 50 per cent of net reckonable capital payments, plus 4 per cent of total debt incurred for capital purpose and outstanding at 31 March 1981. In addition to this offer of 'quota' loans, additional moneys were made available under the categories of non-quota 'A' loans, and non-quota 'B' loans (PWLC Circular 57, March 1981).

THE SHAPE OF THE MARKET IN THE LAST DECADE   During the decade in which these changes in the control of local authority capital finance and borrowing were taking place the severe difficulties of the national economy naturally had equally unfortunate effects on the London market. In May 1976 the report of the Layfield Committee on Local Government Finance (Cmnd 6453) had said 'The scale of local authority borrowing has implications for the control of the money supply, the management of financial markets and international confidence'. An exceptionally high level of both inflation and interest rates, and the sharp increase in total local authority debt, led to a number of devices for reconciling the needs of borrowers and lenders in the local authority as well as other markets. The most significant of these was the introduction of variable interest rate loans by the use of which both borrowers and lenders could be assured that they would not fall into a long-term trap created by violently fluctuating interest rates. Variable interest rates did not require a new instrument, the change was only of borrowing terms. In due course the variable rate base was applied to bond and mortgage rates and to stock issue rates (though here with some difficulty), and in government borrowing measures and, finally, even by the PWLC. The problem was to establish a base for ascertainment of the permitted fluctuations. Several alternative bases were adopted but undoubtedly the most used was that known as LIBOR, the London Inter-Bank Offer Rate, as ruling at given times at given intervals. This is not a fixed ascertainable rate in the way in which at any one time there is no doubt as to what is the ruling bank rate (or its equivalent the bank overnight rate) or commercial bank base rates. Rather it is the rate which though changing each day nevertheless would be ascertainable with a fair degree of certainty at say 10.00 a.m. on any one day. Variable rate loans of this kind were usually agreed at a premium – of the order of 1 per cent – above the LIBOR rate at the time of the agreement and subject to 'roll-over' according to the LIBOR rate at 10.00 a.m. on the agreed review date(s). What the local authorities were getting in this way were long-term loans at short-term interest rates. This was not necessarily a particularly favourable deal, but both lenders and borrowers had the satisfaction of knowing that they had 'hedged' future interest rate variations, in an unstable market. Local authorities had in fact little alternative to this basis as the large sums of money required were simply not available otherwise. The fact that this somewhat shadowy rate was so acceptable is some indication of the way in which the London inter-bank money market had flourished, and of the degree to which the local authorities had gradually begun to rely on bank funds as against the old source of small local lenders. Institutional money from other sources – pension funds, insurance funds and building societies – had also assumed a far greater prominence in local authority capital supply. So large were the sums needed by local authorities, and so reluctant were the banks to lend for the longer periods needed under the new voluntary code, that a new form of lending was established in the syndicated or consortium loan. The essence of these loans was that syndicates were organized, usually by merchant banks in collaboration with various groups of other banks, institutions, and so on – the so-called 'wholesale' market – with in-built arrangements that while the loan was guaranteed to the local authority for, say, five or seven years fixed, the syndicate had its own internal mechanism for allowing its constituent members to move in and out of the syndicate. Naturally such loans were on a variable rate basis, the variation taking place usually every six months (though sometimes more flexibly) and with other variations incorporated in a somewhat 'tailormade' fashion. To the local authority these were simply longer-term bond or mortgage loans for fixed periods, but with variable interest rate provisions.

From this state of affairs, towards the end of the decade, a further type of loan developed known as the 'drop-lock', and even a 'deferred drop-lock'. These loans had a mechanism whereby the 'locking in' of the interest rate to variations in LIBOR could be 'dropped' and a fixed rate established in specified circumstances; they were thus constructed in two parts – one part an ordinary syndicated loan, and the other a formula for determining when the variable interest rate could become a fixed rate, either on the occurrence of predetermined market conditions or the arrival of a selected gilt-edged security at a predetermined level. Such developments illustrate both the growing sophistication of the market and the increasing reliance of local authorities on the large-scale institutional lender.

Although the introduction of these new types of lending arrangements were primarily devices for coping with high and volatile interest rates, their development began to raise concern in the Treasury because of their implications for the growth of bank lending, a factor relevant to the control of the money supply (M3). The Treasury response was to widen the facilities offered by the PWLC. The first stage in the 'softening' of the PWLC provisions was that in August 1982 (Circular No. 63), a variable rate of interest was introduced for loans for from three to ten years as a further alternative. The variations were to be at three-monthly intervals; repayment could be either at maturity or by equal instalments of principal, and such loans could be switched to fixed rate (equivalent to a 'drop-lock') at any time. The basis of the variation was to be the three-month LIBOR rate as declared by the four major clearing banks at 11.00 a.m. on the previous day, with a margin above this rate of initially ⅛ per cent. Then in November 1982 (Circular No. 65) the three-year minimum loan period was extended to other loans (five years for EIP loans). This circular also announced that the '50% plus' quota to local authorities would for the remainder of the year be increased to 75 per cent plus 6 per cent of total debt. The complete formula was that the board would lend the greater of £10 million or 75 per cent of net reckonable capital payments during the year, plus 6 per cent of debt incurred for capital purposes. In January 1983 (Circular No. 66) this same arrangement was promised for 1983/4, confirmed in its major annual circular (No. 67, March 1983). Authorities were also invited to apply for excesses over their quotas if market difficulties were encountered. Yet another improved offer was made in December 1983 (Circular No. 70) in which the 6 per cent of capital debt on top of the 75 per cent of annual needs in the quota formula was increased to 10 per cent, with the promise that this would apply also for 1984/5 and probably for 1985/6.

The calculation of this two-part formula means that at least 90 per cent of its annual requirements are available to a local authority from the PWLC at less than open-market rates, with the offer of the balance if untoward difficulties arise. As the local authorities usually also have internal funds which they can use, and as they have a right of access to the short-term money market for loans of under one year, which they will no doubt make some use of, the wheel has turned practically full circle since 1945, and the local authorities are in effect back with the PWLC for virtually the whole of their longer-term requirements. This would therefore seem to be an exceptionally appropriate point at which to conclude this chronological survey of 320 years of local authority borrowing.

NOTES: CHAPTER 14

1 The local authorities believed that they had been given an assurance that anything found to be unsatisfactory with the provisions as hurriedly passed could be corrected in a further measure planned for 1974, but despite local authority dissatisfaction with certain aspects of the borrowing provisions of the 1972 Act, no changes were made subsequently. This anecdotal evidence is given to explain partially the lack of fresh thinking in the 1972 Act borrowing provisions. (*See* N. D. B. Sage, *Local Authority Capital Finance*, 3rd edn (1977); and information from F. Tolson, then City Treasurer of Leeds, both of these officers being in 1971/2 financial advisers to Local Authority Associations.)
2 The leading figure behind the code was Maurice F. Stonefrost, formerly the Director of the IMTA, but at that time Comptroller of the GLC and later to become Director General of the GLC; he was also a member of the Layfield Committee.

PART THREE

Borrowing Instruments and Associated Techniques: An Historical Analysis

(In this part a number of the examples quoted in the historical survey in Part Two are repeated, so that the picture of each type of security may be considered as a whole.)

Chapter 15

MORTGAGES AND RELATED INSTRUMENTS

A mortgage is a loan instrument of considerable antiquity and some legal complexity. There are even differences of opinion as to the origin of the term, which may be taken to mean a 'dead pledge', in contrast to a 'live pledge', though the original significance of these terms is far from certain. Fortunately there is no need to probe deeply for the meaning of the term in relation to local authority borrowing as, clearly, from its first employment down to modern times in local government or quasi-local government legislation a local authority mortgage has been simply an instrument pledging or assigning certain revenues (sometimes both revenues and properties, but exceptionally the properties only) of the local authority as a security against money borrowed and the interest thereon until the loan is redeemed, with all interest discharged. A relatively simply definition of a mortgage in this context (see W. Collin Brooks, *A Concise Dictionary of Finance*, 1934) is that a mortgage is 'a conditional transfer of property to secure at a given date payment of a sum of money, generally bearing interest'. Even from its earliest uses, as described in this book, what essentially was 'pledged' was not property in the usually understood sense, but the revenues which were expected to be derived from the utilization of the property, the physical property being included only in so far as it was needed to produce revenue. Perhaps Halsbury's definition that 'A mortgage is a transfer or other disposition of property as security for payment of a debt' is nearer to the practice that a local authority mortgage is an attachment not to the physical property of the authority, but to the revenue to be derived from that property. Even so, the local authority security, while it might include some of the properties owned by the authority, and income to be derived from them, is now fundamentally based on its total revenues, including those which the authority is authorized to raise by the levying of a rate, tolls and charges, which by no means are dependent on income arising from the use of assets. In the local authority case what is being mortgaged is ultimately the 'right' to levy a tax, which happens to be based on the occupation of property, and to 'take over' other incomes to support the repayment of the debt, with interest meanwhile. Even if a local income tax or other form of tax supplanted or supplemented the rate, the security would presumably remain the right of access to all revenues.

Semantically the view might be taken that in its local authority context the word 'mortgage' should be regarded as a verb rather than noun; today 'mortgaging', whatever it may have meant in early times or may mean today in other fields, in local government borrowing means the surrendering to a lender of the right of access to sources of revenue in the event of default in loan repayment or periodic interest. In so far as all local authority loan instruments, whatever their form or designation, imply the same promise – or give the same undertaking – then in each the revenues, by being assigned as security, are being mortgaged against the local authority's statutory revenues as a security for moneys loaned. Acceptance of this concept leads to material conclusions about what is the local authority loan instrument 'appropriate to our time'.

The earliest borrowing by a quasi-local authority has been identified in this book as that authorized by Parliament for the construction and operation of a toll-gate at Wades-Mill, in Hertfordshire, in 1663. The words used in the Act were that the

> Surveyors are hereby enabled . . . to engage the profits arising from the said Toll . . . by Indenture under the hands and seals of the respective Surveyors . . . for the repayment of such principal sums of money so lent with interest for the same.

The undertaking given – the pledge – could hardly be more clearly expressed, being not the physical asset, but the revenue to be derived directly therefrom. This extract is from the reprinted statutes of 1818, to which side-notes were added by the editors; the note here says: 'Power to Surveyors, with the consent of Justices, to mortgage the Tolls', a term which does not appear in the body of the Act. Therefore, in the opening phase of local authority borrowing the document involved was not internally designated a 'mortgage', but the process involved was accepted in fact as 'mortgaging the tolls'. Moreover, in the second phase of the introduction of borrowing power the security shifted from the revenue to be derived from the use of the asset to the mortgaging of the tax authorized to be raised for the finance of a particular service – that is the welfare of the poor – in which the creation of a physical asset was incidental and unlikely, on default, to offer a significant source of revenue in itself. The term 'indenture' under 'hands and seals' continued to be used for a considerable number of years as well as the reference to 'assigning' tolls or rates.

The term 'indenture', though nowhere legally defined, is recognized in law as 'a deed under seal between two or more persons' (*Concise Dictionary of Finance*). However, in due course 'indentures' ceased to be 'indented' – the origin of the term was that each deed was written twice on a single skin of parchment, with a sufficient space between the two entries to enable them then to be severed one from the other by an irregular or deckled cut, so that the two parts could if required be 'matched', as master and copy of the same agreement (leaving always the awkward possibility that the words in each might show variations). The term indenture, then, is no more than what the grammarian might call 'the container for the thing contained', in that it simply describes a peculiarity of the piece of parchment on which the pledge is inscribed, though how the curious practice of deckling the edge of documents arose must be a matter of speculation; no doubt, by chance arising in the mists of antiquity from the careless trimming of the edges of the vellum.

In earlier times the word 'chirographum' might be written in the dividing space and cut through in the process of indenting, to facilitate a more convincing 'match'. A three-part indenture might be made by the writing of the third copy at the side of the other two vertically, so that it overlapped both, the third copy also being severed by an indented vertical cut. Indeed this type of three-fold indenture, as already referred to in the Introduction, is of very ancient origin for the identification of a debt. In 1233 the Statute concerning the Jews laid down that loans at interest from Jews to Christians (the only form of lending at interest then legally permitted) should be in this three-fold type of indenture known as a chirograph (simply 'a handwriting'). The Act laid down that one copy of the agreement should be retained by the lender, one by the borrower and the third be held in the 'chests of the Chirographers', that is, the equivalent of the modern registrar; the deed was not valid unless a third copy was so retained. Thus the essential form of a borrowing instrument, with no doubt arrangements for the payment of interest and repayment, was specified some 750 years ago, and examples are still extant in the Record Office. The use of an 'indenture' by the early turnpike authorities therefore comes as no surprise, but presumably it differed from the early chirographs, which were probably secured against property, in that the turnpike instruments specified the security for the loan as the revenues to be derived from the turnpike; nevertheless, on default the 'property' was taken over not for its intrinsic worth, but its earning capacity.

To move some years ahead the same pattern of an instrument as being simply an agreement to assign revenues is clearly to be seen in an Act of 1759 dealing with turnpike roads in Kent (Maidstone to Cranbrook Road) which allowed the trustees

> by any writing or instrument under their hands and seals to assign over or mortgage the said Tolls or Duties as a security for any sums of money to be borrowed . . . to secure the repayment thereof by or out of the moneys collected by the said Tolls or Duties, with such interest upon the same.

Thus 'assigning revenues' and 'mortgaging revenues' is seen to have been regarded as the same process. This phrase was in common use on Turnpike Acts of that time. By 1800 (Bolton) not only were the tolls assigned or mortgaged, but 'also the toll houses and appurtenances', without the use of which the tolls could not readily have been collected, if default had taken place. The Bolton Act actually specifies the form of 'mortgage or assignment' in which comprehensively the trustees 'do grant, bargain, sell or demise . . . such portion of the tolls arising upon the said road and of the turnpikes and tollhouses for collecting the same as the said sum do bear to the whole of the sum due'.

As turnpike roads became more significant and more complex in their organization the terms of the Acts expanded. In an 1820 Act (Stockport to Warrington) 'weighing machines and other engines' were added to the assigned revenues and properties. The Act also specified that all persons to whom mortgages or assignments should be made 'shall in proportion to the sums mentioned be creditors in equal degree one with another'. Later Acts began to specify quarterly or half-yearly payments of interest. During all this time provisions required that registers were to be kept and assignment from one lender to another, with appropriate forms of transfer, authorized.

The wording became more involved as time went on. An analysis of the growth of the technical structure of the mortgage deed would be possible, but probably without much significance. If the deed became more elaborate because problems of interpretation had arisen, there is now no evidence of this available. As will shortly be shown, a peak was reached after which the wording dwindled to the merest skeleton of earlier usages and now so remains.

A series of turnpike 'indenture mortgages' (made available by the County Treasurer of Kent, Mr William Taylor) from 1718 to 1828 show the modification of the mortgage as an instrument over that period. That for 1718 (£1,700 at 5 per cent) which calls itself an 'indenture of mortgage' is a magnificent document written on a sheet of vellum, about 2 ft by 3 ft in area, and begins: 'This Indenture made the 30th day of July in the fourth year of the reign of our Sovereign Lord George by the Grace of God of Great Britain, France and Ireland King, Defender of the Faith'; it quotes not only the list of tolls which would be charged on the road as security for the loan, but also the public houses at which interest would be paid – Bowling Green House and the 'Green Man' in Blackheath. Indeed it also virtually repeats the preamble to the Act explaining (in words quoted earlier in this book) that the reason for borrowing was that the tolls could not be collected until the road was in good order. The tolls in this deed were simply 'assigned over'.

A deed of 1770 (£140 at 5 per cent) is also at great length, and undertakes in another set of words presumably to remove any possible doubt about what is afoot, to 'bargain, sell, assign over, transfer and mortgage' the tolls. By 1821 (£248 at 5 per cent) a much more restrained and less picturesque document is used, but the offer is still to 'grant, bargain, sell and demise' the tolls as security. This deed is of special interest because it declares that a loan by the Public Works Loan Commissioners had priority over the mortgage loans. By 1828 the deeds simply 'grant and assign' the tolls (interest rates then being £4 17s 6d per cent, and £4½ per cent). No doubt, the gradual simplification of the deed is an indication of the growth of confidence throughout the market in the reliability of this instrument. Clearly also, the later administrators regarded the borrowing exercise as something much more commonplace indeed everyday than the pioneers of the system. These developments amounted to no more than refinements of the original concept that the revenues which the tollpikes could earn should be pledged as security for the interest and principal of the loans required to establish the system. From very early times because the principle was accepted that all loans ranked equally without priority, the conception of a mortgage was that each lender had a lien on the security, whether a toll or a rate, in proportion of his loan to the total loans outstanding.

There is a degree of triviality about the titles given to some of these borrowing instruments. The terms mortgage and bond are substantially declarations of the nature of the instrument, while a chirograph indicates simply that the document, whatever it is, is handwritten (although chirographs also involved 'indenturing'); and the term indenture simply implies that there are two parts to a document and therefore two parties to an agreement, and that the document has been divided in such a way that 'matching' is possible. (An 'indenture' is no more than a shape.) In this book a single example was brought to light of a 'one-sided' agreement, that is, a deed poll, which is a declaration (financial or otherwise) by a single party (almost like a local authority money bill or promissory note) which is 'polled' – cut straight along the top edge and not requiring matching indentation because no counterpart is involved (although doubtless copies were retained). This deed poll related to a turnpike trust Act applying to a road in Tiverton, Devon, in 1811. In this instance money was authorized to be borrowed in units of £50, and the necessary number of deeds poll executed to cover the sum authorized. These were then to be issued to lenders, but the documents evidently made clear that the security offered was the mortgaging or assignment of the tolls; in fact instruments in these forms could also be used. Unfortunately the Act did not specify the form of the deed poll, nor do any examples appear to have survived. While indentures traditionally begin with the words 'This Indenture . . .' and follow with the date, a deed poll, being simply a one-part declaration, begins: 'Know all men by these presents . . .', and concludes with the date.

Although the Poor Law borrowing facilities came relatively late (despite the antiquity of the service), similar mortgage terminology was employed from the beginning. The early Poor Law borrowing Acts which have been discovered – those of 1697 for Exeter and Hereford – allowed the mayor and his colleagues by any sealed deed or writing to 'grant, convey and assure' the market tolls as security for such sums as they elected to borrow or take up for setting the poor to work and thereby promoting the public good. After a long gap, in 1756 the guardians of the incorporation of Colneis and Carlford, in Suffolk, were authorized to borrow £6,000 at interest not exceeding 4 per cent and 'to assign over by writing under their Common Seal all or any part of the Poor's Rate . . . as security for repayment of Principal and Interest'. Similar words were used in 1764 (Mutford and Lothingland, in Suffolk), that is, without specific use of the term mortgage. In the City of Oxford's substantial Act of 1771 both annuities and assignments were permitted, the side-note to the assignments clause being 'For mortgaging the rates'.

The early reluctance to use the word mortgage in the text of the Acts is interesting and may be significant. In 1772 the guardians of the parish of St Sepulchre (Middlesex) were authorized to 'borrow and take up at interest upon the credit of the rates by any writings on vellum or parchment' and to 'assign the rates', without using the term mortgage. Perhaps while the concept of mortgaging property was clearly understood, those concerned were less happy with the idea of mortgaging income and preferred simply to assign the right to it. This simpler concept was possibly more appropriate, but gradually the two concepts of 'assigning over' and 'mortgaging' began to coalesce. Guardians in the Isle of Wight, in 1776, were also given two modes of borrowing, 'either by mortgaging the rates . . . or by a Scheme of Survivorship' (that is, a tontine). This Act also describes the mortgage as an assignment of the rates.

By 1782 in the Parish of St Luke (Middlesex) the terminology used was 'to assign over and mortgage' under hands and seals. In 1785 (Tunstead and Happing, in Essex), mortgages, annuities and a tontine were authorized. The mortgages – in sums not to exceed £100 each – were described in the text as assignments, but a draft form was given which was headed 'Form of Mortgage'.

The adoptive Gilbert's Act 1782 has already been described as probably the first Act giving a general, though limited, power to borrow as distinct from private Act powers. Contrary to what might have been expected in the light of the terminology of local Acts, mortgages as such were not specified – what was given was merely a power to borrow in sums not exceeding £50 each, secured upon the poor rate, and the draft form given was simply headed 'Form of Security for Money Borrowed'. In one of the early reports of the Poor Law Commissioners, appointed after 1834, outstanding loans under Gilbert's Act were referred to as 'Gilbert's bonds'. The Poor Law Amendment Act 1819 which authorized further borrowing specified only 'by loan, or by Sale of Annuities'.

Therefore, there seems to have been a period towards the end of the eighteenth century and the beginning of the nineteenth when there was doubt in the minds of the legislators about the appropriateness of the concept of a 'mortgage' for a simple loan secured against rate income, though no doubt, whatever the wording on the document, the loan instrument issued against the security of the rates would be legally deemed a mortgage. As already shown, the Poor Law Amendment Act 1834 and the Municipal Corporations Act 1835 did not provide a basic mortgage system, though other legislation for particular services – for example, the Gaols Act 1823 – picked up the mortgage as a useful and flexible instrument. The Acts which could have established a completely standardized mortgage code were the Companies and the Commissioners Clauses Acts of 1845 and 1847. The establishment of a standard mortgage code would have been precisely in line with the 'model' clauses nature of these two Acts. In the event, the Companies Clauses Consolidation Act, which really related to commercial enterprises but was picked up by the Baths and Washhouses Act among other local government activities, included provisons for both mortgages and bonds; the Commissioners Clauses Act – adopted, *inter alia*, by the museums and libraries legislation – provided adequate facilities for mortgages or 'assignations in security of rates or other properties'. This could have been the beginning of a true mortgage code, but the two Acts were either incorporated erratically by later local government service Acts or ignored altogether in place of specific but often brief provisions within particular Acts. Whether the term 'mortgage' was appropriate or not, the excellent idea of a uniform standardized system as obviously underlying the two Acts did not implant itself, at least in relation to a borrowing code.

The strange situation developed that despite the use of the mortgage from earliest times, it was not only omitted from the Local Loans Act 1875, but while there were numerous Acts which allowed the mortgage as the borrowing instrument for particular services, there was no Act, until 1933, which gave local authorities a general power to borrow by mortgage whenever borrowing was authorized. Local authorities were left to acquire local Act powers for the general use of a mortgage instrument. At the same time, while the use of the Local Loans Act, never great, has dwindled quite away, it nevertheless has survived by inclusion not only in the 1933 Act, but also in the 1972 Act, by which time the mortgage itself was rapidly being superseded by the bond.

Confusion must certainly have been caused by the passing of the twin Acts of 1875, the Public Health Act shortly preceding the Local Loans Act. Each Act was based on a different borrowing code, though they must have been in the hands of the parliamentary draftsmen at about the same time – the Public Health Act following earlier Public Health Acts in favouring the mortgage, while the Local Loans Act introduced the debenture. The mortgage code perhaps attracted most attention because at the time public health functions covered a large proportion of the work of local authorities. Yet, with hindsight, the powers of the Local Loans Act can be seen to have been nearer to what was appropriate for local authority borrowing. What the Local Loans Act did was to provide for loans on security of the local revenues without the complexity of a legal mortgage (though all the same what was being done in offering this security was, to all intents and purposes, the 'mortgaging' of those revenues) which the draftsmen chose to call a 'debenture' – an acknowledgement of a debt. The Local Loans Act speaks of 'A debenture under this Act shall be an instrument taking effect as a deed, and charging the local rate or property in such debenture, which could equally well have been applied to a mortgage or a bond. This debenture was however, on the face of it, more flexible than the mortgage as it could be issued in registered or bearer form. In so far as it involved the use of interest coupons, this may have made it unwelcome to the authorities. But the Act also provided a 'marketable' form in debenture stock which could be issued at a discount, so that the mortgage was to be replaced by practically a 'general-purpose' debenture.

The Local Loans Act also made provision for what it called 'annuity certificates' but these were simply debentures repayable in equal annual instalments of principal and interest, and for a given term of years, that is, terminable annuities. The lack of precise analysis lying behind such provisions is to be seen by comparison with the Public Health Act, where mortgages could be repaid either at maturity, or by equal instalments of principal, or principal and interest combined – but these were not called annuities. The Education Act 1870 (which generally adopted the Commissioners Clauses Act) may be quoted as another Act which provided for the repayment of mortgages by means of a sinking fund or 'by equal annual instalments, not exceeding fifty'. That this could be taken to mean instalments of interest and principal combined is shown by a mortgage (supplied by the City Treasurer of Newcastle upon Tyne), by which in 1884 the Longbenton School Board borrowed £7,187 from the Prudential Assurance Co. with repayment over fifty years by a flat sum to include both elements, the discharge in 1934 being endorsed on the deed in a hand differing greatly from the copper-plate. Mortgages and debentures thus had the same security and the same methods of repayment. In what ways did they differ other than in the form of words?

Except that there was no provision for the issue of the simple debenture at a discount, the Local Loans Act debenture follows closely the pattern of the bond, so that much trouble might have been saved later, if instead of developing the bond, efforts had been made to perfect the debenture. Even without provision for discount, the simplicity and flexibility of the debenture can still explain why the framers of that Act did not consider that a mortgage was called for. Yet it was the Public Health approach and the mortgage which carried the day.

The provisions of the Municipal Corporations Mortgages Act 1860 were directed towards the mortgage as a method of borrowing, but rather strangely the Municipal Corporations Act of 1882, the preliminary to the great reorganizations of local authorities later in the decade, was ambiguous in its provisions. The main borrowing clauses simply gave power to 'borrow at interest' on the security of corporate land, or the borough fund or borough rate, but the repayment provisions referred specifically to the money as being borrowed on mortgage. The powers which occurred later in this Act for borrowing for the provision of borough bridges specifically authorized borrowing for which the borough fund or borough rate might be mortgaged, and the draft form of mortgage given in the schedule to the Act is designed specifically for borrowing for bridge works. The whole procedure was very ragged, and entirely ignored the available provisions of the Local Loans Act. The major reorganization of the Local Government Act 1888 illustrated yet another approach as it permitted borrowing by the new county councils under the Local Loans Act and, if special reasons existed, by mortgage under the Public Healtʰ Act. The limitation on the use of mortgages was withdrawn by the County Councils Mortgages Act 1909. Yet with the completion of that phase of local government reorganization in 1894, the parish councils were only given power to borrow by mortgages as under the Public Health Acts.

Because until 1933 there was no general power authorizing the use of a standard mortgage to fulfil any authorized borrowing, local authorities were again forced one by one to take local Act powers to obtain this facility. The borough of Bolton is believed to be the first local authority to do so in 1872. Certainly, Leeds did so in 1901, allowing the city to 'raise all or any principal moneys which for the time being they may be authorised to borrow or re-borrow by mortgage or the creation and issue of Leeds Corporation Stock'. The draft form of mortgage specified was very lengthy, almost one-third of it being directed to arrangements for renewal at maturity. Leeds Corporation also had an older provision in an Act of 1877, which permitted the issue of bearer mortgages each to be of not less than £5. This power is not now thought to have been utilized, but at least its approval by Parliament indicates that there was no intrinsic reason why mortgages as well as debentures should not be in bearer form.

A succession of authorities took this course of obtaining general mortgaging powers. Manchester did so in 1914, obtaining powers similar to those already quoted for Leeds, but with a more condensed form of mortgage – all such mortgages ranked equally both against one another and against other corporation securities, and were subject to normal practices as to transfer and registration, but without mention of receivership on default. The Manchester Municipal Code, which collates all the city's local Act powers in encyclopaedic form, indicates that this power replaced the use of some twenty mortgage powers for specific purposes. Local authorities continued to seek these general powers; even as late as 1929 with the 1933 Act in the offing, Hendon Urban District Council, for example, took general mortgage powers in an Act which at the same time allowed them to catch up with a later trend – to issue general bonds.

Although mortgages thus gradually elbowed their way into the system as the preferred method of borrowing, they were nowhere given complete recognition as the accepted code, and the variations within the provisions must have given local treasurers many headaches. There is no problem in explaining why many authorities had their own standard mortgage powers. Yet even in 1933, and later in 1972 when the mortgage was very much a recognized instrument, with the intrusion of the bond in 1963–72 and with stock as the longer-term marketable alternative, the debenture provisions of the Local Loans Act were still retained. However, all the indications are that those involved had by then forgotten what the Local Loans Act was really about, and that the possible greater flexibility of the use of Local Loans Act debentures was no longer recognized.

By 1933 the mortgage was certainly the main form of local authority borrowing; it had proved itself to be a versatile (though somewhat wordy) instrument, well understood in the market, and very attractive to the small local lender on whom local authorities then much depended. It had acquired greater flexibility than was perhaps originally intended because term mortgages were often allowed to run on at notice after the first maturity date (a feature which was later frowned on by the Treasury).

In May 1970 the then treasurer of Carlisle wrote to the *Journal of the Treasurers' Institute*, to report that he had just renewed, for the sixth time, a mortgage to a lady who had first invested in 1922 – forty-eight years earlier. The original rate of interest was 5½ per cent, in the mid-1940s 3 per cent and, on this last occasion, 9 per cent. Later inquiry shows that the same lady subsequently renewed in 1975 at 13¾ per cent, and in 1979 at 11¼ per cent. She died later in 1979, but the holding was transferred to a relative of the same name who died in 1981 at which date repayment was taken. A spell of fifty-six years between investment and repayment, with nine opportunities to take repayment, indicates the satisfaction of the small lender with the local authority mortgage. At what stage, asks the city treasurer, had the lady had the best return? He does not ask for views about capital depreciation. There is no doubt that while this is an exceptional period, many similar examples could be uncovered.

Johnson in *Loans of Local Authorities*, written in 1925, reported that some local authorities had developed the use of the Public Health Act mortgage into a 'temporary loan' facility by borrowing on mortgage without the issue of a mortgage deed, lenders of considerable sums for short periods having been persuaded to accept the 'interim receipt' as their security. (Because the mortgage required detailed preparation including duty stamping and official signing and sealing, the practice was to issue an elaborate interim receipt to lenders, to cover the period during which the final deed was under preparation.) Indeed a case went as far as the Court of Appeal in 1911 (1910: 8 LGR 588 (CA) 9 LGR 103), which sustained the argument that while the Public Health Acts authorized borrowing on mortgage, there was no reason for a mortgage deed to be issued in every case, if the lender could be persuaded otherwise; thus much stamp duty was saved on loans of short duration. This may well have been the origin of the temporary loan receipt borrowing procedure. As, according to Johnson, interim receipts in these instances contained a footnote promising the issue of a full mortgage deed if required, this indicates an even earlier origin of the practice than as having arisen under the Financial Provisions Act 1921, even as far back as before 1910.

Extremely simple regulations were made under the 1933 Act (Local Government (Form of Mortgages and Transfers) Regulations – SR&O 1934/621) giving, as the name implies, only the draft form of mortgage deed. This was in the old 'narrative' form with names, consideration, interest and other details to be fitted into the body of the text. Provision was made for renewal, but the deed had of course to be sealed. The regulations issued under the 1972 Act (Local Authority (Mortgages) Regulations – SI 1974/518) were considerably more detailed, although the draft form of mortgage was reduced to what must be the absolute minimum for this form of instrument. Nevertheless, while the wording had been gradually condensed from that used in older mortgages, the design was still in narrative form; moreover, the provision for receivership having been omitted from the Act, this is given in the regulations, allowing approach to the High Court when the aggregate amount of liability is not less than £500.

Some indication of the dissipation of the mystic of the mortgage is to be seen in a comparison of the wording of the form of mortgage in both the Public Health Act 1875 and the 1934 Regulations with that in the 1974 Regulations (sixteen lines as against eight). In the 1875 Act the district council

> do grant and assign unto the said A.B., his executors, administrators and assigns, such portion of the rates arising or accruing by virtue of the said Act from [the rates mortgaged] as the said sum of . . . doth or shall bear to the whole sum which is borrowed on the credit of the said rates

The 1974 wording is

> In consideration of the sum of £ . . . (the receipt whereof is hereby acknowledged) the . . . Council of . . . hereby charge such proportion of the revenues of the Council as the said sum bears or will bear to the whole sum which is or will be charged on the said revenues.

Granting and assigning still formed part of the 1934 Regulations.

Fortunately mortgages designed 'to the like effect' have always been permitted. This allowed the more progressive authorities to use a form of wording in which all the typed data could be added in a schedule at the foot of the document, thus making it easier to prepare and to comprehend. This was on the lines of a simplified mortgage produced in Manchester in the 1950s. The introduction of the simplified Manchester mortgage was accompanied by a decision to print the Common Seal (instead of embossing) as well as facsimile attesting signatures. At the same time, the arrangement with the Inland Revenue had been introduced, in that the document needed no longer to be stamped, provided that it bore a legend that stamp duty had or would be paid. Shortly afterwards stamp duty on borrowing was abolished. The combined effect of these changes was that a mortgage could be completed 'over the counter', or sent by return of post, in place of the six weeks or so delay which had previously been required for stamping, sealing and attesting. This in turn enabled the elaborate interim receipt to be abolished, so that the mortgage became as readily issued as the bond, leaving the only objection to it that its formality still might be seen as implying some difference in status – possibly superior – from the bond, in that the rates were 'mortgaged' rather than 'given as security'.

The 1974 mortgage, though still in 'continuous narrative' form rather than the newer 'scheduled' form, is exceptionally simple and nowhere does it use the term 'mortgage'. It does not require a declaration of the statutory authority for its issue, whereas the bond regulations specify that in the instrument the 'statutory authority under which the bonds are issued' must be declared. The obvious question arises: if two documents are, to all intents and purposes, of the same status and security, terms and conditions, why confuse lenders by offering the choice of instrument?

A remarkable example of both the longevity of local authority investments and of the confusion between mortgages and debentures is to be found in the example (produced with the authority of the Borough Treasurer of Bolton, Mr Arthur Haslam, for many years the borough's Loans Officer) of a deed described in its title as a '6 per cent Mortgage Debenture to be repaid at the end of 999 years'. This was almost but not quite a perpetual annuity; not quite an annuity because while the payments over the period were of interest only, as would be the case with a perpetual annuity, the principal was eventually due to be repaid as a lump sum. This beautifully engraved document, under seal, was first issued by the Haslingden and Rawtenstall Waterworks Co. under the Waterworks Acts of 1853 and 1856, incorporating also the Companies Clauses Act 1845. No doubt, this origin as a 'company' document accounts for its classification as a 'mortgage debenture', unusual in local government. The company was taken over in 1900 by the Bury and District Joint Water Board, a body which in 1935 became the Irwell Valley Water Board, which was itself transferred to Bolton Corporation in 1963. (It finally came under the aegis of the North-West Water Authority.) The investment was for what would now be described as a mere £50, but as there were three deeds for the same holder each for £50, this indicates that the original Acts specified deeds for not more than this amount. Its four 'states' of borrower are paralleled by nine transfers of ownership during the period until it was repaid by agreement in 1967, after serving only 104 of its potential 999 years, as a result of the Bolton treasurer's effort to clear up some of the perpetual debt in his books. Thus during its tenure the £50 investment earned some £312 interest, but how this relates to a loss of capital value is not easy to calculate. Clearly, it was a loan taken out when confidence in the future value of money was greater than it is today; incidentally, it simply 'assigned' the 'said undertaking and all the Tolls and Sums of money arising by virtue of the said Acts' – no question of apportionment of debt.

The conclusion to be drawn from this brief survey of the evolution of the practice of borrowing by local authorities on mortgage must be that the mortgage is neither more nor less than (as indeed its name indicates) a pledge to a lender that, in return for a loan, the lender is given as security access to the 'property' of the borrower – whether this is a physical property or, as overwhelmingly in local government, an 'intangible' property in the right to collect revenues. The earliest examples show that in 'assigning' revenues as security, the borrowers knew that they were in legal terms 'mortgaging' those revenues, even though the term did not appear in the borrowing instrument. Seen in this light, and along with the many undertakings that all securities ranked equally, the mortgage does no more than the bond, which binds the borrower to certain promises, nor

than any other borrowing instrument which equally assure the lender that
his loan is secure on default by access to the revenues of the borrower.
Mortgaging, granting, assigning, demising, bonding and promising to pay
are words which have no specific meaning as long as they attach to the
same remedy – the right of recovery of debt by the taking over of the
revenues. This is entirely different from the situation in the commercial
world where defined hierarchies of debt are created. In local government a
document which in bygone times was 'indented' for matching purposes,
but which in some form assigned the revenues, even though it did not use
the word mortgage, was nevertheless in a legal concept a 'mortgaging' of
the revenues; conversely, a deed which specifically 'mortgages' the
revenues does no more than assign access to these revenues as security.
This spelling out of the status of the mortgage in this tedious way is
necessary to an understanding of how the conglomeration of borrowing
facilities now available to local authorities can be rationalized.

The delay in the production of a standard mortgage for use by local
authorities would be difficult to understand, if it did not have its
counterpart in similar delays in a number of other aspects in the
rationalization of local authority borrowing. This vacillation is all the
more difficult to understand in the face of the fact that the mortgage has
proved a versatile borrowing instrument. The evidence has shown that it
can be repaid by any of the established methods (even though it then
sometimes takes on the attributes of an annuity). It can be (but never is)
drawn as a bearer instrument, and there seems to be no legal or logical
reason why it could not be issued at a discount. Superficially it suffers
from the minor administrative inconvenience that it needs to be issued
under seal, that pointless exercise. No means have yet been devised of
avoiding sealing as with a bond by the issue of a 'certificate'. However, as
the practice is fully established that a 'seal' can be printed in facsimile
when the document itself is presented, this requirement has no practical
effect. This leads to the thought that if these two simple devices for
avoiding the tedium of impressed sealing are acceptable, why is the sealing
requirement officially maintained? (In any event, the 'impressed seal' is
itself a makeshift reproduction of the original wax seal going back to the
days of general illiteracy.) If a case can be made against the use of the
mortgage in local government, it is simply that the concept is outmoded
and that its continued use tends to suggest that, in some way, it is different
from any simple form of loan acknowledgement offering the security of
the revenues.

Chapter 16

ANNUITIES, DEBENTURES AND TONTINES

'Annuity' is a term much lacking in precision of meaning in its application to local authority borrowing procedures. In practice, it is used loosely to refer both to forms of instrument and to a system of repayment of any loan. In general dictionary terms it is described simply as 'an annual payment' (although annuities are often disbursed quarterly or half-yearly). Today the essence of the 'annuity' is that it involves an annual payment which combines a partial repayment of principal with an interest element. Nevertheless, examples have already been quoted of nineteenth-century so-called 'perpetual annuities', where interest only was payable 'for ever', and in which the annual payments did not include an element of repayment of principal, although the holder retained his property in the principal.

Frequent references have been made in this book to statutory provisions for the repayment of loans by any of three methods: at maturity, by equal annual instalments of principal with interest on the declining balance (called the 'instalment' or EIP method), or by equal annual payments of principal and interest combined, calculated on 'annuity' tables (the EAR or annuity method). Unfortunately for clarity loans repaid by either the EIP or EAR methods — even though the instrument is palpably a mortgage — are often found to be referred to as 'annuities'.

Several types of annuity must be distinguished. A term or period annuity is simply a loan with a fixed maturity period, part of the principal of which is repayable each year, so that by the end of the fixed period the loan has been wholly discharged, whether by the EIP or EAR methods. Repayment of such loans continues to the maturity date whether or not the holder survives.

For our purposes such a fixed-term annuity is not regarded as a true annuity, but simply as a mortgage or bond the repayment of which, instead of being at maturity, is spread over the life of the investment — that is, repaid on an annuity basis. An example of such a pseudo-annuity has been already given in the Poor Law Amendment Act 1851 in which a general power to borrow for Poor Law purposes is supported by the pro forma of what is simply called 'deed', providing for a charge on the future poor rates with a provision which required the specification of the number of instalments over which the loan must be repaid. It is thus a combination of a mortgage, with an 'equal instalment of principal' annuity system of repayment written in: is this a mortgage repayable on the annuity principle, or an annuity on which the security consisted of a mortgage on the rates? Similarly, until maturity repayment was recently permitted the instruments covering advances from the Public Works Loan Commission were described as mortgages but were repayable on either of the annuity methods.

Another illustration is relevant as an example of the confusion of terminology. In an extension of the City of Manchester, in 1940, certain houses were taken over from the adjacent Bucklow Rural District Council on which debt was outstanding in the form of several loans from an insurance company for sixty years from 1930 to 1990. They were spoken of in the Manchester treasurer's Loans Office as 'annuities', but an examination of the records shows that they were mortgages repayable on the annuity principle (half-yearly) by an equated amount of principal and interest combined; the deeds are clearly endorsed 'mortgage'. The debts were eventually bought-in to 'tidy up' the consolidated loans fund in 1978. At that date Manchester still held a small number of perpetual annuities (dating from 1872) attached to the waterworks undertakings, which were also later bought-in.

Equally, although the Local Loans Act 1875 made no reference to mortgages, the earlier examination of this Act has shown that the debentures introduced under it were, in effect, mortgages with the added flexibility of 'bearer' status, repayable in full as selected. The annuity certificates contemplated under the Act were similar in all respects, except that they were repayable not at a selected maturity date, but in annual instalments over twenty years (unless some other period was specified). Thus the Local Loans Act regarded as an annuity any investment which was repayable by annual instalments rather than at maturity despite similarity with a mortgage. Life annuities are clearly not contemplated as, among other points, these certificates might also be given bearer status.

The type of security known as a perpetual annuity equally herein is not regarded as a true annuity because, in theory at least, principal is never intended to be repaid. Nevertheless, perpetual annuities continued to appear in statutes for the acquisition of trading undertakings, particularly waterworks, until late in the nineteenth century. The not wholly convincing explanation usually given in textbooks for the use of long or perpetual annuities in relation to public utilities is that, in their early history, these were usually company-operated concerns and had shareholders who considered themselves to have permanent investments in valuable enterprises (even though at fixed interest rates). Thus to compensate these shareholders on a takeover very long-term or perpetual securities were considered essential. Examples of this attitude are to be seen in the Bolton mortgage debentures for 999 years, already examined, and to take another example the perpetual annuities of £10 each available as an alternative to mortgages under the Batley Corporation Waterworks Act 1871, or the issue in the early twentieth century of perpetual annuities by the Bury and District Joint Water Board, in substitution for the preference shares originally issued to investors in the Bury and Radcliffe

Waterworks Co. The line is extremely fine between the older and more remote forms of 999-year (or even 99-year) mortgages to be found in waterworks legislation, irredeemable stock and perpetual annuities. In all forms the holder retained title to his principal; where they differed was that the mortgage-holder had a (remote) promise of redemption which did not apply to the others unless the borrower became impatient and decided to bargain for redemption. 'Perpetual debentures' might have been a better name for this type of long annuity.

The provisions for the acquisition of a gas undertaking by the Coventry Corporation in 1884 have certain interesting features relating to so-called annuities. There were two classes of shares to be acquired by the city. For one class of shares the council was to pay an annuity of £2 a share for fifteen years, plus a sum in discharge of principal of £48 a share at the end of that term. For the other class of shares the annuity was to be £1 17s 6d a share for fifteen years, plus the discharge of principal at the end of the period by £45 a share. The 'annuities' were to be represented by the issue of 'gas certificates' the wording of which described the annual payments as being 'in the nature of interest for forbearing payment of the principal sum'. The security was the gas undertaking and the district fund and general district rate of the city. These 'annuities' were clearly fifteen-year mortgages at 4·17 per cent. The company's bond debt of £20,000 was also to be discharged by the city, which could borrow on mortgage or by debentures, debenture stock, or annuity certificates under the Local Loans Act 1875. Existing city mortgages retained preference over these new borrowings.

The 'deferred annuity' of which rare examples have been encountered is simply a form of investment the terms of which provide for a period during which interest only is paid, until a point is reached at which repayment of principal begins on an annual basis. In the international money markets maturity repayment is sometimes referred to as the 'bullet' method, by which is meant without a system for annual 'amortization', but the situation can be confusing to those not closely involved. For example, at present Dutch (and certain other) government bonds are available in which interest only is receivable for the first five years, but thereafter principal is repaid in ten equal instalments with interest on the diminishing balance; these are never referred to as or considered to be annuities, but the system of repayment of these bonds complies with the deferred annuity principle.

The true form of annuity, that is, the instrument which has a characteristic special to itself, is the life annuity. Life annuities are those which are paid at a flat rate during the life of the lender (or his nominee, or on joint lives) however long, and cease on his death however soon. The flat rate sum to be paid annually for this indefinite number of years is determined at the outset on the basis of the estimated life expectation of the lender or nominee, a contingency which varies with age at commencement, sex and on speculation as to the long-term trend of interest rates. The annual payment thus includes both an interest element and a speculative element. Consequently, if the lender died within the period of expectation, the borrower was the gainer; if the lender survived longer than expected, the borrower was the loser. In so far as a borrower could be expected to have borrowed under the scheme on a variety of lives, he might hope to balance gains and losses 'on average'; he must of course take account of the continuing tendency to greater longevity in the population, with more people living to a greater age, than shown by earlier experience, as a result of greater attention to public health, better hygiene, diet, increased success of medical science, and so on.[1]

The beginning of the reign of William and Mary in 1689 is regarded as the starting-point of the National Debt in an organized and funded form. The early methods of central borrowing were certainly unscientific – by crudely calculated annuities, lotteries and tontines, and sometimes a mixture of all three – a far less stable approach to the problem than the general run of early local authority borrowing. The principle of the life annuity, so readily adopted, was quite imperfectly understood, depending as it did on the life expectations of various age-groups. The problem was that the necessary basic statistics for this form of borrowing were simply not available. In 1693 the astronomer Halley produced a table of life probabilities at five-year intervals, based on figures for births and deaths in the City of Breslau. At this time the British government was borrowing on 14 per cent annuities irrespective of age and sex, which implied a general life expectation of around ten years. Halley's figures showed that at age 10 a seventeen-year purchase would have been appropriate, while at age 75 four-and-a-half-years' purchase would have sufficed.

In 1725 Demoine put forward a theory that of eighty-six children born in the same year, one would die on average each year thereafter until the final survivor reached age 85 or 86 – perhaps not an unreasonable though rough-and-ready basis. Only in 1798 did the government adopt a table based on the ages at death in Northampton between the years 1735 and 1780. Bills of mortality (often mentioned in statutes) had been collected from parishes since the fourteenth-century Black Death and the basis of these had been improved from time to time, particularly in the seventeenth century. Nevertheless, a firm basis for the calculation of reliable tables did not become available until registration of births, marriages and deaths, under the Act of 1836, made a start with the systematic collection of the necessary statistics on an efficient basis, and some years were needed before these figures produced an adequate data-base for calculations. The early local authorities can hardly be blamed if they followed to some extent the lead of the government's practices in borrowing by means of life annuities, and indeed they are to be congratulated, in that they are thus seen as having made some attempt to tailor annuities to the circumstances of nominees. However, a survey of their methods of borrowing shows that, after fifty years of experience to 1800, they decided that better borrowing alternatives less speculative than life annuities were available for their purposes. Having once given up life annuities, they never went back seriously to that system.

Although organized borrowing for Poor Law purposes began in 1756, these early loans – like those for turnpike development – were simply assignments of the revenues, that is, mortgages. The use of life annuities as an alternative in the substantial Act of 1771 relating to the relief of the poor in Oxford has been referred to earlier but here is enlarged upon. The terms of the Oxford Act immediately illustrate the problem of assessing the value of a life annuity at that date, in the absence of reliable life tables; the relevant terms of the Act were:

That it shall and may be lawful to or for any person or persons to contribute, advance and pay into the hands of the Treasurer any sum or sums of money not exceeding in the whole the sum of ten thousand pounds for the absolute purchase of one or more annuity or annuities to be paid and payable during the full term of the natural life of every such contributor respectively, or the natural life of such other person as shall be nominated by or on behalf of such respective contributor at the time of payment of his respective contribution money; which annuity or annuities shall not exceed the rate of Nine Pounds per annum for every One Hundred Pounds and so in proportion for any greater or lesser sum. [Payment was to be made quarterly.]

Which annuities shall be publically sold by the Guardians of the Poor in the said Council Chamber or some other public place [after notice] to be best bidder for the same.

Let it be said that whatever the form of the loan, the practical exercise was the 'mortgaging' of the revenues available for an indefinite period; the problem lay in the selection of 'best bidder'.

The maximum rate of interest permitted at that date under the laws for the control of usury was 5 per cent, and had been so since 1713. The rate offered on the Oxford annuities of £9 per cent would conventionally be described as 'eleven years' purchase', although this is a dubious method of assessment because it implies that all the annual payments were towards the repayment of principal, whereas in fact 5 per cent on the diminishing amount of outstanding principal should be regarded as normal interest.

Today an annuity is quoted on the basis of what annual sum a payment of £100 will buy, according to the age and sex of the applicant (the insurance companies making their own estimates of the trend of interest rates). The Oxford offer (and many like it which followed) seems to have been on the basis of an offer of an annual sum (in this case £9 per £100 nominal) for life, and an invitation for the would-be annuitant to declare what sum in cash he would pay for the nominal value of £100, representing this annual return to him of £9 for life. The 'yield' of this 9 per cent would thus depend on the price which the buyer thought it worth his while to pay – in the same way as the yield on 'gilts' is calculated today. Both sides to the bargain would be speculating without the benefit of life expectancy tables for reference. Therefore, in these early days the annual annuity was fixed, and the variable was the purchase price, in contrast to the reverse approach today. Using no doubt what would now be called 'their best endeavours' the Guardians of the Poor would have been required to assess, for example, which was the better offer for a £9-a-year annuity for life between, say, in contrast, £110 offered on behalf of a 10-year-old female and £90 by a 65-year-old male.

There is another indication in the Oxford Act that variable sums of money per £100 nominal were involved; a later clause says that each purchaser was to have a receipt 'importing the receipt of so much purchase money as shall so be paid'. For his deed the purchaser was also to have 'an order on parchment or vellum for payment of the said security for and during the life' of the person nominated. This 'order' would specify the units of £9 a year which the buyer was to receive. A further possible complication was that the annuity (that is, the annual sum received by the purchaser) could subsequently be assigned 'to any person whatsoever'; but although this is not said, the assumption must have been that the annuity continued to depend on the life of the person originally nominated, even though such nominee outlived the investor, indeed this was the reason for the adoption of young nominees. The security of the rate was not expressed specifically, but the treasurer was required to 'pay the same out of the first monies which shall be in his hands arising by the rates' – which no doubt means that the annuity payments had at that stage priority over all other debts.

In 1774, a Poor Law Act for the Liberty of the Tower of London declared that borrowing by annuities was 'the most speedy and effectual method to accomplish the good ends and purposes intended by this Act'. These annuities were also on a 9 per cent basis, but 'the rate at which the said annuities shall be purchased . . . shall be settled and adjusted by the Trustees . . . as they think proper'. This phraseology certainly indicates that the guardians were required to strike a price with each bidder, which would no doubt roughly have regard to his age and condition. Unfortunately evidence has not come to light to illustrate how the guardians went to work in these circumstances.

The guardians at Stow, in 1778, in undertaking to pay life annuities, were to 'assign over and charge the Poor's Rate', a typical mortgaging formula here applied to annuities. Thus the guardians were mortgaging the rate and making repayment and paying interest in the form of a speculation on the lives of the lenders on an annuity basis. By contrast, an Act of 1781 applying both to poor relief and streetworks at Plymouth Docks granted and assigned a yearly sum out of the rates and assessments to be paid 'in every year for ever' – a perpetual annuity; in this instance the rate is not 9 but 5 per cent, for the obvious reason that no repayment of principal was involved. As was shown in Part 2, the dangers of excessive 'bargains' were avoided in a Poor Act of 1775 at East and West Flegg (where a tontine was also used) by the provision that annuities were not to be sold to anyone less than 50 years of age, and for more than £5 p.a.

Again to repeat earlier examples, in 1782, for poor relief in the parish of St Luke (Middlesex) there appeared an early – possibly the first – crude but real attempt to relate annuity payments to life expectancy. In this Act annuities were not to be granted to any person of less than 45 years of age, at which point the annuity was on an £8 per cent basis; for those aged 50 and over the rate was 10 per cent and for those of 60 and over 12 per cent. In a case of this kind apparently a price would not need to be negotiated; the price of £100 was fixed, but the yield depended on what was not the variable, that is, the commencing age of the annuitant, but still apparently without a sex differentiation.

Thus although primitive efforts were being made to relate the value of annuities to life expectation, the otherwise workmanlike Act for relief of the poor at Tunstead and Happing, in Norfolk, in 1785 which provided for borrowing by mortgages, life annuities, term annuities, deferred annuities and a tontine, and moreover gave draft forms for each type of security, did not attempt to base annuities on starting ages, nor say how the price was to be fixed. The words providing for annuities were 'for life, or a term of years, or to take place at the end of a certain number of years' and to meet these the rates were to be 'assigned over and charged'.

The Manchester Poor Relief Act 1790 illustrated a slight variant on the system of matching rates to ages but not sex; 45–49, 9 per cent; 50–59, 10 per cent; and 60 and over, 12 per cent. An Act in 1791 for the welfare of the poor at Ellesmere Port, in Cheshire, contained a scale for age 20 and above: to age 30, 7½ per cent; under 40, 8 per cent; under 50, 9 per cent; under 60, 10 per cent; and 60 and over, 11 per cent. As late as 1819 a Poor Law Amendment Act introduced some general annuity powers but confined these to persons over 50 years of age, or for a certain term not exceeding fifteen years, that is, the alternatives of either life or term annuities.

A Manchester Act of 1817 for the building of the Blackfriars Bridge over the River Irwell gave power to borrow by annuities (with the suspicion of a suggestion that a tontine might be used), but said that 'for preventing any improvident Grants of Annuities under this Act' the annuities should be linked to age at commencement, and laid down a nine-stage scale beginning at £8 3s 0d for any person not over the age of 35 and running to £18 10s 0d at age 75, for £100 of consideration. At long last the significance of life expectancy was becoming recognized for its supreme importance.

These rough-and-ready annuity provisions of the early Poor Law are matched in other services during the period, as already quoted. In 1772 streetworks in the parish of St Sepulchre (Middlesex) could be financed by life annuities, charged on the rate and 'sold to the highest bidder at a public sale'. In 1774 the extension of a burial ground in Bristol could be financed by 8 per cent life annuities, but not issued in favour of any person less than 48 years of age. An Act for streetworks and general improvements in Reading, in 1785, is of interest for the contrasting descriptions of the securities. The commissioners could 'mortgage or assign over the rates for money borrowed', or they could sell annuities 'secured upon and payable out of the rates' – both methods to rank equally. These were life annuities at 10 per cent without age specification but were to be issued on public sale to the best bidder. On the death of an annuitant further annuities could be sold presumably to permit further work without specific sanction.

Improvements at Cambridge in 1788 could be financed by mortgages (by which the commissioners could 'mortgage, demise, grant or assign over' the rates, duty and tolls) or by annuities ('secured upon and payable out of' the rates), and these 10 per cent life annuities could be 'by way of tontine or otherwise', although the tontine alternative was not acted upon. Examples of Cambridge 10 per cent life annuities have been described earlier in which, although the ages of those involved are not given in the records, the precision of the annuities paid suggest a careful examination of the circumstances.

One other example is of particular interest. The Edinburgh Corporation Debts Act 1838 was passed to 'regulate and secure the debt due by the City of Edinburgh', to confirm an agreement between the city and its creditors, and to effect settlement of the affairs of the city and the town of Leith, the city's finances having 'for some years been in a state of general embarrassment and various difficulties have therein arisen in relation to a settlement with the creditors of the City'. Thus it was 'most desirable that a remedy should be provided against the great injury and inconvenience coming from these causes'. By agreement, one-quarter of the value of earlier bonds was 'written off', and the remaining three-quarters converted into Liferent Annuities. These seem to have been ordinary life annuities but (and Mr Walter Cowan, the present Deputy Director of Finance, agrees) they may have been simply bonds at interest but maturing only on the death of the holder, at which date principal would be repaid. However, 3 per cent Bonds of Annuity were also issued and there were specifically perpetual annuities over which the liferent annuities took preference.

However, despite this later date, life annuities in England although obviously popular for a time never appeared in general local government legislation and seem to have disappeared by about 1800; even in the Companies and Commissioners Clauses Acts they find no place as an alternative to the mortgage and the bond, although amortization on either of the annuity systems continued to be acceptable. The 'insurance-risk' element of life annuities seems to have come to be considered inappropriate to local government borrowing. In any event, a distinct uneasiness in the minds of the central authorities about life annuities is apparent in an Act of 1777 requiring the registration of grants of life annuities. This seems clearly to be related to the control of usury; the preamble said:

Whereas the pernicious practice of raising money by the Sale of Life Annuities hath of late years greatly increased, and is much promoted by the Secrecy with which such transactions are conducted . . .

The underlying implication seems to be that the control of interest rates was being flouted in this way by obscurity about the make-up of the returns offered.

The conclusion in relation to annuities must therefore be that the 'true' annuity, that is the form of instrument which has a specific identifying characteristic, was the life annuity, the speculative element of which – and in the absence of reliable life expectation tables – finally drove it from favour after a brief period of popularity, though the principle remained as a basis for the calculation of amortization. What is perhaps strange is that this method of borrowing lost favour only shortly before the data necessary for the compilation of adequate statistics began to be formed (in 1836).

DEBENTURES   Except that the name persists in current legislation by reference to the Local Loans Act 1875, debentures merit little attention in the consideration of local authority borrowing. Yet the term continues to crop up. The several definitions of a debenture available all indicate its generalized character. In the Mortgage Debenture Act 1865 it is 'a deed under the Common Seal of the company, duly stamped, as a mortgage of the amount secured'. In the County Debentures Act 1873 it is 'a security for a principal sum and interest to be charged on the county rate in such debenture specified' and may be payable to bearer. The Local Loans Act stipulates that: 'A debenture shall be an instrument taking effect as a deed and charging the local rate or property in such debenture specified . . . with payment of the principal sum and interest', and is also to be available in bearer form. For the purposes of the stamp duty due on a debenture the Stamp Office of the Inland Revenue relied on a case, in 1881, in which a learned judge said: 'In my opinion a "debenture" means a document which either creates a debt or acknowledges it, and any document which fills either of these conditions is a "debenture".' This virtually means that any local authority borrowing instrument is in the nature of a debenture – for whatever that is worth.

The conclusion has been reached that these debentures are akin to simple mortgages, with the added facility not usually associated with mortgages that they might be issued in bearer form. The Treasury's reactions to a local authority which might decide to exercise the 1972 Act powers to issue debentures under the Local Loans Act and chose the bearer type would be interesting. The 'debenture stock' also mentioned in the Local Loans Act seems in no way to differ from ordinary stock.

In central government borrowing debentures, at the early dates in which they were used, seem to have been loans which were expected to be repaid in due course, and though transferable/assignable did not have an organized market in contrast with 'government annuities', which were the predecessors of 'gilts' and for which there was an organized market through the Stock Exchange even in its primitive form. For example, an Act of 1804 provided for the raising of money in Ireland both by annuities and debentures for which £100 contribution produced holdings of £112 7s 3d to earn 5 per cent.

The County Debentures Act 1873 for a brief number of years allowed the use of this instrument in either nominal or bearer form by counties (though of course this was before the creation of the elected county councils). These seem similar in most respects to the mortgage. An unfortunate provision in the 1873 Act was that debentures issued under it took priority according to date, but fortunately this did not apply under the 1875 Act. Under the Local Government Act 1888 this power was replaced by the right to issue debentures under the Local Loans Act 1875, a power which seems to have been largely ignored.

The 1873 Act provided that unless a local Act provided otherwise, debentures should be discharged by equal annual instalments with interest on the balance, which puts the instruments in the category of term annuities which again, to all intents and purposes, are mortgages repayable on an annual basis. The repayment provisions of the 1875 Act, as already described, were more widely drawn to provide for maturity repayment as well as by equal annual instalments. The conclusion must be that if there is or was such an instrument as a 'debenture', it is capable in local government of having a form which puts it close to the mortgage or bond, or even to certain types of annuity.

Certainly, there is no tradition of borrowing by debentures by local authorities, although some use may have been made at some time of this power. However, if there had been more co-operation (or even any co-operation) between those who drafted the Public Health Act and the Local Loans Act, both of 1875, the generalized term debenture – simply, a loan – might well have emerged as the designation for an all-purpose, or nearly all-purpose, local authority borrowing instrument.

TONTINES There are numerous variant types of tontine, but especially in application to local government a tontine fundamentally is a scheme in which a fund is created by a group of subscribers who share its earnings, but in which as time goes on the shares of those subscribers who die do not fall out, but are apportioned among the diminishing number of survivors, until the final survivor receives the whole of the interest (or other earnings) for the remainder of his life. The final survivor may also in certain tontines – generally those of a privately organized character – acquire the whole of the remaining capital, or the asset which has been provided by the capital (for instance, an hotel).[2] There seem to have been tontines where the income was not distributed, but accumulated, thus vastly augmenting the capital sum falling to the final survivor, or where interest was not distributed for a number of years (the tontine period) while the fund and its income 'built up', but the number of participants diminished, so that in either of these systems the capital fund ultimately available to the survivor could be substantial. In a public tontine, organized by a public authority, the capital sum was used immediately for the purposes of a public service (for instance, the building of a workhouse) and was never returned to the subscribers, who nevertheless in their diminishing numbers shared the whole sum of the interest. This form of raising funds had only a minuscule effect on local authority borrowing, but it is such an extraordinary device to have found its way into local government finance at all that a brief reference to the examples discovered seems justified.

The idea was introduced into France in 1653 by an Italian (Neapolitan) banker, Lorenzo Tonti, but apparently such a device is known to have been used in Italy before this date, so the name of the original genius behind the idea is lost. The modest use of the tontine in local government was preceded by its use in central government, combined with lotteries.

In a private tontine, particularly where the interest was accumulated, a situation of great tension naturally developed as the surviving members dwindled to a mere handful especially among those interested in the estate of a possible final survivor, and there are horrific tales in the records of the use of physical violence employed to narrow down the competition for the final prize. The increases in income alone on the death of one of the last few survivors in a 'distributing' tontine could itself be a source of temptation for the use of skulduggery.[3] R. L. Stevenson, with his stepson Lloyd Osborne, exploited this theme in The Wrong Box, where a tontine was established in which interest was not distributed, but accumulated, so that the survivor was eligible to receive a very substantial capital fund. More recently Thomas B. Costain based his long novel The Tontine on the problems involved in this form of speculative fortune-hunting.

Under the title heading 'A very bad man has a very good idea' Costain says:

> I can explain how it works in a few words. Generally there are six or eight classes, starting with children and winding up with people over fifty-five. Each class is run separately. Suppose we consider boys and girls from twelve to eighteen years. They are entered by parents at one hundred guineas apiece. For twenty years – that's what we call the tontine period – the money is kept in active use and the profits are applied to [that is, added to] the principal, except, of course, such sums as are needed to pay the operating costs. At the end of the tontine period the total has rather more than doubled. At this point the payment of interest begins. Each participant gets an equal amount. And now . . . we come to the gimmer. When the holder of a share dies or falls out of sight, his part of the interest reverts to the others and his payments thereafter are divided equally among all the survivors. As the years pass and the members begin to die off faster, the survivors begin to enjoy handsome incomes. It becomes fantastic as things narrow down; because, you see, the full amount must be paid no matter how few there are to receive it.

Costain fails to consider the effect of the classes, and is vague about the future of the capital sum.[4,5]

The object of a public tontine, with which we are concerned, was to raise a capital sum for the creation of an asset. Such schemes were occasionally called in the statutes 'Annuities with the benefit of survival' or

'Schemes of survival by classes'. Reference to 'survival by classes' meant that subscribers were divided into broad age-groups in order to equate the chances of survival (as mentioned above by Costain), perhaps with higher interest rates for the older age-groups. This, in effect, created a group of small tontines, operated as a single overall scheme.

The general rate of interest on tontines was usually in the region of 5 per cent, a rate which seems to make little allowance for any element of repayment of the capital sum invested as on the more straightforward annuity schemes. Assessment of 'gainers and losers' is not easy – depending on 'contingencies' even more than in normal life annuities. The borrower continued to pay this total interest on the original sum of capital appropriated to each group, so long as any survivor remained in each group. After a certain point, survivors therefore received a good deal more on their original investment than they would have been likely to receive on a straight life annuity, but such profit as they made was really at the expense of those who had fallen by the wayside, and not at the expense of the borrower. Because the borrower continued to pay full interest as long as a single contributor survived, his retention of the capital sum did not necessarily assure him of a profit against a similar number of investors in life annuities. On the other hand, the borrower was better off than he would have been with an annuity scheme because of the lower rates on tontines than on equivalent annuities (e.g. 5 per cent rather than say 9 per cent).

A volume made available by courtesy of the National Debt Office, entitled *Early Years of the Funded Debt* (author unknown), describes three central government tontines of 1693, 1766 and 1789. None was considered to have been successful (except, no doubt, by the later survivors). The first, designed to raise £1 million, collected only £108,000. There was no division into classes, and the annuities distributed were 'frozen' when the survivors reached seven in number. The oldest male died at age 93 and the oldest female at 100, thus early confirmation of the pattern of greater longevity for women; the final survivor dying in 1783 had an 'annuity' of £1,080 (£108,000 at 7 per cent divided between 7 = £1,080).

The 1766 tontine was part of a package deal in which subscribers received a block of 3 per cent annuities, a £10 lottery ticket and a 3 per cent tontine share in which there were six classes. Only 138 lives were nominated by contributions of the trifling amount of £18,000, and the shortfall had to be made good by the sale of ordinary annuities. Any subscriber who failed to apply for the payment of his annual sum within twenty days of the year-end forfeited it. Nevertheless, the survivor who died in 1859 had been in receipt of the whole of the annual sum of £540 for four years (3 per cent on £18,000) on an original contribution which would seem to have been £130. The main central government tontine was that of 1789, provided for in an Act of George III intended to raise £1,002,500. The classes and the annual payments which each was to receive at the start were as follows:

age at the date of nomination	annuity per £100
20-29	£4 5s 6d
30-39	£4 8s 6d
40-49	£4 13s 6d
50-59	£5 1s 6d
60 and above	£5 12s 0d

to be paid half-yearly out of the consolidated fund. And:

> upon the death of any nominee the Annuity falling in shall be distributed among the several persons interested whose nominee shall survive in the class in which the person dying shall be nominated but the Annuity of any one share which shall by survivorship amount to £1,000 shall so continue to be payable ... during the life of such nominee.

Thus the scheme made some attempt to provide against excessive profits by survivors – which simply meant that the possible 'excesses' remained with the (government) borrower.

A total of 5,733 shares were taken up, but during the life of the scheme many shareholders became disillusioned and were allowed to exchange for long annuities at 3 per cent for the peculiar term of 69¼ years. The places of those who exchanged in this way were filled by 'dummies' to keep the scheme on an even keel. The final survivor died in 1887 at the age of 99, by which point she or he was receiving £1,000 p.a. for an initial contribution of £100.

During the researching of this book a form of 'Life Certificate' for a nominee in the 1789 tontine has come to light.[6] This is more elaborate than, but similar to, that used in present pension funds, whereby some person of standing is required to certify that the nominee has 'appeared before me personally on ...' (that is, is still alive). A footnote to the certificate quotes an Act of 1832 about the penalties for false witness, so that the 1789 tontine was flourishing at that later date, yet still had a half-century to run.

This may seem an overelaborate introduction to the minimal references to tontines in local government but the curious feature is that where tontines were actually used in local government, they do not seem to have been sanctified by statute, and where they were authorized by statute enthusiasm seems to have run out on the passing of the Act, so that authorized schemes were not in fact implemented. Nevertheless, the foregoing evidence shows that where local authorities used tontines, they were simply following central government practice.

The oldest local government tontine scheme which has been discovered during the writing of this book was launched at Chester in 1757; it appears to have been without statutory sanction and was not in fact described as a tontine, although it was clearly a scheme of 'survivorship' on what was undoubtedly a tontine basis. As earlier described, a committee had been appointed by the city council to raise £6,000 'to answer the City's exigencies'. The scheme produced by this committee and approved by the council involved the granting of annuities on lives; 120 persons were expected each to invest £50 for which at the outset they would receive £6 p.a. (12 per cent) until the number of survivors was reduced to 80 persons. At this point each surviving investor would receive £7 p.a. and so on in a crudely diminishing scale of numbers of survivors until the last four would receive £100 each, the last two £200 each and the final survivor £400 p.a. Survivors were to appear in person or 'be certified as being alive on 24th December'. The weighting of this scheme in favour of the borrower meant that, for a large part of the time, savings through deaths fell to the benefit of the city, and at the end the city was expected to pay only £400 p.a. for the use of £6,000 without having any liability to repay capital. As security each contributor was to be given a bond, and another bond was to be given to three unnamed gentlemen assuring them of access to the income from a property worth £440 p.a., if the city defaulted for three months on interest payments; from this income the three gentlemen were to make good the default. When a contributor died, his entitlement immediately 'sank'; part-year apportionments of the annuity were not to be made. It is hardly surprising that this scheme was not particularly successful; it raised only £4,000, which was used to repair the Exchange, discharge a debt to the Charity School, help towards the erection of a workhouse and the construction of a quay on the River Dee. Any balance was to be held by the mayor. What could apparently be done with £4,000 is some indication of the value of the pound in 1757.

A series of local authority tontines was discovered by Dr Anne Digby (see her *Pauper Palaces*, 1978), while investigating Poor Law incorporations in East Anglia. In studying Poor Law incorporations in that area, she has thrown light on borrowing practices for that purpose, including what so far seems to be the first use of the tontine by a quasi-local authority, though as borrowing was not her theme, she leaves unanswered some of the questions which a treasurer would like to have had answered, particularly as to the final outcome of the tontines used.

In discussing the East and West Flegg Poor Law Incorporation of 1775 (not the first incorporation, as we have already noted), she says: 'The Flegg Incorporation, like several other East Anglian incorporations, was financed in part by a tontine scheme, which was a form of life annuity which increased in amount as other subscribers died.' Of the £6,000 authorized by the Flegg Act, £2,500 was in fact raised by twenty-five shares or bonds of £100 each in a tontine scheme. A nominee was to be registered for each share on whose life the interest of the subscriber to such share was to depend, and as the nominees died the shares and interest depending thereon were to vest in the subscribers or names of the surviving nominees: 'There was no shortage of shareholders, who found it an irresistible method of satisfying their gambling instincts while salving their consciences by subscribing to a good, charitable cause.' However, reference to the Act itself shows that it makes no reference to a tontine. It simply provided for the mortgaging ('assigning over') of the rate and by borrowing on life annuities, provided that no person of less than 50 years was sold an annuity, and that no annuity was to exceed £50 per annum.

Obviously in this area of Norfolk there was an underlying non-statutory use of tontines, which is certainly worthy of further investigation. This non-statutory aspect is borne out by the experience in the Forehoe incorporation of 1776. Dr Digby says that the entire capital was raised by a tontine scheme in which 110 shares of £100 each were sold. The initial interest was 5 per cent, but by 1800 there is evidence to show that there were eighty-five shareholders alive who were receiving 6·4 per cent and that by 1836 the numbers had been so further reduced that the interest rate was 15·3 per cent to each. Yet again no authority appears in the Act for such a scheme where only mortgages, and not even straight life annuities, were authorized.

Nine years later, in 1785, the Act for the Incorporation at Tunstead and Happing, in Norfolk, contained specific powers for a tontine. The Act said: 'If the Directors and Acting Guardians shall think proper to raise any portion of the money ... by a Scheme of Survivorship, the same may be raised in the following manner.' The scheme outlined provided for 5 per cent interest 'all of which said interest shall be fairly divided amongst the contributors during the lives of their respective nominees'. Interest was to be half-yearly:

> Upon the death of a nominee the share or shares which was or were payable during his life shall be equally divided among the rest of the contributors whose nominees shall still be living ... so that from time to time the whole interest agreed to be paid to the said contributors for the sum by them advanced shall be divided and paid among the contributors whose nominees do survive until such time as there shall be no nominee living.

The provisions made clear that the interest continued so long as the nominee lived, even though the contributor died, but the conclusive statement was that 'on the death of all the nominees, all interest in and for the said sum of money so contributed shall cease'. The units were to be not less than £50 each, and there was to be only one nominee per £100. A form of agreement printed as a schedule to the Act was headed 'Form of Agreement and Mortgage by way of Tontine', thus further confusing the classification of this type of instrument. This described the security as the rates to be raised for the relief of the poor 'in the said Hundreds'.

A tontine was also authorized in a scheme of incorporation for poor relief purposes in the Isle of Wight. Money could be borrowed on mortgage at 4 per cent, but for the purposes of a tontine at 5 per cent, a very modest additional incentive. The wording was almost identical to that used for the Tunstead tontine. Information supplied from the Isle of Wight (by Mrs Johanna Jones, a researcher into the history of Poor Law provisions on the island) is to the effect that the power was never exercised, as the rate of 5 per cent was (not surprisingly) considered to be too low. This view is substantiated by the fact that a central government tontine in 1778 was organized on a 7 per cent basis (not listed in the National Debt Office record).

A similar non-event was provided for at Cambridge in an Act of 1788 for streetworks. The power to borrow on the rates and tolls was 'by the granting of annuities for lives by way of tontine or otherwise', but the draft form in the schedule to the Act provides for standard life annuities only. The city treasurer and county archivist have unearthed minutes which record that the commissioners authorized the printing of a proposal by a Mr Haggerstone, but no copy of this can be found, and there are doubts as to whether the proposal was in fact ever printed; however, no doubt the enthusiasm of Mr Haggerstone caused the inclusion of the clause in this Act, although that was as far as he managed to persuade his colleagues.

Plymouth seems to have been a town much interested in tontines as a way of raising capital funds for public purposes, but there is no record of this in statutes. The Devon Record Office has supplied most interesting details of a scheme as late as 1811 for the building of 'an elegant ballroom, a theatre, and a commodious hotel', and possibly a public library, at the modest cost of £20,000. On the face of it, although according to the announcement annuities were to be 'secured by bonds under the seal of the Corporation thereby binding the whole of their very large properties to the performance of their obligations', there is doubt whether the borough had statutory powers to provide such buildings or to raise the funds by a tontine. There was indeed a Plymouth Corporation Act of 1811, but this makes no mention of this project or of a tontine.

Nevertheless, the scheme was obviously a success in raising the £20,000 because, by the time the proposal was advertised, the subscription of £100 shares had already exceeded £17,000. Each subscriber was to receive 'an immediate annuity of £5 clear of property tax' as well as a ticket for a lottery which thereby afforded 'a chance of an immediate ten-fold return on their subscription' – a top prize of £1,000. The nominees were 'to be arranged in ten classes of twenty according to their ages', with an added provision that a special class was to be formed of persons 'upwards of 50 years', who would receive £7 per cent clear from the start, as well as the lottery ticket. The advertisement pointed out, as an inducement, that a similar scheme for the provision of a market launched a few years earlier already gave surviving contributors a net income of nearly 7 per cent. An earlier Plymouth Corporation Act of 1805 makes no mention of this project either. This is precisely the type of scheme which might have been the subject of a private tontine, but the security of the property of the local authority and the implication that the ultimate ownership of the property was with the corporation makes clear that this was a municipal project. The mayor and his relatives figure so prominently in the list of contributors that both the lottery and the survivorship might easily have come their way.

Copies of the receipts from contributors for the payment of interest to them are available for 1811 and 1841; these show that while contributors started off with £5 of interest in the opening year, by 1841 some classes were receiving £28 p.a. and others over £32 p.a. Unfortunately the later history of this tontine is not available, but may yet be awaiting exhumation from the records.

A very few years later, in 1817, an Act for the building of the Blackfriars Bridge in Manchester, referred to earlier, used the phrase that such annuities 'shall be granted and made payable either with or without Benefit of Survivorship', which must be understood to mean that the proprietors could use the tontine system if they so wished. The form of annuity written into the Act refers to 'the natural life, or natural lives (if more than one), and the life of the survivor of them (as the case may be)'. This could conceivably refer to joint annuities on two or possibly three lives, but the phrase 'benefit of survivorship' almost certainly left the door open to a tontine scheme of some kind. However, there is no record of borrowing in this form.

No doubt, there were a number of tontines organized by local authorities in this period, details of which are now lost; tracing them is something of a matter of chance. However, an interesting variant occurred at Kingston upon Hull in 1806 when the borough borrowed – apparently without statutory sanction – £12,000 by way of tontine in shares of £100 to build a market and shambles. In this instance interest was paid initially at 5 per cent, but the repayment of the whole amount of capital was also promised to survivors at the end of twenty-one years. The advertisement announcing the scheme suggested that survivors might hope to receive a 50 per cent increment in their capital at the end of this time and an increasing rate of interest meanwhile. The result was less sanguine. The records show that the survivors in 1828 received only £115·78, which indicates that of the original 120 contributors there were still 103 persons benefiting; the calculation does not work out exactly, perhaps because the final payment included also the final payment of interest, which would by then on these numbers be in the region of 6 per cent.

In addition to the sum raised in this way, the borough promised to expend a further £4,000–£5,000 on a scheme to provide 100 butchers and other shops from which an income of £1,050 p.a. could be expected, thus giving an income of £450 in excess of the annual interest charge and increasing the security to the investors. The surplus of income after payment of interest to the tontine-holders, even if accumulated at interest, would certainly not have been sufficient to provide the full capital sum after twenty-one years, particularly after bearing management expenses. However, records are available which indicate that a short-term loan of £8,384 from the borough's bankers was raised to supplement the available surplus in 1829 to meet the tontine payment and also that this bridging loan with other debt was funded by a bond issue in 1830. Incidentally, the original tontine borrowing was acknowledged by an overall 'mortgage bond', so that the terms annuity, mortgage and bond are all associated with this speculative borrowing device.

Even Adam Smith in his *Wealth of Nations* spoke not unkindly of tontines, and Robert Hamilton in *An Enquiry into the Management of the National Debt* (1814) says:

> Tontines seem adapted to the passions of human nature, from the hope every man entertains of longevity, and the desire of ease and affluence in old age; and they are beneficial to the public, as affording a discharge of the debt, although a distant one, without any payment. They have been extensively adopted in some foreign countries, but seldom in Britain. The last and almost the only scheme of this kind now subsisting among us is that of 1789. Although the sum proposed to be raised in this way was only £1,002,500 the persons who contracted with the Government for the whole were unable to complete it without loss ('farming out' the management); and an alternative was afterwards allowed them of a long annuity.

(It is a footnote to this quotation that shows that the annuities used to complete the sum required were for the peculiar term of 69¼ years at £4 5s 0d per cent.

There seems to be little more to be said on this topic. It ill-behoves a generation which buys premium bonds where the interest is shared by lot (even though the depreciated capital is refundable), and favours municipal lotteries, to criticize a scheme for the combination of the sharing of interest with (sometimes) a lottery incentive.

The proper classification of a tontine as a system of local authority borrowing is not easily determined. A tontine involves the mortgaging or assignment of revenue as security, but 'life survival' is an essential element. In this they are similar to annuities; the similarity goes further, in that payments made during the existence of a scheme should, as with annuities, represent both the payment of interest and the repayment of capital – unlike the private tontines, the final survivor of a local government tontine did not acquire the asset, rather this remained with the local authority. However, rates on tontines do not seem to have been sufficient to have incorporated a full return of capital. In so far as some survivors gained mightily by the increase in their return this was provided less by repayment of their original capital, but more by the re-allocation of the interest otherwise due to others. Investors seem nevertheless to have been attracted to tontines, and the reason seems to have been the lottery element involved, an element far more significant than in any conventional annuity. The most that can be said for them is that they do in a peculiar way include an element of life annuity, but annuities, mortgaging rates and tolls 'modified on a lottery principle' seems to be as good a classification as any. One thing seems certain: local government is unlikely to see their like again. The Revd Dr Trusler, writing in 1790, had no doubt about his views: 'Of all the phantoms to entice and deceive the multitude, nothing are more mischievous than Tontines!'

NOTES: CHAPTER 16

1   The latest conjecture is that the gap between the life expectation of males and females, which is in favour of females, is tending to increase, thus further reducing the annual value of annuities on offer to women (information from Mr Geoffrey Heywood, Consultant Actuary).

2   There is a Tontine Hotel in Cleveland created by this means and another in Peebles which claims the added distinction of having been constructed by French prisoners from the Napoleonic Wars; another is close to Iron Bridge, in Salop. Tontines hotels are said to suffer from the problem of raising adequate maintenance funds during the life of the tontine; see also Sheridan's *School for Scandal*: 'I hear he pays as many annuities as the Irish tontine.'

3   Various dictionary and encyclopaedia references consulted indicate that foul play was not infrequently attempted in an effort to influence entitlement to the final capital sum, particularly in certain French schemes where vast fortunes were involved. There is a reference to tontines and tontine certificates in *Scripophilly* by Keith Hollander (1982) in which the author claims that tontines are now illegal because of the threats of violence inherent in them; however, it has not been possible to substantiate this allegation of prohibition.

4   This author is now deceased; his family were unable to elucidate his scheme further for me.

5   By a strange coincidence the ghost of a tontine haunts an area less than half a mile from my address in South Manchester. The Victoria Park Residential Estate was established by Act of Parliament in 1837, 'The Company was formed on the basis of a tontine . . . whereby each holder of a £100 share could nominate a "life". If the person nominated died within the first three years another life could be chosen . . . When only fifty lives remained, the whole assets were to be divided between the shareholders . . . The [tontine] scheme came to nothing, for the company did not survive for a long enough period' (Maurice Spiers, *Victoria Park, Manchester*, Chetham Society, 1976). However, the residential development scheme itself did flourish, and for many years entry to the area was protected by toll-gates; ultimately, in quite recent years the area was acquired and 'liberated' by the city council.

6   The discovery of this certificate in a volume of statutes in which it appeared to have been used as a place-marker was one of a number of examples of serendipity which occurred during the course of writing this book.

Chapter 17

STOCK

Although today its meaning in relation to borrowing is well understood, the truth is that the origin of the term 'stock' is somewhat obscure. In commercial use it relates to the capital of a company – as stocks, shares and debentures (loans), all of which are sometimes also described overall as the company's stock. In the governmental sense it relates to the long-term 'funded' debt the securities for which are issued under arrangements which make them as readily marketable as commercial stock. Both forms represent a liability of the borrowers to the stockholders and investors.

Webster's International Dictionary claims that in its financial sense the term originates in the extraordinary system of use by the Exchequer over centuries of wooden sticks known as 'tallies'. These were notched to record financial transactions. The tally was then split down the middle, one half – the stock – going to the creditor, and the other half – the foil, hence counterfoil – remaining with the government as debtor. *Collins' English Dictionary* gives one of the many meanings of stock as '[formerly] the part of an account or tally given to a creditor; the debt represented by this'. Though tallies occur before 1644, an Act of that year (16/17 C.ii.1) that is, before the foundation of the National Debt, provided for a system of Crown borrowing by which a 'Tally of Loan' would be struck by the Exchequer (bearing interest at 6 per cent). These loans were also to be registered and an order on paper for repayment and a warrant for interest on forbearing to take repayment were also given to the creditor. If the portion of a tally given to the lender was indeed the 'stock', the transference of this term to borrowing by the government by the issue of stocks does not require much stretch of the imagination. These orders on paper were a means of facilitating the negotiability of the stock. 'Government paper' is still a term in colloquial use. Thus stock had from the start an implication of negotiability, and the evolution of the present-day Stock Exchange from meetings in coffee-houses, where stocks were bought and sold presents a natural sequence.

On the other hand, the *Oxford Etymological Dictionary* does not include the 'tally' meaning for stock, but records use of the term from the fifteenth century as 'fund, store (of money)'. Furthermore, in local government legislation clear statutory uses of the word 'stock' from early times both for stocks of materials (for example, for use in employing the paupers in a workhouse) and for stocks or supluses of money have already been quoted. The famous Statute of Elizabeth 1601, after dealing with general responsibilities for poor relief and the rates to be levied to finance those activities said that all fines and penalties collectable for non-compliance with the requirements of the Act should be used for the general purpose of the Act and 'towards a Stock'. That this meant a 'fund' created by surplus moneys is made clear by a final section of the Act adding further duties of a general and somewhat optional character of poor relief, for example, aid to those suffering misfortune by fire, flood, or the sea, and the provision of county hospitals, which should be financed by the use of 'all surplusage of money which shall be remaining in the said Stocks of any County'. The use of the term (with a reference back to 1601 and other Acts) is to be found over 100 years later in an Act of 1710 for 'ratifying several purchases lately made with the Public Stock of the County of Devon and for making further purchases for the use of the said County with the Public Stock thereof'. This Act seems to have been necessitated by doubts as to whether some of the expenditure which had been financed from the 'public stock' was really within the authority of earlier statutes; ratification was therefore sought. Another example of the use of the word stock in this context occurred in 1778, where the borrowing of money was authorized for the provision of a gaol at Bodmin, in Cornwall, on the security, both for principal and interest, of the 'County Stock' – which seems to embrace that fund into which the precepts from the parishes were paid, in modern terms the 'county fund'. The same phrase also occurred, in 1700, in regard to harbour works at Minehead, in Somerset. An Act of 1705 for work on the pier and harbour at Parton, in Cumberland, allowed trustees to borrow to raise 'such sum or stock of money' as was necessary on the security of the tolls. Thus the need to borrow to augment the 'stock' of money available may equally well be the origin of the term.

Whatever the real origin of the term (and in remoter history these alternative origins might conceivably coalesce), a book published in its fourth edition, in 1761 – *Every Man his own Stockbroker*, by T. Mortimer, an author consumed by a hatred of those who formed what was clearly the origins of the Stock Exchange – says that 'the word Stock in its proper signification, means, that capital in merchandise, or money [thus combining goods and money as materials of trade] which a certain number of proprietors have agreed to make for carrying on an united commerce'. Mortimer also defines those bodies who have united together to form their own stock or capital as companies. He sees this capital as the assets rather than the liabilities of the companies and therefore takes strong exception to the designation of government debts as 'stock' because they are, in his view, the opposite of stock; government stocks are not capital, but liabilities. However, Mortimer acknowledges that government borrowing mainly by 'annuities' was nevertheless then called the 'Government stocks' and he speaks highly of the British government security for its debts. What is perhaps surprising is that local authority borrowing by stock was not introduced until late in the nineteenth century.

Local authorities began to borrow by the issue of stock in 1869, based on the experience and practices of two centuries of stock issuing by commercial companies, by the central government's success in borrowing on the 'public stocks', and the rules and practices of the evolving Stock Exchange. Now that local authority stocks, mortgages and bonds have (and have had for many years) equal priority in local authority debt portfolios and rely on the identical security of the rates and revenues of the authority, they are in effect to that extent identical securities. The difference between local authority stock and the other forms of local borrowing arises entirely from the *different provisions for marketing* and the characteristics which arise directly from this marketing facility which is the hallmark of 'stock'. The situation is slightly obscured because as nothing is in fact 'issued' with a stock issue, 'stocks' are intangible, in that they are represented not by a deed, but simply an entry in a register. Although such entries are now supported by the issue of a certificate, this has not automatically always been so, and despite the certificate and some confusion about evidence of title in the eventual Stock Regulations, the stock itself lies not in the document issued, but in the register entry. In making a stock issue, the borrower guarantees that the Stock Exchange will establish a daily market in the security, with quoted buying and selling prices, immediately on issue. Certain consequences follow from this immediate and continuous facility for marketability.

In the first place, a stock issue needs to be for a relatively substantial amount; otherwise its regular availability on the market cannot be guaranteed. Secondly, because the market is expected to be in operation within a very short time of issue, arrangements must be made for the whole of the stock to be made available virtually instantaneously with 'issue'. This is achieved by 'underwriting', a system in which various financial institutions agree (for a fee) to acquire any stock not taken up by the initial applications; the normal intention of the underwriter is to re-sell any stock he finds left on his hands, if possible at a profit, as soon as the market develops. Alternatively, an issue can be 'placed' with one financial house who will immediately make it available for sale through the usual channels; this is equivalent to single-handed underwriting. One of the consequences of 'instant issue' is the possibility of 'stagging', which means that certain buyers believing that an immediate post-issue rise in the value of the stock is likely to take place apply for an allocation of stock on issue, so that they can sell as soon as the expected rise occurs. This is encouraged by the practice of requiring only a modest payment for the stock at the time of issue, followed by further payments, to complete the full amount over the first few months of the life of the stock. Although some government stocks are issued 'on tap', this does not mean that the whole of the stock is not issued immediately. The system is that arrangements are made for the stock to be acquired by other government surplus funds, and released on to the market as required. In this way central government is, in effect, underwriting its own issue. Again to sustain a ready market stock needs to be available over the longer rather than the shorter period, so that a stock issue is a 'funded' debt – an undefined term but meaning 'with a long life'. The early stocks were in some instances perpetual, but this proved unpopular, and redeemable stock, but with a fairly long life, quickly became and remains the norm. Yet another characteristic of a marketable security of this kind is that buyers expect the issue to be made other than at par – almost invariably at a discount – though of course the price after issue may rise to a premium. This system introduces an element of capital profit, and naturally gives a changing yield as distinct from the nominal rate of interest – the 'coupon' rate.

In addition to issue by 'placing', stock can be issued by open offer to the public at a fixed price, or by tender, where lenders are invited to state the price at which they will buy, usually subject to a fixed minimum price. Although local authority stocks are not now issued as bearer documents, earlier issues, as will be shown, did provide for this further aid to marketing. Nor are government stocks issued to bearer, but arrangements for rapid transfer make them highly negotiable; the freedom of government stocks from capital gains tax if held for longer than a year is a self-created preferential treatment for central borrowing.

The provision made in early local government Acts that stock could be made available in either registered or bearer form followed the policy laid down by the Stock Certificates Act 1863, although this was a commercial measure. Although local authority stocks are not now issued in these alternative forms, this Act and the early practice led to a development which had an impact on the later issues by local authorities of money bills (see pp. 271–7). The Stock Certificates Act established the principle that a stock certificate in which the name of the holder had not been inserted entitled the bearer of the certificate to the stock described and the interest thereon. This meant that, in such cases, coupons to cover the interest needed to be attached to the instrument, and this in turn led to the use of the term 'coupon' rate as the nominal rate as distinct from the rate of 'yield'. The development of this practice thus throws further doubt on the rationality of the central government view that 'blank' money bills are not really bearer documents, as discussed in Chapter 19. This same Act of 1863 provided that a bearer certificate could be converted to a nominal certificate by the insertion and registration of a name and, *per contra*, that the holder of a registered certificate could have it converted to bearer form. These facilities were broadly repeated in the National Debt Act 1870.

The first stage in the emergence of a county-type administration for Greater London (a flexible term having different meanings in different contexts) was the formation of the Metropolitan Board of Works under the Metropolis Management Act 1855; the board's borrowing powers were initially limited to the use of mortgages on the security of the rates. In 1869 the Metropolitan Board of Works (Loans) Act gave the first local authority powers to borrow by the creation of

> capital stock to be called metropolitan consolidated stock and to be issued in such amounts and manner, at such price and times, on such terms, subject to such conditions, with such dividends, and redeem-

able (at the option of the board) at par at such times and on such conditions as the Treasury, before the creation thereof, may from time to time approve.

All issues were to be of equal priority and charged indifferently on the whole of the lands, rents and property belonging to the Board, 'and on all moneys which can be raised by the Board by rates under this Act'; subject to certain limited priorities relating to an earlier improvement fund, the stock was to be a first charge on those assets and revenues. Dividends were payable out of the metropolitan consolidated rate.

The intention was that the 1869 Act should authorize a number of successive issues, but the Act had a curious flaw as described by Sir Harry Haward in *The London County Council from Within*. The specified period for redemption was sixty years 'from the time of the first creation'. The first issue in 1869 (at 3½ per cent) took advantage of this long maturity period, but later issues (there were nine in all) were all constrained within the period of sixty years from 1869, so that, for example, the issue in 1880 could be made for only forty-nine years – surely a long enough period, but certainly not what the originators of the Act had had in mind. This provision meant that all the issues (a total of £17 million) were due to come to maturity at about the same distant date (if they were each for the maximum period available). New powers were taken in 1881 for a sixty-year 3 per cent stock (of which seven issues totalling £10·8 million were made), and in 1889 a further issue at only 2½ per cent; this issue gave the council power to redeem after thirty years, if they so determined (a requirement which seems to have been necessitated by limitations on the borrowing period for fire brigade purposes). The trend of interest rates is to be seen (and, by present-day borrowers, marvelled at) from the fact that at the end of the century the original 3½ per cent stock stood at a price of £128 for £100 nominal. This encouraged the LCC to take powers in 1896 to issue 2½ per cent consolidated stock, redeemable only at the discretion of the council, in imitation of government consols; three issues were made. By 1900 the interest rates were rising again and new consolidated stock powers were taken for 3 per cent London consols. By 1907 interest rates had crept back; an issue of consols had to be made at 3½ per cent. Liverpool Corporation also made an issue of irredeemable stock, but thereafter irredeemable stocks lost favour with central government. Nevertheless, the major LCC (Finance Consolidation) Act 1912 still gave the council power to issue both dated and undated stock; perhaps the term 'undated stock' was intended to mean something less categoric about intentions than 'irredeemable stock'. (The Metropolitan Board of Works (Loans) Act 1869 gave reasonably comprehensive details on stock management, and in particular incorporated the 'bearer' facilities of the Stock Certificates Act 1863.)

In Chapter 23 we deal with the introduction and operation of consolidated loans funds (CLFs), but attention should be drawn here to the requirement of the 1869 Metropolitan Board of Works (Loans) Act for the establishment of a CLF specifically for the handling of the stocks. This was not the comprehensive CLF of today, rather a pooling account to accommodate a conglomeration of stock borrowings. Nevertheless, this development is without doubt relevant to the introduction of CLFs in later times. The irony of the situation is that because the concept was then established of using a consolidated account for stocks when the idea of a CLF for other borrowings was mooted, stocks were excluded from the wider concept because they already formed part of their 'own' CLF, thus handicapping the total CLF concept for many years. These consolidated loans funds, confined to stock, became the general practice in the Acts promoted by other authorities.

Other authorities took powers to issue stock after the example of the Metropolitan Board of Works in 1869, but the first efforts of these authorities seem to have been directed to irredeemable rather than long-dated stocks. In 1872, for example, the Swansea Local Board of Health Act introduced perpetual debenture stock (before the 1875 Act, then) at the same time as giving powers for term, life and perpetual annuities. These borrowings were in relation to waterworks activities where perpetual annuities were already popular. On the face of it, perpetual stock (the term 'debenture' can be ignored) is simply a marketable form of a perpetual annuity. In any event, no evidence has come to light that these stock powers were used, certainly not at this early date.

Indeed the tradition is that Manchester was the second authority to issue stock, and this again was by perpetual stock in support of waterworks activities. The powers were obtained in Manchester Corporation Waterworks and Improvement Act 1872, which gave authority for the conversion of perpetual annuities, mortgages and bonds to perpetual stock; an issue was made in 1872. The form of certificate was specified in the Act, obtainable on demand by investors, emphasizing the 'registered' nature of stock, though both the register and the certificate were said to be prima-facie evidence of ownership. A charge of 2s 6d could be made for the issue of a certificate. The early history of Manchester stock powers is clearly set out in the Manchester Municipal Code. In 1875 there were two further clauses in the Act of that year, relieving the borrower of responsibility for making inquiries as to the bona fides of a stock borrowing, and incorporating the trustees investment provisions of the Debenture Stock Act 1871. These initial powers were for irredeemable stock only, but in 1886 redeemable stock powers were granted, the date of redemption to be at the borrower's option – what would perhaps better be called undated stock, though in fact redemption dates were announced at the dates of issue. In Manchester's 1891 Act the redeemable stock provisions were more extensively set out, with a full code of borrowing practices similar to the general Stock Regulations which were issued under general legislation in the same year. A significant point was that the Manchester 1891 Act withdrew the powers for the issue of irredeemable stock, which confirms the view expressed above that this type of stock was by that time no longer in favour with central government. The fact was that irredeemable securities were not consistent with the growing development of the policy that local authorities must begin to make provision for repayment immediately on borrowing. This situation was finally consolidated when, in 1899, Manchester was given power to borrow to extinguish such irredeemable stocks as were still outstanding, showing that the term 'irredeemable' was not to be taken altogether at its face value.

Another example, selected here almost at random, was the Lancaster Corporation Act 1880 which, *inter alia*, contained powers for the municipalization of a local gas company, though the stock powers were not limited to that purpose. The corporation was authorized to borrow, for any authorized purpose, by stock, or to convert into stock any existing mortgages or bonds. The stock was to bear 'such fixed and perpetual interest' not exceeding 4 per cent as the corporation should determine on the security of the borough fund, borough rate and revenues of the gas, water and market undertakings. Again as in the Manchester Act eight years earlier, any proprietor of the stock could demand a certificate under seal, but was required to pay a fee of 2s 6d for it. Several pages of provisions were needed to spell out the details of management, in anticipation of the Stock Regulations which were not to come for a further decade. This stock could be redeemed by agreement, but its perpetual nature was borne out by the receivership provisions which related to arrears of interest only. This same Act also authorized the corporation to utilize the powers of the Local Loans Act 1875 to issue debentures, debenture stock and annuity certificates. There may be little new in the above provisions, but they do spell out the tedious confusion arising from the lack of a rationalized general borrowing code for authorities carrying out local government functions even as late as 1880; indeed the first steps towards rationalization had still to wait until 1933.

That a number of authorities were taking powers to issue stock from 1870 onwards is shown by the Local Loans Act 1875, which set out a borrowing code for debenture stock and which could only be exercised by those authorities who had or later obtained private Act powers to issue stock. It did not, that is to say, itself give stock-issuing powers. Nor were powers to issue stock to be found in the Public Health Act 1875. The first general power was that given to county councils in the Local Government Act 1888. In this Act the borrowing period for stock was limited to thirty years, with the curious counterpart, already referred to, that if stock powers were exercised, mortgage borrowing was limited to a five-year maturity period. The omission in the Public Health Act 1875 of powers to allow borrowing by stock was put right by an amending Act of 1890 whereby municipal corporations, local boards and improvement commissioners, who were urban authorities, were given power to borrow by stock subject to central regulations. Thus specific stock powers were not required in the Local Government Act 1894, which established the county district authorities. Power to borrow by stock was not given to rural districts until 1933. The issue of stock under the 1933 Act could only be carried out with the approval of the Minister unless the local authority had specific powers. The 1972 Act included stock powers without the need for Ministerial consent, but subject of course to the Stock Regulations, and required also Bank of England approval in certain respects. The history of the central control of stock after 1890 is really the history of the successive Stock Regulations, which are now examined.

Two sets of Stock Regulations were first published in 1891 (SR&O, November 1904), one applicable to counties and the other to the remaining authorized authorities – although by all appearances not much ingenuity would have been necessary to produce a combined set, except perhaps that those for counties were issued under the 1888 Local Government Act and those applicable to the rest under the 1890 Public Health Amendment Act. They are excessively detailed, each taking up with the elaborate draft documents attached over forty pages, with some fifty-one articles (with subsections) in one and fifty-seven in the other. Why such excessive control as this should have been applied when this was not found necessary for the other modes of borrowing is not easily understood, but this degree of control has continued through to current legislation (1972). It is now somewhat simplified (for reasons which will be examined), but it also embraces bonds and mortgages (but not 'temporary' borrowing, represented by 20 per cent of the total debt). By 1934 (following the improved and joint provisions of the 1933 Act) joint regulations had been produced, but forty-seven articles and a schedule were still required. However, the 1891 Regulations certainly established the fact that the minutiae of borrowing and managing large sums of money was thoroughly understood.

An example of uncalled-for detail (and variation of wording) may be illustrated by one requirement which has persisted throughout the regulations' life. The system called for the establishment of a dividends fund into which regular sums were to be paid for a fairly obvious purpose. However, for the avoidance of doubt, article 10 gratuitously finds it necessary to say: 'The local authority shall from time to time apply the dividends fund in paying the dividend on the stock.' Article 8 of the County Regulations has a similar requirement with this variation: 'The county shall, from time to time, pay the dividends on the stock, and charge the same to the dividends fund account.' Even in the (by then) joint 1934 Regulations article 5(3) requires that 'The local authority shall from time to time pay the interest on the stock and charge the payments to the interest account'. This directive does not form part of the 1974 Local Authority (Stocks and Bonds) Regulations because by that time the use of a consolidated loans fund in its comprehensive form was statutorily required and this covered the interest payment provisions. However, the argument will later be advanced that the 1974 Regulations are still over-detailed, and that this stems purely from the exhaustive nature of the ancient 1891 Regulations. The main features of the 1891 Regulations, which were frequently but not substantially revised throughout the years to 1974, are now summarized. Despite the excessive detail, some important principles were determined.

With the approval of the Local Government Board, authorities could create redeemable stock, to run for not more than sixty years. The issue price was (for no apparent reason) to be not less than 95 per cent, a figure no doubt 'picked off the wall' but still applicable. This had later to be amended (1901) by the addition of the words 'except where the Board otherwise consents'. In recent years this minimum has had a special significance in the light of the tax treatment of capital gains. The amount which could be raised was permitted to take account of the shortfall of cash receipts which would arise from issue at a discount. All stock and other securities were in future to rank equally, subject to any priorities already established, and the dividends (and presumably interest on equally ranking borrowings) was to be a first charge on the supporting security. This supporting security was to be 'all the revenues of the authority' indifferently. These revenues were defined as 'all revenues arising from any land, undertakings, or other property . . . and the rates leviable by or on the precept of the local authority' – a paraphrase of the original Metropolitan Board of Works provisions. This was either a subtle shift of ground or clarification that earlier references to the security on land and property really meant only the revenues to be derived from those assets. A noticeable omission was that revenue from government grants was not referred to. Consolidation of stock was permitted. A dividend and a redemption fund were to be established, with a repetition of the requirement that if the redemption fund were used to buy in stock prematurely for redemption, then notional interest which might have been earned by the utilized redemption moneys was to continue to be paid into the fund (with the further proviso that if stock were bought-in at a premium, the notional interest to be paid in was to be at par value only). Provision was made for the paying in of capital receipts and the investment of the redemption fund in statutory securities.

Stock issued could be used to repay other borrowings, at which stage earlier sanctions to borrow were automatically cancelled by a like amount. Stock was to be registered, but while the register entry was to be prima-facie evidence of proprietorship, certificates could be issued which would have a like effect; the want of a stock certificate did not affect the holder's title; and transfer was provided for, but there was a peculiar provision that dividends would only be sent by post on written request. The old verbal oddity that payments of interest and dividends were to be made by warrant was met by the provision that every warrant was deemed to be a cheque, as is now common practice.

Bearer certificates, with coupons to be attached (fresh supplies of which were to be issued from time to time) and transferable by delivery, could be claimed by investors, but with a right of later holders to reconversion to registered stock. Later regulations retained this provision to convert to bearer, but with the provision that this could be overridden by the terms of issue. Extensive provisions along these lines persisted until 1934, but although they remained for this long time, they are not believed to have been used. They do not appear in the 1974 Regulations where more general arrangements for bearer documents are made in the main legislation (and countermanded by the Control of Borrowing Order).

A curious feature about the power to apply for the appointment of a receiver was that, in the 1891 Regulations, this related to dividends only, and after two months delay (with no minimum amount of debt specified). However, a receiver was required to maintain the redemption fund as well as the interest fund, and to make any payments required by the regulations, so that this point of principle seems to have been met by implication. The 1934 Regulations still made this provision, although power for a lender to apply for the appointment of a receiver was in the 1933 Act itself; the debt required by the regulations had however to be £500 before the provision operated. (As already mentioned, the power to apply for such an appointment was omitted from the improved provisions of the 1972 Act, on the very sensible ground, it is understood, that it never had and never would be required in practice, but so great was the concern in the market at this omission that the provision was reinstated in the regulations under the Act – a technique which causes some confusion as temporary debt is still not enforceable in this way.) Stockholders were relieved of any responsibility for inquiring into the propriety of the borrowing or the utilization of funds borrowed. Requirements were also imposed for annual returns to the Local Government Board, the handling of unclaimed dividends and redemptions, and draft forms for most conceivable purposes.

The consequence of this determination to specify the conditions of issue in minute detail meant five amending issues of regulations up to 1902, with three more to 1934 and a further five before the current 1974 regulations, all of which were no doubt essential for clarification of wording but did not affect the underlying significance of borrowing by stock. Stock issues must also of course comply with the strict regulations of the Stock Exchange.

Setting aside the 'bond' aspects of the 1974 Stocks and Bonds Regulations (SI 1974/519), the principal provisions of that instrument relating to stock are that registered and not bearer stocks are permitted; the register may be kept 'other than in legible form' – a concession to the computer age; and a certificate must be issued (but there is no sealing requirement), yet both the register and the certificate continue to be prima-facie evidence of proprietorship. There are other extensive provisions relating to transfer, unclaimed interest and principal, and, as already mentioned, to make good the shortcomings of the principal Act provision is made for application for the appointment of a receiver when the sum 'which remains unpaid' after two months is not less than £500. Amending regulations in 1983 (SI 529) were issued to permit the use of variable rates of interest.

In this book little attention has so far been paid to local authority borrowing provisions in Scotland, where the range of authorities is somewhat different and where the statutory provisions although close to those in England and Wales have significant variations in certain respects.

These variations of practice became of some significance in the late nineteenth century and, in consequence, the comparison is now taken up with the Local Authorities Loans (Scotland) Act 1891. The title of this Act indicated that it was intended to give increased facilities for the raising of money by local authorities in Scotland 'by the issue of Debentures, Stock or otherwise', but in fact it deals only with the issue of stock. However, in the section covering the power to convert other borrowings to the stock now authorized reference is made to 'any mortgage, bond, debenture, debenture stock, annuity, rent charge or other security', which indicates that similar instruments to those developed over the years in England and Wales were also operative in Scotland.

The Act is long and complex, mainly because it seeks to incorporate, in the Act itself, the greater part of the detail dealt with in England in supporting regulations. That incorporation directly in the statute in this way was overambitious is proved by the necessity for an amending Act in 1893 in which the Secretary of State for Scotland was empowered to make regulations which could in fact amend the original Act.

The powers of the 1891 Act follow closely the provisions in the English Act and regulations, subject to the observance of special Scottish practices. Special reference was, for example, necessary to the security which might be offered by the 'common good according to the law and usage of Scotland' – the 'common good' being a fund of some antiquity generally accumulated by Scottish authorities from a variety of non-statutory sources and without a counterpart in England. The power to issue redeemable stock at an agreed price in the initial statute was modified by the 1893 amending Act to a price 'not being less than 95%', that is, as in England. Another peculiarity of the Scottish Act was that in requiring payments to be made into the consolidated loans funds now to be established, from the various funds or rates of the authority, provision was made that if these sources were temporarily inadequate to meet the required contributions, the loans fund could itself make loans to them at an interest charge of 5 per cent to enable them to make the payments back to itself. There was a further 'fall-back' provision that if any rate or fund continued to be inadequate, a general 'guarantee rate' could be levied to assure that the loans fund received its proper contributions. This rate was to be levied half on occupiers and half on owners – another Scottish variant practice. 'Equal ranking' and 'first charge' provisions were included. The provisions for the operation of the loans fund were more detailed than in England and this has continued through to current practice. The loans fund was not specifically divided into a redemption and an interest fund, but the parliamentary draftsmen could not resist making clear that:

The local authority shall, from time to time, apply the loans fund, first, in paying the dividends on all stock, and secondly, in redeeming stock according to the terms of issue and in purchasing stock for extinction.

The establishment of a register was required, and this again was to establish 'the title of the persons entered therein as holders of the stock', but certificates could be issued in either registered or bearer form with coupons, as in England. Obviously the bearer certificates had to be the evidence of ownership, but the registered certificate could also be used for this purpose, presumably in dealing, though lack of a certificate did not prevent the holder of the stock from selling or transferring. As in English practice, steps could be taken, if there was two months' delay in the payment either of principal or interest, to apply to the court of session for the appointment of a 'judicial factor' (receiver). Extensive draft forms were given in a schedule to the Act, and these were similar to those in the English regulations.

Conclusions

A stock issue can be attractive to a local authority needing a very substantial sum of money at one time arising from the state of its borrowing portfolio, or from a sudden expansion of its capital expenditure on major schemes, or to enable it to take long-term advantage of low interest rates. On the other hand, the receipt of a substantial sum of loan moneys at one short interval of time, even though on favourable terms, can be an embarrassment, if the whole of the money cannot be utilized immediately. This problem is, as already explained, partly met by the system of making issues subject to 'calls', by which a successful applicant for the stock makes an initial payment followed by two or three further instalment payments over the next few months, although the facility for a lender to receive an allocation of a stock without immediately paying the full cost encourages 'stagging'. Being in negotiable form, theory would have it that stock should be marginally cheaper to the borrower, but this has always proved difficult to establish because of the imponderables of calculating the true cost of stock, particularly the problem of 'front-end loading' – that is, heavier initial costs of issue which need to be readjusted over the full life of the issue to enable the real cost to be ascertained. There are also likely to be greater management costs with a stock issue which, by definition, is expected to change hands more frequently than other types of loan, particularly at the start and towards the end of the stock period. As earlier discussed, this was a particularly important feature when transfer stamp duty was payable and usually borne by the borrower.

Fixing the appropriate price for an issue continues to be a matter of great skill. Until recent times the terms of an issue were required to be fixed several days before the issue, and changes in market conditions in that interval could have effects which were sometimes disastrous to its success and vice versa. A successful issue in the view of the market is one which is oversubscribed (sometimes heavily) as this indicates that the price has been pitched too low. An unsuccessful issue in market terms is one which is left substantially with the underwriters as this indicates that the borrower has obtained his funds rather cheaply, to the market's disadvantage. Without doubt, as in most money and stock market situations, a result which satisfies both sides is the best result over the long term, but is not easily achieved.

Before an issue can be made, the extensive controls in the 1972 Act (which require the operation of a loans pool for all who borrow by stock) and in the Stocks and Bonds Regulations (on the management of stock) have to be met. There is also a requirement that the terms of stock issues must be approved by the Bank of England. Under this restraint the Bank of England has set a limit of £12 million for a placed issue (previously £7 million) and imposes a 'queuing' system when pressure on the market is heavy. Finally, there are the regulations of the Stock Exchange itself, which it imposes (no doubt very wisely) before it will accept the responsibility for establishing the necessary daily market. A local authority treasurer must pick his way very carefully through these various controls but of course there is a body of stockbrokers, forming part of a structure almost as old as his own, eager to assist him.

The stringent controls applying to stock issues do not really impose problems on local authorities wishing to enter this particular market; local authorities have nothing to hide and are not seeking to find loopholes in the general provisions. However, this cautionary attitude has given to local authority stock issues an overriding mystic which, particularly today, is not justified when equally vast sums of money are being borrowed by local authorities from institutions with, if need be, variable rates of interest and various alternatives as to repayment or redemption.

Present high interest rates combined with, no doubt resulting from, high rates of inflation have brought a 'new look' to local authority borrowing. Developing from this, central government's wish to control monetary growth, rates of interest and local authority spending have caused it to offer such facilities from the Public Works Loan Commission that stock issues by local authorities, if not a thing of the past, are at least in abeyance for a considerable time.

In the final analysis, whatever the terminology used, the conclusion is difficult to avoid that the local authority mortgage and general bond are to all intents and purposes the same instrument, and that the negotiable bond and stock are the marketable forms of this same 'conceptual instrument', the negotiable bond for shorter and stock for longer borrowing periods.

Chapter 18

TEMPORARY (DEPOSIT) LOAN RECEIPTS

The history of the use of temporary borrowing, in support of both cash-flow revenue needs and in anticipation of funded borrowing, has been so entwined with the general development of borrowing practice since the end of the First World War that it has in the main already been dealt with in chronological sequence in this book. There is not therefore a great deal now to be added about the techniques, as such, of this form of borrowing. However, the development of temporary borrowing since the first general statutory mention in the Local Authorities (Financial Provisions) Act 1921 and the subsequent change in the nature of this form of capital financing may perhaps be recapitulated with benefit and slightly expanded upon, to allow conclusions to be drawn.

As described earlier, the 1921 Act powers though originally introduced for a limited period of five years were gradually extended to 1932, after which the Local Government Act 1933 took over. These powers were for borrowing in anticipation of revenue only, but gave this borrowing the same security and ranking as capital borrowings generally. The total to which they could be exercised by a local authority was subject to the consent of the Minister of Health. However, there are indications of much earlier borrowing under the heading of 'temporary loans' in certain authorities. While this book does not embrace the earlier history of borrowing in Scotland, reference has necessarily been made to borrowing by Edinburgh and Glasgow as these two authorities were early in the field in the issue of money bills and promissory notes. The documents examined in that respect show that while in 1895 Edinburgh did not have any temporary loans listed in its loans fund balance sheet, by 1900 the capital liabilities listed included nearly £½ million due to 'Sundries on Temporary Loans'. This may have included an amount on overdraft from their then bankers – the British Linen Company Bank – but an amount of £55,000 is also shown as specifically due 'to the Bank on Current Account'. The 1901 accounts show more than £¾ million of 'Temporary loans received from the Public'. No statutory authority for this borrowing has been traced. A similar situation has not been discovered in Glasgow, but the article by the City Registrar quoted earlier, published in 1914, refers to the 'Common Good Fund' – that useful and extra-statutory facility exercised in Scotland – as having borrowed on mortgage and also on bills and promissory notes as early as 1607, and states that the promissory notes were replaced by mortgages in 1873. This indicates that although the statutory powers for borrowing in this way were only established late in the nineteenth century, as described in Chapter 19 on money bills, non-statutory temporary borrowing of several kinds was a common practice in both of these cities and no doubt elsewhere in Scotland.

Statements by Johnson and Burton written in the early 1920s and referred to earlier can now be recognized as being of considerable significance – that some of the larger local authorities had long revoked the practice of borrowing substantial sums for short periods theoretically on mortgage but without the issue of a mortgage deed, but with the promise to issue a deed if called upon. There is a field here for further investigation as this suggests that 'temporary' borrowing for capital purposes goes back much further in practice than is at present thought. Equally the use of the term 'deposit receipt' and the principle underlying the 2d or 6d stamp duties are also of much earlier origin than is generally recognized.

Of less remote interest to us is the experience in the City of Leeds which was one of the principal users of temporary borrowing in the middle 1950s and early 1960s, forerunners in the development which ultimately led to the White Paper control of temporary borrowing described earlier. Chapter 19 shows that Leeds was almost certainly first to borrow for capital purposes by bills (ignoring the extra-statutory activities of the authorities north of the Border). What is equally interesting is that, by the Leeds Corporation Act 1913, the city was empowered 'to borrow by way of temporary loan or overdraft from any bank or on temporary loan on deposit receipt from any person' for the purposes of 'providing temporarily for any current [that is, revenue] expenses' up to 25 per cent of the amount of such expenses. These are almost exactly the words which later appeared in the general 1921 statute. The security for the Leeds borrowing was 'the properties, rates and revenues of the Corporation *pari passu* with all other mortgages stock and other securities'. Another section of the clause permitted the temporary use of accumulated sinking funds for the same purpose, subject to payment of interest at a rate not less than 3 per cent. Such borrowings towards current expenses were to be repaid from the revenues of the year. Thus the 1921 Act provision was merely making available for general use provisions which had been conceded to Leeds eight years earlier and in all probability to other enterprising towns evidence of which is now lost in early local Acts. The Leeds temporary borrowing powers were limited to a five-year period subject to extension, which was given – for a fifteen-year period – in the Leeds Corporation Act 1919.

The use of the term 'deposit receipt' in the Leeds provision for borrowing by temporary loan was not taken up in the later general legislation. The term deposit receipt popular with local authorities in the 1950s seems on the face of it an attempt to employ Scottish terminology as a more reassuring phrase in the ears of lenders than 'temporary loan receipt'. Because of this exclusion from general statutes, after the White Paper local authorities seem to have reverted to the term temporary loan receipt, as now used. *Thomson's Dictionary of Banking* (10th edn) describes a 'deposit receipt' as 'A receipt given by a banker where moneys are lodged on deposit account and no passbook is issued. It will express the money to be repayable at a certain number of days' notice or at call or at the end of a fixed period.' It was liable to stamp duty of 2d. This is a reasonable definition of the modern temporary loan, but applicable to any lender of temporary money to a local authority and not only to deposits with a bank, and clearly the Leeds deposit receipt was for use with the general public. At least this reference seems to establish that the term was not imported into England from Scotland in the 1950s, but was already in use in Leeds, one of the principal operators in this field (though Leeds of course may have picked it up from Scotland).

The general power to borrow by temporary loans in anticipation of revenue given in the 1921 Act has already been described. The inclusion of similar powers in the 1925 Rating and Valuation Act with the addition of powers also to borrow temporarily for capital purposes has also already been dealt with (see p. 163). However, an important point to be noted here is that the capital borrowing was not specifically in anticipation of later funding, but straightforwardly for any sum which the authority might temporarily require and which 'they are authorised to raise by loan'. What has not yet been pointed out in this book is that the revenue-borrowing powers were thus contained in two statutes at the same time, the difference being that under the 1921 Act the consent of the Minister was required for their exercise, while this was not a requirement of the 1925 Act.

There was however a very significant switch of principle in the 1925 Act. The earlier Act gave the temporary borrowing, though for revenue purposes, the security and ranking of other forms of (capital) borrowing, but this situation was not repeated in the 1925 Act where section 12(2) uses the curious phrase: 'The treasurer of a local authority may advance to the local authority any sum which the authority may temporarily require', as though the treasurer held money which he himself could lend to the local authority temporarily. What exactly was in the minds of the legislators is not now clear; this concept may have been a throwback to the time when a local authority treasurer was often a local banker. Certainly, in practice, this provision was taken to mean that a local authority had power to borrow temporarily for capital or revenue purposes, but that such borrowings were not given the security or ranking of other forms of borrowing which applied to revenue borrowing under the 1921 Act.

This withdrawal of security was not only maintained in the 1933 Act, but two points of clarification were added. First, borrowing temporarily for capital purposes was expanded to mean 'for the purposes of defraying, pending the raising of a loan which authorities have been authorised to raise, expenses intended to be defrayed by means of the loan'. In other words, temporary borrowing for capital purposes was in anticipation of funding, just as temporary borrowing for revenue was in anticipation of the receipt of revenue, both provisions forming a logical conception in the circumstances of the time. The other point of clarification was that under section 197 the provision for charging all moneys borrowed indifferently on all the revenues of the authority specifically excluded 'any money borrowed by way of temporary loan or overdraft without security'. This seems to mean somewhat tautologically that all money borrowed without security shall have no security, though whether the words 'without security' apply to 'overdraft' or to both terms is a matter which the courts would have to decide – but have never been required to do so. There is a vague possibility that 'security' in this context meant a 'borrowing instrument', particularly an official mortgage. Temporary loans were therefore, without question, no longer 'secured debts', and remained in this invidious position for forty years.

When the upsurge of temporary borrowing took place in the mid-1950s, the lack of this underlying security made popular the older practice of adding a footnote to temporary loan receipts giving the holders the right to require that a mortgage should be issued to replace the receipt on demand (this event would then require the payment of stamp duty on the new instrument), whereupon any mortgage issued in replacement of the receipt automatically gave the security of the revenues and access to receivership, if called for. No cases of the exercise of this right to call for a mortgage have been brought to light. Why this complexity should have been tolerated in relation to substantial sums of money for so many years may be wondered at. The simple course would have been to give temporary borrowing the necessary security in the Financial Provisions Act of 1963.

The development of the short temporary loan would have been considerably handicapped by stamp duty at more than 2d or 6d. The irony of the situation is that by the time the fifty years had elapsed from the first general statutory temporary borrowing provision in 1921 until the 1972 Act, which gave both capital and revenue temporary borrowing full ranking with other forms of borrowing, the situation had so far developed in other directions that the temporary loan as a separate method of borrowing was by that time outmoded for reasons enlarged upon below. Despite this, it still flourishes, though needlessly in its present form, which treats it as some special kind of instrument with attributes of its own.

From 1933 onward the temporary loan receipt was a useful instrument for short-term borrowing; although it did not have 'written-in' security, this problem could be overcome in the shape of the 'exchange for a mortgage' footnote described above, and the stamp duty of 2d or 6d was negligible. When the modern bond was intoduced in 1963, the limitation to one year still made the temporary loan receipt the appropriate instrument for periods of less than one year. But when stamp duty was abolished, and when in 1972 the one-year minimum was withdrawn from all bonds (except in negotiable form), the bond in its rationalized form was quite capable of serving all the purposes of a temporary loan receipt. In fact by this stage the bond certificate had, and still has, a superiority over the temporary loan receipt. This is because through Whitehall's stumble over the matter of the provision of receivership availability, access to a receiver does not cover 'temporary loans' because there are no regulations for such loans, the device which was used to reinstate the receivership provision for bonds, stock and mortgages. Thus a temporary loan receipt is still not as entirely satisfactory as a bond certificate, and can only be made so by the reintroduction of a footnote offering conversion to a bond/mortgage on demand.

The lack of complete understanding about what was really being achieved in the 1972 Act is a source of some surprise. The appearance is that Whitehall was in fact making a great effort to come to terms with the evolving situation, but nevertheless had not grasped the change in the nature of 'temporary' loans after 1963. The way in which the borrowing provisions were hurried into the Act at the last moment has already been described; if the original plan of dealing with the financial aspects separately had been followed, the logic of the proposed changes might – might – have been followed through.

Since then a handful of authorities have indeed adopted the bond as the all-purpose instrument for all 'term' borrowing (for example, Croydon and South Kesteven), replacing the temporary loan receipt and the mortgage, but most local authorities continue to use the temporary loan receipt as well as the bond – and, in a declining number of cases, as well as the mortgage. There are still many thousands of outstanding mortgages of great age which have been renewed frequently. However, 'bond' authorities take every opportunity of replacing these documents with bonds at times of renewal.

Dealers in the market do not of course speak of the temporary loan receipt in their transactions, but of 'two-day', 'seven-day', 'seven-plus-seven' and 'one-month' money. All concerned know that normally a deal will be followed by the issue of a temporary loan receipt, but no one objects if a few authorities issue a bond certificate because, if the loan was for anything more than 364 days, a bond certificate would be the normal issue (except for the few who have still not outgrown the ancient mortgage). Temporary loans are subject to frequent changes of interest; a loan running at seven days' notice may well be put under seven days' notice of change on one day, and given a second notice of change a day or two later, when the market is in a volatile state, each notice having to work through its term. Because of circumstances of this kind, and particularly following the entry into the local authority market of many overseas banks in London, a number of operational problems not surprisingly have arisen. Such large sums are involved and the periods are often so short that special arrangements are necessary for transmitting the money involved. Such short loans always therefore pass by bank transfer, and many disputes have arisen about how many days interest are due, particularly when non-banking days fall within the period. For many of the points of dispute the solution is simply a matter of accepted convention, but often differences of practice in different countries are involved.

Eventually accepted conventional interpretations began to emerge, and in November 1963 the then Institute of Municipal Treasurers and Accountants (now CIPFA) issued a series of Recommended Procedures for Temporary Borrowing, which have subsequently been refined and expanded through discussions with affected parties. These are not binding, but general agreement has been reached that unless a variation from Recommended Procedures is endorsed on a borrowing instrument, then these will be followed. The procedures deal with such matters as effective dates of notice, where the time of day on which notice is given (by telephone) can be material, and the treatment of non-banking days which can also make a good deal of difference to interest due. A surprising amount of heat was at one time generated by disputes about the proper treatment of leap years where American practice differed from that normal in England. In the end agreement was reached that even in leap years, daily interest is to be arrived at by dividing the total yearly interest by 365, while a multiplier of 366 may be used.

The form of instrument was also a problem in the early days of the development of the market. Because of the curious birth and development of temporary borrowing, no draft form was or has ever been specified in a statute, whereas all other forms have been so specified, 'or to the like effect'. Writing in a letter about his early experiences as a money broker to local authorities, Mr Norman Woolley, one of the earliest in this field, says: 'The instrument of receipt given for temporary loans [in the early years] was typewritten on the Authority's notepaper, but I have seen many non-descript documents on plain paper which caused some misgivings among our lenders.' The form used now is set out in the Recommended Procedures and is, to all intents and purposes, on the same lines as a bond certificate.

Once again the conclusion is difficult to avoid that the history of the temporary loan receipt as a borrowing instrument illustrates a lack of appreciation by both the central and local authorities of the full implications of what was being done and, perhaps more important, of what needed to be done. The pattern wavers over a period which is of at least seventy years' duration (if Leeds was the first authority to obtain the power), from the giving of full security and equal ranking to temporary borrowing for revenue purposes (1913 and 1921), through a second stage of double provision for revenue borrowing and the introduction of capital temporary borrowing (1925), with the disappearance of a security provision at that point, to a further stage (1933) where both provisions were more precisely set out with a specific exclusion of security and ranking, and where for the first time it was clear that capital temporary borrowing was simply in anticipation of longer-term funding.

Some forty years later (1972) – after the 'Battle of the White Paper' – when the illogicality of this situation was at last recognized, security and ranking were reinstated, without the realization that concurrent alterations by the introduction of the bond without its one-year limitation, and the abolition of all stamp duty, had made the provision for temporary borrowing (at least for capital purposes) redundant. Even at this point, the receivership provision was fumbled. (Receivership may be only a token offering in the light of the history of stability of local authority debt management, but so long as nervous lenders attach significance to it the provision should not have been neglected.) The Scottish legislation has seen the point clearly (since 1947), and the Scottish Act of 1975 says simply that temporary loans may be used 'for the purpose of the raising of a loan in the exercise of any statutory borrowing power'.

The latest legislation continues to adhere to the concept that temporary borrowing is an interim measure pending the raising of longer-term loans, but this attitude however appropriate it might have been half a century ago is at variance with the philosophy underlying the 1963 White Paper in the recognition that up to 20 per cent of a local authority's portfolio might be in loans with an initial borrowing period of less than one year. In addition, such an attitude is not consistent with the accepted principles of the consolidated loans fund which contemplate a fund fed by borrowings from 'overnight' – and a more 'temporary' loan than overnight cannot be conceived – to an indefinite number of years, irrespective of arrangements for amortization. At most what must now be seen simply as the ultra-short sector of a local authority portfolio may be regarded as a 'buffer' element giving the treasurer flexibility in tailoring his portfolio to market conditions. In other words, to purloin a phrase often used in the field of education, a local authority borrowing portfolio is a 'seamless robe'.

Two features of the temporary loan receipt may be advanced as an argument that it is of a different nature from other borrowing instruments: one is that interest can be paid gross (without deduction of tax), and the other is that the volume of temporary borrowing is subject to overall control. Neither of these points is significant in this respect. The payment of gross interest is not a feature of the specification of a temporary loan; it is a tax concession or provision which relates to any loan for less than a year – that is, local authority money bills and even to a mortgage or bond, if such were issued for less than a year. The percentage controls on 'less than one-year borrowing' do not affect the security, as such, and they have their counterpart in the maturity code applicable to all other forms of borrowing and described elsewhere in this book.

In the return published by CIPFA for local authority debt as at March 1982, the total for the United Kingdom was £41,757 million, of which 12·2 per cent is described as 'temporary debt', equivalent to £5,087 million. Probably about £3,300 million was with an initial borrowing period of not more than three months. The Treasury and the Bank of England feel that borrowing by three-month money bills is not proper for capital purposes – at least that is what they thought in the 1930s and they do not yet appear to have revised this view. Three-month capital bills would provide simply a small fringe of negotiable paper at the edge of nearly £4 billion of so-called temporary borrowing, just as negotiable bonds provide a small fringe on bond term borrowing. A fair conclusion would seem to be that the bond could readily be used as the instrument to replace the temporary loan receipt, and that a negotiable fringe of capital bills can no longer be conceived as an improper feature at the short end of the local authority portfolio. This point will now be examined in greater detail, in Chapter 19.

Chapter 19

MONEY BILLS AND
PROMISSORY NOTES

Despite a somewhat obscure etymology, the term 'bill' in its application to a local authority borrowing instrument denotes basically a simple documentary acknowledgement of a debt, originally under seal but not so in recent years, with an assurance of discharge in the short term (not more than one year, usually much less) and capable of ready negotiability, implying an organized market. The local authority money bill shows marked differences from the commercial bill of exchange to which it is sometimes likened; it is nearer to but still not quite the local equivalent of the central government Treasury bill. The first statutory mention of the local authority money bill in 1877 coincides with the introduction of the short-term Treasury bill (proposed by Walter Bagehot), which was intended to replace in due course the unpopular, somewhat clumsy and longer-term Exchequer bill. The history of the borrowing instrument called in the relevant local government statutes simply 'bills', but in terms of market use 'local authority money bills', exhibits several peculiar features. While statutory powers to borrow by this means were first given to a local authority (the Metroplitan Board of Works) in 1877, they were not used for twenty years and only after another eighty, in 1972, was a general power to borrow on bills given to local authorities and even then subject to close regulation by overriding statutory and administrative means. In particular, the use of the bill, permitted in the 1972 statute for both capital (the original function) and revenue purposes, is at present confined by administrative action to use only 'in anticipation of revenue', that is, as an aid to revenue cash flow. The original capital function has thus been nullified. Despite these restrictions, the bill is nevertheless the only local authority borrowing instrument which by a peculiarity of wording and practice is available in bearer form, even though the Treasury have not so far exercised the power given them under the 1972 Act to authorize the use of bearer instruments by local authorities.

The difference in the nature of the local authority bill from that of Treasury bills and bills of exchange seems never to have been fully appreciated. The argument will later be examined that this tendency to confuse local authority bills with other types of bill has led to the uncalled-for imposition of certain of the present restrictions. Indeed the evidence is that the major Treasury restriction, that on the use of money bills for capital purposes, nullifies the exercise of a power originally given by

Parliament over a century ago and repeated in many local Acts, and used for many years and reaffirmed in the 1972 Act, simply because the Treasury adhere to the view first expressed in the early part of this century that the power to issue bills is simply not appropriate to local authorities. This attitude is maintained by the Treasury despite the approved development of wide-scale capital borrowing on equally short, or shorter, terms for a long period of time. Because of this view local authority money bills are unable to play their part as the 'marketable' form of temporary borrowing, in the way that stock and negotiable bonds form the 'marketable' counterpart of mortgages and general bonds. Money bills are significantly cheaper than temporary capital borrowings. The tight restriction imposed on the quantity of revenue money bills might be seen to be inappropriate, if the capital form of bill were to be accepted by the Treasury.

Because the maximum amount of bills which a local authority might have on issue at any one time has until recently been small and lacking in flexibility, local authority money bills have formed only a minor part of local authority borrowing portfolios. In recent years the maximum amount of bills which may be on issue instead of being a designated amount has been related to expanding rate income/expenditure; at least while the bills are limited to revenue purposes, this is a more appropriate method. A recent Treasury report says that while the current formula would have permitted the issue by local authorities of £1·8 billion of bills, at the end of 1980/1 only £0·8 billion had been issued (Report of Treasury/Local Authority Borrowing Committee, 25 February 1982). The Treasury seem to feel that this implies a lack of interest by local authorities in bills, but beyond question this shortfall arises because of the problems involved at present by the restriction of the use of bills to revenue purposes, and the strict definition of what is meant by this. By and large, local authorities do not need bills in anticipation of revenue.

Before bills are dealt with generally in this chapter, reference should be made to a peculiar provision (mentioned in passing earlier) in an Act of 1793, under which the City of Liverpool was authorized to issue negotiable notes. Details of this brief exercise do not survive, but the terms of the Act give the following information:

> In consideration of the state of credit in the Town of Liverpool it is expedient that the Common Council . . . should be enabled to issue for a certain period such Negotiable Notes for different sums of money and of such amount in the whole as are hereinafter specified.

Consequently, for two years from May 1793 notes payable to bearer could be issued for cash for £50 and £100 with interest 'at any rate not exceeding legal interest' payable after one year. A second issue was permitted on expiry of the first period. The third – and most curious – provision was that for a period of two years and five months notes to the value of £5 and £10 could be issued for cash, but would not earn interest.

These seem to have been in the nature of bank notes; they were to be 'negotiable in the same manner as notes of bankers or other persons made payable to bearer'. The total to be issued was not to exceed £300,000. Whether these issues were made to assist the council's finances or as a means of stimulating trade remains a mystery. Further details of this brief interlude might be most enlightening, particularly as it coincides in time (1793–5) with some borrowing by promissory notes in Bristol, referred to in Chapter 5.

The earliest reference to bill powers is in the Metropolitan Board of Works (Money) Act 1877. Despite their inclusion there and in successive Money Acts, these powers were not exercised until 1896, as will shortly be described. From 1899 onwards a number of the larger English local authorities obtained capital bill powers by local Act; the date of the first statutory powers in Scotland was 1897. Shortly after the Local Government Act 1972 had given the general powers, all local authority provisions (except those relating to London) were repealed by the Local Authorities, etc. (Miscellaneous Provisions) No. 2 Order (SI 1974/595) with the object of creating 'standard' bill conditions for the convenience and reassurance of the market. At that time, some 120 local authorities had obtained bill powers. This was no doubt a logical move, although the local Act powers had been strikingly uniform: 1899, Leeds; 1900, Sheffield, Croydon, Halifax, Liverpool, Nottingham and Southport; 1901, Manchester, Hull and Blackpool; 1902, Birmingham, Birkenhead and Lancaster; and so on. Thus Leeds appears to have been first in the field in England and Wales, after London. Later amendments of local Acts introduced slight simplifications, and increases in the amounts authorized to be raised. The major and much later change was the addition of powers to issue bills in anticipation of revenue, in addition to bills for capital purposes. The year in which the revenue function was introduced has not been established, but it was probably in the 1960s. There appears to have been a long gap between the early 1920s and the mid-1960s during which no local authorities were given money bill powers.

Although the features constituting a bill are specified in some detail in the local Acts, and although from the beginning bills were authorized for capital purposes, the exact status of the local authority bill has never been fully grasped. Megrah, in *The Bills of Exchange Act 1882* (1957), and the excellent handbook *The Bill on London* (1952), make no mention of either Treasury or local authority bills. Griffiths, in *Municipal Capital Finance*, refers to them as bills of exchange, as do Hardacre and Sage in *Local Authority Capital Finance* (1965), but this they are certainly not; Johnson in *Loans of Local Authorities* (1925) says that although they are generally looked upon as being identical to commercial bills of exchange, they have little in common with such instruments and are only analogous to Treasury bills, as issued by the government, in their issue procedure. In fact they do seem to be quite close to the central government's instruments in design and general treatment. An article on the Treasury bill in the *Bank of England Quarterly Bulletin* (September 1964) says categorically that the Treasury bill is a bearer security of great simplicity, but that it is neither a bill of exchange nor a promissory note. Certainly, the Treasury bill does not follow the Bank of England currency note in 'promising to pay'.

The bill of exchange and the promissory note are possibly the only two commercial borrowing instruments which are defined specifically, and in detail, in a statute (at least since the 'chirograph' of the Act of 1233). The two instruments have the well-known definitions given them in the Bills of Exchange Act 1882. The essence of a bill of exchange is that it is an order to pay, normally involving three parties: a drawer, a drawee and an acceptor; the essence of a promissory note is obviously that it simply 'promises to pay' – almost a 'deed poll'.

The standard form of money bill issued by local authorities is not framed as an 'order to pay' and cannot be said to involve an 'acceptor' even though, at the present day, redemption may be on presentation to a named bank (who have been authorized to meet it) rather than as earlier at the offices of the local authority. It is simply a document worded to say that: 'This [name of local authority] bill *entitles* . . . or order, to payment of . . . amount . . . at the [address of Town Hall, or named bank] on . . . date . . . out of the revenues of the Corporation.' Nowadays the final words are often replaced by the phrase 'secured on all the revenues of the Corporation'. Thus the word 'entitles' is the hallmark of a local authority bill, a word also used on Treasury bills but not in bills of exchange or on other local authority borrowing instruments.

In fact the local authority bill is by nature more akin to the promissory note (or even the simple IOU) than to the bill of exchange; this is borne out by practice in Scotland. The City of Glasgow obtained powers in 1896 (Glasgow Corporation (General Powers) Act) to issue Glasgow Corporation bills *or* promissory notes. In 1897, six days before the LCC issued its first bills, Glasgow made an issue of what were called promissory notes, and has continued to do so under this terminology since that time. In the Glasgow Corporation (Gas, etc.) Order Confirmation Act 1902 appear the words 'The term "bill" shall include "promissory note" '. The form of promissory note is given in the 1896 Act, in which the 'Corporation of Glasgow promise to pay . . . etc.', and provision is made that if the name of the holder is not shown, the note will be paid to bearer. While Glasgow continues today to designate their issues as promissory notes, of which there is no mention in the general statutes, they also continue to comply with the current legislation and directions relating to bills. In 1899 the City of Edinburgh obtained similar powers to issue promissory notes, and did so. Dundee have also been involved from an early date. The powers of the Leeds Corporation Act 1899 were for the issue of 'corporation bills or promissory notes'; Leeds elected to use the term 'bill' and immediately issued the maximum permitted (£300,000), by 'placing' rather than by open offer, and have continued to do so. Is there a significant or legal difference between 'a promise to pay' and granting an 'entitlement to holder'? If not, why cannot lenders have the reassurance of conformity of wording?

The function of local authority bills (in their capital aspect) is the same – or would be, if their use were not prevented – as that now used extensively by local authorities under the so-called 'temporary loan receipt'. However, the mechanics of management have always been very different as the bill is a marketable instrument and, in practice, is issued and circulates in bearer form under the auspices of the discount houses. It could thus easily be seen as the marketable alternative to the non-marketable 'temporary loan'. As a borrowing instrument it may be described, especially now the complications of the Stamp Act have gone, as a very short-term debenture – perhaps even a mortgage debenture as its security is, in effect, derived from the mortgaging of the revenues of the authority, with the peculiarity that interest is paid by the device of issue at a discount and repayment at par. It has the peculiarity already mentioned that though designated to be issued in nominal form, in practice, it is converted into a type of bearer instrument. As its issue, like that of stock, presupposes a 'market', it has vague undertones of 'stock', although the market for bills is not the Stock Market, but generally the London discount market, which has a traditional responsibility for the handling of Treasury bills as well as normal commercial bills. While there is a going market rate for local authority bills, the daily rate is available but not published as are stock market prices. Because they provide the market and can always be relied upon to take bills on issue, at a price, as with Treasury bills, the discount houses expect to be given a portion of every issue even though their tender may not always be the highest.

For the greater part of their existence local Act powers and regulations required the bill to be under seal, but in recent years that requirement has been dropped and the signature of the treasurer has sufficed; and even this may now be mechanically impressed. The rate of interest is not stated on bills or promissory notes because the effective yield on the security is calculated from the 'discount' – the difference between the sum accepted by the borrower on tender, which may vary from one tenderer to another, and the amount paid to the lender on redemption at par, which of course being for a period of less than a year is paid without deduction of tax. As the borrower initially receives less than par, the true yield is slightly more than the discount rate.

In modern times there is a problem about the upper maturity limit. The powers to issue bills provide 'not more than 12 months' as the maximum period. In practice, a bill issued for a full 12 months would fall into the trap that the 'interest' would in fact be 'annual interest' under the Income Tax Acts, and would therefore necessitate the deduction of tax at source, something which would be likely to make the bill unattractive to the market. The maximum operational period for a bill would therefore have to be one day less than a full 12 months as it is for 'temporary' loans. Another extraneous problem is that if a bill were of a capital nature (which is not at present permitted) and for one day less than one year, it would fall within the temporary debt limitations; if it were for a full year, it would fall under the recent maturity control code.

Bills have always been designed with provision for entry of the name of the holders. However, when the bill was required to be used as a bearer instrument, this has been achieved simply by the omission of the name and an indication by a footnote that the 'blank' bill will in these circumstances be paid to bearer on maturity. Scottish promissory notes use the same device. This is in some degree consistent with the provisions of the Stock Certificates Act 1863 which was concerned with the form of public securities. This Act defines the method whereby government stock can be converted to bearer form by the omission of the name but also contains other provisions, for example, method of reconverting to transferable nominal stock, which have never been adopted for bills. A similar practice is incorporated in the Local Loans Act 1875. This appears always to have been the form in which Treasury bills have been designed.

There is a peculiarity in this local authority bill procedure. This is that the Bank of England does not appear to regard a 'name blank' certificate, which is treated in the market as a bearer bill, as a true bearer instrument, although Treasury bills so designed are described as such in the Bank of England article quoted above. The Bank and the Treasury appear to take the view that local authority bills are, in practice, revenue bills and that the restriction on bearer documents in the 1972 Act relates only to capital instruments. This is apparently why the 'bearer bill' persists in present times, when no other form of local authority bearer instrument is permitted. The truth of the matter probably is that over the course of time the market expects this type of instrument to be in bearer form if it is to be acceptable.

The history underlying the development of local authority bill procedure may be illustrated in the evolution of the powers granted to the first bill-issuing authority, the Metropolitan Board of Works, and in one of the group of authorities which obtained these powers in the first years of this century, namely, Manchester.

The Metropolitan Board of Works Bill powers occurred initially in their Money Act of 1877 and certainly stemmed from the creation of Treasury bills in the same year. The initial powers were sweeping. The board was authorized 'to raise any part of the money which they are authorised by this Act to raise, not exceeding £4,622,007, by the issue of bills under this Act'. These metropolitan bills were to be from three to twelve months and to be used 'for the purposes for which the same are by this Act authorised'. Thus not only were the bills made available for capital purposes, but for the whole of the capital expenditure planned for that year, totalling the precise figure quoted in the clause and detailed in a schedule to the Act. They were to be repaid either from the county rate or out of moneys to be raised by a stock issue. As to repay them out of the county rate a few months after issue would have been equivalent to meeting the whole of the year's capital expenditure from revenue, the only practical alternative would have been to meet the repayment (bearing in mind that there was not yet power to renew them) from a stock issue. Thus to borrow these sums by bills would have been tantamount to an announcement that the council was planning a stock issue, six months hence, something which for market reasons was and is usually kept secret. At least this is the reason given by Sir Harry Haward, a later Comptroller of the LCC, in *The LCC from Within*, as to why the bill-issuing powers were not exercised for many years; this explanation is hardly convincing because borrowing by stock issue was the standard method of raising funds by the Metropolitan Board of Works (MBW) at that time, and the market must have been fully aware that regular issues of stock were bound to follow all major expenditures on capital account. However, the power continued to be included in annual Money Acts of the MBW, and after 1891, of the LCC, with the important (and more realistic) provision that after the first open-handed year, the maximum amount which might be covered by bills was reduced to a mere £½ million each year. Thus the bills were clearly considered to be a 'pump-priming' measure in anticipation of longer-term funding by stock. Still the authority refrained from utilizing the facility until 1896 when a significant change in attitude took place. By this Act the bills ceased to be simply a pump-priming facility for the capital expenditure of the year, as power was given for renewal of the bills in place of the earlier provision for their discharge on maturity by means of a stock issue.

In other words, the issue of bills was no longer seen as a measure applicable only to the current year's capital expenditure, but as a continuing operation for capital finance, if the authority so wished. Even so, action was still deferred until 1897 when the powers were repeated but with the maximum raised to £1 million. Sir Harry Haward describes the procedure whereby an issue was made on 22 May 1897 of £600,000 at a discount of £1 1s 11½d per cent, with a true yield of £1 2s 3d per cent. Sir Harry's account includes a note of regret that the issue was preceded by an issue of Glasgow promissory notes some few days earlier, so that despite being the first local authority to obtain the powers, London missed by a narrow margin the opportunity of being the first local authority to make a bill (promissory note) issue. Nevertheless, evidence has already been quoted to show that Glasgow was borrowing for its non-statutory 'common good fund' as early as the middle of the seventeenth century by what seem to have been promissory notes. A clause in the 1897 Act permitted the seal, hitherto embossed, and the signature, hitherto added manually by the Clerk, to be engraved on the bills as a matter of convenience. Some sixty years later when the City of Manchester introduced a 'simplified' mortgage deed, what was then believed to be the innovation of a printed seal and signature was introduced. Nevertheless, despite the establishment of this simplified method, the GLC today continues to impress the seal on its mortgages.

The 1897 issue of bills raised stamp duty problems: the Inland Revenue Stamp Office proposed to charge 10s per cent duty on three months bills (that is, 2 per cent p.a.) as on a 'marketable security'. This would have killed the financial benefit of borrowing by bills had not a clause been inserted in the Finance Act of that year, making all local authority money bills subject only to stamp duty of 1s per cent as promissory notes.

Writing in 1932, Sir Harry Haward expressed some doubts about the use of such short-term borrowing for capital purposes – he expressed similar doubts about the use of short-term temporary borrowing for the same purpose – and says that the Treasury were at that time 'discouraging this form of local unfunded debt'. How wrong he was in the first conclusion, but how right in the second.

The parallel history of the evolution of borrowing by bills in a representative authority may be illustrated by the experience of the City of Manchester. There were other authorities who were marginally earlier in obtaining the original powers, but Manchester achieved a post Second World War breakthrough in this field, accumulating powers which were no less than those of any other authority by the time the local bill powers were abolished in 1974.

Manchester obtained capital bill powers in 1901, under the Manchester Corporation Act of that year; the introductory clause said:

> instead of raising for any purposes by the creation and issue of stock or of mortgages money which they are authorised to borrow (whether under this Act or any other Act of Parliament or otherwise howsoever) the Corporation may if they see fit raise for these purposes such money by the means of bills subject to the following provisions.

The Bills were to be known as 'Manchester Corporation bills', and were to be in a form prescribed by regulations (to be made by the corporation itself), which form should show the amount involved and the period, which was to be not less than three or more than twelve months. The bills were to be offered by tender after public advertisement. The authority for the issue of the bills was to be a warrant officially sealed by the corporation. The amount of any bill was to be not less than £1,000; why a minimum was needed to be specified is not clear, but although this minimum remained in the specification until 1972, the unit of issue was by that time usually £25,000 and multiples thereof. The bills themselves were also to bear the seal of the corporation and a register was to be maintained. (The later use of bearer bills reduced the significance of a register.) The right of inspection of the register was given to 'any creditor of the corporation' without fee. This provision also remained throughout the life of the provisions but, in practice, must have been without significance.

At this initial stage the issue of bearer bills was specifically prohibited, which originally gave some meaning to the need for a register. The regulations to be made by the corporation, in addition to designating the form of the bill, were to make detailed arrangements for the mode of issuing and cancelling bills, replacing lost or damaged bills, means of avoiding fraud (counterfoils and special paper) and proper discharge. Arrangements with a bank were permitted for the handling of issues and redemption, at a suitable remuneration. In practice, for the greater part of their history Manchester bills were habitually sold to the then District (now National Westminster) Bank, who either held them to maturity or sold them in the market. Later a tendering system was adopted. The Act specified that the amount of money actually received for the bills was to be regarded as principal money, and the difference between this amount and the amount repayable was to be deemed interest. A curious clause in the Act showed that there was still a lack of understanding of the difference between the periods for which particular loans had been taken up and the loan sanction period over which the debt incurred for a project was to be redeemed. The provision for redemption where specified by statute clearly relates to the loan sanction period which although somewhat erratic at the time could be as long as fifty or even sixty years. The amount to be set aside for redemption was one-fiftieth of the sum borrowed each year (except if by annuities). This annual sinking fund provision bore no relationship to the amount required at any one time for the repayment – or 'roll-over' – of an individual loan, which might be for three months, or three or thirty years, if not for the full fifty years. Yet this (and the other bill Acts) contained a provision that a sinking fund was to be provided in the same way as if the money had been borrowed by mortgage. The point has already been made that a sinking fund has no connection with the method by which money is borrowed but relates to the period sanctioned for the writing off of the debt incurred. This situation is even clearer when a fully fledged consolidated loans fund is operating. In that case annual provision for redemption is a matter between the CLF and the service to which an advance has been made to meet an item of capital outlay; and the feeding of funds into the CLF by borrowings and the periodic repayments of these borrowings whether overnight or for a long period of years is irrelevant to the redemption payments by the accounts to which advances have been made. Yet this peculiar clause remained in the bill Acts and was repeated at various times down to 1972. This is yet one more indication that capital finance by borrowing was not thought through as techniques changed.

The next provision was that the maximum amount at issue at any one time was not to exceed £½ million. The money raised was to be employed for the purposes of the several statutory borrowing powers in respect of which the bills were issued. The first Manchester issue of £½ million was allocated between the Parks, Waterworks, Tramways and Electricity departments. These requirements were part of a system of doubtful validity even at the time when borrowings were earmarked to authorized projects, if not to sanction periods, but it also remained in the terms of bill provisions through to 1972 when the whole concept had long been altered by the use of the CLF. Another anachronism was that the provision for repayment of the bills was permitted to be by the issue of stock or borrowing on mortgage or the issue of further bills, but if stock or mortgages were used, then the borrowing powers available for the stock or mortgages were to be suspended while this purpose was covered by bills. This odd provision again survived throughout the life of local Act bill powers.

The holder of a bill was to be entitled at maturity to the sum expressed in such bill, which was to be charged against all the revenues of the corporation. These revenues were defined as those arising from time to time from any land, undertakings, or other property and rates leviable by or on the precept of the corporation. Finally, the city treasurer was to make a return to the Local Government Board within twenty-one days of the year end containing such particulars as the board required.

The amendments made to these arrangements over the next seventy years were few but of significance. The maximum amount was raised from £½ million to £1 million as early as 1903. In 1920 an attempt to increase the sum to £5 million was rejected by the House of Lords on the advice of the Ministry of Health. After a long gap, in 1965 it was increased to £3 million; in 1967 alternatives were introduced of either £3 million or one-fifth of the estimated rate product for the year; and in 1970 this was rephrased as one-fifth of the gross rate income as defined in the General Rate Act 1967. The need to advertise the issue was dropped in 1908. An important change in 1920 was that power to issue bills to bearer was obtained. As already mentioned, this did not result in the production of specially designed bearer bills, but the use of the existing form of bill with the name entry left blank. These bills could be (but as far as is known never were) 'nominalized' by the insertion of the holder's name at any stage.

After the Local Government Act 1933 had consolidated the local authority borrowing code, but continued to omit bill powers, the bill-issuing powers of Manchester Corporation were repeated in the local Act of 1934. The Manchester Corporation Acts of 1965 and 1967 saw a considerable modernization of the provisions, though without the removal of anachronisms previously described. The need for a 'warrant' of the council before the making of an issue was replaced by a simple council resolution (which in fact was achieved by a general resolution authorizing the Finance Committee to borrow by this means as necessary); the sealing requirement was replaced by the signature of the city treasurer or other authorized person; the maximum (as already mentioned) was increased; and most important of all, the use of 'revenue bills', that is, borrowing by bills in anticipation of the receipt of revenue, was also authorized. The underlying security definition was tidied up by the omission of references to properties and concentration on 'all the revenues', these revenues were to be as defined in the Local Government Act 1933. The 1970 Act removed the three-months minimum – which need never have been there in the first place – and generally consolidated the amendments made over the years into a fresh code. This new code was short-lived, being repealed under the 1972 Act and replaced by the provisions shortly to be described.

These developments may be generally accepted as representative of the actions taken by most other authorities having such powers. The revenue bills power is of some interest as at that date (1967) the Treasury was restricting capital bill issues by local authorities. Revenue-issuing powers were not so restricted, but do not seem to have been exercised by those few local authorities which had them. When Manchester obtained the revenue bill powers in 1967, a number of other authorities which already had these powers seemed to believe that revenue bills also came within the Treasury's embargo on bills. Manchester sought the powers simply as a step towards giving the city full options for some later date, but discovered during the process that the Treasury had no objection to the exercise of revenue bill issuing powers which, to use their expression, were 'self-financing by the receipt of the revenue in due course'. Thereupon Manchester once again began to issue bills, now in anticipation of revenue; those authorities with similar powers followed suit, and other authorities promptly sought revenue bill powers in local Acts. Even as late as 1970, when the 1972 Act must have been in the preliminary drafting stages, a dozen or more local authorities (Northumberland, Cumberland, Yorkshire West Riding, Hampshire, Bolton, and others) obtained a 'package' of local Act borrowing powers – including capital and revenue bills, the use of bearer bonds and the right to borrow abroad in foreign currencies – all of which powers, except the right to issue revenue bills, were subject to immediate frustration by the withholding of Treasury approval despite the statutory sanction.

Local authority money bills are acceptable to the Bank of England as overnight collateral, and this of course increases their popularity with the discount market. The history of this facet of the status of bills reveals a most interesting situation (information supplied by Mr Murray Erskine, Bank of England). Although a number of local authorities had bill powers by 1930 little use seems to have been made of these during the early years of that decade. However, towards the end of the decade the market began to expand because bills were issued not only by those local authorities with statutory powers, but by other authorities in the (presumably erroneous) belief that section 215 of the Local Government Act 1933, permitting borrowing without sanction in anticipation of either revenue or capital, automatically permitted such temporary borrowing by the issue of bills.

In the financial crisis consequent upon the outbreak of war in September 1939 the London clearing banks experienced problems with the quantity of bills being offered. The Committee of London Clearing Bankers determined that they would not accept bills unless they were also acceptable to the Bank of England as security and for deposit. In fact the Bank had recognized only a handful of local authority bills as collateral. (Names are now unobtainable but related to local authority 'customers of the Bank' – probably those who used the Bank as 'registrars of stock' – though Glasgow is known to have been one of the acceptable authorities.) This would have meant a severe restriction on local authority bill borrowing, even for those authorities with specific powers. The Bank of England therefore announced that henceforward it would accept local authority bills as collateral subject to terms. These were that the bills were issued under specific and limited statutory powers, for periods of not more than six months; that there must be a period of sixty days in each financial year when each authority did not have any bills on issue; that the issue would be advertised in London within three days of issue; and that the Bank would be given seven days' notice before issue. These terms were set out in a confidential notice to the banks and customers affected, dated 8 December 1939. In press reports of the time this move was welcomed, though not by those local authorities whose bill borrowing was thus discouraged if not specifically forbidden.

In 1969 (by which time the restriction of all local authority bills to anticipation of revenue had been firmly established by the Treasury) the Bank of England issued a similar notice, with the alteration that the sixty-day break rule was withdrawn. In June 1983 a further Bank notice was issued in which the specification of six months maximum period was amended to 187 days. In practice, the majority of bills are issued for ninety-one days.

Despite the undeniable but modest benefits to be derived by local authorities from this method of borrowing, the issue of money bills under the current powers of the Local Government Act 1972 cannot be described as otherwise than complicated and hedged by restrictions. There are three . areas of restraint: in the Act itself, through the use of the Control of Borrowing Order, and by Bank of England regulations. The Act's schedule 13 (para. 5) allows a local authority whose annual rate income is not less than £3 million to borrow by the issue of bills payable within 12 months of issue (a small but relevant clarification), for an amount not exceeding 20 per cent of the rate income attributable to its own purposes for any purpose for which the authority is authorized to borrow or for defraying expenses pending the receipt of revenue within the financial year. Two comments arise at once from this apparently simple and straightforward authorization. First, the use of the word 'payable' instead of 'repayable' suggests an attitude to bills as 'deferred payments', as are commercial bills, whereas local authority bills are repayments of loans. Secondly, the attachment of the amount of bills which may be issued to a revenue, rather than a capital, base-line suggests a revenue, rather than a capital, function despite the fuller intentions expressed in the Act. By contrast, the amount of borrowing by temporary loan receipt is linked to capital requirements and total debt.

With this underlying emphasis on revenue purposes the continued countermanding of the use of bills for capital purposes by use of the Control of Borrowing Order and the Consent comes as no surprise. The Bank of England rules for acceptability by them as collateral, and the Treasury definition of what constitutes a revenue bill, continue to apply.

These rules make no reference to the use of bearer bills (although the bearer nature of bills is a recognized market essential) as the power of local authorities to use bearer instruments is controlled by para 6 of schedule 13, which makes such facilities dependent on the consent of the Treasury which has not yet been given. Nevertheless, local authority money bills do in fact circulate in bearer form as they are revenue bills to which the Treasury embargo does not apply. Once the parameters within which bills may be issued is understood, their placing on the market is a reasonably simple operation, and they have proved to be a comparatively cheap source of borrowing.

The practice of using local authority bills as bearer instruments is of interest. There was no indication in the early London Acts that bearer bills might be issued, but neither was there any prohibition. The form of bill illustrated in the London Regulations made under the Act had a footnote to say that: 'If this blank be not filled in the bill will be paid to bearer.' The draft form of Glasgow promissory note had a similar provision. Yet in the English Acts giving bill powers of around 1900 the issue of bearer bills was specifically forbidden. Johnson in his *Loans of Local Authorities*, written in 1925, says that in earlier days the issue of bearer bills was prohibited 'except in the case of a few favoured authorities' but that the restriction, which was designed to prevent forgery, is not now considered of importance and that a clause repealing it can generally be obtained in a private Act. As explained, Manchester did obtain such a clause in 1920, but instead of issuing bearer bills, as such, relied upon the footnote technique as in Glasgow. Therefore, there seem to be grounds for believing that this long-recognized practice in relation to certain kinds of instruments crept into local authority money bill use gradually and was certainly established by the early 1920s. This footnote device was apparently regarded as superior to fully fledged bearer bills both by the authorities and the market, perhaps because it had the advantage that the bill could be used in either form – that is, nominalized, and thus made secure by any holder who so desired, by the addition of his name (though in that case he would require to have the bill registered) – and it followed a pattern of practice used for other instruments in the Local Loans Act 1875.

Because this option remained with the holder, thus demarcating such bills from true bearer documents, the Treasury and the Bank of England seem content today to allow the practice to continue outside the restriction of schedule 13 (para. 6) to the 1972 Act. In a letter (24 February 1983) a representative of the Bank repeated the view that the restrictive clause on bearer instruments was not intended to apply to revenue borrowing, but admits that this is not what the schedule says. However, in the light of past experience doubt may be expressed whether, if central authorities do ever allow the use of capital bills by local authorities (as conceivably they might, at least in special circumstances), such permission would need also to extend to the long established use of the footnote device on bills. Ten years after the Act, the Treasury show no inclination to permit the use of bearer documents by local authorities. Bills which were not in bearer or quasi-bearer form would certainly not be popular on the market.

Nevertheless, there is evidence that the Bank of England has in the past been in two minds about this matter because until exchange control was abolished in 1979 the Bank had laid down Exchange Control Regulations which, among many other things, made rules for the handling of bearer instruments designed to avoid their unauthorized acquisition by foreign holders. Under Exchange Control Notice No. 8 bearer securities were required to be lodged in the custody of 'an authorised depositary' – namely, a bank or solicitor, etc – who was responsible for seeing that any change of ownership took place within the regulations. That this requirement applied to local authority 'open' bills was made clear, in a letter to the author (29 April 1975); thus the bills were bearer documents for one side of the Bank, but not for another, perhaps understandably. The same letter pointed out that also under the Exchange Control Rules, 'The specific approval of the Bank of England is required for each and every issue of these Bills'. When the Exchange Control Department was thereupon informed that the practice of local authorities was to obtain Bank of England approval for each bill issue for 'acceptance', but not 'exchange control' purposes, this point was not pursued by the Exchange Control Department, though local authorities did in fact issue bills on the understanding that they would be lodged with authorized depositaries until exchange control was abolished.

The Treasury attitude towards local authority capital bills is worthy of further examination; it appears to be consistent but anachronistic. Capital bills have been under embargo both before and after the general powers of the 1972 Act. Why has this ban been maintained when an equal quantity of bills as might have been issued as capital bills is readily allowed as revenue bills? The only effective difference is that, if the bills permitted had been for capital purposes, they would simply have reduced the volume of borrowing permitted by temporary loan receipts. Nevertheless, the Treasury adhere to the view in 1982 that short borrowing of this kind is somehow improper for the financing of capital expenditure. This is despite the fact that Parliament has authorized this use as recently as 1972, and that a maximum of 20 per cent of local authority debt of less than 12 months' initial borrowing period has been accepted by one and all since 1963 for capital expenditure, and despite the operations of the recent Maturity Code.

Griffiths (for many years City Treasurer of Sheffield), in his *Municipal Capital Finance*, reports that Sheffield were refused power to increase the amount of bills from the £½ million granted in 1900 to the £3 million sought in 1928. This refusal was based on Treasury advice to the Committee of the House dealing with the proposal that 'the Lords Commissioners of the Treasury view with disfavour any extension of the power of local authorities to raise money on short-term bills'. Griffiths continues by saying that attempts to discover the reasons for the Treasury's view elicited the opinion that local authorities should not use this type of borrowing for capital expenditure, which should normally be financed by securities with a currency of not less than five years. The purpose of bills was in its view to tide over periods of financial stress.

In 1920 Manchester was refused an increase of bill issues from £1 million to £5 million, but in 1965 an increase to £3 million was allowed when the Treasury had established a policy that revenue bills only would in fact be permitted. Sir Harry Haward says in his *London County Council from Within* that 'In recent years the policy of the Treasury has been to discountenance this form of local authority unfunded debt'.

This objection to the use of bill borrowing for capital purposes was still the opinion expressed by Treasury and Bank officials in 1975 (personal interview). The Treasury resisted arguments that the Exchequer was issuing bills without regard to purposes by saying that Treasury bills are issued only for revenue cash-flow purposes. This is factually doubtful as Treasury bills are used mainly as a means of market and monetary control and in so far as they are a financing item, they finance the public sector borrowing requirement (PSBR), in which capital and revenue purposes are not separated – PSBR borrowing being simply a financing of a budget deficiency. (This view has been reiterated in response to inquiries during the course of writing this book.)

The Treasury and Bank of England views have thus remained frozen between the late 1920s and 1982, although a completely new approach has been adopted to local authority temporary borrowing – initial period less than 365 days – and a Maturity Code has been introduced which extends the recent average life of local authority borrowing considerably. The Treasury and Bank views need reconsideration in the light of these changes. The effect could be, by allowing the issue of capital bills, that the total amount of really short local authority borrowing would be reduced, not extended. The 'self-financing' aspect has become immaterial. Incidentally, lenders probably do not realize that the receivership provisions applicable to mortgages, bonds and stock do not apply to bills, as they also do not apply to temporary loans. Treasury obstinacy is all the more inexplicable against the acceptance of the use by building societies of short-term loans for long-term lending. The Bank has also recently suggested that the market is chary of bills not supported by revenue receivable. This view may be substantially doubted as capital bills have exactly the same security as revenue bills – all the revenues of the authority. There must be very few buyers of local authority money bills who are interested in whether they are for revenue or capital purposes.

Just when a complete embargo on capital bills was first effectively applied is not now clear. However, borrowing by local authorities, except for a small margin on mortgages, was prohibited other than from the PWLC, as already described, from 1945 to 1952. In 1958 the Control of Borrowing Order forbade the use of local authority capital bills without Treasury consent (this may have been the first official ban on these instruments). The Order allowed local authorities to borrow by revenue bills if the expenditure was not capital expenditure, the money was repaid within one month of the financial year-end (increased in 1975 to three months – SI 1975/12) and the amount outstanding at any one time did not exceed one-half of the total revenues received or receivable during the period. This suggests that there were local authorities with revenue bill powers by 1958, though none is known to have exercised this permission under the Order at that time. The General Consent of April 1964 (repeated in the Consents of 1968 and 1974) withheld consent from capital bills, which remained subject to specific consent. This has not since been given. The withdrawal of the sixty-day break rule by the Bank of England has already been described; the change was conveyed to the Local Authority Associations in a letter dated 31 January 1969.

While the granting of revenue bill powers to Manchester in 1965 seems to have signalled the beginning of a wide use of revenue bills by authorized local authorities, the gaps in the story are the date when the issue of capital bills was finally suppressed and that when the revenue bill powers were first obtained by a local authority. The specific mention of revenue bills in the Control of Borrowing Order suggests that such powers were extant in 1964 but evidence has not been found of their use.

In October 1969 the Treasury refused the request of the local authorities that district councils should be allowed to seek bill powers without opposition, but said that county councils seeking such powers could include power to borrow by bills on behalf of their districts. In January 1971 the Treasury issued a letter of guidance setting out the terms on which county councils and county borough councils might seek bill powers without Treasury opposition. These were that the authority must have a rate call of over £3 million, the expenditure must be for revenue and not capital purposes, repayment must take place within one month (later three months) of the period end and, most significantly, the total on issue must not exceed 20 per cent of revenue receivable rather than the 50 per cent of the Control of Borrowing Order.

But there had been a more tortuous outcome of the prohibition of capital in favour of revenue bills. Whichever type of bill was to be issued, the overall amounts permitted would be the same as the limits prescribed in the Acts applying to both forms of bill. In practice, because of the way in which local authority revenue flows in, aided by the regular and frequent payment of government grants (though now slightly impeded as a result of the right of domestic ratepayers to pay in ten instalments), local authorities have little real need to borrow money in anticipation of revenue and can, in any case, borrow temporarily or by overdraft for that purpose if they need. To assist their borrowing requirements treasurers have therefore sought to use the proceeds of revenue bills to 'underwrite' a portion of their capital needs, while excluding the bill proceeds from their loan account transactions. The general practice of local authorities is to use a single consolidated bank account, at least for their main funds, thus avoiding overdraft problems between one internal subaccount and another. Any surplus revenue balances within such a consolidated bank account have for long been regarded and used as available to allow the capital portion of the bank account to fall into theoretical overdraft, without any payment having to be made to the bank, though there may be internal interest adjustments made. This has enabled an element of capital borrowing to be deferred. Local authorities are permitted by law to finance borrowing temporarily by bank overdraft, and by the use of internal funds, and this utilization of revenue bill proceeds falls exactly within this process. Therefore, in a roundabout way treasurers have found a means of taking advantage of the cheaper interest for bills.

The Treasury are not unaware of this practice of making a roundabout use of revenue bills in support of capital expenditure. In the letter to local authorities of January 1971 setting out the terms on which local authority revenue bill powers would not be opposed a relatively simple definition of the scope of revenue bills was also laid down – the proceeds must be taken into revenue and not capital account, the interest must be charged against rate fund account (and not the loans fund) and the authority must be able to demonstrate that, at some time within the currency of the bills, the total revenues receivable will not be less than the amount of bills on issue.

The conclusion about local authority bills, then, must be quite simple. The fifty-year-old Treasury view that bills are not an appropriate way of financing capital outlay has been bypassed by the subsequent 'permanent' acceptance of 'substantial' local authority temporary borrowing and the introduction of the Maturity Code. Now there is no reason at all why capital bills should not be permitted and recognized as the negotiable fringe element of the temporary (short-bond) borrowing, just as negotiable bonds are the negotiable fringe of the medium-term bond issue. This would mean that the volume of capital bills issued would narrow the volume of 'temporary loan' (short-bond) issues. If local authorities need a cash-flow borrowing facility other than bank overdraft (which is doubtful), some other means of providing this can be introduced. But the overall operation will be much clearer both to borrowers and lenders, if revenue borrowing is not confused with capital borrowing. There is no reason why capital bills should not be allowed as an element in the total control over 'less than one year initial borrowing', and some measure of revenue bills allowed for an authority which needs a cash-flow facility. What is not acceptable is a view of capital bills dating from the 1930s which takes no account of the material changes of practice that have since taken place.

Two final thoughts may be expressed at some risk of overstating the case. The Treasury believe that the attraction of revenue bills is their 'self-financing' nature, as rate income is collected. This same rate income is by statute the security applicable to capital bills; receivership provisions are not applicable to either form. The Treasury also appears to believe that the present revenue bills are either not bearer instruments, or that, if they are, they somehow fall outside the restrictions of the 1972 Act. The reality is that the practice of leaving the name line blank, thereby creating a bearer document, has precedence of 100 years, and that there can be no harm in having a fringe of local authority capital borrowing techniques which use bearer instruments. In consequence, when local authority bills are accepted as capital bills, they also need by the same token to be accepted as bearer documents; otherwise they do not have the true chracteristics of the 'bill' as a borrowing instrument. The problem is, why have so many impediments been maintained for so long?

Chapter 20

BONDS

As a borrowing instrument the bond has two distinctions: it is extremely ancient, and its title expresses its content. It has perhaps a third distinction, in that it has become in recent years the borrowing instrument now most used by local authorities. Two types of bond are generally used in the money markets, the simple and the double or conditional bond. The simple bond, which is the form now used in local government, is indeed simple, being the straightforward acknowledgement of a debt with an obligation to pay interest. The conditional bond imposes a penalty for non-fulfilment of the bond, and does not necessarily apply to a loan – for example, public works contractors today give 'bonds' for due performance of contracts. Structurally the conditional bond begins by binding the giver of the bond to the penalty, with the added proviso that this is held in abeyance and becomes void if the consideration is fulfilled. Of course the classic case appears in Shakespeare's *Merchant of Venice*, when the debt but not the penalty was in financial terms. The great age of the bond in its conditional form is shown by inference in the quotation, given in the Introduction to this book, from the Act of Henry III, in 1233, which specified the form of the chirograph: 'No Jew may lend anything by penalty', which must certainly be a reference to the conditional bond.

A bond is defined in *Halsbury's Laws of England* (3rd edn) as 'an instrument under seal, usually a deed poll, whereby one person bonds himself to another for the payment of a specified sum at a fixed or future date'. This reference to a deed poll, as distinct from an indenture, identifies the bond as being a 'one-party promise' as distinct from a two-party agreement. This is echoed by the *Encyclopaedia Britannica*, which gives a more generalized definition of a bond as 'A type of promissory note . . . specifying an obligation to return borrowed funds'. Thompson's *Dictionary of Banking* (10th edn) defines a bond as 'a document under seal whereby a person binds himself to pay a certain sum of money or to fulfil a certain contract'. Thompson adds that a reference is usually made in a bond to a penalty for non-fulfilment, as, for example, for a loan of £100 the borrower binds himself to pay a penalty of £200 to cover principal, interest and charges, with the proviso that as long as the interest on the original investment is paid and the loan ultimately discharged, the penalty will not come into operation. In *A Concise Dictionary of Finance* (1934) a bond is defined by Brooks as 'a promise under seal defeasible [subject to cancellation or withdrawal] upon a condition subsequent, that is, it imposes a penalty for the non-performance of a condition, which is avoided on the performance of the condition, such performance being the real object of the bond'. Conditional bonds are certainly still in use but the bond as used by local authorities is not only of the simple type, but by a device which we shall describe it also now evades the common law tradition that it should be under seal. In fact it is the conditional type of bond which gives this instrument its individual character; otherwise, and as used in local government, it is now no more than an instrument of debt acknowledgement in more or less common form.

For an up-to-date, thoroughly pragmatic definition of what a bond is considered to be today that contained in M. S. Dobbs-Higginson's *Investment Manual for Fixed Interest Securities* (Credit Suisse First Boston Ltd, 1979) may be referred to; the bond here is given two meanings:

(1) an interest-bearing certificate of debt, under the terms of which a borrower contracts, *inter alia*, to pay the holder a fixed principal amount on a stated future date, and a series of interest payments during its life;

(2) a long-term debt instrument – in this sense may also be referred to as a debenture.

Definition 1 certainly describes the present local authority bond perfectly, but it could also embrace other local authority instruments. Finally, the Stock Exchange motto 'Dictum meum pactum' ('My word is my bond') confirms the straightforward implication of a binding undertaking or promise – except that lenders like also to have a document for good measure.

Bond provisions have cropped up erratically in the examination of borrowing by local authorities in this book, though such references have been rare when compared with the powers to borrow by assignments, mortgages and annuities. Specimens of bonds supplied by the City Archivist of Kingston upon Hull (G. W. Oxley) date from 1640 until almost the end of the following century (the *Merchant of Venice* saw the light of day about 1600). The oldest of these examples (though whether it relates to a city debt is not clear) established a penalty of £290, unless the borrower repaid £145 on the due date. A later example of 1696, which certainly refers to a municipal debt, established an obligation on the borrower to pay £80, unless £40 was repaid within two months, in which case 'then this obligation to be void'. A third example in 1700 established a bonded obligation for £400 unless the mayor and burgesses paid £200 with interest on the due date 'without fail or further delay'. The obligation portion of these bonds is written in Latin, while the condition is in English. Finally, a bond of February 1782, written wholly in English and with a 10d document stamp, began with the deed poll words 'Know all men by these presents' and set up a penalty of £260 which became void if £130 with 5 per cent interest was paid by August 1782.[1] When the first quasi-local authority borrowing powers were introduced in the establishment of a turnpike in 1663 with the assignment of the tolls as a security against the borrowing, doubts about the reliability of the new venture were such that the money could only be raised when the gentlemen involved in the undertaking gave their personal bonds in further support.

In the late eighteenth century when mortgages and annuities were well established as the means of borrowing for Poor Law purposes, an Act to provide a workhouse at Marylebone (1775) gave the guardians power to borrow up to £10,000 'at the lowest rate of interest that can be procured ... such money to be borrowed upon bonds of One Hundred Pounds each'. This Act is also of interest for two other financial provisions. The debt was to be repaid at the rate of £500 a year, the lenders to be selected by lot, and the guardians might repay and replace loans if they could reborrow at a lower rate. In the same year a workhouse was provided at Clerkenwell by money borrowed 'by [life] Annuities, or upon Bonds or other Securities'. In 1783 the guardians at Birmingham were authorized to raise £15,000 'upon Bonds of not less than £50 each'. Repayment could be at the rate of £750 a year. Life annuities were offered as an alternative.

An excellent example of a local authority bond occurs in the Coventry Waterworks Act 1844 where the form of bond, which is of the 'conditional' type, is given in a schedule to the Act on the following lines: 'Know all men by these presents ... We, the Mayor, Aldermen and Burgesses of the City of Coventry ... do bind ourselves and our successors unto the said ... in the penal sum of ...' which penalty was avoided if the original consideration was repaid, with interest meanwhile. In this draft bond the security is not mentioned, which gives an interesting comparison between the bond and the mortgage also provided for in the Act, for which the security was specifically set out. The Act provided that every bond and mortgage 'for securing money borrowed by the said Corporation shall be by Deed under the Common Seal of the Mayor, Aldermen and Burgesses duly stamped, and wherein the consideration shall be duly stated'. The bond was to be in the form already given above, but the draft form of mortgage was somewhat more explicit in saying that 'Every mortgage of the said Waterworks, Rates, Rents or Premises may be in the form in Schedule B or to the like effect'. Thus the mortgage expresses the security which is 'mortgaged' but gives slightly greater latitude in the design of the loan instrument. For what it is worth in reality, the difference at that date was clear: the bond was a 'binding undertaking' relying on a penalty for non-fulfilment, whereas the mortgage was an assignment of access to properties and revenues, so that in effect a lender on a bond did not know precisely what security stood behind his loan other than the binding words of the city fathers. Annuities also available under the Act were given the same specific security as the mortgages. No doubt, similar clauses could be found in other of the many nineteenth-century local Acts giving powers for the establishment or takeover of trading undertakings.

To recapitulate, the Company Clauses Consolidation Act 1845, which was later applied to some local authority services but not others (for instance, to Baths and Washhouses 1846, but not Libraries 1855), provided for both bonds and mortgages. The form of bond in this Act was of the 'conditional' type and bound the commissioners 'in the penal sum of . . .' unless they repaid the principal as promised with interest meanwhile. The Commissioners Clauses Act 1847 provided only for mortgages. The Public Health Acts favoured mortgages only, by reference to the Commissioners Clauses Act. The Municipal Corporations Act 1882 mentions neither mortgages nor bonds, but in so far as borrowing was to be on the security of the properties and revenues, mortgages were implied. The Local Loans Act 1875 included neither mortgages nor bonds. The reorganization Acts of 1888 and 1894 provide for borrowing as under the Public Health Acts, that is, by mortgage.

The nature of the simple (non-conditional) bond may be clearly seen in the Poor Law Loans and Relief (Scotland) Act 1886, in which parochial boards in any parish or combination of parishes with a population in excess of 100,000 might borrow for the purposes of the Act and

assign the assessments present and future leviable by them for the relief of the poor in security of the money so borrowed and the interest thereon; and the bonds to be granted on such borrowings and transferences or assignations and discharges may be in or near to the forms contained in the schedule.

The instrument envisaged, though called a bond, was thus the precise equivalent of a mortgage, by assignment of the rates. The scheduled form was headed 'Bond for borrowed money', but the content made no reference to bonding or promising, but simply to the assignment of revenues, and sealing was not called for. There was no question of a penalty clause, nor was there any peculiarity about repayment provisions; these could be either 'in one sum or by instalments as may be arranged', with a maximum loan period of thirty years.

The indications therefore seem to be that the use of the conditional type of bond for local authority borrowing lapsed some time shortly after the middle of the nineteenth century, and that the simple bond was quietly absorbed into the mortgage form from whence it has recently re-emerged.

A curious example has come to light of a handsome bond issued by the Yorkshire West Riding County Council in March 1906; this was for a (pre-printed) amount of £100 at 3½ per cent, repayable fifteen years later. It claims to have been issued by the council 'By virtue of the Local Loans Act 1875, the Local Government Act 1888, and all other statutes enabling them'. Neither of these principal Acts conveyed a power to borrow by bonds, and inquiries of the present county treasurer (C. S. Pollard) indicate that there were no local Act powers relating to the county council until the 1940s. The minute-book of the Finance Committee at that date discloses that the decision was to raise £123,000 'by the issue of West Riding Debentures or Bonds (subject to the rules of the County Council under the Local Loans Act 1875)', and that the fiteeen-year bonds were against thirty-year loan sanctions. Clearly, these loans were Local Loans Act debentures in nominal form which the county chose to designate as bonds, thus indicating a certain lack of respect for precision of nomenclature. Needless to say, the bonds were in the simple and not the conditional form. They were a charge on the county fund and the county rate.

The bond as a fully fledged borrowing instrument for local authorities owes its origin to the limited provisions of the Housing (Additional Powers) Act 1919. The bond introduced by that Act (confusingly called in the statute 'local' rather than the more appropriate 'housing') was the outcome of a Treasury-appointed committee under the chairmanship of W. H. N. Goschen. Unfortunately it contained the provision of a minimum borrowing period of five years, which materially handicapped the later effective adoption of a general bond for local government purposes for half a century. This five-year minimum can now be recognized as part of the Treasury's long battle to lengthen local authority maturities.

The opening paragraph of the Goschen Report (Cmd 444/1919) referred to the committee's duty to consider 'the steps that should be taken by Local Authorities to facilitate the raising of capital to defray the cost of housing schemes and in particular to make suggestions for a model long-term security for this purpose', so that local authority debt would not interfere with the funding of the government's postwar debt. The attitude expressed towards the borrowing abilities of local authorities (which was no doubt also a reflection of the Treasury view), despite their 250 years of borrowing experience, gives grounds for some surprise:

> Many local authorities, unaccustomed to conduct loan operations on a large scale, were proposing to obtain money for housing by means of short-dated loans from banks and others from whom they had previously been able to obtain such advances as they required. Your Lordships considered that this course was calculated to undo much of the good which might be anticipated from the process of funding the floating debt of the State and if indulged in on a large scale was in itself certain to defeat its own object, viz: the conversion of such loans in a few years time into long-term securities at more favourable rates of interest than could now be obtained. The very fact that a large volume of short-dated indebtedness was awaiting an opportunity for consolidation would in itself keep the terms for long-dated securities high.

Although the committee made a half-hearted attempt to produce a 'long' security, the members seem to have had doubts about the practicality of such a project and felt compelled to remind the Treasury that the well-established mortgage had raised large sums in the past, though mainly for three, five, or seven years; the report added 'it has been common experience that about 70% of such mortgage loans have in the past been renewed on maturity and could ordinarily be regarded as almost permanent loans'. Incidentally, in the light of this cogent observation, it was particularly unfortunate that because of a drafting flaw the new bond when it became law was so designed that it could not be renewed on maturity, so that if renewal was desired a new instrument had to be prepared. The committee said bluntly that they did not feel that a long-term security was likely to raise the sum of money considered to be necessary (estimated at £430 million to build 535,000 houses). The committee's recommendations began, in effect, with a declaration of allegiance to the mortgage (and stock) by saying that the largest authorities should continue to raise money as they had in the past and that mortgages should be given trustee security status, where the local authority had also power to issue stock in this category. To strengthen existing powers the committee recommended that the temporary Public Authorities and Bodies (Loans) Act 1916, which gave power to borrow abroad, should be made permanent (although, as explained previously, advantage does not seem to have been taken of this facility). However, subject to the sanction of a central department, authorities (in combination if need be) were to be authorized to issue 'local bonds' on the security of the rates and revenues, and consideration was to be given to the possibility of county councils borrowing by such bonds for lending-on to smaller authorities. Access to the PWLC was considered inappropriate – local authorities were to be expected themselves to find the capital for housing development. In the event, the commissioners lent a great deal of money for housing purposes.

The recommended specification of the bond was that it should be issued at an interest rate of 5½ per cent, in denominations of £5, £10, £20, £50 and £100 and multiples thereof for periods of five, ten and twenty years (a vague and vain attempt at long-dating) secured on all the revenues (including rents and government subsidies receivable). The bonds were to be on continuous (tap) issue and interest to small lenders (holders of not more than £500) should be paid gross. Transfers should be free of cost and bonds should be Trustee Securities; they should also be accepted for value at par as payments towards the cost of any local authority houses built for sale.

Despite its search for a long-term security, the Treasury accepted the greater part of the recommendations. Interest was however to be as specified by the Treasury, initially 6 per cent (the responsibility for interest rate decisions was not transferred to the local authorities until 1936); and the issue period was to be not less than five years (no mention of ten and twenty years) and the multiples of units to be as recommended. The bonds were to be free of capital/stamp duty.

Regulations were made under the 1919 Housing Act in February 1920 (SR&O 1920/197); these were in fair detail. The significant provision was that the record of title to be issued to the holder was not itself to be a bond, but a certificate that the lender was registered as a bond-holder by the local authority. This provision, which had important consequences, meant that the bond was 'intangible' and that the certificate, not itself being a bond, did not need to be sealed. If the interest on a local bond was not paid within two months of demand in writing, the person entitled thereto could apply to the High Court for the appointment of a receiver. There was no reference to delay in payment of principal. The holder of a bond was relieved of responsibility for assuring himself that the loan had been properly raised and applied.

These powers were re-enacted in the consolidating Housing Act 1925. In the same year the Trustee Act confirmed the inclusion of local (housing) bonds as trustee securities, and extended this status to mortgages (not stock) issued by local authorities authorized to issue bonds. This led to comment by the Lord Chancellor's Committee on Trustee Securities in 1928 that this provision meant that trustee status was being given piecemeal, with the extraordinary consequence that further consents to the issue of local bonds were thereupon withheld. Not until the Local Government Act 1958 gave general trustee status to all investments with a local authority was the Minister able, in March 1959, to give general consent to the issue of housing bonds, by which time they were virtually moribund. Even in the Housing Act 1957, when the housing bond powers were again re-enacted, the security remained the rates, properties and revenues of the local authority, although the 1933 Act was considered to have settled security once and for all as 'all the revenues'. Perhaps 'properties' remained in the housing bond security because the loan money had been used for house building? The 1925 Act regulations continued to operate under the 1957 Act.

Writing in 1932, although his LCC service had ended ten years earlier, Sir Harry Haward spoke highly of the success of the LCC activities in raising funds by housing bonds; he also said that although the short term of local bonds made them in his opinion 'unfunded debt', they were in effect indistinguishable from registered stock. This statement was apparently based on their form of registration and transfer. He also claimed that a Stock Exchange quotation was obtained for the London issues, but in general there was not an organized market with daily quotations for housing bonds. In fact, as will be shown, bonds overlap in concept both mortgages and stock, depending upon the marketing arrangements which apply. Sir Harry also said in general reference to local authority borrowing other than by stock (the Metropolitan Board of Works and the LCC had never issued mortgages by the time Sir Harry left the organization) that: 'those authorities which depend almost entirely on short-term loans [by which he seems to mean borrowing for less than, say, fifteen years] fared no worse with regard to the rate of interest they had to pay than did those who followed the funding policy.'

The County Borough of Bolton (Lancashire) were enthusiastic users of housing bonds from 1920 right through to 1964, during which period over 15,000 loans of this kind were taken up.[2] A method of extracting the maximum advantage from the facility for gross interest on up to £100 of bond investment was apparently for husband and wife to invest £100 each and a further £100 jointly, which was deemed to allow a holding of £300 at gross interest to one household.

Perhaps one other reference to the 1919 Housing Act should be made.

Section 8 of the Act made permanent the section of the Public Authorities and Bodies (Loans) Act 1916 which gave to certain authorities power to borrow money by bearer securities, whether within or without the United Kingdom. This power was never used and was rescinded by the 1933 Act, to appear again in 1972, but still under Treasury embargo. Despite the modest and confused nature of the housing bond concept and the thirty-year hiatus in its life history, the supposition must be that the bond powers consolidated in the Housing Act 1925 led to the general bond powers contained in the Coventry Corporation Act 1927.

The Coventry treasurer of that date (Sidney Larkin) was like certain later treasurers of that city clearly of an enterprising mind. The resolution of the Finance Committee, made on recommendations of the treasurer in a report to the city council in the run-up to the city's 1927 Act, was that the council should seek powers to establish an insurance fund and a consolidated loans fund, to authorize the investment of reserve and similar funds in the corporation's own securities, and to rationalize sinking fund provisions. (The recommendation which the committee did not accept was that powers should be sought to establish a municipal savings bank similar to that of their neighbour, Birmingham; this decision was possibly influenced by word which had been passed round that any repetition of the Birmingham experiment was not acceptable to Whitehall.) The other recommendation, which was acted upon, was that the council should seek powers 'to authorise the issue of bonds, similar to housing bonds, for the general purposes of the Corporation'. Unfortunately there is now no record of the advantages which the treasurer claimed for these instruments, but there is no doubt that this lifting of the housing bond into a broader sphere was to have impressive consequences in the long term.

What stimulated the then Coventry treasurer to take this step? Possibly it was the suggestion by J. R. Johnson, the Birmingham treasurer, in his *Loans of Local Authorities*, written in 1925, that there was scope for a general bond. The treasurers of these two authorities must frequently have met. The suggestion made by Johnson was for a much more ambitious instrument than the housing bond, involving Stock Exchange participation, but it was Coventry and not Birmingham which took the initiative with a bond which followed the housing pattern and not Johnson's proposal. The Coventry bonds were to be called 'corporation bonds', to be covered by a certificate and with a five-year minimum period, at a rate of interest to be determined by the council. Unlike housing bonds, they were liable to capital duty and did not have the 'gross interest facility'; their security was the rates and revenues of the authority. The only apparent administrative advantage over the mortgage was that by the issue of a certificate they avoided the necessity of sealing, but the five-year minimum made the instrument less attractive and less flexible than a mortgage. A break with tradition was that the treasurer was to be registrar rather than the town clerk. The appointment of a receiver was attached to a delay of two months in the payment of interest. To all intents and purposes, then, these were wider-purpose housing type bonds, without the limited gross interest facility or the exemption from loan capital duty (which gave housing bonds a saving in cost equivalent to ⅛ per cent).

What must now be made clear is that in the subsequent history of the emergence of the bond as a major instrument the significant (handicapping) feature was the imposition of the minimum issue period imposed by the statutes. Sealing was not a matter of significance – some authorities preferred to give their bonds the dignity of a seal, while others were happy to take advantage of the loophole offered by the facility to issue a 'certificate'. Some used a 'certificate' but also sealed. In his description of the issue of London housing bonds Sir Harry Haward confirms that the imposition of the five-year minimum on the bond arose from the Treasury's great reluctance to allow local authorities to borrow short. Yet this reluctance had not shown itself in relation to the mortgage, though Treasury uneasiness about short money bills has already been described.

Hendon took bond powers in 1929, to be called 'council bonds', but the powers were identical to those of Coventry. Thereafter there was in most years a steady trickle of authorities seeking bond powers, mainly the smaller boroughs, some urban districts and an occasional rural district, but from time to time a county. For example, according to Institute of Municipal Treasurers and Accountants (IMTA) returns, some thirteen authorities took powers in 1933, the year of the vital local government Act, when the expectation might have been that if the bond showed promise as a borrowing instrument the appropriate powers would have been included in that general Act, an opportunity which was not taken.

Bonds of this period were based on a £5 unit of issue and a minimum period of five years. For reasons which cannot now be identified the five-year minimum was increased to seven years in the Reigate Corporation Act of 1945 and this figure still ruled in subsequent Acts, for example, the Orpington Act of 1954 in which council bonds required sealing, whereas the housing bonds issued by the same council did not. (There was however at least one intervening exception – Doncaster 1950, where a three-year period was introduced.) East Ham in 1957, and the Borough of Wallasey in 1958, had the seven-year minimum.

A short-lived breakthrough occurred in 1958 which might have had considerable consequences, but did not. On grounds which cannot now be established (despite considerable efforts by the county treasurer) Kent County Council obtained bond powers in the latter part of 1958, in which a minimum period of issue was not prescribed, it being simply as the local authority should determine. However, the county treasurer reports that his authority simply resolved that bonds should be for five or ten years, although in fact no bonds were issued until 1966 at which point the period was re-determined as two to five years.

In the Reading and Berkshire Water, etc. Act 1959 the water authority also obtained powers to issue unrestricted bonds for 'such period as the issuing authority may from time to time determine'. Berkshire County Council, which already had bond-issuing powers for seven-year bonds, took the opportunity to insert in this same Act a clause to remove its seven-year minimum. But again no action was taken to exploit these new powers. There is some indication in surviving records that inquiries in the London money market were unenthusiastically received on the ground that the new powers made the treasurer and not the county clerk the registrar. If this were so, it is not easily understood as by this date many local authorities had transferred registration from the clerk to the treasurer for loans generally (Manchester as early as 1925). Two other authorities – Oldham in 1960, and Cardiff in 1961 – also obtained unrestricted bond powers, but again appear to have made no use of this opportunity.

At about this time the Association of Municipal Corporations (AMC) were pressing for a standard clause for bonds to relieve local authorities of the tedium and expense of arguing the case whenever new bond powers were sought. In 1961 the Model Clauses Committee of the Ministry of Housing and Local Government, which included lay representatives, considered and produced a model clause. Notes of this meeting which have been examined indicate that while the lay members were suggesting that a limitation to a minimum number of years was unnecessary, the Ministry representatives opposed this view and ultimately inserted a five-year limitation in the model clause. What does not seem to have been put clearly before the committee was that a nil-limit had already been established in several Acts, although there are indications that the Cardiff Act was mentioned, but without effect, during the committee's deliberations.

In addition to the five-year minimum, bonds under the model clause were still related to a £5 unit. These could be issued at a discount but only with the consent of the Minister. They had another curious restriction that repayment could only be made by a sinking fund (which presumably excluded the use of instalment repayment despite the inclusion of all methods under the 1933 Act). There were the usual administrative details and as before (despite expressions of doubt in the Model Clause Committee) both the entry in the register and on the certificate were to be prima-facie evidence of title. The certificate – 'This is to certify that . . . of . . . is the registered holder of a bond', etc. – was to be under seal. It gave the rate of interest and repayment date, but not the interest dates nor, more important, the underlying security. All that this amounted to was that the bond was a less flexible form of mortgage and that such progress as had been made in improving the bond was negated.

Immediately following the publication of the model clause, Devon in 1961 and Liverpool in 1962 had the five-year minimum imposed in their newly acquired bond powers. Perhaps if the few authorities which by means now unknown achieved the no-minimum powers had brought these into operation, the reimposition of the five-year restriction might have been avoided. However, the decisive changes needed to bring about the rationalized all-purpose bond were about to be made – though the full refinement was still to be deferred for another decade.

The local authority bond in its present two forms – non-negotiable and negotiable – stems from the Manchester Corporation Act 1962 in which an optimistic but deliberate attempt (involving myself) was made to construct the 'ideal borrowing instrument'. Although this endeavour has had obstacles to overcome, it has at last reached a point very close to its goal. The Manchester bond originated in an exercise in form design not of a bond, but of the older form of mortgage. In 1960 the form of mortgage in Manchester was much simplified (see p. 219 dealing with the mortgage) and from this exercise was conceived the idea of analysing all forms of local authority borrowing instrument in use, in order to extract the 'best' features of each. The aim was to construct the ideal instrument, looked at both from the lenders' and the borrowers' points of view – clear, simple, rapid in completion and with maximum flexibility, and based on a somewhat more modern approach than the formal 'mortgaging' of an authority's revenues. The documents analysed in this exercise were the mortgage, the local and housing bonds, stock, temporary loan (deposit) receipt and bills. On extraction of the best features of these forms the result was patently a combination of the then local bond and the mortgage, leaving aside for the moment the question of negotiability.

Powers for the introduction of a rationalized bond were sought in the Manchester Corporation Bill of 1962. There is little doubt in the minds of those concerned that Treasury acceptance of it, together with the emergency steps which they then took to give similar powers to all authorities, was influenced by central government's wish to offer improved borrowing facilities to local authorities as part of the deal for their acceptance of the control of temporary borrowing which at that time was being debated.

By their analysis of other forms of borrowing instruments and the extraction therefrom of the 'best features', Manchester achieved useful indeed vital improvements in the bond, but did not succeed in jettisoning all the older restrictions. The Treasury insisted that a £5 multiple unit should be retained, and that some minimum period of issue must be specified. The Treasury did however agree to a one-year minimum which Manchester, perhaps mistakenly, regarded as acceptable on the ground that there was at that time no intention of issuing bonds for less than this period. What must be clearly recorded is that by an unfortunate hiatus those in the Manchester Treasurer's Office responsible for this exercise were guided by the model clause and were unaware that since 1957 there had been precedents for bond powers without the specification of a minimum (no doubt because these powers, having been obtained, had not been exercised). The Treasury agreed that the Manchester bonds need not be sealed (after all, the housing bonds had not required this archaic symbol), and the confusing sinking fund requirements of the model clause were dropped. (This was not actually of any importance for an authority using a CLF.) The conflicting provision that both the certificate and the register entry were prima-facie evidence of ownership was retained (another restriction which proved of no significance in practice).

However, the unnecessary one-year minimum restriction did immediately give rise to a minor operational difficulty. There are circumstances in local authority borrowing in which a loan, though entered into for a period of years, needs to make provision for immediate repayment in certain emergencies, and such emergencies might occur within the first year of the borrowing period. For example, some authorities agree to make immediate repayment of a loan to the estate of a deceased lender, to assist the winding up of the estate (although there are other ways of dealing with this problem). Such emergency repayments on death were technically not now possible within the first year of a loan if a bond, rather than a mortgage, had been used. In practice, all parties tended to turn a blind eye to this situation,[3] but there were more intractable difficulties. Building societies and trade unions are two organizations which may in an emergency find themselves in cash-flow difficulties at short notice. Consequently, what are called 'six months stress clauses' were in practice introduced into the deeds for loans from such bodies, so that they could demand repayment on six months' notice, not in order to improve terms, but to meet an established cash-flow emergency. As such situations could also arise within the first year of a loan, there were thus legal objections from these bodies to lending on a bond with a one-year minimum, and a mortgage had to be used which could be repaid in less than a year in an emergency. This again, while not a serious dilemma, meant a restriction on the flexibility of the bond and was most inconvenient for an authority which wished to discontinue altogether the use of the mortgage in favour of the simpler bond. Manchester went to the length of obtaining a clause in the Manchester Corporation Act 1967 to allow a one-year minimum restriction to be overridden in such cases. In an obsession with removing all restrictions from the bond, Manchester also eventually persuaded Parliament to remove the £5 multiple requirement. In 1970, in further efforts to make the bond truly flexible, in the Manchester Corporation Act 1970 powers were obtained to issue bonds (and other instruments) in bearer form, subject to Treasury consent which has never subsequently been given. Manchester did not succeed in getting the one-year minimum withdrawn, but efforts to do so finally persuaded the Treasury to exclude this limit when the powers reached the Local Government Act 1972. However, two important developments took place before that date.

The two immediate developments, following upon the introduction of the Manchester bond, both constitute significant landmarks in the history of local authority borrowing techniques. The first was the granting of statutory powers to all local authorities to issue bonds on the lines of the Manchester bond, and the second not requiring any statutory action was the evolution of a negotiable form of the bond as a market instrument.

At the time of the granting of the improved bond powers to Manchester in 1962 I was the city treasurer and also honorary financial adviser to the Association of Municipal Corporations and, in the latter capacity, was involved in central discussions on the restriction of temporary borrowing which led to the 1963 White Paper on Local Authority Borrowing; thus I was given ready and direct access to the Accountant-General of the Ministry of Housing and Local Government (at that time F. L. Edwards) on whom the suggestion was pressed that local authority bond powers should be given to all local authorities in the improved form. The Accountant-General warmly welcomed this proposal, which he described as 'opening up the prospect of very useful country' and said that the government were already committed to giving bond powers when a suitable opportunity arose (letter to Manchester, 15 March 1962) and had already available a model clause (as already discussed). However, the Ministry's enthusiasm for a more liberal bond was such that a Member of Parliament who had been successful in the Private Members' Bill Ballot (Mr Rupert Spiers) was persuaded to 'adopt' a small local government Bill with promise of government support. This ultimately became the Local Government (Financial Provisions) Act 1963. It contained about a dozen minor but helpful provisions of a general financial character (expenses of councillors, the power to spend a rate of 1d on matters of local benefit, and so on) but also a major provision giving all local authorities power to add borrowing by means of bonds to their existing methods; these were to be known as 'local authority bonds'. A schedule to the Act gave standard details, but while the multiple of £5 requirement was retained the minimum period was reduced to one year as in the Manchester provision. This provision also made clear that a bond was renewable at maturity, that is, that the period could be extended by agreement – an aspect about which there had been some legal doubt. Bonds were charged against the revenues of the authority and could be issued at a discount with the consent of the Minister. Regulations in some detail were issued later (Local Authority Bond Regulations, SI 1964/983). These again were in standard form; a certificate was to be issued to holders (the bond remained 'intangible') and a register maintained, both of which continued to be prima-facie evidence of title to a bond.

A letter from the Minister (9 July 1964, Circular 33/64) issued with the regulations went over the general ground but clarified several points. It gave a General Consent to the issue of bonds at a discount subject to the requirements of the Control of Borrowing Order (5 per cent maximum), and also confirmed that local authorities could use different registrars for different issues. These were matters of considerable interest in the next phase of the bond – the evolution of the 'negotiable' bond. The circular letter also drew attention to an amendment of the 1933 Act which had been contained in the London Government Act 1963 (schedule 4, para. 39). This said that signatures to local authority documents could be in facsimile form, and that the Minister had been advised that a bond certificate did not need to be sealed. Thus several useful simplifications were made available in the issue of the new local authority bond. The simplicity and flexibility of this instrument was further improved when the capital duty on local authority borrowing was abolished by the Finance Act 1967.

The second development from the Manchester bond was of a quite unexpected character. In 1963 a member of the merchant banking firm S. G. Warburg & Co. (John Nott, later Sir John Nott and Secretary of

State for Defence at the time of the Falklands crisis) wrote to the City
Treasurer of Manchester to say that, if the new type of bond used by
Manchester and then about to become generally available could be made
readily transferable in London, he believed that the discount houses (with
whom he had initiated discussions) would be prepared to create a daily
market in it, and that this facility for rapid negotiability would produce a
saving of interest to the local authorities of up to ½ per cent p.a. against
comparable periods on less negotiable instruments. If the system of
negotiability, transfer and re-registration could be organized to take place
within the day, this would give the one-year bond almost the same
negotiability as bills, the speed of transfer making good the bond's lack of
bearer status which the Treasury would not sanction.

This 'same-day negotiability' could be achieved by the use of a London-
based registrar for this type of bond, a matter relatively simple to arrange,
though not the general practice of local authorities. Manchester explored
this proposal with a number of the larger local authorities who were
prepared to support the experiment. In November 1963 the Treasury and
the Bank of England raised no objections. There were certain security
problems to be overcome, but, in the event, an issue of £½ million was
made in February 1964 by the City of Manchester using its local Act
powers, that is, at a date after the passing of the general powers, but
before the necessary Bond Regulations had been issued under the 1963
Act. The issue was taken up by two of the discount houses – Union
Discount and Jessel Toynbee – who proceeded with the scheme despite
uncertainties about the Bank Rate which loomed as the date of issue
approached. Bank Rate did in fact rise by one point on the day following
the issue, which made the loan a cheap one for Manchester and something
of a burden for the two discount houses. However, they accepted this as
part of the cost of establishing a new security in the market. This issue was
made at par, but the discount facilities available in the Act were later used
extensively for the new negotiable bonds.

Two controversies immediately emerged. Although the central authorities
had not sought to suppress this proposal, they were not overpleased with
the unexpected creation of new 'negotiable paper'. The Bank of England
countered the enthusiasm of the discount houses by refusing to accept
these bonds as overnight collateral, for which local authority bills are
acceptable, and which those involved had hoped to obtain for the bond.

This dampened the enthusiasm of the discount market for the negotiable
bond, but did not kill it. Steps which were taken under the Control of
Borrowing Order will shortly be described, but a more immediate impact
was on the Stock Exchange. The idea of the negotiable bond was originally
that it should be a 'money market' and not a 'stock market' facility, and
this was why Warburgs had solicited the support of the discount houses.
However, the Stock Exchange immediately saw that important business
might elude them and took steps to make arrangements for bonds also to
be issued and dealt through the Stock Exchange machinery, with the daily
quotation of rates. Because there was a minimum period of one year, for

which negotiable bonds were first issued, the term 'yearling bonds' was coined in the market and is still in use even though bonds are now often for periods of more than one year.

Because of the determination of the central authorities to control bonds of this type through the use of the General Consent, an attempt was made in 1964 to define it in a way which readily distinguished it in its negotiable form from the general bond. The first attempt to describe the type of bond which was excluded from the Consent was extremely clumsy and lacked grasp as to the instruments' scope. The Consent in this early form excluded 'the issue of any bonds whereby the funds raised in a single operation total £1m. or more', unless details were approved by the Bank of England on behalf of the Treasury. This was based on the assumption that the negotiable bond would normally be used for what were then the large loans, and the general bond for small local loans, in practice, a completely erroneous distinction. By 1968 the inadequacy of this definition had been recognized, and a revised Consent excluded

> (b) ... the issue of any bonds for which a quotation is to be sought from the London Stock Exchange, or any bonds which are to be issued in whole or in part to a bank, discount house, or broker in the City of London

unless the timing and terms had been given Bank approval on behalf of the Treasury. Those involved in making this definition understood that 'issued to . . .' meant that such bodies would be the issuers of negotiable bonds on behalf of the local authorities. However, from time to time newcomers in the field of local authority finance in the Bank and the Treasury have attempted to enlarge this field of control by reading into these words that, for example, no London bank could invest in even a general local authority bond without Bank approval, and various ingenious reasons have been advanced as to why this is what the definition really intended. However, generally the matter is now clearly understood and is indeed set out in a Treasury letter (31 January 1968), which says that the revised General Consent

> is not intended to alter the present position under which authorities are required to get Bank of England approval to the terms and timing of issues in the London Stock Exchange or to the London Discount Market, and do not need to obtain approval to the issue of other bonds.

Following the exclusion of negotiable bonds from the General Consent, the Treasury have periodically issued letters informing local authorities of the volume of such bonds which they might have on issue at any one time. Initially this was a flat sum of £1 million, but in August 1967 a scale was introduced which set the ceiling of bond issues by each authority in relation to outstanding loan debt. This has been revised from time to time;

the latest scale (letter, 1 March 1978) confines even an authority with over £400 million of debt to no more than £15 million of negotiable bonds – a figure well overdue for revision. The Bank favours a minimum issue of £¼ million, little enough in these days, and a maximum period of five years for the so-called 'yearling'. These are no more than administrative impediments to the full use of this instrument, in the interests of what the central authorities call an 'orderly market' – that is, one perhaps which does not interfere unduly with the management of government borrowing. Without these restraints, there might at certain times be something of a mêlée among local authorities in this field, but the market might be expected to influence this by the rates it was prepared to offer. There have been occasions when the rate offered for negotiable bonds was less favourable than for non-negotiable investment. This has been the market's method of indicating that it was oversupplied with that form of security, and a natural adjustment has usually quickly followed.

While the Treasury lays down the scale of maximum permitted issues, the Bank in conjunction with the market operators regulates the weekly flow to such proportions as it believes can be readily absorbed. This system has had the effect that all bonds issued by all authorities, irrespective of 'name', have been issued at the same price. Anything other than this would lead to indescribable confusion in quoted prices. Thus a buyer of a local authority bond in this market may find that it comes from any one of a large number of local authorities and he has been expected to accept it without protest whoever the borrower might be.

The battle between the discount houses and the Stock Exchange continued but with the latter gradually gaining the upper hand. The situation developed that different prices were being quoted for similar bonds according to whether the quotation came from the discount market or the stock market. Gradually the unsatisfactory nature of this situation came to be recognized by all, with the result that in March 1974 the Bank announced that an arrangement had been made that all bonds would have a 'Stock Exchange quotation' whether they were issued by the discount houses or through the Stock Exchange and this is the compromise which operates today.

Despite these teething problems and the Bank's continued refusal to give the negotiable bond recognition as collateral, the fact is that, unexpectedly, in the provision of a general bond with the object, at least in the minds of the Manchester bond creators, that it should replace the mortgage, a new form of borrowing in negotiable paper came into being, one which has strong elements of 'stock' in it. Therefore, the bond not only overlaps the mortgage, it has the attributes of a simplified stock issue.

The historical development of the bond thus moves to the Local Government Act 1972 where it was picked up from the 1963 Act, given a further polish by the dropping – at last – of the minimum one-year period and finally incorporated in the list of instruments by which a local authority might borrow. (What can now be seen is that, if the draftsmen had thoroughly understood the significance of what they were doing, they would have omitted both the temporary capital borrowing powers and the use of the mortgage from the list, both being superseded by the bond.) No distinction was made in the Act between the two types of bond but the regulations, required under the Act before the bond could be used, differentiated the negotiable type of bond in the words of the General Consent, and reimposed a one-year minimum period on the bond when used in that form. Probably this could equally well have been done by the use of the Consent without reference to the regulations.

However, the main advance was that the niggling requirement of a £5 multiple and the minimum period had both been dropped from the local authority bond now available for general borrowing. Naturally, as the regulations also applied to stock in which the confusion first started, the dual prima-facie evidence of title – both in the register and on the certificate – was retained but this fortunately, in practice, has never yet caused any problem.

The receivership provisions omitted from the Act were reincorporated in the regulations (as also in the Mortgage Regulations). Instead of referring to principal and interest in this context, the regulations used the words 'if at any time any money due in respect of . . . bonds issued by a local authority remains unpaid for a period of two months after demand in writing'. The local authority was given freedom in the appointment of the registrar and sealing of the certificate was dispensed with. There were many other standard details in the regulations.

The claim can hardly be made that the bond in this all-purpose form suddenly emerged to the surprise of all. The period between 1962 and 1972 had been one of intense behind-the-scenes agitation for the removal of such impediments as remained on the bond.[4] The bond powers described in the model clause in 1961 were virtually the same as those granted to Coventry in 1927, and these were not noticeably different from the local housing bonds of 1919. The Treasury's rearguard action, plus a certain lack of enterprise by the local authorities involved, had resealed the temporary breakthrough in 1958–61. The reduction of the issue limit to one year achieved by Manchester, followed by the general powers in 1963, finally put the bond into active service but another decade passed before the 'all-purpose bond' was ultimately established. All this delay can now be seen to have stemmed from the Treasury's determination to lengthen the maturity of housing debt in 1919, a determination which was carried over to the use of the bond for general purposes in the first Coventry bonds, despite the freedom then and still available to mortgages. Indeed why bond powers continued to be sought when that instrument had less flexibility than (and no advantage over) the mortgage is now difficult to understand, but the inadequacy of the restricted bond is proved by the lack of utilization of the powers by those who went to the trouble and expense of obtaining them, until the restrictions were lifted.

The outcome of this saga is an instrument which can do more simply, and in a manner more easily comprehended, all that the mortgage can do. It is seen to be capable of use in negotiable form, and (if permitted) it is certainly capable of being adapted to bearer form. Now that 'temporary' borrowing is accepted as a permanent part of a local authority borrowing portfolio and the temporary loan receipt has been given equal status with all other instruments, the conclusion emerges that the bond is quite capable of playing a role as a more formal (and secure) instrument in place of the temporary loan receipt as well as the mortgage. Many local authorities have now used the bond in place of the mortgage, but only a handful have taken the further step of using it in replacement of the temporary loan receipt (partly because the market has not yet recognized this potentiality, nor realized that the 'short' bond, being covered by receivership provisions, is theoretically more secure than the temporary receipt).

Is, then, the bond truly the apotheosis of the local authority borrowing instrument? There would seem to be a good case for so regarding it. The bond as now established has the following characteristics:

(1) it is a simply understood and simply prepared acknowledgement of debt arising from money loaned to a local authority;

(2) its security is all the revenues of the authority both as to principal and interest, and it ranks equally with other forms of capital indebtedness;

(3) it is subject to receivership on default;

(4) the title of the holder is represented in a certificate, which does not require to be sealed, and may be signed in facsimile;

(5) it is recorded in a register maintained by an officially appointed registrar;

(6) its issue and transfer are no longer subject to duty;

(7) it is not limited in amount or duration (except in negotiable form), and if issued initially for less than a year, interest would be payable gross;

(8) its term can be extended by agreement on maturity, that is, it is renewable without the production of a new instrument;

(9) yet it can be repaid before maturity by agreement in an emergency, and may therefore include a 'stress' clause;

(10) it may be issued at par or at a discount (limited at present) or at a premium;

(11) it is a trustee security in the narrow range;

(12) it is capable of being assigned or otherwise disposed of to any person or willing buyer;

(13) it is also capable of use in negotiable form as a daily quoted marketable instrument through the stock market (Stock Exchange), or the money market (discount houses) (though in this form it is at present subject to restriction to a minimum maturity of one year and to such volume as the Bank of England approves);

(14) it is convertible into bearer form, transferable by delivery, if the Treasury would lift their ban.

This list is not a specification for an instrument for the future – this will occupy the final part of this book – it is a description of the current bond, an instrument for which all of these features are already provided by statute or practice. There are other borrowing instruments which have some, or many, of these facilities, but the bond possesses them all. The various recent developments in terms of issue – variable rates, drop-locks, and so on – do not affect the nature of the instrument itself. Indeed the probability is emerging that there is only one local authority borrowing instrument, variations in which are in mode of issue and degree of negotiability. The Treasury seems to manage very well with a single instrument, or two if the Treasury bill is added.

The one further rationalization which might be sought is that the confusing arrangement for an 'intangible' bond, covered by a 'certificate', should be abolished. There is no reason why Parliament should not provide that the unsealed certificate may itself be called a bond, if this would help to a better understanding of the instrument. Money bills/promissory notes are not now sealed; is there any difference between a 'promise' and a 'binding undertaking'?

The only reason for this arrangement seems to be an ancient legal understanding that a bond is an 'instrument under seal'. Is there any reason other than ancient tradition why a bond must be sealed in every instance? The possibility emerges also that there is a confusion of a bond with 'stock' and that the use of the term 'an issue of bonds', like an issue of stock, somehow tends to obscure the essentially simple nature of a bond in local authority finance, where it is now simply an acknowledgement of a debt and an undertaking to repay under certain conditions, and no more.

Would not local authority borrowing be the better for having one all-purpose and simple instrument than the three which are permitted, all of which are identical in security and ranking? Anecdotally an overseas banker (United States) operating in London has been heard to say that he lends half of his local authority money in bonds and the other half in mortgages as there *must* be some difference, otherwise the two types would not be available.

The London market, fully occupied with its own affairs, has done nothing to help develop a clear understanding of the two forms of the bond, calling the negotiable bond, first, the 'yearling', and later the 'LAB', when in fact the vast majority of what the Act calls LABs are of the 'over-the-counter', 'town hall' non-negotiable type.

NOTES: CHAPTER 20

1   Since this chapter was completed a non-local authority example of a conditional bond has been acquired, dated 1686, the year in which the National Debt was first organized, which shows the well-established nature of this type of instrument. This has the penalty clause in Latin with the consideration clause in English; the debt acknowledged was £15 with a double penalty of £30. This example is of further interest, in that it is a pro forma document, pre-printed not in type but apparently from the copper-plate, in facsimile

writing, with the details of the loan added by hand. The borrower signs with 'his mark'.
2 Information from Mr Arthur Haslam, for many years Loans Officer in the Borough
   Treasurer's Department.
3 That this particular problem is not without significance is shown by a clause in the 1974
   General Consent, which agrees that provisions for repayment on death, even in less than a
   year, do not bring the bond into the temporary loan category.
4 See my articles in *Local Government Finance* during the 1960s.

Chapter 21

THE PUBLIC WORKS LOAN
COMMISSION

The Public Works Loan Commission (PWLC)[1] played an increasingly important role in the provision of capital funds for local government since its function was established in 1817, that is, since well before local authorities in the modern sense had been brought into being. The extent of provision has varied considerably – and erratically – over the years, in accordance with government policy objectives, from *ad hoc* decisions on special cases through restriction to 'last-resort' facilities to the provision of full requirements. The state of play at present (1984) is that the board is prepared to supply almost 90 per cent of a local authority's needs (even 100 per cent for smaller authorities), with a supplementary facility for special applications in addition. The rates of interest have on the whole been related to government borrowing rates, with an addition for administration costs, but at certain times have been related to open-market rates and even above for some or all of the advances; eventually even a system of variable interest rates has been offered as an alternative. In recent times the methods of repayment have developed from the narrow and restrictive to the highly flexible, and the machinery of administration from the slow and cumbersome almost to 'instantaneous loans'.

The commissioners appointed in 1817 for making loans for public works to public and private bodies (but also to individuals) had their roots in a temporary system set up in 1793 for lending money to 'worthy persons in need of financial aid', meaning in practice manufacturers and traders of repute – an encouraging gesture though made against a requirement of substantial collateral. The activities of these first commissioners were terminated as early as 1794, but other temporary bodies of commissioners followed for the making of short-term loans for specific purposes; for example, in 1799 loans to merchants in Liverpool and Lancaster, and in 1811 loans of up to the substantial total of £6 million to manufacturers of cotton goods and various importers. These were short-term loans for specific purposes largely to alleviate hardship arising from war conditions.

Thus the commissioners appointed in 1817 for the making of government loans for public works – and not merely for such works as were provided by what might have been regarded as 'local authorities' – similarly were set up originally as a temporary measure to make relatively short-term loans; but they were soon seen to have a permanent role for longer-term and ultimately very long-term lending. Because of the original short-term concept of this body, the commissioners do not seem initially to have had a precise or at least concise title; however they were colloquially known as Exchequer Loan Commissioners – it was not until 1842 that the title Public Works Loan Commissioners was established. (There was a separate body for Ireland.)

A strange feature of this situation is that although this body is commonly referred to as the Public Works Loan Board (PWLB), circulars and reports being regularly issued under this name, in no statute are the commissioners referred to as constituting a board (Public Works Loan Act 1853: 'any such loan by the said Commissioners called "The Public Works Loan Commissioners"'; and the National Loans Act 1968: 'The Treasury may issue out of the National Loans Fund such sums as are required by the Public Works Loan Commissioners (in this Act called the Loan Commissioners)'). In practice, the commissioners must be regarded as forming a 'board', and the two terms PWLC and PWLB regarded as synonymous. The present Secretary confirms this interpretation; his Annual Reports are signed 'By Order of the Board'.

The preamble to the 1817 Act referred to the great advantages which might arise by the advancing of £1¾ million for affording employment for the labouring classes of the community by the carrying out of works of a public nature – an early Keynesian concept, surely? – from the encouragement of fisheries and the support of collieries and mines, and from the employment of the poor in the parishes of Great Britain (an oblique reference, presumably to the provision of 'self-supporting' workhouses). This rather curious sum of £1¾ million, perhaps the result of internal disputes and compromises, was to be provided by the advance of Exchequer bills and from the consolidated fund but initially, in practice, the funds came only from the issue of the Exchequer bills, current for between one and two years.

The twenty-one commissioners appointed were to decide the purposes and amounts of loans. Persons and bodies to whom loans were advanced were to provide such security as satisfied the commissioners. This could be either in written and clearly enforceable form or by the deposit of government securities. In addition to the personal securities to be given on loans for public works, collieries and mines, additional security could be required by mortgages or assignments of 'rates, tolls and receipts' accruing or likely to accrue from the works; the proprietors of such works were accordingly authorized to mortgage or assign such revenues for security of both repayment and interest.

If the public works on which an advance was made seemed likely to produce from rates, tolls and rents or profits a 'clear actual surplus', after payment of management expenses of not less than double the amount of interest due, then provided the commissioners were satisfied with the practicality and utility of the work and with the estimates of income likely to accrue, and subject also to rules about the amount of capital provided by the proprietors of the undertaking, then personal securities could be dispensed with. The rules about security from parishes were somewhat obscure. In the first place, parishes were under the general requirement that personal securities must be provided by the applicants. In addition, the parish poor rate could be mortgaged/assigned. While the provision that personal securities need not be required if the 'rates, tolls or receipts' were more than adequate to cover interest payments also applied to parish loans, there was nevertheless a further provision that a supplementary rate must be levied, if adequate funds were not available to meet interest and repayment. Furthermore, parishes could not borrow unless there was a majority of persons paying the rate in favour, and these must also represent three-quarters of the total sum assessed to the poor rate; and even so the consent of justices of the peace was to be obtained.

Parishes were also under strict rules as to how much they could raise in loans, related to current rates and the average of the previous three years. The purpose of this clause was to ensure that borrowing was not resorted to unless the rate required to provide the asset out of revenue would have been excessive. Unfortunately this clause involved the use of a double negative, of which one negative was omitted by the printer in error, thus necessitating an amending Act some weeks later. Despite the intention of allowing borrowing by parishes only if otherwise an excessive rate would have been required, the Act provided that loans to parishes should be repaid in any event within two years; indeed the Act specified that all such loans should be repaid within two years after Easter 1818. Such an arrangement represented no more than an aid to cash flow during construction for parishes who made application immediately the Act had come into force.

As a further means of safeguarding interest and provision for repayment, turnpike trustees were authorized to increase tolls by 50 per cent over their statutory provisions if needed for this purpose. The interest rate for all loans was to be 5 per cent, and in addition a 5 per cent sinking fund was to be provided. As the Act required a system of repayment by annual instalments, this meant not an accumulating sinking fund, but annual provision for amortization over twenty years. Shorter or longer periods could be arranged by agreement. With the interest rate on Exchequer bills at 3½ per cent p.a. (actually 2½d per cent per diem), a charge to borrowers of 5 per cent p.a. gave an adequate margin for administration costs.

The commissioners wasted no time; the Act was passed on 27 June 1817 and the first loan was approved only eleven days later for works at a number of collieries and mines. The applicant sought a loan of between £35,000 and £40,000; that he received only the lower sum does not come as a surprise. The second loan, a fortnight later, was for the substantial sum of £200,000 to assist in the construction of the Regent's Canal, made dependent on the simultaneous provision of funds by the proprietors; the commissioners employed the great engineer Thomas Telford as their investigating surveyor. Local authorities were not far behind. In August of this first year of operation a loan was granted to Sir Robert Heron for the erection of a 'House of Industry' (workhouse) at Claypole, between Grantham and Newark, to serve a group of six parishes. This loan was repaid as promptly as May 1819. A loan also made in the first year to a turnpike trust (the Birmingham–Wolverhampton road) is of interest because as the statutory life of the trust was due to expire before expiry of the loan period, and although the lives of such trusts were invariably extended, nevertheless a group of local worthies was required to give personal securities. Another feature which added excitement to the board's first year was an attempted fraudulent application by a private individual. In its first year the commission approved 205 loans totalling just over £2 million, of which £338,000 was actually advanced during the period. The greater part of this was to undertakings of a 'transport' nature – canals, roads, harbours and bridges. Aid to parishes and burial boards was almost negligible.

Acts following that of 1817 were frequent (mainly for the extension of the commissioners' power to borrow for relending), though the first of particular significance was that of 1842 (the Advances for Public Works Act). This made the Commissioners for the Reduction of the National Debt the trustees for the PWLC, and this close link has been since maintained, the two commissions sharing the same staff and headquarters. (The two staffs were merged in 1980, since when the organization has been known as the National Debt and Loans Office, NDLO.) Equally, perhaps more important, in 1842 the method of financing the loans was switched from the cumbersome system of Exchequer bills to the logical basis of the consolidated fund, and as an indication of the permanence of the system the title of Public Works Loan Commission was formally adopted.

The purposes for which the commission could lend were extended in the great Poor Law Act 1834. By this Act the newly established Poor Law authorities, whether still parishes or the new unions, were authorized to borrow on the security of the rates for the provision of land and buildings for workhouses on a ten-year basis, soon altered in 1836 to twenty years. They could also borrow from the commission for the purpose established in that Act of assisting emigration. The commission was not referred to in the Municipal Corporations Act of 1835, presumably because it was already authorized to lend to bodies corporate, but the Prisons Act 1842 made special provision for borrowing from the commission. The commissioners' powers were slightly extended in their Act of 1842 to include, by an unfortunate juxtaposition, power to lend for the building of county and town halls and for lunatic asylums.

Much of the work of the commission in the first half of the century was for purposes other than local government, as such, but from the middle of the century local government proper began to take the lead. An interesting example occurred in the Public Works Acts of 1863–4 the objectives of which were similar to those delineated in the 1817 Act. In these money was authorized to be lent to local authorities in Lancashire, Cheshire and Derbyshire for works of public utility and sanitary improvement to alleviate unemployment resulting from the shortage of cotton imports during the American Civil War. These were cheap loans at 3½ per cent with a thirty-year repayment period. In 1866 the first of the Acts to provide houses for the labouring classes permitted local authorities to borrow from the commission. Similarly, the Education Acts of 1870 and 1873 authorized School Boards to borrow from the commission with a maximum repayment period of fifty years; and the Public Health Act 1872 did likewise.

The year 1875 – of particular financial significance for its Local Loans Act and the great Public Health Act – was also a key year for the PWLC with an Act of consolidation and amendment of the commission's powers. From 1817 to 1875 the commissioners had approved loans of over £30 million the bulk of which was by that time for purposes of a distinctly local government character; the rate of lending was clearly accelerating as in 1875/6 loans of £3½ million were approved, again mostly of a local government nature and particularly for schools. In 1875 what were originally designed as two Bills were amalgamated during their passage through Parliament into one Act to consolidate, with amendments, the Acts relating to loans for public works. While the parliamentary committee examining the Bill expressed the nation's gratitude to the commissioners for the care and attention with which they had administered their funds, nevertheless representatives of the commission in giving evidence to the committee expressed their frustration at the amount of interference they were experiencing from the Treasury. (This complaint clearly fell on deaf ears as the PWLC of today is even more entirely the tool of the Treasury.)

The 1875 Act established the important simplification that the commission might lend to any body which was authorized to borrow by Parliament, though they were also to continue to have regard to the sufficiency of the security and whether the loan would be of such benefit as would justify it in the light of the funds available. The interest rate to be charged was to be not less than 5 per cent unless another rate was specified in an Act, repayment was to continue to be by either of the instalment methods and for not exceeding twenty years, unless otherwise specified. The commission was to prescribe its own form of mortgage deed, and was authorized to accept premature repayment of loans. From 1875 the commission was required to report annually to Parliament; its hundredth report (1974/5) contains much fascinating historical information.

In 1887 the National Debt and Local Loans Act once again separated the PWLC funds from the consolidated fund (and the budget), by establishing the 'Local Loans Fund', to be financed by local loans stock issued by the Treasury (and from repayments from earlier borrowers). This was to enable the PWLC funds to be put on a clear self-supporting basis, independent of general government borrowing transactions. By 1895 interest rates had fallen substantially, and the power given to borrowers in 1875 to make premature repayment of loans was widely exercised by local authorities to the embarrassment of the commission and the local loans fund. Rules were therefore introduced to impose a penalty on local authorities making premature repayment, to safeguard the commitments which the fund had undertaken when rates were higher. Restrictions of this kind still apply, though they are of less significance. However, by 1900 rates had fallen so dramatically that the PWLC ceased lending to larger authorities and to any local authority wishing to borrow for a quasi-commercial purpose.

Little local authority capital activity took place during the First World War but there was great pressure on the commission's funds after 1919, particularly for the extended local authority housing duties; in 1921/2 £49 million was advanced for housing purposes alone. For the next twenty years the limited amount of funds made available to the PWLC caused them to restrict their lending to local authorities with a rateable value not exceeding £200,000 (£250,000 in Scotland), although larger authorities could still borrow for education purposes and for expenditure under the Small Dwellings Acquisition Acts. Local authorities have always been substantial borrowers from local lenders. This market was diminished by the growth of the National Savings Movement from 1916 onwards. Therefore, from 1919 local authorities of all sizes were also allowed to borrow from the PWLC the equivalent of one-half of the money raised locally from national savings certificates.

A complete reversal of this policy took place after the Second World War, in that the Treasury wished to control more closely the immense demands expected to be made on the capital market after 1945. The Local Authorities Loans Act 1945 not only instructed the commission once again to lend for any purpose for which the local authority was authorized to borrow, but as earlier described prohibited authorities from borrowing elsewhere (with narrow exceptions related to the amounts raised locally during the war and by the use of internal funds). This restriction lasted for seven years, until the end of 1952. During this period, local authorities needed three approvals from central government to any act of borrowing: sanction from the authorizing central department, from the Capital Issues Committee (under the Control of Borrowing Order) and an (automatic) consent from the PWLC; all three were issued to an applicant local authority at the same time. After 1952, local authorities were permitted to return to the market though access to the PWLC remained available. In 1947 separate funding of the local loans fund by local loans stock was abandoned and funding reverted to the consolidated fund.

Yet another turn of the wheel occurred in 1955. In the government's view the open-access policy had meant that local authorities had less incentive to consider capital expenditure carefully because they knew that capital funds would be readily available from the PWLC and that these would be at preferential (near government borrowing) rates; the enthusiasm with which the local authorities had exploited this situation meant that government monetary and credit policies were placed under additional pressure. The local authorities had not sought such a policy in the first place; nevertheless, they were in effect suddenly switched from the ready-money policy to the other extreme of a policy of lending at 'last resort only', and were required to prove that they could not otherwise easily obtain money in the market before they could expect assistance from the PWLC. If they did manage to prove this point to the PWLC and thus extract a loan, this was made not at government borrowing rates, but at the rates at which large authorities of good standing were able to borrow in the market. The figures are striking; local authority capital borrowing between 1955 and 1964 was about £5,000 million, of which the PWLC advanced only £641 million (against applications for £780 million). Because of the rising level of interest rates, this was the period during which local authorities began to develop, with increasing enthusiasm, the short-term (temporary) money market, a policy which they defended as resulting from high interest rates and from being suddenly 'thrown on to the market', left to their own devices, by the Treasury. As described earlier, the success of the local authorities in this area was such as to create a further panic in the Treasury (many treasurers were not too happy about it either), with the result that in 1963 another change of policy was announced, this time after extensive consultations with the local authorities. The PWLC was partially reopened in exchange for the acceptance by the local authorities of sharp restrictions on such of their borrowings as had an initial maturity period of less than one year.

This change of policy, announced in the White Paper of 1963 (Cmnd 2162) and which has had far-reaching consequences, has already been discussed. It marked the beginnings of the now dominating PWLC policy which offers local authorities nearly 90 per cent of their borrowing needs. On 6 March 1964 the board issued the first of its continuing series of circulars which each year outline the lending arrangements for that year and have become increasingly sophisticated as the policy has developed. The White Paper's promised timetable of a 20 per cent start, increasing annually by 10 per cent until 50 per cent of loan requirements was reached in the fourth year was not precisely maintained, but events have subsequently far exceeded expectations. In 1964 the quota was established at 20 per cent of 'longer-term borrowing needs'. While the board would not 'guarantee' local authority borrowing in the market – the argument being that the security underlying local authority borrowing was such that a guarantee of this kind was not required – a 'last resort' facility was also offered in addition to the basic quota. The words of this offer are worth quoting – they have been repeated annually from the start, with minor amendments of terminology:

Each authority will be expected to make all reasonable efforts to obtain the remainder of its borrowing requirements from sources other than the Loan Commissioners. The Commissioners will however continue to act as the lender of last resort and will make additional loans if satisfied that an authority cannot raise the money elsewhere from local sources or in the centralised money market.

(The word 'centralised' was later dropped.) This was taken to mean 'cannot raise at reasonable cost'. There was a two-level interest rate structure – a near government rate for quota advances and a higher rate for 'last resort' loans. Although 'last resort' facilities were rarely sought (but if needed they were promptly supplied), the existence of this 'fall-back' had a very reassuring influence on the money market institutions, particularly those with a foreign base. The minimum loan period was ten years but reborrowing was freely permitted and the board no longer required evidence of the existence of loan sanctions. (A further simplification in this period was that the Public Works Loans Act 1965 promised that loans from the board became an automatic charge on the revenues of the authority. This meant that formal mortgages were no longer necessary and a simple letter from the board accompanying a loan and recapitulating the terms became adequate documentation – PWLB Circular No. 7, 10/8/65.)

This simple beginning soon required refinement of detail. A more precise definition of 'longer-term borrowing' was introduced as well as terms for carry-over of quotas from one year to the next. A guaranteed minimum was introduced for small borrowers (£50,000 soon raised to £100,000, later to £500,000 and now £10 million). Each year quota allocations were revised to absorb surplus funds available when some authorities did not take up their full quotas. The quota percentages crept gradually upwards; in 1965/6 the figure was 30 per cent, with the addition of a further 10 per cent for less wealthy areas as defined in Circular No. 5 – broadly Scotland, Wales and the north of England. As some authorities were slow in reducing their short-term debt – the other side of the deal to reopen access to the Board – the permitted percentage of borrowings from the board was increased in 1967/8 to include a quota of 34 per cent (40 per cent in the designated areas), plus a bonus of 30 per cent of 'the reckonable reduction in temporary debt' during the year (Circular No. 11). This meant that authorities who had begun with a high percentage of temporary debt and had been slow in reducing this were offered a carrot rather than a stick to persuade them to conform. Steps were also taken to ensure that local authorities spread their applications over the year to assist the funding mechanism of the board. By 1969/70 the quotas were 40 and 50 per cent (Circular No. 23). These remained the basic quotas for a number of years, but in 1975/6 an important supplementary facility was offered as an alternative to the 'last resort' safeguard.

The minimum period of PWLC loans having been ten years since the start of the quota system, and the greater portion of loans having been taken up on this period (in the unfulfilled hope that interest rates would be bound to fall shortly), this meant that by 1974/5, a decade after the start of the new scheme, the commission were collecting substantial repayments. As a result, ample funds were available in their hands for the introduction of an offer of further help as an alternative to 'last resort' loans – now re-designated non-quota A loans. This alternative was of non-quota B loans which were to be available without the authority having to prove inability to raise funds on the market as required for the non-quota A loans

(Circular No. 42, July 1975). Therefore, there were now three classes of loans – quota, non-quota A and non-quota B loans – the last two being alternatives. This new non-quota B offer was available without further restriction to any local authority relinquishing its right to 'last resort' non-quota A loans (though a switch back could be made after adequate notice). A local authority opting for non-quota B loans had merely to declare that it would shortly need additional capital finance; local authorities were still at liberty to borrow on the open market, if they so wished. Quota loans were at near government rates; non-quota A loans were at open-market rates; and non-quota B loans were to incorporate a penalty – initially at 1 per cent over the (open-market) rate for A loans. The interest rates required by the board for ten-year loans, extracted from the appendix to the circular introducing this development, show under the alternative arrangements for repayment the following:

quota		non-quota A		non-quota B	
instalment	maturity	instalment	maturity	instalment	maturity
(%)	(%)	(%)	(%)	(%)	(%)
$11\frac{1}{8}$	$12\frac{5}{8}$	$12\frac{7}{8}$	$13\frac{3}{8}$	$13\frac{7}{8}$	$14\frac{3}{8}$

There were four other 'loan periods' available from which the borrowing treasurer had to select, giving a possible choice of thirty interest rates on offer; and of course he had still to compare these with the best available market rates. If he elected for instalment loans, he still must decide which of the two methods to adopt (EIP or EAR), a far call from the days when Acts permitted borrowing at 'legal or lesser rates'. These complexities necessitated revision of the 'penalty' calculation for premature repayments.

By 1979/80 the basic quota had been redefined at $3\frac{1}{3}$ per cent of capital debt, plus 35 per cent of net redeemable capital payments during the year (4 and 45 per cent to designated areas). This reference to capital debt as well as to current borrowing was directed to helping those authorities who had a substantial debt which was 'turning over' but which had little or no current capital expenditure (Circular No. 52). In 1980/1 (Circular No. 55) the quota reached 50 per cent, plus 4 per cent, or if more favourable £5 million; consequently, the difference in favour of less wealthy areas was abandoned.

Tedious though this recital may be, it indicates the significant march from 'last resort only', in 1963, to over 50 per cent, in 1980, and the increasing complexities of the choices with which a borrowing treasurer was faced. However, the most radical changes were still to come. In 1982/3 the time taken by the board to advance a loan was reduced from ten to two days (Circular No. 61); the maximum lending period was extended from forty to sixty years (Circular No. 62); a further alternative of variable rates of interest was introduced in line with the then emerging market practice (Circular No. 63), involving an elaborate formula for ascertaining the rate at a point between LIBOR (London Inter-Bank Offer

Rate) and the government borrowing rate. Later reversion from variable to fixed rate was also possible. But the surprising change in 1982 (Circular No. 65) was the increase of the quota during the year to the greater of £10 million or 75 per cent of net reckonable capital expenditure, plus 6 per cent of total capital debt. Bearing in mind that local authorities could have 20 per cent of their debt in 'less than one year' money, and usually also had internal funds available, this in effect meant that local authorities no longer needed to use the general market for other than short-term funds. Moreover, not only had the maximum period been increased to sixty years, but the lower minimum, generally ten years, was reduced to five years for instalment loans and three years for maturity and variable interest loans.[2] The offer was also made of higher advances to any local authority which could make a case. Thus the need for 'last resort' facilities and A and B non-quota loans disappeared. These provisions were extended to 1983/4 in Circular No. 67 of March 1983, but in December 1983 Circular No. 70 amended the formula to 75 plus 10 per cent of outstanding capital debt (instead of the former 6 per cent) even for that year, and added the promise of similar provisions for 1984/5, coupled with 'the Commissioners' expectation' that the same terms would apply (with Treasury consent) to 1985/6. This formula must be the equivalent of almost 90 per cent of local authority longer-term requirements – much to the chagrin of the institutional lending market. Only time will tell whether this move once again to an almost complete dependence on central funds is in the long-term interest of local government.

The closing words of the 1963 White Paper are extremely apposite to the situation now reached twenty years later: 'These proposals are made in the belief that in present circumstances they represent the best way of reconciling the needs of monetary management with the natural desire of local authorities to have ready access to capital as cheaply as is compatible with prudent finance.'

The board's attitude over its lifetime to methods of repayment is of interest, in that it focuses attention on the basic question of the propriety of pushing the burden of cost on to later generations. The original very short (two-year) loans were repayable at maturity, but the twenty-year loans also permitted by the 1817 Act were required to be repaid by equal annual instalments of principal (EIP) with interest on the declining balance. (There was a useful provision later, of general application, that certain repayments did not need to begin until five years after the date of the loan.) After 1844, the alternative of the 'annuity' method of repayment (EAR) was allowed under which equal instalments of principal and interest combined were accepted. With the EIP method, the principal is discharged more quickly at the beginning, so although the annual sum starts at a higher yearly level than under the annuity system, it declines each year until at a certain point it drops below the fixed annual annuity payment. As a result, the total amount repaid including interest is lower on an EIP loan than on an EAR loan, and the proportion of the total repaid in the early years is greater. This feature of the EIP method means that a greater part of the debt is cleared while the building is more or less new and acceptable as a modern and efficient asset, and that as maintenance charges begin to grow with the passage of time the debt amortization charge is falling. The commissioners were not happy about the use of the annuity method, particularly for longer-term loans (over thirty years) because of the increased burden which it placed on posterity, who would be likely to have problems enough of their own. Their annual report for 1891/2 made the forceful comment that

> the present ratepayers should not ease their own burdens by the double method of (a) taking the maximum period for repayment allowed by Parliament, and (b) then repaying by annuity, the lighter mode of payment as regards themselves but the more expensive in the aggregate of the two methods.

In repeating this earlier statement in their report for 1966/7, the commissioners indicated that they still favoured this point of view. Both methods have been allowed to operate since 1844, though the Commission have continued to seek to discourage the use of the annuity system. The maturity method was admitted only from 1964 as part of the deal on the restriction of temporary borrowing, in order to give treasurers complete flexibility in the handling of their loans, particularly as consolidated loans funds by then in widespread use favoured the adoption of this method. (As will be described, the CLF leans towards EIP methods of repayment to the fund from the borrowing departments, but maturity repayments from the fund to lenders.) This argument about deferment of the burden of capital cost is fundamental to the whole concept of borrowing to finance capital expenditure and will be examined in Chapter 24.

The establishment of a minimum borrowing period has been a less pressing matter; there was in fact no prescribed minimum until 1942, when seven years was introduced under the Defence Regulations. In the period after the Second World War when all borrowing was for a time channelled through the PWLC, loans were required to be for the full sanction period unless the use of a CLF or other loans-pooling system disassociated borrowing from individual projects, in which case the minimum seven years operated. This minimum remained when the local authorities were given freedom to return to the market (except where loan sanctions, for example, for vehicles, some plant and machinery, were for less than this period). As already described, the quota system from 1964 adopted a ten-year minimum since reduced to three.

An interesting table appeared in the 102nd Annual Report of the Board (1976/7), which showed the changes in preferences for these methods (and hence the value to borrowers of full flexibility of choice) from 1964 to 1975. As this was a period of steeply rising interest rates, there was as might be expected a swing from the newly introduced maturity method, in which principal is retained for the maximum period, to the EIP method, in which the principal is repaid most quickly, with the annuity method – the middle course – holding a relatively steady place (Table 21.1).

Table 21.1   *Proportion of total sum advanced which was repayable*

	(a) By equal instalments (%)	(b) By annuity (%)	(c) By maturity (%)
1964–5	9·5	29·8	60·7
1965–6	11·3	27·0	61·7
1966–7	8·2	26·1	65·7
1967–8	10·2	26·2	63·6
1968–9	20·1	25·8	54·1
1969–70	29·6	27·3	43·1
1970–1	42·9	34·3	22·8
1971–2	39·3	34·9	25·8
1972–3	36·5	34·1	29·4
1973–4	40·8	29·6	29·6
1974–5	58·2	35·2	6·6

Repayment periods allowed by the PWLC have borne a general relationship to the loan sanction periods granted by government departments. Where they have differed, the commission has of necessity been lower than the sanction period. In the early years, periods of two, eight, ten and twenty years, with twenty as the standard period, were used with authority to the commission to extend periods if they considered this to be desirable. The 1844 Act brought in thirty years, and after 1858, fifty years was available for certain purposes. The 1875 Act required the commissioners to have regard to the desirability of the work for which the loan was granted and to the expediency of the cost being borne by generations which would immediately benefit. This suggests the possibility of a difference of view between the sanctioning department and the commission. From 1870 School Boards were inclined to use the full fifty years allowed to them, but the commission considered that this encouraged recklessness and was intended to be used only in special cases, thirty years being more reasonable. Nevertheless, fifty years seems to have been the common practice for schools and of course very many schools built in that period have been in use for much longer. The Commission tried to adopt a policy of charging a higher interest rate for longer loans and of insisting on the EIP method of repayment for loans over thirty years. In 1895 the central Government Education Department adopted a thirty-five-year period.

In 1907 loans for eighty years were permitted for land for smallholdings provided by county councils, a step regarded by the commissioners 'with much apprehension'. A somewhat erratic policy then followed – sixty years for schools, eighty years for housing (but restricted in practice to land, buildings being given sixty years). These variations were of course forced on the commission by government policy, not adopted on their own initiative. The way in which this loan period policy was ultimately rationalized will be examined later.

The initially prescribed rate of interest of 5 per cent was reduced in 1822 to 4 per cent, but reverted to 5 per cent in 1826. In 1853 rates as low as 3½ per cent were allowed, or the then current yield on 3 per cent consolidated annuities. In the middle of the century different rates for different services were introduced, always with an eye to avoiding loss to the Exchequer, and from 1870 rates relating to repayment periods were used. These were all rates laid down in Acts of Parliament but in 1897 the Treasury were at last given power to fix interest rates at their discretion.

For the greater part of the PWLC's existence the rates have been simply based on government borrowing rates, with an addition for administration. Earlier paragraphs describe how different interest rates have formed part of the quota policy in recent times. An interesting exception occurred in 1919, when under the major Housing Act of that year a substantial government subsidy was given; the cost of the provision of housing to a local authority was limited each year to the amount of a rate of 1d in the pound – a system soon abandoned. The PWLC rate was fixed for housing purposes at the local authority open-market rate, so that there should be no further hidden subsidy in the interest rate.

The twenty-one commissioners appointed in the early days were later reduced in number to sixteen and now twelve. They are, and always have been, unpaid. They were originally appointed from bankers and business-men, together with a small number of Members of Parliament. After 1948, a levening of retired municipal treasurers was added; the first treasurer so honoured appears to have been Frank Walter Rattenbury, the former County Treasurer of Gloucestershire. Why the Board remains in existence must be a matter of some wonder; it does not fix the amount of money available, the purposes for which it may be lent, or the amounts which authorities may borrow; it is not now concerned with assessing security, nor does it have any influence on the interest rates to be charged or on major changes in PWLC policy. All these are dictated by Parliament or the Treasury. Virtually its only function is to approve the action of its officials, who are themselves carrying out Treasury instructions. Perhaps if it had been a paid board, it would have been abolished long ago. Nevertheless, over the years, particularly when the Board had a more positive role, much dedicated service has been contributed by commissioners.

Table 21.2 shows that ever since the outbreak of the First World War the PWLC has played a prominent part in the capital finance of local authorities. Apart from the peak period after the Second World War when all current borrowing was required to be from the commission, the pattern is surprisingly regular – between one-third and something much less than one-half of local authority debt has been with the commission. The rapidly growing debt of local authorities (mainly housing), and the equally impressive rise in the PWLC's annual interest rate for new advances and consequently the rise in the overall average rate are also striking though rather more painful. The figures are taken mainly from a table in the 102nd Annual Report of the Board; the figures for the last five years have been supplemented from the annual debt statistics published by CIPFA Statistical Information Service. These two sets of figures are not calculated on exactly the same basis but are adequate as an indication of the trend.

By manipulation of PWLC lending policy, the Treasury has been able to exert some influence on local authority capital finance and to protect local authorities against the possibility of market exploitation. There is simply no doubt that the aid given by the PWLC and the existence of the 'last resort' facility has created a considerable confidence about local authorities in the market. From a somewhat confused and halting pattern of operation during the first half – perhaps longer – of its life ('bumbling' would be an appropriate description) the PWLC has emerged since the 1960s as a highly professional, sophisticated and efficient machine.

Table 21.2 *PWLC Share of Local Authority Debt*

Year ending March	Total local authority debt, billions (£)	Debt with PWLC, as percentage of total	Average rates of interest	
			New loans (%)	Overall average (%)
1914	0·6	9·0	3½	3⅜
1924	0·9	16·4	4¾	5
1934	1·6	19·4	3⅝	5
1944	1·7	18·4	3¼	4½
1954	3·9	64·4*	4	3½
1964	8·6	34·6	5¾	3⅞
1968	12·7	36·4	7	4¾
1969	13·9	36·7	7¾	5⅛
1970	14·9	37·8	8⅞	5⅜
1971	16·2	38·9	8⅛	6
1972	17·6	40·3	6⅞	6⅛
1973	19·6	41·0	8½	6¼
1974	22·2	40·6	11⅝	7¼
1975	25·6	39·6	12½	8⅛
1976	28·0	40·4	11½	8¾
1977	31·0	38·4	12¼	9¼
1978	33·1	38·1	10⅛	9⅜
1979	34·8	36·7	12	9¾
1980	36·6	36·0	12⅞	10¼
1981	39·5	37·0	—	—
1982	41·8	32·6	—	—

* This variation from the trend was caused by the restriction of local authority borrowing to PWLC for the period.

This evolution has been, to some extent, a result of pressure from municipal treasurers and also an attempt by the PWLC to adapt itself to techniques which were being developed in the local authority market generally (for example, variable interest rates). Where the commissioners were slow in coming into line – reluctance to accept maturity repayment – their attitude was not without a sound financial basis in the interests of ratepayers.

Clearly, there is a case to be made that while the PWLC continues to operate with an imaginative and flexible approach and to show a willingness to evolve new techniques, the finance of local authority capital expenditure at near government rates and with the avoidance of competition between local authorities is economically sensible. At the present time the amount of government borrowing is so large that the extra requirements imposed on it by the local authority demands do not appear to necessitate a noticeably higher rate for funds for central use than if the local authorities were operating separately. Indeed the withdrawal of the local authorities from the market may possibly make the government's task easier. This is particularly true now that the old-fashioned 'local lender market', on which local authorities relied so heavily until, say, 1930, has been so seriously eroded by other forms of investment made available to the small investor – by National Savings, building societies, unit trusts, and so on.

The worry to local authorities is that which has exercised central-local relations generally over the centuries since Henry VIII. Although centralized borrowing may produce economies in cost and administrative effort for local government, is local government wise to surrender its liberty – its personal initiative – in this way? After all, the case for a reasonably independent local government rests fairly substantially on the value of inter-reaction (even if abrasive) between central and local authorities. Is economy really the overriding criterion? The foregoing account of the history of the PWLC has shown that an on-off policy has been adopted at various stages during the last 100 years, and that local authorities have been switched at short notice between policies of 'all from the board' to 'board at last resort only', as suited government policy. Local authorities have adapted themselves to this sort of change with considerable agility, but only by adopting methods which have twice in recent times called for urgent corrective action from an alarmed Treasury: first, the imposition of restrictions on temporary borrowing, and secondly, the insistence on the adoption of a 'voluntary' Maturity Code which was, in effect, simply an elaboration of the short-loan restriction.

The Treasury may fairly combat these fears of surrender to central borrowing by the argument that while the greater part of local capital needs is readily and promptly available with flexibility of conditions and methods of repayment from the PWLC, local authorities are not in fact prohibited from going to the market either locally or in London to safeguard their independence. But what would be the reaction if a substantial proportion of local capital needs was raised by local authorities at open-market rates, despite the availability of cheaper PWLC money? The problem is not likely to arise. Suspicious or uneasy though municipal treasurers may be of long-term Treasury motives they are unlikely to be able to justify themselves (or their authorities) in the eyes of the public by paying more for their capital than they need, even in the cause of defensive action against central encroachment.

At one time the view was current among treasurers (wishful thinking, perhaps), that the Treasury's need to restrict its borrowing was such that it would not wish to add to its problems by excessive assistance to local authorities. Indeed that the rate of progress of entry to the PWLC after 1964 was slower than promised in the White Paper was directly because the Treasury was not prepared at that time to find the extra money required. However, as Treasury concern with public borrowing now embraces not only direct government needs, but also those of the nationalized boards as well as local government, this separation of demand is no longer significant.

Some years ago, in the 1960s, there was a school of thought among treasurers – particularly in the smaller authorities where borrowing though smaller was more of a problem in the open market – which advocated the use of a central borrowing agency for local authorities, operated by local authorities rather than central government. (This suggestion was influenced by the development at that time of a central investment organization for local authority pension funds – Local Authority Mutual Investment Trust, LAMIT.) This proposal for an independent central borrowing agency found no favour with the Treasury (nor was it welcomed by treasurers of the larger authorities) on the ground that a single borrower on the scale which would have been necessary would have such an influence on the market that government regulation would be inevitable; the idea failed to prosper.[3]

The advance to '75% of expenditure plus 10% of debt' comes at a time when severe restrictions are being placed on local authority revenue expenditure, and government sanctions in the form of substantial withdrawal of grant and prohibition of rate increases are being imposed on alleged high-spending authorities. Thus at this moment local authorities are moving into a situation where both revenue and capital finances are very much in the grip of Whitehall. Peculiarly enough, at this same moment ministers concerned with local government (Department of the Environment) are criticizing local authorities for a short-fall of expenditure on capital works below levels which the government would be happy to approve. The local authorities account for this short-fall very simply by the old adage that 'the capital expenditure of today is the revenue expenditure of tomorrow', and that in consequence with severe and increasing restraints on revenue expenditure, they are reluctant to incur capital expenditure. The government seem to have a theory that there are avenues of capital expenditure which will not impinge heavily on future revenue – except for debt charges! – but the local authorities remain unconvinced. Perhaps the expansion of PWLC assistance is related to a wish by central government actively to encourage local capital development in the interests of provision of employment, a policy local authorities do not at this moment seem disposed to adopt.

Nevertheless, depending upon how long it is maintained, the recent expansion of PWLC lending must have a marked impact on the pattern of the local authority capital market. For a certainty, stock issues are unlikely to find a place, nor large bond or syndicated loans. Negotiable bonds must also be affected unless as part of the very short end of the local authority borrowing portfolios. Less than one-year money will no doubt continue to flourish and the availability of the PWLC may help to keep rates down in this area. Money bills will continue as short and revenue-financing instruments. The mortgage/bond market is unlikely to see much action unless local lenders will accept low rates for the convenience of investing at the local town hall. The counties, in particular, are likely to manage wholly from the PWLC and their internal funds, with the short market as the regulator, as by tradition the local market is usually left to the district councils.

NOTES: CHAPTER 21

1   The greater part of the history of the PWLC as described in this chapter has been derived from a scrutiny of the many statutes involved, but also from 'A general note of the history and current activities of the Commission' published in March 1976, and from articles on various selected aspects of the commission's history – interest rates, methods of repayment, and so on – included as appendices to Annual Reports of the Board and largely collated in the 100th Annual Report (1974/5). The series of numbered circulars issued by the PWLC beginning in March 1964 has also been used. The present Secretary to the Commission, Mr P. A. Goodwin, has been most helpful in supplying material and in replying at length to many searching inquiries; he is of course in no way responsible for any of the views expressed in this chapter. His predecessor in this post, I. de L. Radice, was also for many years a good friend to local government.

2   In July 1984 (Circular No. 72) after the completion of this work, the PWLC announced: 'The minimum period for new loans from the Board will be reduced to one year for maturity loans and to 2 years for those repayable by annuity or equal instalments of principal (EIP).'

3   From the 1950s voluntary loans bureaux under the auspices of branches of the IMTA played a useful part in inter-authority lending, particularly that in the north-west run by the borough treasurer of Nelson, Mr J. Knight, and his associates. In the late 1960s these were replaced by a central full-time Loans Bureau established by the institute in London which continues to operate, now in a wider field, as a broker for local authority capital finance. The bureau plays an active role but is limited in its operations, as compared with the commercial money brokers, by its lack of ready access to markets and sources of funds outside the local authority area. (In an attempt to widen its facilities for access to other sources of funds the Loans Bureau has now – July 1984 – entered into a commercial agreement with a local authority money broker for a measure of joint co-operation. What effect this will have on the local authority links between the bureau and local treasurers remains to be seen.)

Chapter 22

MISCELLANEOUS SOURCES OF
CAPITAL FINANCE

There are several sources of finance for local authority capital expenditure
other than by direct borrowing, some of which are and some are not
relevant to this book. For instance, the bulk of government financial
assistance to local authorities has been, and continues to be, in the form of
revenue grants (particularly housing), and in so far as the revenue costs
towards which the grants are made include debt charges, the grants are a
positive aid to capital expenditure though they do not reduce the overall
amount of borrowing. But some grants have been given as direct aid to
capital expenditure, thus reducing borrowing and the accompanying loan
charges. Over the course of time direct capital grants have been made to
highways, housing, sewerage and sewage disposal, planning, drainage,
river conservancy and coast protection, other minor rate fund services and
even to trading undertakings. Before and during the Second World War,
substantial capital grants were made towards air-raid precautions,
particularly the provision of shelters. The most significant grants have been
towards expenditure on the provision of roads, scaled in relation to the
local, regional, or national importance of the roads concerned, and finally
reaching the point where the main network of trunk-roads and motorways
has become wholly a central government expense, even though carried out
on a local agency basis. The use of capital grants as a form of capital
finance is not enlarged on here as it is relevant to borrowing only in the
sense that local borrowing is reduced by this means.

Methods of capital finance which are more directly related to this book
are through capital and (similar) funds, the use of internal funds,
borrowing abroad and, to a lesser extent, direct revenue provision through
capital purposes rates and in recent years leasing.

CAPITAL FUNDS A capital fund is a device whereby income from certain
miscellaneous sources is set aside and used for capital rather than revenue
purposes, with the intention of reducing the amount of a local authority's
external borrowing. In its most extended form money which is provided from
a capital fund for a borrowing service is the equivalent, so far as that service
is concerned, of funds provided by normal borrowing, as the borrowing
account is required to repay these advances over the loan sanction period,
with interest meanwhile. There are simpler forms of the application of a
capital fund (to be described), but when the fully developed form is
adopted, the long-term objective is to create an internal fund which will in

due course be large enough to provide the capital needs of the authority from year to year without resort to external borrowing. In other words, the full use of a capital fund involves the ploughing back of interest into the local authority's own budget instead of paying it out to private lenders. Depending upon how the capital fund is financed, it may very well involve taxing present ratepayers through the rate, in order to build up a fund for the use of future ratepayers. These principles apply whether the fund is called, as it now generally is, a capital fund, or a capital reserve fund, or a land fund as this type of device was originally known.

The first local authority to establish a capital fund has not been categorically established, but the event probably occurred in the late 1920s or early 1930s. There is no mention of capital funds in Johnson's *Loans of Local Authorities* (1925), nor even in Carson Roberts's *Local Administration – Finance and Accounts* (1930). Such funds found no place in the Local Government Act 1933. A. B. Griffiths, in his *Municipal Capital Finance* (1936), shows that capital and similar funds were obviously well established under private Acts by this date. In fact Griffiths writes of a 'lands fund' as 'authorised by a number of Acts' and quotes that of Sheffield as having been authorized under the Sheffield Corporation Act 1928. Wolverhampton Corporation established a 'capital fund' by local Act in 1932, in what seems to have been very near to the standard form followed thereafter (for example by 'land funds' set up by both Bury and Cambridge corporations in the same year), and this may be the first of its kind.

The Sheffield land fund involved simply the setting aside each year of an amount not exceeding a rate of 2d in the pound, subject to a maximum in hand at any one time of £50,000, for the purpose of buying or leasing land for civic purposes. This was therefore simply a land capital purposes rate but with power to carry forward balances from one year to another. (The point should be made clear here that without specific power to 'carry forward', balances at year-end would have had to be used for the credit of the following year's rate.)

Capital reserve funds were similarly formed from sums set aside annually for any purpose 'to which capital is properly applicable' – usually for rate fund departments only. In the example of a capital reserve fund quoted by Griffiths no one transaction was to exceed £5,000, the amount set aside annually was not to exceed the proceeds of 2d rate and the maximum in hand was not to exceed £25,000.

These modest schemes led to the wider conception of the capital fund proper. A typical local Act capital fund could be formed from the proceeds of sales of corporate property and, much more important, from the transfer of rate fund balances at year-end, and indeed from the annual surpluses of 'any undertaking of the Corporation', together with 'such other sums as the Corporation may by resolution direct'. Transfers from the rate were limited to a maximum of 2d each year, and sums could not be transferred from a corporation 'undertaking' (and never from a water undertaking) unless adequate reserves were in being. Such a capital fund could be used in the exercise of any statutory borrowing power or to expedite repayment of debt already incurred in earlier borrowings (but not to make annual sinking fund payments in respect of earlier debt). There was no maximum limit to the total of the unapplied fund.

The shortcoming of the capital fund provisions in this early form was that adequate facilities were not given for recovery from borrowing accounts over a period of years of the sums advanced with or without interest. The only provision made in these early examples was that if the money advanced from a capital fund to a borrowing account had originated from a sale of council property, that is, a capital receipt, then this sum was subject to annual instalment repayment with or without interest. This was apparently an offshoot of the tradition that capital once created should not be dispersed, but it meant that separation of sources of origin of moneys in capital funds had to be maintained.

Presumably, although the point of change has not been identified, development of this feature took place, as is indicated in a general Act of 1945. The adoption of the concept of capital funds was such that when under the Local Authorities Loans Act 1945 local authority borrowing was for a time permitted only from the Public Works Loan Commission (PWLC), a clause was necessary to allow those local authorities which had a capital fund to continue to operate this for capital purposes. The term 'capital fund' used in this clause was very widely defined as

> any fund established for the repayment of debt, or as a reserve, or for the maintenance, renewal or repair of property, or for superannuation of staff, or for insurance or otherwise for meeting expenditure of a capital or non-recurring nature or any like purpose.

This omnibus definition was clearly designed to allow the continuation of the practice of using, temporarily, any internal funds of the local authority.

The 1945 Act allowed advances from a capital fund for any purpose for which a local authority had power to borrow, and required that the advances made 'shall be repaid to the capital fund' either (remembering the wide definition of capital funds under this Act) when the lending fund required the money or, more specifically, in relation to a capital fund 'proper', within the loan sanction period. Interest 'at the appropriate rate' was to be paid by the borrowing account on outstanding balances. Thus a capital fund as operated under these provisions was very much of an accumulating nature.

Positive recognition of the benefits of a capital fund followed relatively speedily in a Private Member's Bill, the Local Government (Miscellaneous Provisions) Act 1953 which, *inter alia*, allowed a local authority (county council, county borough, metropolitan borough, county district, and the City of London) to establish a capital fund (and a repairs and renewal fund). The granting of these facilities to all local authorities indicates the passage of a growing number of local Acts seeking this power, and of increasing sophistication.

A capital fund established under the 1953 Act could be used 'for defraying any expenditure of the authority, to which capital is properly applicable' – indicating that loan sanction was not required for such expenditures – or in expediting the repayment of debt. The capital fund could not be used for the purpose of a trading undertaking or, surprisingly, the education functions of the authority (this restriction stemmed from problems with the then specific grant for education purposes). The moneys which might be paid into the capital fund were any sums derived from the sale of corporate property, annual surpluses on the county or rate fund and 'such other sums as the local authority may by resolution direct'. The annual sums which could be transferred by way of rate surpluses or 'such other contributions' were limited to 4d for county boroughs, 3d for county councils and 2d for other authorities. Under powers given him under the Act the Minister later determined (Circular 47/1953) that the maximum unapplied amount of any fund at any one time was not to exceed the equivalent of a 1s rate, and that the maximum which could be applied to any one transaction was not to exceed the product of a 5d rate.

Local authorities were still required to arrange for repayments from borrowing accounts of any moneys originating from the 'sale of land', but had a discretion to do so with other funds, in both cases the charging of interest being optional. Maintaining the old principle that land once acquired should be preserved, the Act required that any money coming into the capital fund from the sale of land could only be used to acquire further land, unless with the Minister's consent. This reflected provisions of the 1933 Act designed to control the disposal of land by local authorities.

A brief Institute of Municipal Treasurers and Accountants (IMTA) research study on local authority borrowing, first published in 1957 and revised in 1962, reported that by 1953 over 100 authorities had obtained local Act powers to operate a capital fund, twenty-eight of which were during the period 1945–50. The main differences between local Act provisions and those of the 1953 Act related to the amount of annual contributions, and the determination of size of fund and 'single transactions' in specific amounts rather than rate equivalents.

Though now well out of date, some of the statistics given in the institute study are of interest as indicating the variations in practice among local authorities. The 1953 Act powers were in addition to and not in substitution of local Act powers. Consequently, some local authorities operated both a local Act fund and a 1953 Act fund. Thus of 100 authorities investigated, seventy-one operated eighty-four funds, thirty-three under local Acts and fifty-one under the 1953 Act. Moneys fed into funds originated in a variety of ways as allowed by the Acts. Of the seventy-one authorities having funds, only fifty-one required annual repayments (of which only thirty-nine also required interest on balances) from the accounts to which advances were made. Annual repayments were almost invariably required over much shorter terms than the loan sanction period, often as short as ten years.

The City of Manchester fund, established under the 1953 Act in 1958 (but see p. 322 on a capital purposes rate), had an unusual origin. The initial contribution to the Manchester capital fund consisted of a once-for-all transfer from reserve of approximately £¼ million 'severance money' received as compensation on the nationalization of the gas and electricity undertakings. An annual rate contribution to the fund was not made in the ordinary way, nor were annual rate surpluses transferred. However, a sum of £160,000 had become available each year from a fixed interest investment made in the early 1890s in the Manchester Ship Canal Co. to assist it through various financial difficulties. Amortization had just been completed of the loan incurred to on-lend to the Ship Canal (after a sixty-year period) but because the investment in the canal company was permanent the interest was no longer needed to discharge the corporation's initial debt. The city council therefore decided to use this interest as an annual contribution to the capital fund; this was, quite coincidentally, almost exactly, at that time, the equivalent of a rate of 4d.

The Local Government Act 1972 repealed and re-enacted the earlier provisions for capital funds and the use of other funds temporarily for capital purposes. The exclusion of trading undertakings continued, but that relating to education expenditure ceased. The limit of the amount which might be transferred in any one year was fixed at 5p. The facility to require repayment, with or without interest, from a borrowing account remained, but there was no longer a requirement that income from the sale of land should be used again for that purpose.

But a material change was made in the Local Government (Miscellaneous Provisions) Act 1976. This withdrew specific provisions for capital and repairs funds, and gave a general power for the establishment of such funds as local authorities considered necessary to meet their expenditures, without restrictions as to amounts of transfers or sizes of funds (except that trading undertakings still could not participate). However, advances from capital funds are now regarded as capital expenditure, within the restrictions on overall annual capital spending as described in Chapter 23. This change is in fact a considerable simplification of the concept of the capital fund, but it lacks a clear statement about repayments (with or without interest) from borrowing accounts. However, in theory, local authorities can make such provision in determining the amounts of annual transfers to the capital fund.

A capital fund set up from rate contributions, or from moneys which would otherwise go to relieve a rate levy, is the equivalent of a capital purposes rate, with the added facility for the carrying forward of balances at year-end. If a capital fund of a local authority is in such a form that instalment repayments and interest are required, then the present ratepayers are being placed under the burden of having to meet the annual levy and also to pay debt charges as though the money had been borrowed externally. In so far as this leads to the accumulation of a fund which will ultimately meet all capital requirements without external borrowing, and allows the ploughing back of interest into the local authority's budget rather than its payment to outside lenders, this may be judged a good thing (leaving aside the 'fructifying' theory that ratepayers should be allowed to make their own use of their own money). But nevertheless, however sound as a measure of long-term finance, this system is burdensome to present ratepayers in imposing a double charge. Not surprisingly, although the facility has been available now for fifty years, it has not made much impression on local authority debt portfolios (most of which in any event relate to housing). Debt statements published annually by CIPFA show that in Britain the proportion of total debt which related to capital funds was no more than 6·5 per cent for the year ended March 1982, though it had risen from 5·1 per cent in the previous year. This rise in the use of these internal funds was possibly stimulated by the high levels of interest rates in the market generally at that time.

In 1979 the then Comptroller of the GLC and now its Chief Executive (M. F. Stonefrost) reported to his Policy and Resources Committee that, as a result of the annual increase in the amounts allocated from revenue to the council's capital fund (£68 million in 1978/9, giving a balance in hand of £104 million), the sum available in the fund was 'close to the total of outstanding debt on GLC services other than housing', so that 'An opportunity therefore presented itself for the GLC to adopt a policy of "no debt/no borrowing except for housing" by using the capital fund balance to expunge all non-housing outstanding debt'. This the council agreed to do; after this date, all non-housing capital expenditure has been met from revenue and there is no outstanding debt other than for housing. This happy outcome of the bold use of a capital fund must be encouraging to treasurers, but it is less dramatic when set against the statistics given in the report which show that 80 per cent of the GLC debt related to housing, and that the total housing debt was equivalent to 77 per cent of the total loan debt of all other county authorities in England and Wales (both metropolitan and non-metropolitan).

This book has shown that early expenditure of a capital nature was automatically borne from current revenue. The first break from this system occurred when a capital asset was to be created for which revenue was not available until after the asset had been brought into use, that is, the turnpike road, but even after that, much expenditure of a capital nature continued to be a direct charge on revenue. The direct charging of some portion of capital expenditure against revenue has continued throughout the history of local government. The concern here is not with the use of temporarily surplus revenue funds for capital purposes; that is simply a source of borrowing (for example, the internal investment of pension or fire insurance funds and the like). The question now to be examined is one of direct use of annual revenues for the creation of capital assets without recourse to borrowing and extended repayment.

The lack of a firm definition of capital creates something of a problem, but the general concept of expenditure on those items the cost of which can reasonably (or in a Minister's view) be spread over a number of years is adequate. The importance or cost of an asset is not the deciding factor.

When a new school is established, the crockery in the canteen, some of which may be broken on the day on which the school is commissioned, is as much capital expenditure in the first instance as the lathe in the workshop, or the bricks of the wall. The principle is that the capital asset once created is thereafter maintained from revenue.

But there are many capital assets for which borrowing would be inappropriate and the effort involved tedious. An authority which needed ten fire-engines to meet its responsibilities, each of which has a working life of about ten years, would not normally wish to borrow for these appliances. Rather it would so try to organize its affairs that one appliance could be provided or replaced each year – that is, programme provision. Nor would any authority but the smallest wish to borrow and set up repayment for minor items such as typewriters and other office equipment (a computer or a word processor might now be a different matter, but even so the short effective life of such devices might raise special considerations). Such items might however be purchased from borrowed money in the initial establishment of a concern, as part of an overall capital provision.

The finance of some expenditure of a capital nature from revenue has therefore always been a common practice, and the line between what should be borrowed for and what not is impossible to draw precisely. Practice varies according to the cost of the asset concerned and the resources of the authority – and no doubt the views of the treasurer. This is therefore not a subject for a study of borrowing – it is anti-borrowing – but in certain instances such practices impinge on the edge of the field of borrowing. The IMTA study of local authority borrowing contains statistics (extracted from Local Government Financial Statistics, published by Whitehall) on 'Revenue contributions'. These show that in 1935/6, on a capital expenditure of £35 million, 9·5 per cent was met directly from revenue. In 1959/60 capital expenditure was £230 million, with no less than 14·6 per cent borne from revenue. The peak year in the period was 1947/8 when of a low capital expenditure of £34 million, 19 per cent was met from revenue. This was almost certainly because local authority services had not resumed their stride after the war, so that rate revenue was more easily available. The same statistics indicate that counties and metropolitan boroughs were the classes of authority most likely to rely on the revenue financing of capital expenditure.

The IMTA study shows that the practices of authorities varied considerably. Some authorities charged to revenue all expenditure of a capital nature below a certain amount, for example, from £2,000 to £10,000 in counties and up to £5,000 in county boroughs. The study records a tendency for the maxima to increase, but this must have been partly the result of inflation. Other authorities adopted a system of identifying items which although of a capital nature were regularly recurring; minor capital works forming part of a longer-term programme – for example the provision of public conveniences – might also be charged to revenue on the same principle.

Other authorities either fixed a ceiling of a round figure of revenue to be allocated to minor capital expenditures each year or elected to levy a fixed rate of a few pence in the pound the proceeds of which were to be used for capital expenditure or in the writing off of outstanding debt. Such a practice is close to that already described in this chapter in respect of the early capital reserve funds. A capital reserve fund, usually based on the annual proceeds of a 2d rate, differed from a capital purpose rate (CPR), in that the balance of the capital reserve fund could be carried forward under statutory authority to following years, whereas the proceeds of a CPR the levying of which did not require specific statutory authority had to be expended during the year; otherwise any balance at the year-end would constitute a normal rate fund surplus which the law required should be absorbed into the following year's budget in the determination of a 'sufficient rate'. Because of this prohibition of the carrying forward of earmarked balances in a CPR, any such balances were normally used up in expediting the repayment of debt.

Manchester's practice of levying a CPR is probably fairly representative of authorities using this device. In 1930 the city council resolved to levy a CPR of 3d in the pound for minor capital works; this decision arose from the deliberations of a special committee appointed to review the council's financial prospects, which produced a five-year forecast of potential rate rises which while modest by today's standards horrified the city council. Once this CPR was launched, informal records were maintained of the debt charges which would have been necessary if the items financed from revenue had been the subject of borrowing. By 1943 the accumulated notional annual debt charges which had been avoided amounted to the product of a 3d rate, so that the moment was considered right for the increase of the CPR to 6d each year. This situation repeated itself by 1959, when the CPR was increased to 1s in the pound despite the increase in the penny-rate product resulting from a recent rating revaluation. The progress of the capital fund for Manchester, and of the systematic approach to the meeting of capital expenditure from revenue has been sadly disrupted in the recent years of financial stringency.

The conclusions of the institute study are today still valid: 'Clearly there are sound practical reasons for financing capital expenditure from revenue particularly at times of high interest rates.' Whether a CPR should be utilized for minor items or for items on which the amortization periods are usually long and the interest cost high seems never to have been resolved. The institute's final conclusion was that: 'Many authorities could, with advantage, increase their present provisions from revenue for the financing of capital expenditure.' This conclusion was reached long before the advent of 'rate-capping', and the overall control of capital outlay by local authorities irrespective of the methods by which it is financed.

But there are also views about the benefits of 'pay-as-you-go' for capital purposes in the light of the ruling rates of inflation and interest – is it better to borrow now and repay over a long term of years in depreciated pounds? Many with house mortgages will have decided that it is, apart from tax benefits. In his presidential address to the Treasurers' Institute, in 1971, the then City Treasurer of Birmingham (Francis Stephenson) taking certain assumed rates of inflation and interest, indicated that the trend of education capital expenditure in Birmingham was such that after eighteen years annual debt charges would exceed annual new capital expenditure. This led to a brisk correspondence in *Local Government Finance* during the following months, especially from those who sought to prove that by applying discounted cash flow (DCF) to the savings through borrowing in the early years the 'real' date at which debt charges would overtake expenditure was pushed very many years ahead. On the whole, while the mathematical correctness of the DCF figures was conceded, the overall view seemed to be that the ratepayers of the future would show little interest in the savings made by ratepayers in the early years of the demonstration. There are clearly philosophic as well as mathematical arguments behind decisions to finance capital expenditure from revenue. As the institute's president said in concluding the correspondence: 'All present generations wish to defer payment; all future generations rue the deferment.'

Writing in the *Journal of the Institute of Public Administration* in 1928, I. G. Gibbon of the Ministry of Health referred to the 'refreshing indications' of the devotion of a greater amount of attention by municipal treasurers to the possibilities of meeting more capital expenditure from revenue – the policy of pay-as-you-go; however, he added:

> Some theorists are inclined to preach the pay-as-you-go policy to futile extremes. It is manifest that many of the great public improvements would not have been made without loan. The local authority is a continuing community. A local authority must lay its course not just for this generation but also for the generations to come without unwise sacrifice of the present generation.

Today's financial administrators might prefer a more precise spelling-out of these generalizations.

Over the last twenty years a further device has been resorted to, as a means of avoiding borrowing, which allows local authorities to take advantage of tax concessions not normally available to them, but readily available to commercial companies. This is the adoption of 'leasing'. Statutory authority is not needed by a local authority wishing to adopt this method. It arises because local authorities, not being subject to tax, cannot take advantage of depreciation and similar allowances available against tax assessments, whereas companies owning similar equipment can do so. The outcome of this is that many substantial items of equipment, and even buildings, can be provided by a company and 'leased' to the local authority, which pays the leasing costs annually instead of debt charges. In effect, the value of the depreciation allowances which the lessee can obtain is shared with the local authority through the lease and results in lower annual charges to the authority than would be involved in straight borrowing. There are many variants of leasing contracts – leasing, lease and lease-back, and 'deferred purchase'. In some cases the local authority never obtains ownership of the subject of the lease; in others ownership passes to the local authority at the end of the lease period. Leases are sometimes drawn so that the provider of the equipment recovers his cost quickly, after which a reduced leasing fee is payable by the authority. This method has been widely used for such equipment as computers, buses, ships, motor vehicles, plant and fire service equipment; less frequently is it used for buildings, but it has been used to finance the building of town halls.

In 1969 the government showed some enthusiasm in the direction of encouraging local authorities to borrow abroad in foreign currencies, where interest rates were relatively low.[1] (Nationalized industries had already been in this field for substantial sums.) The motives behind this are thought to have been that the government had considerable short-term liabilities overseas which could perhaps be 'funded' if local authorities borrowed longer-term from these sources. Local authorities had of course, particularly since the end of the war and with the increase in short borrowing, attracted considerable sums from foreign sources, but these borrowings had been in sterling and through the London branches of foreign banks. The rush to borrow abroad directly was something of a storm in a teacup as the situation making this activity favourable rapidly changed and the whole exercise was over by 1975 (although later it was restarted in a small way to allow borrowing from European Economic Community institutions).

Reference has been made in our historical review to the Public Authorities and Bodies (Loans) Act 1916, which gave powers to local authorities to borrow abroad and to use bearer securities 'by means of the issue of bearer bonds or other securities to bearer whether within or without the United Kingdom and, if thought fit, in any foreign currency'. Sir Harry Haward, in his *The London County Council from Within*, has described the pressures which the government of the day brought to bear on the LCC to borrow abroad and the speed with which the necessary parliamentary powers were rushed through. A $15 million fifteen-year 5 per cent 'gold bond loan' was negotiated by the LCC with bankers in New York, but the final price had not been fixed by the time America elected to enter the war and the need for the loan fell through, greatly to Sir Harry's relief. Later London apparently made other attempts to raise foreign money – including one in pesetas – but none of these, in his words, 'came to fruition'. There is no evidence of any other local authority taking advantage of these temporary powers. Problems of fluctuating exchange rates are known to have caused local authorities to view this area with extreme caution.

But the Act was not only unproductive in its results, it had also a curious negative or prohibitory effect on local authority statutory borrowing half a century later. When in 1969 the government decided that the national finances might be helped by local authority foreign borrowing, there was a statutory obstacle. The first public indication that the government was interested in a development of this kind by local authorities was in the Finance Act 1969. A clause was inserted in this Act to enable local authorities to pay interest on a foreign loan gross – that is, without deduction of income tax – a necessary preliminary. At the same time, the Treasury announced that the government would assist in protecting local authorities who borrowed abroad against exchange rate fluctuations.

Nevertheless, having announced these concessions, the Treasury immediately cautioned local authorities that they could not borrow abroad, and in a foreign currency, without express Parliamentary power. In the local government statutes authorizing local authorities to borrow to meet capital expenditure, nothing is said as to where and in what currency loans might be raised. Thus, on the face of it, treasurers might have been excused for thinking that the source and currency of the loan was a matter for the exercise of their own expertise. However, the Treasury took the view that because Parliament had once (in 1916) expressly given powers to borrow abroad in a foreign currency, and as these powers had now lapsed (by their 'non-re-enactment' in the Local Government Act 1933), Parliament had clearly established the rule that to borrow in this way was subject to their express consent. Obviously this seems to have been an extreme case of the rule that British local authorities are only able to do what they are expressly authorized to do, and may not assume powers merely because they have not been specifically forbidden to use such powers. This produced the odd situation that local authorities might pay interest on foreign loans gross and seek government aid against exchange rate fluctuations, but they could not raise foreign loans because they did not have power to do so, nor issue the bearer bonds required in this market. Actually a small number of county authorities had taken such power in local Acts – perhaps the heritage of the idea mooted in 1916 – and a number of other authorities immediately took steps to obtain local Act parliamentary powers in short statutes for that purpose, including the necessary authority to use bearer bonds. The Treasury agreed that they would not oppose the taking of such powers, authority by authority, provided that they were given subject to Treasury approval as to use; the Treasury also said that local authorities should not assume that such approvals would be readily forthcoming.[2]

Admittedly this was an area in which great caution would need to be exercised by beginners, but the following of the prompting in the Finance Act by the discouraging indication that the use of this power required local Act legislation and even then would be subject to Treasury approval, reluctantly given, is not easy to understand. Something like 100 local authorities felt the need to take the necessary powers by local Act; how many of them used the power is not known, but it was certainly a small proportion. Local authorities had not been pressing for this power, and those few who had it, had not been seeking permission to exercise it. Either this type of borrowing was of assistance to the national finances or it was not. The indications are that the Treasury became alarmed by the enthusiasm which their tentative encouragements had created and sought immediately to dampen it down. Perhaps there was a conflict within the Treasury about the whole idea; and the international financial situation was so volatile that a decision made one day could be inappropriate ten days later. Nationalized bodies including the Electricity Council and the Post Office were early in the field. Perhaps the Treasury's vacillation regarding the local authorities arose from a growing belief that this area should be left to the nationalized bodies. Nevertheless, despite waning central enthusiasm for this type of borrowing by local authorities, the power was included (subject to Treasury consent) in schedule 13 of the Local Government Act 1972. The need for 100 local authorities to take local Act powers before, seems a very cumbersome way of 'experimenting' but is entirely in line with the borrowing practices of the previous century.

The Treasury's offer to protect local authorities who wished to be so covered against losses from exchange rate fluctuations was originally on the following basis. The offer applied only to local authorities with a loan debt of over £100 million (lesser authorities could proceed subject to consent but were not eligible for this protection). The loan was required to be in US dollars (this was later extended to include the Deutschemark and other currencies) and for a minimum period of five years. A number of consents were required – that of the Bank of England to control the flow on to the market, and that of the Treasury for the issue of bearer certificates, gross interest payments and under Exchange Control. Given these approvals, the guarantee was not of the loan itself (which is what the continental market would have liked), but of the costs arising from a deterioration in exchange rates during the course of the loan. Local authorities were to be permitted to buy the necessary foreign currency for interest and repayment at the rates which had been ruling at the time the loan was introduced. There was naturally a charge for this cover; it fluctuated with each loan, being pitched at such a level that the gain in interest to the local authority was a mere half of 1 per cent below that payable for PWLC borrowing at that date for ten-year loans. Thus the major part of the immediate interest gain from a foreign loan was absorbed by the Treasury and every authority, no matter what rates it negotiated, was left with a 'profit' of this narrow margin below that at which it could have borrowed at home, if it still had a quota margin available. For those authorities who had used up their PWLC quotas and would otherwise be in the institutional market the gain was a good deal greater. However, there was no incentive for the local authorities to fight with the foreign lender for the best rates available, and to any lender aware of the circumstances (that they all were aware must be axiomatic), there was distinct encouragement to force up rates in the knowledge that the local authorities would not be any worse off.

The local authorities were left to make difficult decisions. Loans were available in currencies other than those in which the Bank and the Treasury were interested in promoting, and the margin even in those which could earn the guarantee was well below those of the PWLC. In 1973 the GLC decided to take up a loan in Swiss francs – not admissible under the guarantee. The rate at 7½ per cent was well below the corresponding PWLC rate of 12 per cent. Yet when repayment became due in 1978, the GLC were reported as having lost £25 million because of the movement in the exchange rate, even after taking account of the interest benefit (*Financial Times*, 30 June 1978).

Before powers could be obtained by those other than the few who already had them (including the GLC) and loans organized, the market changed dramatically and adversely, and no progress was made. Indeed early in 1972 the Treasury guarantee against exchange rate fluctuations was withdrawn, only to be reinstated in the Chancellor's budget speech in March 1972, but then in relation only to loans in US dollars. In the meantime, as already indicated, general powers had been given both for foreign borrowing and the use of bearer bonds (both subject to Treasury consent) in the Local Government Act 1972. In December 1973 new rules were announced with a widening of the types of currency. The profit on interest rates which could be retained by the borrower was lifted from the ½ per cent then ruling to a figure to be determined by the Treasury according to the currency involved. But because foreign borrowing even without guarantee was becoming popular by local authorities, to prevent a flooding of the market, the debt limits required for exchange guarantees borrowing were then applied to all foreign borrowing. Finally, in 1974 as a result of debt amalgamations following reorganization, a further revision was made. The authorities who could benefit by the guarantee were defined as the GLC and counties with a net debt of £400 million, with the curious exception that the cities of Manchester and Liverpool could take the 'lead' in their counties because their names were better known than their counties' names on the continent. Scottish authorities with a debt of over £100 million continued to have access to the guarantee, but this admitted only a narrow field. Both floating and fixed rate loans were admissible.[3] Despite these changes, only a little foreign borrowing took place over the period; the total does not probably much exceed £500 million. The big borrowers in this area have been the nationalized boards.

The latest development in what must be classified as foreign borrowing is the provision for loans (and grants) which the European Economic Community has made to assist various organizations, including public (local) authorities. These are made through the European Investment Bank either direct to the organization concerned or through an appropriate agent in the borrowing country. The general theory is that this assistance is to be given to enterprises which benefit the development and operations of the Community. There are nine broad classifications of objectives of which those which apply to local authorities are: (1) loans for economic development; (2) finance for energy; (3) aid to coal and steel regions; and (4) selected educational, social and cultural objectives. Examples of assistance given are: for energy, a loan to Devon County Council for a solar-heating experiment in a school; and for aid to coal and steel regions,

£7 million of low-interest loans for local authority houses for steelworkers and coalminers. Under the 'miscellaneous' category a grant of £54,000 has been made for conservation work in the Edinburgh City Art Centre. Funds of this kind, not directed specifically at economic development, are said to be 'very small'.[4]

NOTES: CHAPTER 22

1 A most useful article on this subject by Dr (now Sir) Laurence Boyle, the then City Chamberlain of Glasgow, is in *Public Finance and Accountancy* (February 1974); also see my 'Appraisal of foreign currency borrowing by Manchester', *Public Finance and Accountancy* (February 1970).
2 Letter to the Association of Municipal Corporations (December 1969) said, *inter alia*, 'authorities who are seeking these powers [should be] under no illusions about the immediate prospects of their being able to use them'.
3 Treasury circular letters of 10 December 1973 and 21 March 1974.
4 *Finance from Europe – a Guide to Grants and Loans from the Economic Community* (London: Commission of the European Communities, July 1982); and correspondence with various local authorities.

Chapter 23

MANAGEMENT AND AMORTIZATION
OF DEBT

An history of local authority borrowing is incomplete without reference to the evolution of provisions for the management and amortization of such debt. The history of debt administration shows the same hesitation, uneven and delayed development as the history of borrowing itself, but success has at last been achieved in the official adoption of the consolidated loans fund (CLF), though even this is still less than whole-hearted. This aspect of the subject embraces authorization to borrow, the loan periods permitted, the provisions for amortization required to be made and the methods of amortization, and the development therefrom of such devices as sinking funds, loans pooling and finally consolidated loans funds.

INTEREST WARRANTS   This opportunity may perhaps be taken to clear up what is meant by an interest warrant, the term once generally used by local authorities to describe the document used for the payment of interest. Originally a warrant was an order from a superior to a subordinate instructing him to do something under authority (and such a meaning is still applicable in various uses). A warrant, as such, was thus an order, and in the local authority context an order by a board or a body of justices to its treasurer (or to some other officer if for a non-financial purpose) to make certain payments or carry out certain duties. The term in due course became attached, in financial terms, to the document by which the payment was made, so that a treasurer made a payment of interest by warrant in consequence of an order made by his superior body. In the event, the treasurer himself made an order – issued a warrant – on a bank instructing the bank to make a payment in compliance with his order. The National Debt Act 1870 defines a warrant as including 'a draft, order, cheque or other document used as a medium for the payment of dividends'. Therefore, in effect, in current usage a warrant is simply a cheque, and this more modern term is now generally in use, particularly when interest payments made by computer are no different from other payments by the authority.

AMORTIZATION   The justification for the finance of certain local authority expenditures by borrowing will be examined in the conclusion to this chapter. As to local authorities' right to finance by borrowing, the principle seems to have been taken for granted since the beginning that, as borrowing was a form of 'deferred revenue expenditure', and as the levy of taxes for revenue purposes was a function of the Crown (but which could of course be delegated), then the right to borrow especially as a pledging of future revenues must also be subject to central control. Another overriding principle of the greatest importance, again established more by implication than direct statement, has been that from first to last, except for minor cash-flow purposes, borrowing could not be resorted to for annual revenue expenditures. Charter boroughs seem to have believed for a period of time that, having been given (or having bought) the power to tax their inhabitants on behalf of the Crown, they could proceed to borrow in an attempt to spread the burden of taxation without specific approval. Even so, except for rare crisis periods, such borrowing was generally seen to have been for longer-term projects, and not for general annual revenue purposes.

One difference has been apparent between the nature of the central approvals of revenue raising and borrowing. Once approval had been given to the principle of levying a rate to meet local community responsibilities – poor relief in the original instance – the parishes were left (subject only to the approval of the local bench of magistrates) to determine their own level of rates. At least this has been so until 1983/4 when for macro-economic reasons government pressures have been strongly exerted to limit rate expenditure. This culminated in what is colloquially called 'rate-capping' – for the time being at least – of the so-called 'high-spending' authorities. Rate limitations were certainly occasionally imposed on various new services in their early days, but this has not been the general practice. But borrowing, even though statutorily permitted, has always been subject to detailed control by specific projects. This still remains so; and although recently there has been some relaxation, it has been mainly on minor services and always within overall totals. The reason for the difference between these two degrees of control seems fairly obvious. Ratepayers could be relied upon to keep the annual rate levy within reasonable bounds by pressures exercised through the electoral system. (Even this simple statement is suspect today when a somewhat greater proportion of the rate is paid by non-voting commercial undertakings, and when a large proportion of the voting ratepayers receive substantial rebates according to their lack of means.) However, there has always been a suspicion that today's ratepayers have a financial interest in pushing as much expenditure as possible on to tomorrow's ratepayers, and that finance by borrowing with repayment over a long term was an obvious way to do this.

Central approval of each specific project intended to be financed by borrowing (an approval not required if the same project were to be financed directly from revenue) with the gradual development of techniques for establishing the principles and periods of amortization have thus been the means whereby the ratepayers have been prevented from unduly deferring their responsibilities. Whether these restrictions have been sufficiently tight is another matter.

The central government's approach has been suspect in this area on two counts. First, the very lengthy amortization periods allowed to local authorities, which lessen the immediate burden but not the total cost, seem to have been used by central departments as a means of persuading local authorities vigorously to develop new services. Secondly, there is clear evidence that the central departments have used the sanctioning procedures to influence local policies, and even the operational details of local schemes, in aspects unrelated to finance.

As has been shown, borrowing was not contemplated in the earliest Acts authorizing the levy of a local rate. When borrowing came to be regarded as a necessary aid to expenditure (for a variety of reasons), the approval of the 'King in Parliament' was initially given not in general Acts, but in the private local Acts relating to individual authorities or groups of authorities. Later the power in the local Acts was given subject to the consent of a central department to its detailed exercise, and later still the necessity for central departmental sanction became the rule even in general legislation.

The earliest Act authorizing borrowing by a quasi-local authority which has been identified in this book, namely, the Wades-Mill Turnpike Act of 1663, required that the loan taken up for the purposes of putting the road in good order before the tolls could be levied should be repaid within nine years. This period was almost immediately extended to twenty-one years. In 1695 when the flood of Turnpike Acts began, a fifteen-year period was generally specified, shortly developing to nineteen and twenty-one years. This cautious restraint had disappeared in the various Turnpike Acts around 1760, where the authorization extended the period to borrowing 'for such time or term within the life of the power to collect tolls'. However, the toll-levying period was itself often restricted. As has been shown, the original theory that once a road had been put in good condition and debt paid off tolls should cease did not have a basis in reality, largely because of the impossibility – and inequity – of properly operating the 'statutory voluntary service' system of road maintenance. Consequently, the short-life Turnpike Acts were regularly continued by the innumerable 'extension' Acts, so that tolls and borrowing continued well into the nineteenth century. The general approach was that the loan moneys should be used to repair the road, and the tolls collected to administer the road and repay debt, but how this repayment was to be organized was not specified.

That provisions for repayment were not at first prescribed is surprising because the method of borrowing – perhaps because it assured the underlying security – was specified from the start and has continued so, with a growing number of alternatives, throughout the history of local government. Originally, as shown, it was by assigning/mortgaging the tolls or poor rate, and later also by annuities, bonds, stock, and so on, which also depended upon the assignment of revenues as security.

Apart from the minor borrowing activities of the charter boroughs, the first Poor Law borrowing has been shown to be in the Acts of the 1760s setting up the various incorporations. At that stage borrowing by these organizations was restricted only as to amount and rate of interest. No provision was made for periods of borrowing or for repayment. The assumption seems to have been that the loans would be repaid as quickly as possible subject to the availability of revenues from rates at not too unreasonable a level.

In 1771 the Westminster Act for paving purposes, as we have described, provided in spite of its glaring typographical error that the security for borrowing should be only five-sixths of the rate, while the remaining one-sixth should be set aside as a sinking fund. However, this prudent provision was somewhat spoiled by the addition of the words 'or used for other paving purposes', unless this can be regarded as a recognition in advance of its time of the propriety of using sinking funds for further capital works.

However, in the same year the substantial Act for poor relief functions in the City of Oxford provided for borrowing by the local authority both by the issue of mortgages and the sale of life annuities. Again no maturity period was specified for the mortgage borrowing; as to the life annuities, perhaps an average lifespan of thirty to forty years for the likely nominees may be conjectured which, if this is a reasonable assumption, would coincide with the periods later considered reasonable for borrowing for the erection of buildings such as workhouses. The annuities would thus have a built-in though variable amortization period, with capital repayment provision incorporated in the annual payments. Though no provision was made for amortization of mortgages, lenders on this instrument were entitled to repayment on giving twelve calendar months' notice – a lender's option. The implication of the Oxford Act is that repaid mortgages could be replaced within the original total sum authorized to be borrowed.

The first specific though halting provisions for organized amortization seem nevertheless to have been around the 1770s. There is certainly such a provision in the Act of 1771 for setting up a Poor Law incorporation for the Isle of Wight (which in 1776 had the abortive provision for a tontine). This Act called for amortization based on what appeared to be the common assumption at the time that the new workhouses, staffed by pauper labour, would produce a margin of profit. Therefore, the Act provided that one-half of the money 'to be saved out of the rates . . . by the profits of the work of the poor' should be retained by the treasurer to the incorporation and applied 'yearly and every year towards paying off and discharging such sums as shall be borrowed upon the credit of this Act until the whole of such monies shall be paid off and discharged'. The other half was to go in rate relief. This can hardly be called a guaranteed amortization provision, but it at least recognized the liability positively. Whether any profit ensued and how the debt was eventually redeemed is not known. There were certainly no such profits from workhouses in later years.

From 1770 the use of life annuities with their in-built though variable amortization provision became common. However, even such Acts as those already quoted for the provision of a workhouse and paving works in the

Liberty of the Tower of London (1774), which provided for self-redeeming life annuities, also provided for assignments (mortgages) without specific provision for the setting aside of funds for repayment. Nor did the Marylebone Act of 1775, which contained an early reference to borrowing by bonds, make provision for their repayment, although they could be 'rolled-over' if bonds at a cheaper rate became available – a 'borrower's option' again in modern terminology. Gilbert's Act (1782), with its narrow borrowing provisions, had a similar sanguine provision for repayment out of workhouse profits. However, the second amendment to Gilbert's Act of 1803 provided that poor rates could be lowered only if at least one-twentieth of debt was repaid each year.

The 1785 Act for Poor Law incorporation at Tunstead and Happing, in Norfolk, provided for borrowing on assignments for unspecified periods, but the draft mortgage concluded with the words that interest would be paid 'until the principal should be discharged' without saying how or when this would come about. As well as life annuities, term annuities were also permitted under this Act, which were the equivalent of fixed-period mortgages repayable by instalments. Also in 1785 an Act for various purposes in Richmond, Surrey, authorized borrowing by bonds and required that £500 should be repaid each year, selection being by lot.

Even by 1790 the provision for amortization, though taking shape, was still sketchy. The Manchester Poor Relief Act 1790 authorized borrowing by assignments of rate or life annuities. Under a side-heading, 'Payment of principal', the Act provided that the churchwardens should levy a yearly rate sufficient to maintain the poor, pay interest on money borrowed and meet the annual annuity payments and 'the payment and discharge of at least 5% of the principal sums borrowed on mortgage', the lenders to be repaid being selected by lot. The Gilbert's Act amendment mentioned above and this Act indicate that a twenty-year loan period was considered appropriate. Yet the Poor Relief Act 1819 actually specified a period of fifteen years for any borrowing, without further details of the amortization.

The beginning of organized overall central control of the borrowing function and the introduction of formal and general amortization provisions seems to have been the Poor Law Amendment Act 1834. Thereafter all borrowing and repayment of money for Poor Law purposes was subject to the consents and conditions of the Poor Law Commissioners. Initially the repayment period was restricted to ten years, but as promptly as 1836 this was extended to a twenty-year period (which complied with the PWLC lending arrangements from whom the Poor Law authorities were authorized to borrow). Repayment was to be by the single method of equal annual instalments of principal (the EIP method) and overall limits on borrowing were imposed. Thirty years later, in 1867, the amounts which could be borrowed were increased, and in 1869 the period was extended to thirty years, with the addition of the alternative method of repayment by equal instalments of interest and principal combined (the annuity method), again a development which fitted the PWLC arrangements. The thirty-year period was extended in 1871 to apply to existing older loans still on a twenty-year maximum, with power to introduce half-yearly instalments. Not until 1897 – after over sixty years of experience of the system – was the period extended to sixty years, with yearly or half-yearly instalments of either kind, and with the addition of the third method of repayment, that is, at maturity with the use of a 3 per cent accumulating sinking fund, as under the Local Loans Act 1875.

The development of arrangements for amortization were equally ponderous and even less systematic in the rest of local government. The Gaols Act 1823 specified repayment within fourteen years, extended in 1842 to thirty years, but repayment was confined to the sinking fund basis. As the Municipal Corporations Act 1835 made virtually no reference to borrowing, the first relevant Acts of general significance were the Companies and the Commissioners Clauses Acts of 1845 and 1847 with their generalized provisions.

In the Commissioners Clauses Act 1847 the period was to be whatever the commissioners chose to express in the mortgage deed, but if a period was in fact not stated, repayment could be demanded by the lender or effected by the borrower at any time after twelve months on six months' notice. In any event, an accumulating sinking fund for not more than twenty years was to apply, with investment in government securities. The somewhat broader Companies Clauses Act again left the period for insertion in the deed, and if this was not done, the twelve months option applied; but there was no mention of a maximum period or of the creation of a sinking fund, presumably because of the different concept of a company as compared with the quasi-local authority system of commissioners.

There was inconsistency in the various service Acts during the middle part of the century. For example, the Public Health Act 1848 specified a thirty-year period with a sinking fund and interim repayments selected by lot. The 1858 Public Health Act increased the period to fifty years with instalment or sinking fund repayments. At about the same time, the Municipal Corporations Mortgages Act of 1860 adopted thirty years and the sinking fund (maturity) period, whereas the curious and short-lived County Debentures Act 1873 left the period open but required repayment by equal annual instalments unless some other system was specified in any special Act in which the provisions might be incorporated.

Inconsistencies between the approaches adopted in the Local Loans Act and the Public Health Act, both of 1875, have already been examined; the amortization provisions were also inconsistent. The annuities allowed by the Local Loans Act were of course repaid by yearly instalments, but other loans were to be repaid by the sinking fund method, with selection by lot of early repayments. The Public Health Act was far more positive and progressive; a sixty-year period was authorized with repayment, although the borrowing was by mortgage, to be on either of the two instalment methods or from accumulated sinking funds invested in government securities. Similar inconsistencies of approach were to be found in the Acts covering the major reorganizations of the last years of the century. The

Municipal Corporations Act 1882 allowed the three methods of repayment, but adopted a maximum period of thirty years. The Local Government Act 1888 adopted a similar basis for counties. The Local Government Act 1894 allowed the new county districts to borrow 'in the like manner and subject to the like conditions' as under the Public Health Act, that is, with a sixty-year maximum.

Activities governed by the Municipal Corporations Act 1882 and the Local Government Act 1888 – largely provision of premises and land – were thus on a thirty-year basis, while those on the Public Health Act basis could have sixty years (although the full period would not necessarily be authorized by the sanctioning department). There were independent service Acts some of which used thirty years and others sixty, but where land was involved the government was anxious to encourage development, and even eighty years was authorized by statute, for example, under the Small Holdings and Allotments Act 1908 and the Housing Act 1925. As a result of these inconsistencies, police stations, for instance, had a thirty-year sanction period, while fire stations could be given up to sixty years.

When the conflicting amortization provisions are set against the assumed requirement that borrowings should be earmarked against sanctions, and when other service Acts introduced their own controls on borrowing periods, the confused and complex situation in the treasurers' Loans Offices can be imagined. And this situation lasted – except for local Act provisions – right through to 1933, and in some respects even beyond.

A further complication, until 1925, was the continued existence of different 'rates' which were to provide the underlying security in each authority. By the Rating and Valuation Act 1925 all rates (except water rate) were consolidated into a general rate. Until then, except under local Act provisions, the security for borrowing was the rate authorized for the service for which the capital asset was to be provided – the poor rate, the district rate, the borough rate and other minor provisions.

The attitude of the PWLC during this period has already been described. The commission was unhappy about the annuity method of repayment of their advances and preferred the EIP method. The PWLC have only recently accepted maturity repayment as part of their 'new look'. Their anxiety was to see substantial repayments of their debt being made from the start of the advance. They frowned on the use of sixty years and sought to encourage forty years, in effect, contrary to the attitude of the sanctioning departments.

In 1902 a parliamentary Select Committee on the problem of amortization provision (under the chairmanship of Sir John Grant Lawson) positively recommended that the thirty-year periods of the local government Acts should be extended to sixty years. It also recommended what is now standard practice, that in certain cases (revenue-producing works) the start of amortization might be deferred for a short period. The committee believed that the method of amortization, as well as the period sanctioned within the overall statutory period, should be decided by the sanctioning department, but this principle has never been adopted. The

curious recommendation was made that while the housing operations of
the Working Classes Dwellings Act 1890 should be given an overall loan
period of eighty years, this period should apply to land transactions under
the Act only if the instalment repayment system was used; the reverse
would have seemed to be the more logical approach in view of the
indestructible nature of the asset.

The variations in practice laid down in the Acts do not seem to have
been the result of deliberate policy, but rather of a lack of appreciation of
the techniques of loan management. The Commissioners Clauses Act 1847
and the Public Health Act 1875 provided for repayments during the course
of the sanction period, although any reborrowing under the Public Health
Act required further government sanction. Yet the Municipal Corporations
Act 1882 contained no provision for partial repayment and reborrowing,
which was taken to imply that the loans raised were to be for the full
sanction period – a system which was possible, particularly using
borrowing from the PWLC, but highly restrictive. Throughout the
consideration of borrowing seems to have been based on a failure to grasp
the essential difference between the period in which the outlay on a capital
scheme was to be amortized, and the periods for which money might be
borrowed from individual lenders and, if necessary, repaid and reborrowed
even several times during the life of the sanction. This confusion seems to
have been further confounded by the concept that the finance of a
particular capital expenditure by borrowing was a separate, 'one-off'
occasional exercise rather than simply an incident in a continuous capital
programme. This is rather like the early turnpike schemes, originally
envisaged as short-term projects but which ultimately became continuous
operations. Hence the attachment to the principle of earmarked loans,
never clearly expounded, and the complications of separation of sinking
funds thereby involved.

Although of lesser importance, the lack of a common form of mortgage
because of the specification of the form of mortgage in so many Acts,
added to the confusion. There appears also to have been a belief among
lenders in the early days (now completely reversed), that attachment of a
loan to a particular capital scheme gave added security. The result of all
this was that both local authorities and Whitehall recognized over a period
of time that common sense could be allowed to override the precise
statutory provisions, and in consequence a situation evolved in which
some but not all borrowings were 'pooled'.

A point which also needs to be remembered is that until the 1933 Act
lenders were not officially excused from the need to seek assurances that
money borrowed was with authority and that once borrowed it was
correctly used. This meant that lenders ought to have sought to know the
sanction under which each loan was raised before they parted with their
money.

There was, then, a lack of a systematic approach to the determination of
amortization periods and to methods of amortization; and the idea of
earmarking loans also persisted, despite the provision for 'roll-over' at the

desire of either borrower or lender. The implications of the fact that local authority borrowing had become a continuous, not a once-for-all process, and that loan management should be organized accordingly on that basis, was not effectively comprehended. Above all, there seems to have been a strange lack of understanding of the implications of the separate processes of borrowing on a 'turn-over' basis, with amortization against a long-term loan sanction period.

The solution, the climate for which was ripe from early in the present century (if not before), was fundamentally simple, all money borrowed for whatever period and on whatever basis and terms should have been pooled within each local authority. Advances from this pool of money to the services requiring it within each local authority should have been made as expenditure took place. The services should have made annual provision for repayment to the pool, from the revenue account, over the period required by law or practice, and such repayments while lying in the pool should have been used to make further advances as long as these were the subject of annual repayment provision as if they had been made from newly borrowed money. Similarly, interest due to lenders should have been pooled and averaged over borrowing accounts.

Such a system is automatically self-balancing. Services within each authority would only undertake expenditure of a capital nature after having been given central loan sanction. Borrowings by the authority through the pool and advanced to the service as expenditure took place would thus automatically be within the total of loans sanctioned. The re-use of annual repayments from borrowing accounts to the pool, for new capital expenditure in place of fresh borrowing, simply means that the total indebtedness of the authority stays within its loan sanctions. If at any stage fresh borrowing is required to repay earlier loans, this is simply the established 'roll-over' provision and in no way embarrasses the operation of the pool. As long as borrowing accounts make annual repayment provision within the authorization periods, no problem can arise, and repayments to lenders can be by either instalment system or at maturity. This of course is the simple philosophy of loans pooling and of the consolidated loans fund.

This is not simply the wisdom of hindsight; such a method was in fact instituted in a limited sense as early as 1869 and the mechanics of the processes involved fully understood and operative by the close of the nineteenth century. Yet consolidated loans funds proper did not become part of the general law until 1958 and, in a wider sense, 1972. During the last forty to fifty years of this 'century of progress' there had been widespread but by no means universal acceptance, both in local and central government, that earmarking was not called for and that unofficial loans pooling was acceptable. From the late 1920s a gradual adoption of CLF powers took place; but why was the simple idea of the CLF so long in gaining universal acceptance?

An approach to this uncomplicated mechanism for the pooling of loans is to be found in the Metropolitan Board of Works (Loans) Act 1869. The capital stock authorized to be issued under this Act was to be called the metropolitan consolidated stock and the various issues under these powers were to be merged in one common pool. Because it was so called, the fund into which this stock was channelled was naturally called the consolidated loans fund and was specified as being 'for the purpose of paying dividends on and redeeming the consolidated stock'. To this extent it pre-empted a name more applicable to the pooling of all types of loans, and in doing so led to Stock Regulations which frustrated full consolidation for many years. The moneys to be paid into this original CLF were capital receipts from the disposal of assets, 2 per cent of the total nominal amount of consolidated stock whether this had been cancelled or not (which surely implied a fifty-year amortization period), and such greater or lesser sum as the Treasury approved to pay dividends and redeem the stock in sixty years – a very peculiar series of provisions overall. Funds in hand were to be invested in government securities. Rather oddly, the key utilization of the fund of moneys – the financing of new capital expenditure – was not specified, being no doubt considered as self-evident. This Act also allowed the board to borrow by terminable annuities, and the word 'stock' was consequently to be construed to include such annuities. This meant that the annual annuity payments were to be passed through the CLF, but excused the annuity borrowings from being earmarked to particular expenditures. There were of course many further detailed provisions covering the transitional arrangements and special cases.

Subsequently the provisions of the London County Council (Finance Consolidation) Act 1912 relating to the CLF were in very similar terms, the emphasis still being on redemption of consolidated stock and the paying of dividends, but regulations to be prepared under the Act were to make provision for separate accounts 'in respect of income and capital'. Though stock could be issued on a sixty-year basis, annual contributions to amortize debt were still to be made within any lesser loan sanction period. The 2 per cent contribution requirement did not reappear.

The 1912 Act also made clear that any moneys in hand in the CLF could be applied to new-sanctioned capital expenditure, subject to the making of annual repayment provisions as though this money had been newly borrowed. The provisions for borrowing by annuities to be treated as stock for CLF purposes were repeated.

Meanwhile rather more comprehensive provisions had been made in the Glasgow Corporation Loans Act 1883. Under this Act the Glasgow Corporation loans fund was to be established the purpose of which was

for payment of all interest dividends and sinking funds established by or payable under the City Acts and this Act, and also of dividends on all Glasgow Corporation stock, and for redemption and extinction or purchase and extinction of all Glasgow stock, and also for repayment of the principal moneys borrowed and remaining unpaid, under the City Acts and this Act.

Unfortunately early operational details of this scheme are now lacking but the scheme in improved form has operated since then.

Leaving aside for the moment the general Stock Regulations of 1891, Edinburgh seems to have been the next in chronological sequence in the Edinburgh Corporation Stock Act 1894. The Edinburgh Corporation loans fund established in that Act was solely for the payment of dividends on corporation stock and for stock purchase and redemption. It did nevertheless spell out arrangements for averaging interest charges over the borrowing departments. However, it led to a further Act in 1897 to allow the use for capital purposes of 'any money standing to the credit of the Consolidated Loans Fund on Capital Account', provided that annual repayment provision was made just as for new borrowing – in other words, the key requirement of loans fund management and the re-use of sinking funds. A further Act in 1899 which provided for Edinburgh money bills also provided that 'all moneys borrowed for Corporation purposes by Mortgage, Bond, Annuity, Cash Credit, Simple Acknowledgment, and by Edinburgh Corporation Bills and Promissory Notes' were to have the same security as stock under the 1894 Act, and that the earlier Acts were to apply to such moneys 'insofar as the Loans Fund was concerned'. This was, to all intents and purposes, the first true and comprehensive consolidated loans fund, though in practice the earlier Glasgow fund may have been almost as comprehensive.

Because of the development by this date of local Act powers authorizing the issue of stock, and the advent of general powers for stock issue by counties in the 1888 Act and other authorities in the Public Health Act 1890, the Stock Regulations 1891 (SRO 1904/1891) had been passed. The reference in these regulations to 'consolidation of loans' is simply to some equating of existing borrowing periods. There is no specific mention of a consolidated loans (stock) fund, but provision was made for the establishment by each issuing authority of a 'dividends fund' and a 'redemption fund', which in effect served the same purpose as a consolidated stock fund; the amending regulations of 1897 were a retrograde step, in that they required separate dividend and redemption funds for each class of stock. Funds in hand were to be invested in government securities, until in 1901 further amending regulations empowered the re-use of stock sinking funds for other statutory borrowing powers. Modest powers for the re-use of sinking funds had been obtained by the Metropolitan Board of Works in 1881, 1884 and 1889. The first authority to obtain such powers for re-use of sinking funds outside of the metropolis was Birmingham in their Waterworks Act of 1892, in which the London powers were incorporated. In 1897 Leicester obtained fuller powers which became the model.

In 1898 St Helens Corporation was the first authority to obtain powers specifically to create a common sinking fund for mortgages and for the re-use of this money for new capital purposes. All the principles for the consolidation of stock and mortgages and the re-use of sinking funds had thus been conceded by the turn of the century under general Acts for stock and under local Acts for other forms of borrowing, but integration of the various principles was still lacking in English legislation. The City of Leeds in their General Powers Act 1901 attempted to establish a fully fledged consolidated loans fund but the Act included a clause which required separate accounts to be maintained within the redemption fund for each purpose for which money was raised and statutory borrowing power exercised. This appears to have invalidated the true operation of a consolidated fund. In a lecture to the Yorkshire Students Society of the Treasurers' Institute, in 1910, the then Assistant City Treasurer of Leeds (J. Mitchell) enlarged on the problems of such a restricted fund and also outlined the requirements of a complete CLF as called for in local government. Nevertheless, no progress was made until the early 1920s.

At that point R. A. Wetherall, the newly appointed Borough Treasurer of Swansea, gave a paper to the annual conference of the Treasurers' Institute under the title of 'A true consolidated loans fund'. This paper made no reference to a correspondence on the topic which had taken place a few months earlier in the *Financial Circular* (the journal of the institute), but Carson Roberts, a district auditor of great repute, in commenting on Wetherall's paper, in a submission almost as long as the paper itself, referred extensively and favourably to this correspondence.

This correspondence had begun with an article by W. H. Ashmole (the Swansea treasurer about to relinquish his post) in November 1922 on clauses obtained in a Swansea Act of that year which allowed the combination and re-use of sinking funds, a principle already well established. Robert Paton, the then Chamberlain of Edinburgh, wrote to point out that these clauses fell short of the full consolidation of loans funds in the form which had been operating in Edinburgh for many years; his comments were accompanied by a diagram of the operational details of a CLF and set out in a few brief lines what Paton called 'the attributes of a consolidated loans fund', which together with his diagram, gave a picture of this device virtually as it operates even today; these attributes were:

(1) that all corporation loans of whatever nature should be credited to one account;
(2) that this account should make advances to the various undertakings on which capital expenditure is being incurred;
(3) that there should be one security for all loans which should rank *pari passu* and that that security should be the whole property and assets as well as the rates, revenues and other income of the authority;
(4) that the rate of interest charged against the various undertakings or purposes to which advances have been made should be the average rate of interest paid on all the loans of the corporation treated as a whole.

Despite its failure to take notice of the exchange of letters in the *Financial Circular*, Wetherall's paper was a clear and robust advocacy of a CLF. Among other things, he doubted whether any treasurer of the time still believed that a separate sinking fund was required for each separate loan raised by a local authority, and that the amount of such sinking fund could be used only for the redemption of that loan.

Carson Roberts, as well as referring at length to Paton's earlier exemplification of the CLF (of which he said somewhat extravagantly 'nothing more lucid have I ever seen') claimed that for twenty-nine years, that is, presumably from about 1894, he had been 'engaged in preaching the advantages of loans pools', as a result of which many mortgage pools had been created and much sinking fund moneys freed. He added significantly: 'The Local Government Board of that day had full knowledge of this and raised no objections.' Wetherall did acknowledge in his paper that at that moment the Borough of Torquay was seeking parliamentary powers to set up a consolidated loans fund.

In the discussion the then Borough Treasurer of Torquay (E. C. Riding) explained that his authority already used a pooling scheme for stock and a separate pool for mortgages; their new power was to enable them to effect the combination of the two schemes. The discussion on Wetherall's paper brought out some of the doubts in some treasurers' minds the chief of which was about the equity of charging the annual average rate of the scheme to all borrowing accounts. Although Riding agreed that this was not a fundamental issue, the majority of the members at the conference clearly accepted the averaged interest system. Nevertheless, CLF schemes do provide that in special cases particular advances can be excluded from interest averaging and charged a prescribed rate. Over the long term there is no doubt that the preponderance of housing debt in the accounts of local authorities has meant that all other borrowing services have been influenced by the rates required for heavy housing borrowing. However, there is no evidence to show that by and large this has been either burdensome or otherwise over the period.

To anticipate, there was in 1948 some unrest among treasurers about the effect of the preponderance of housing borrowing, leading towards thoughts that housing capital finance should perhaps have its own pooling arrangements, but the Ministry of Health came out strongly in favour of the comprehensive character of loans pools in a statement which also throws doubt on the earlier assumed legal need for the earmarking of loans. The words are worth quoting (*Local Government Finance*, May 1948):

The matter should be regarded as primarily a matter of administrative convenience rather than of law; and there is no question but that the substitution of loans pooling for the antiquated system of loans earmarked to services is an out-standing advance which has benefited local government finance and the services to be financed, with housing in the forefront. Any proposal to abandon loans pooling now would be retrograde.

It would also be short-sighted. There have been occasions in the past when housing have been borrowers on a rising market, and there may

well be such occasions again. It would be ill-advised, bearing that in
mind, to seek the abandonment of pooling because the borrowing rate
is a little lower than the pool rate. It will not be overlooked that the
market rate has ceased to fall, and some have said that it must rise
appreciably above that now being charged by the PWLB. Apart from
the loss in local government finance generally which would result if
pooling were abandoned, it may well be in the interests of housing
that it should be retained.

This was clearly at a time when borrowing rates for housing were
currently lower than general pool averages; in recent years the situation
has been very much reversed. Are the Ministry still quite so convinced about
the desirability of loans pools? They have not yet made the CLF
compulsory for all borrowing in England and Wales.

Although Torquay was the first of the English authorities to obtain these
powers, the borough did not bring a CLF into operation until some years
later; similarly, Macclesfield which also obtained the power to set up a
CLF in 1923 did not do so until 1934. Manchester and Leeds obtained the
statutory authority in 1924, and Leeds was the first authority actually to
bring a scheme to fruition in 1927; Manchester did not bring its scheme
into effect until 1934/5. Swansea, despite Wetherall's advocacy, did not
take the necessary parliamentary powers until as late as 1947, under the
treasurership of H. K. Greaves. However, the City of Dundee obtained
powers in 1926, publishing its first accounts for the operation of a CLF for
the (Scottish) financial year ended May 1928. There was no form of loans
pooling before this event in Dundee.

The general enthusiasm was such that in 1929 the then Institute of
Municipal Treasurers and Accountants published a model scheme for a
CLF in full detail. This has been slightly revised, in 1953, 1958 and 1974,
to accommodate changes in the law. The original model scheme was
sufficiently elastic to fit variations in the existing debt structures of local
authorities, but basically it followed and has continued to follow the
simple outline established from the first and described above.

The reasons for the delay in bringing CLF powers into operation may
well have been that many authorities had by that time unofficially adopted
loans pooling for all borrowing except by stock (not widely used by
smaller authorities) or from the PWLC (in any event, on an annuity system
of repayment). This is certainly the explanation given by those involved at
the time for the late acquisition of CLF powers by Swansea, from which
authority the movement had been given so great an impetus. This is also
the explanation for the procrastination in Manchester during 1924–34; in
that city a consolidated stock account and a mortgage loan pool had been
in operation for many years.

In 1930 an influential document, the Boroughs and Metropolitan
Boroughs Accounts Regulations (SRO 1930/30), made under the District
Audit Act 1879, specified in its schedule 2 a scheme for the operation of
loans pooling, although there was no direct statutory authority for this

principle. In his *Local Administration – Finance and Accounts* (1930) Carson Roberts repeated his support of the common sense of pooling, but while admitting that local authorities issuing stock needed a local Act clause before stock redemption money could be amalgamated with other funds, he wrote: 'the loan pooling system has now been fully recognised by Parliament and the Ministry of Health and its advantages are open in no small measure to local authorities, large as well as small without requiring specific statutory powers.' As there had in fact been no alteration of the law, except the issue of the Account Regulations in 1930, peculiarly enough simply as the outcome of district audit legislation of many years before, this seems to justify the conclusion that pooling of some sort had always been an acceptable system within the law.

Why in the light of these official developments the situation was not incorporated in the Local Government Act 1933 is difficult to understand. The reason may be that there was still some uneasiness in certain parts of central government about the re-use of sinking funds for new capital purposes. Reference has already been made to the powers obtained by St Helens Corporation in 1898 for the use of sinking funds set aside for mortgage repayments for new capital purposes, and the Select Committee of the House of Commons in its report in 1909 (Cmd 193) had approved the controlled use of sinking funds (including loans funds and redemption funds) for capital purposes. Yet according to Drummond and Marshall in *Consolidated Loans Funds of Local Authorities* the issue of the 1929 IMTA model CLF, prepared in consultation with the officers of the Ministry of Health, had been delayed because of the qualms of the chairman of the ways and means committee about the soundness of a policy of the re-use of sinking funds.

Until 1945 there was no statutory provision for PWLC advances to be carried to a loans pool, but as PWLC loans were repayable by annual instalments this was not a serious impediment. However, when under the Local Authority Loans Act 1945 local authorities were required to take practically the whole of their borrowing from the commission, the Act had perforce to allow the inclusion of PWLC transactions in consolidated loans funds and general loans pools. The only borrowings consistently excluded from consolidation were the housing bonds under the 1919 Act and later consolidations. Neither did this create much of a problem because the proceeds of these bonds were specifically for a single purpose and the interest rate, at least for a time, was determined by the Ministry of Health which had a considerable stake in the financing of this work.

The first general statutory provision on loans funds appeared in the Local Government (Scotland) Act 1947; this allowed a county or a town council in Scotland to establish a 'loans fund' applicable to all money borrowed. Complete operational details of such a fund were set out in schedule 8 of the Act. The use of averaged interest rates was prescribed. The Institute of Municipal Treasurers and Accountants (IMTA) published in 1960 a report on loans pooling (by W. W. Ayling and J. A. Neale), but this was preceded by an interim report in 1957, urging the granting to

English local authorities of similar powers to those given to Scotland ten years earlier. By this time some ninety authorities had obtained local Act powers. In the 1958 Local Government Act the IMTA recommendation was acted upon. The power was given primarily to counties and county boroughs, but it was also to be available to any county district with a population of 60,000 and to other county districts and metropolitan boroughs but then only with the consent of the Ministry; the terms of this statutory power were that:

> the council of any county or county borough may in accordance with a scheme made by the council and approved by the Minister establish and operate a consolidated loans fund for defraying any expenditure which the council is authorised . . . to meet out of moneys borrowed by the council and for the repayment and redemption of debt.

The provisions of this permissive Act were in broad terms and did not spell out the details as in the Scottish legislation. This difference in practice has been maintained. The final step was in the Local Government Act 1972, where a general power in similar words was given for the establishment of such funds without further Ministerial consent even for the smaller authorities.

The broad generalization of this provision was disturbed in the Local Authority (Stocks and Bonds) Regulations (already examined) which said (para. 15) that: 'A local authority who issues stock or bonds *shall* make a scheme in accordance with paragraph 15 of Schedule 13.' This insistence on a loans pooling scheme for only these classes of security undoubtedly stems from the establishment of this principle for stock issues through the long-standing Stock Regulations. The necessity for a loans fund is not included in the Mortgages Regulations, and of course there are no regulations relating to 'temporary' loans or bills. Nevertheless, loans pooling is now the general practice.

The consolidated loans fund in Scotland, now embodied in the Scottish 1975 Act, is not permissive and is related specifically to 'all money borrowed by the local authority and the redemption and repayment thereof and the payment of interest and dividends thereon'. Detailed provisions are then spelled out.

Some form of loans pooling, either officially or unofficially, was inevitable, at least from the point at which the local authorities were thrown back on the market after their brief spell under the PWLC. Loans pooling was particularly unavoidable to an authority which had any large volume of short, rapidly circulating debt to handle. Fundamentally what loans pooling achieved was a final severance of the uneasy link between borrowing and repayment from and to the public on the one hand, and amortization of advances by spending services of the local authority on the other. The loans fund constituted thenceforward the interface between these two components of capital finance. Borrowing from the public could thereafter be by any method and for any period and subject to repayment by either instalment method or at maturity; discounted money bills were as simply absorbed as long-range stock issues. The one essential on the other side of the coin was that the borrowing services, that is, the services to whom advances of capital funds had been made from the accumulated funds of the loans pool, should make annual repayments on the basis of the predetermined sanction periods and should bear average annual charges on their outstanding advances arising from all the interest paid by the fund, and a similarly averaged management charge.

There remains one decision on amortization policy – repayments must be annual, or semi-annual, and to that extent they are on an annuity basis, but the local authority may choose the arithmetical base on which it spreads these payments over the sanction period, that is, whether it adopts the EIP method or the 'true' annuity method. The simple fact is that in setting aside, say, £10,000 over ten years, any variation of 'spread' of annual amounts is possible according to the arithmetical assumptions made. The annexed tables from Johnson's *Loans of Local Authorities* (1925) show that the issue is simply whether on a ten-year loan of £10,000 the authority sets this aside in ten equal instalments of £1,000, or ten varying instalments starting at £833 and ending at £1,186, the total still of course arriving at £10,000, but the starting and finishing points depending on what 'assumed' rate of interest the fund is based.

Tables 23.1–23.3 show the comparative costs of loans repaid on the instalment (EIP) and 'annuity' methods. Figure 23.1 on page 347 shows the operation of a consolidated loans fund in simple terms, but is not fundamentally different from that produced by Robert Paton in 1922.

Table 23.1 *Annual Instalments of Principal and Interest Payable on a Loan of £10,000 at 4 Per Cent Interest Repayable in 10 Years on the Instalment System*

Year	Instalment of principal (£)	Amount of interest (£)	Total annual payment (£)
1	1,000	400	1,400
2	1,000	360	1,360
3	1,000	320	1,320
4	1,000	280	1,280
5	1,000	240	1,240
6	1,000	200	1,200
7	1,000	160	1,160
8	1,000	120	1,120
9	1,000	80	1,080
10	1,000	40	1,040
	£10,000	£2,200	£12,200

Source: J. R. Johnson, *Loans of Local Authorities* (London: Knight, 1925).

Table 23.2 *Annual Instalments of Principal and Interest Payable on a Loan of £10,000 at 4 Per Cent Interest Repayable in 10 Years on the Annuity System*

Year	Instalment of principal (£)	Amount of interest (£)	Total annual payment (£)
1	833	400	1,233
2	866	367	1,233
3	901	332	1,233
4	937	296	1,233
5	974	259	1,233
6	1,013	219	1,233
7	1,054	179	1,233
8	1,096	137	1,233
9	1,140	93	1,233
10	1,186	47	1,233
	£10,000	£2,329	£12,330

Source: As Table 23.1.

Table 23.3 *Repayment of a Loan of £10,000 over Periods of 30, 40 and 50 Years by (a) the Instalment System and (b) the Annuity System at 4 Per Cent Interest by Annual Payments*

Period	Method	First payment (£)	Last payment (£)	Total payment (£)
30 years	instalment	733	347	16,200
	annuity	578	578	17,349
40 years	instalment	650	260	18,200
	annuity	505	505	20,209
50 years	instalment	600	208	20,200
	annuity	465	465	23,275

Source: As Table 23.1.

RECENT DEVELOPMENTS IN CENTRAL CONTROL OF CAPITAL EXPENDITURE

Although methods of local authority borrowing have in recent years been made a great deal more coherent, and the management of debt has been thoroughly rationalized by the general adoption of the consolidated loans fund, government control of capital expenditure, though taking a different form, cannot be said to have been moderated. Detailed control has been partially relaxed, but broad overall control has been intensified in the name of the national economic interest. Whitehall has not so much relaxed as shifted its grip. Indeed the law continues to require it – in England and Wales 'a local authority . . . may borrow money for any . . . purpose or class of purpose approved . . . by the Secretary of State' (1972 Act, schedule 13). The implication of this is certainly that they may not borrow for any purpose(s)

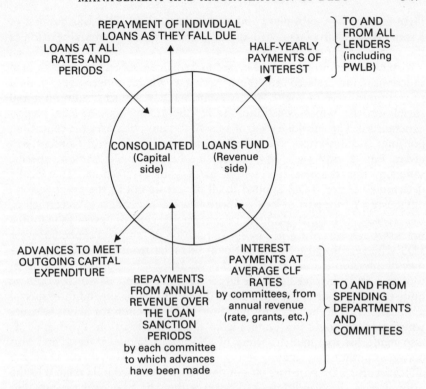

Figure 23.1   *The operations of a consolidated loans fund.*

Source: Sir Harry Page, *Money Services for Local Authorities*, 3rd edn (London: Butler Till, 1982).

not so approved. The Scottish law is even more dogmatic: 'It shall not be lawful for a local authority to incur any liability to meet capital expenses except with the consent of the Secretary of State' (1973 Act, section 94(i)). Until 1970 control by individual loan sanctions as to amounts and loan periods continued for all expenditure of a capital nature which was to be borne initially from borrowed money. Such expenditure when met from a revenue or capital fund did not require central sanction.

This detailed control was certainly considered onerous by local authorities, particularly when central departments often concerned them-selves not merely with the financial soundness of schemes, but used their sanctioning powers to control quite technical and often minor detail as well as the social implications of proposals. After many years of agitation by the local authorities for greater freedom of choice, a scheme was introduced by Ministry of Environment Circular 2/1970 on the subject of 'Capital programmes', which went a limited way towards freeing local authorities from detailed supervision of capital schemes, though still within overall controls of expenditure. Capital works were divided into three sectors: key, subsidiary and locally determined. This was the first of a series of such circulars issued annually until a further material revision of the system of control in 1981.

Capital expenditure in the key sector remained subject to specific loan sanctions, and related to those services where longer-term annual programmes were in vogue, in any event, namely, housing, education and social services, which constituted by far the greater part of local capital expenditure. The subsidiary sector related to land purchases for education, housing, social services and transport, to which a General Consent was given, but as any such land could not be developed without specific sanction, this did not represent a great gain in freedom. The locally determined sector (LDS) applied to all proposals not in the other sectors, obviously a minor part of local authority capital expenditure. Nevertheless, this represented some detailed relaxation of control, even though the breakthrough was restrained by the imposition of limits on expenditure for LDS schemes. Because of the national financial troubles of the time, the overall allocations were modest, although as most authorities would from time to time be involved in some larger scheme the cost of which would be quite out of proportion to their normal annual capital expenditure, special applications could be made to the Ministry for sanction for major schemes which feasibly could not be met from the LDS allocation. Provision was also made for marginal transfers of allocations between years, and also between authorities, mainly on a county basis. The amount of the allocation for LDS purposes was initially based on a formula related to the average capital expenditure on services within the LDS over the previous three years, with a weighting for expenditure in relation to population and developments in the key sector area which would be likely to have repercussions on the LDS. After a few years (from 1975/6), the formula was abandoned and replaced by a negotiated allocation of a centrally determined overall sum. The system was reviewed and somewhat broadened in Circular 66/1976, which reiterated that the basic purpose of the control of borrowing which the government exercised was to regulate public sector demand in the national interest. A far more logical system was introduced in 1981. Prior to that, the government had finally conceded in the Green Paper on Local Government Finance (Cmnd 6813), in 1977, that:

The Government believe that local authorities should be freer to determine their own priorities for capital expenditure within general policy guide-lines laid down by central government. The project-by-project controls exercised under the present system are unnecessarily detailed.

Amazingly this was almost precisely the argument put to the central departments by local negotiators for relaxation of controls in the 1963 White Paper discussions.

The fundamental change, in 1981, was introduced in part viii of the

Local Government, Planning and Land Act 1980. The new arrangements were on a broader basis, though complex in detail. They exhibited a deadly logic in their grasp, not as in the past on local authority expenditure to be financed from borrowed money, but on all local authority expenditure deemed to be 'of a capital nature' whether or not financed by borrowing. They did not therefore merely control borrowing, but all capital investment. The new system also adopted the principle of cash control within each financial year, in contrast to earlier systems under which, once a sanction was given, expenditure was not confined to the year of sanction. The institution of this scheme required not only a lengthy provision in the Act, but Prescribed Expenditure Regulations (SI 1981/348) and a lengthy circular (Department of the Environment, 14/1981).

Each year all local authorities are to be given an expenditure allocation for capital works under five heads: housing, education, transport, personal social services and other services, but once given, these allocations may be aggregated and used for almost any capital purpose; the block allocations are apparently given only for 'monitoring' purposes – much the same underlying philosophy as that appearing in the calculation of the block revenue grant pools. Allocations must be used within the year, with provision for slight overlap, any serious overlap being charged against the following year's allocation. The allocation is set against all expenditure of a capital nature, with the exception of minor items, whether financed from borrowed money, capital funds, or direct from revenue or capital receipts. In addition, profits from trading undertakings may be used for capital purposes, but restraints are placed upon the growing practice among local authorities of financing capital works and equipment by leasing, depending upon whether the ultimate possession of the items pass or do not pass to the authority.

The scheme is too recent and too complex to permit an assessment of its success at this point. Undoubtedly it represents a logical development, if overall control of local authority investment is needed in the national economic interest and as seems difficult to deny. Certainly, inconvenient though it may be for local authorities, if there is to be effective control of investment on a year-to-year basis, then cash control rather than approval by sanction of expenditure which may be incurred at some indefinite date is reasonable. Within this type of control, and subject to 'yard-stick' limitations on various services (for example, housing costs), local authorities are for the first time left to determine their own priorities. A great deal will depend on how local authorities are able to cope with what they feel to be their needs within the overall totals allocated; much more systematic control of work flow will be essential.

One interesting and obvious provision in both the 1970 and 1981 schemes was that at last they included a schedule of specified maximum loan sanction periods, varying from ten years for minor items of machinery, through twenty years for plant and more enduring items of machinery to forty years for special building works and sixty years for land, house-building and other major long-term constructional schemes.

CONCLUSIONS ON THE MANAGEMENT AND AMORTIZATION OF DEBT   Two
questions immediately present themselves: why was the transition from
earmarking to pooling so long in the making? Indeed why was earmarking
ever resorted to in the first place? The likely explanation for the adoption
of earmarking seems to be that early loans were taken up for single,
isolated projects such as a turnpike road, a workhouse, or a scheme
of street improvement. Hence the natural attachment of provision for
repayment to the project and its loan, the whole being seen as an 'entity'.
This conception of the scheme, its finance and repayment, did not
essentially necessitate lendings for the whole of the life/amortization period
of the asset (though many loans, particularly where the PWLC was
involved, were for the full period); loans could be repaid and renewed,
within the sanction period, while remaining conceptually part of the self-
contained initial project. Consequently, when multiple projects overlapping
in time came about, the 'separate entity' concept seems to have clung to
each project. In due course there were Acts aplenty requiring the setting up
and investment of sinking funds such as the Commissioners Clauses Act
1847, but examined closely, these are not seen to require literal
segregation of the sinking funds and their investment, one project from
another. Project-by-project loan sanctioning may have encouraged the
'segregation' line of thought. Certainly, from the start (and still today) one
of the great assurances to lenders to local government is the legal
requirement that specific annual amortization provisions must be made for
each project financed by borrowing, but this does not imply that each will
be handled separately. Even the Local Loans Act 1875, although it speaks
of each loan expenditure having a sinking fund, does not specify that each
sinking fund is to be treated as a separate entity. All that is required by
such Acts is equally, *mutatis mutandis*, performed under a pooling system.
Nor is the Public Health Act 1875 any more insistent on the separate
maintenance of sinking funds.

In other words, the attachment to segregation seems to have stemmed
from an origin in single projects. Local authority capital investment only
gradually became a continuous process, and when it did there was a failure
to recognize the full implications of the development. Was this a lack of
perception on the part of local treasurers? Possibly so, but the government
attitude was ambiguous on the issue, especially about the re-use of sinking
funds.

On the one hand, progressively from 1866 Whitehall allowed local
authorities to take local Act powers to consolidate stock and other types of
borrowing, and to re-use sinking funds, and themselves included pooling
in Stock Regulations and (much later) in the Accounts Regulations. They
co-operated in the preparation of a model CLF. On the other hand, they
did not take statutory opportunities to encourage general funding or to
dispel the idea that separation of sinking funds was required either at an
early stage in the Acts of 1875 and even fifty years later in the Local
Government Act 1933. Only in 1972 (though earlier in Scotland) was the
CLF given full official blessing, still with the reservation in England and

Wales that it was only essential for stocks and bonds. The right to re-use sinking funds was never categorically spelled out. Scores – even hundreds – of local Act provisions could have been avoided, if the proper lead had been given.

However, this vacillation and these puzzling delays are things of the past. The PWLC is now wholly rationalized and tuned to rapid and efficient administration; the full flowering of the CLF is to be observed, with government controls confined to overall limits – though on a cash basis and applied to all capital outlay, not merely to capital financed by borrowing. Maximum loan sanction periods have been stabilized on the one side, and borrowing periods controlled on the other, by the limitations on 'short' money and the requirements of a minimum average seven-year maturity on annual borrowings; and of course the flexibility of the borrowing portfolio is modified by the limits on the amounts of borrowing by the negotiable systems of money bills and negotiable bonds and strict surveillance of the terms of stock issues. The government's control of borrowing methods still has its roots in the past and leaves something to be desired and that key-stone of local authority borrowing, the necessity for annual provision for amortization, may be less sound than is generally thought. Both of these issues will be examined in Part 4 of this book.

PART FOUR

Analysis and Conclusions

Chapter 24

BASIC PRINCIPLES

In the light of the examination of the origins and evolution of local authority borrowing in this book, now brought to a conclusion, the answers to a number of questions which originally appeared difficult if not intractable seem relatively simple, at least in their practical and pragmatic application to local government. Equally seen against this historical background, the framework of a rational system for the future of local authority borrowing (assuming there is to be a future) is virtually self-evident, without the need for any substantial heart-searching.

There are two motives for the distinction of capital from revenue expenditure in local government (compared with central government expenditure where the two are not normally separated). The first is the professional reason, that the books of account should show separately the expenditure which is not attributable to a single accounting period (without going into the problem of the feasibility of the application in local government of the principles of current cost accounting). The second is the financial motive, that only capital expenditure may be legally met initially from borrowed money, subject to annual amortization (except for a degree of short-term borrowing for revenue cash-flow purposes, to be discharged within the year). These two motives are linked; expenditure may still be of a capital nature and so treated in the accounts, even though financed from revenue. However, the reverse of this is not permitted; expenditure of a revenue character may not except within the same year be financed from borrowed money. This important rule, that day-to-day ongoing current expenditure must be met from current income, is a bulwark of the system.

There is no statutory definition of capital expenditure in local government. Expenditure which is deemed to be of a capital nature is that on the provision of assets which are required for the operation of a service and which have a 'duration-in-use' extending beyond the year in which they are acquired, so that the cost may in equity be shared by the changing corpus of ratepayers who 'benefit' from them. This is by no means a completely objective definition and there are wide variations in practice. A definition put forward by the Treasurers' Institute in 1973 ('Form of published accounts of local authorities') suggested as capital expenditure: 'All expenditure for which the local authority concerned could reasonably expect to obtain a loan sanction, regardless of the way in which it is actually financed.'

The Accountancy Panel of the Treasurers' Institute (*Financial Informa-tion Service*, vol. 6.1.05) currently puts the point in the following terms, but in reference to the accountancy treatment of capital outlay:

> Any outlay which is of value to the authority in the provision of its services beyond the end of the year of account should be recorded as a capital asset. The following schedule of classes of expenditure would form the major components of capital expenditure – Acquisition of land and existing buildings; construction or improvement of buildings and civil engineering works; acquisition, renewal or replacement of vehicles, vessels, major plant, furniture and equipment and similar items ... These examples are not exhaustive and there will be other items within the definition. There will be occasions when the appropriate category for an item of expenditure is far from obvious. An example may be expenditure on an existing asset which comprises both a repair and an improvement element. The Institute of Chartered Accountants has recommended that an asset has been improved if its efficiency, earning or production power has been increased, although other accountancy bodies appear to have left this problem to individual interpretation.

This more detailed definition is close to but not quite the same as that given for 'prescribed expenditure' regulations under the new capital controls as introduced in the Local Government, Planning and Land Act 1980. One variation is of interest. This relates to housing expenditure where the definition adds the repair or maintenance of land and dwelling houses, but hedges this inclusion with the words 'to the extent that the expenditure is defrayed by borrowing'. The possibilities that borrowing might be authorized for repairs and maintenance is an outcome of the special nature of the housing revenue account. The Act introduced a further change in the nature of the control which is of considerable significance. This was that central government approval of asset creation was extended to all expenditure of a capital nature, whether or not power to borrow was sought, and was related to annual cash disbursements.

In practice, despite the impossibility of achieving a definition of capital expenditure in precise terms, difficulties are not encountered or at least they have not been encountered so far before the introduction of the cash limits, whether or not the expenditure is financed from borrowings. In local government the simple statement is that the capital expenditure which may be financed by borrowing and amortized over an agreed period of time is that expenditure which the Secretary of State declares to be so, against the background of a general understanding of extended duration of use.

This book has not been concerned with the forces which create the capital moneys – the 'loanable funds' – which local authorities seek to borrow, a matter which economists debate at length; nor with philo-sophical speculation about the nature of interest. Today even the ancient theory that saving is the deferment of consumption is looked upon with suspicion. The simple classical theory that the factors of production are land, labour, capital and business enterprise, for which the respective rewards are rent, wages, interest and profit, may suffice for this purpose, although even Adam Smith was inconclusive about the distinction between interest and profit.

The approaches of the economists to interest naturally vary from the simple to the highly sophisticated; while one economist considered that 'Interest is a price determined by supply and demand; interest is the price of money', Keynes preferred to regard interest as 'the return for parting with liquidity'. Whether or not these declarations are as far apart as they may at first seem the simpler approach will certainly appeal to the municipal treasurer.

However, the fact is that loanable funds are available to local authorities. In local authority experience, while these were once produced substantially from the local market of small savers, since the Second World War the amounts needed are so large, and the alternatives available to the small lender so attractive, that the local authorities must now rely, leaving aside the Public Works Loan Commission (PWLC), on the major institutions – the banks, insurance companies, pension funds, building societies and other 'wholesale' lenders in the money markets. The Act of Elizabeth of 1571, 'agaynst Usurie', permitting (for the second time round) a maximum of 'tenne poundes for the hundred for one yere . . . for the lone and forbearing of money' (the 'deferment' theory), is a sufficient indication to the municipal treasurer as to why he is paying for the use of someone else's money, whether these funds have arisen as a surplus or are created by the active deferment of current consumption in favour of equally immediate consumption (by a local authority), but with a longer-term objective.

The justification for the earliest local authority borrowing was slightly ambiguous: 'Forasmuch as the money so to be collected . . . by the said Toll will not at present raise such a stock or sum of money as may be sufficient for the speedy repairing of the said premises [road].' If by this was meant that tolls would have to be collected for several years before sufficient money would have been available to finance the roadworks, then that would have been self-evident; the underlying motive for borrowing should be more properly understood as the realization that there could be no grounds for collecting tolls in the first place, until the state of the road justified them. There could then be no argument but that the work should be carried out expeditiously from borrowed funds, which could be repaid by the toll which could then be justified. If because of this order of events those using the road had also to bear the burden of interest, they were clearly compensating the lenders for forbearance of the use of their money and its utilization in a social context. Despite the burden which interest places on projects financed by borrowing, this is still the most obvious justification for the financing of longer-term projects by borrowed money – that is, that income cannot be expected to accrue until the asset comes into use. This justification is as sound today for the borrowing of money for municipal housing or a municipal airport as it was three centuries ago for toll-roads. If there is a principle to be observed here, it is that where there is direct benefit received over a period of time those deriving the benefit should finance it, and all activities of a trading nature (using the term to include such subjects as town development schemes and the creation of trading estates) would come under this rule. These may be considered as 'self-financing' activities and are reflected in the provision that amortization payments may be deferred for an initial period until earnings commence.

The second reason justifying finance by borrowing that emerges from early legislation was simply the avoidance of an excessive rate charge (but this argument was not stretched to cover annually recurring expenditure). This principle again was not stated categorically, but it is implied in, for example, the 1756 Act relating to the relief of the poor at Colneis and Carlford, in Suffolk. In this Act a limit was placed on the amount which might be levied for Poor Law purposes (by relation to the level of earlier poor rates). Such rating limits could not be observed if non-recurring capital expenditure was to fall on the rate in the year in which it occurred, so that borrowing became inevitable. As an approach to this principle the earlier Act at Bristol (1695) had not sanctioned borrowing, but it had required that the cost of providing the workhouse should be spread over three years or more, to minimize the annual cost. Later direct references were made to the need to avoid excessive rate levies in the early years of provision. Early in the eighteenth century also, particularly for county purposes, borrowing was considered proper, if there were 'inadequate surpluses' in the county stock, and the rate authorized to be levied annually would be insufficient for the purpose. The need to avoid a heavy initial rate charge is seen in the County Buildings Act 1826, 'when it shall appear that the [cost of building the shire hall] shall exceed one half of the amount of the ordinary annual assessment' then borrowing might be resorted to.

The third stage in the recognition of borrowing – as exemplified in the Public Health Act 1875 – was that instead of putting forward a reason to justify borrowing, the Act set out the condition on which resort might be had to borrowing – that is, that the expenditure was approved as being suitable for this purpose by the central authority. This is the current philosophy, the concept of borrowing is wholly accepted and no longer needs to be excused; what needs approval is the types of expenditure to which it may be applied.

The second and third references described above to the propriety of borrowing involved a general acceptance of the accumulation of debt by local authorities. The question is, was this assumption a proper one? Both central and local government accepted the feasibility of pushing costs on to future generations with some enthusiasm, as is indicated by the increasing length of loan sanction periods in the statutes and the tendency of local authorities to adopt the annuity method of amortization (rather than the EIP method) which maximized the deferred proportion of total cost. Only the PWLC struck a cautionary note in requiring repayment of debt on an annual basis, preferably by the EIP method, and in urging (without success) that loans should not necessarily be sought for the full loan sanction period available.

The other extreme in capital finance would of course have been a general policy of 'pay-as-you-go' (PAYG). I. G. Gibbon has already been quoted as saying that the widespread use of this policy, however theoretically sound, was impractical. This was almost certainly true at the time of the rapid development of local government from about 1870 to the First World War; there is, for example, no way in which it could have been applied to housing. On the other hand, if the 'continuous development' theory of local government had been accepted, the PAYG policy can be seen as the prudent course for general services. Today when local government is in a contracting rather than expanding phase (and heavily influenced by high inflation), what is the proper course? Although local authorities are on the whole in a muted phase most services are of an age when a steady programme of renewal and replacement, at probably materially improved standards, is inevitable. Even the first municipal housing is now sixty years old. However, what now seems certain is that local government cannot afford to renew its major assets every forty or even sixty years, and that need for improved standards apart, properly maintained assets do not need such 'frequent' replacement. The time does seem reasonably ripe for some reappraisal of an automatic capital borrowing policy.

The argument has been offered above that borrowing and reborrowing for 'self-financing', semi-trading activities is acceptable, and indeed proper. If this case is accepted, then certainly the bulk of present debt is accounted for. A decision needs to be made as to whether local authorities should be influenced by inflation in determining their borrowing policies, buying at today's pound value and repaying in depreciated pounds. While this might well suit a house-owner, acquiring one major asset in a long period of years, on balance it does not seem to be a suitable policy for a 'continuing' local authority. On the other hand, local authority debt is a fact of life, so that a transition from borrowing to not-borrowing cannot be made instantaneously and without effort. The compromise for the non-self-financing activities seems to be a combination of methods: the use of a capital purposes rate (CPR) in conjunction with a fully operating capital fund, and a prudent policy towards loan sanction periods and the system of amortization.

There is an obvious practical case to be made for carrying minor items of a capital nature on revenue account to the extent of some equated annual amount. This policy would automatically embrace 'programmed capital' in the shape of such items as police and fire vehicles, public cleansing equipment, office equipment, and the like, but it can also be contemplated for any programmed development such as the building of a series of old people's homes, day nurseries, public conveniences and other items of modest capital outlay and longer-term development of this kind.

By contrast, a CPR is not suitable for 'one-off' projects such as an occasional swimming-bath, public library, or town hall. The policy is more easily adopted by larger authorities, so that recent reorganizations which have abolished the really small local authorities make general use of a somewhat heroic approach to capital finance easier.

The equation of capital burden each year in this way can be materially assisted by the use of a fully operative capital fund, that is, a fund which involves annual repayment and an interest charge. These two devices in combination can go a good way towards providing a buffer against violent fluctuations in annual capital outlay. The building up of a capital fund in this way and the use of a capital purposes rate represent the opposite policy to using maximum loan sanction periods and slow methods of amortization. However, as there are no grounds for a belief that the financial affairs of local authorities will ease for the next generation, and as active expansion is not at present the policy, today there are strong grounds for adopting a very prudent approach to borrowing. When borrowing does take place, the short amortization periods and the EIP method of discharge seem to be indicated.

Borrowing, with the relatively modest annual charges which result – the longer the period, the more modest the annual burden – can be a deceitfully easy policy for elected representatives concerned with showing the maximum public impact of their policies, with minimum annual financial repercussions. Any policy which can persuade councillors to take a realistic view of what they are doing, and to shun the discounting of the future, is likely in the long run to make for more responsible and financially sounder local government. Apart from the old adage that the capital expenditure of today is the revenue expenditure of tomorrow (in general running costs), the cumulative debt effects of a multiplicity of modest-seeming capital activities is not readily acknowledged by councillors with ambitions for social development not backed by financial awareness. If it were practicable, there are grounds for the belief that capital expenditure in a 'continuing' local authority should not be undertaken unless it can be borne from current sums available. This is not practicable with the occasional major development, nor in services such as housing, but as such major services are excluded from this treatment there is all the more a case for a firm policy of financing the lesser schemes on the basis of 'pay-as-you-go' or do without.

The GLC policy of borrowing in future only for housing purposes has already been described (see p. 320). Rugby is another authority which has achieved this status and, no doubt, there are others who are either at or near this point. Perhaps it is simply the prudent treasurer's view, but there seem to be grounds for the belief that if and when local government emerges from its present crisis and period of restraint, both in general and financial policies, the transition of most authorities to a basis that their debt should be related only to 'self-financing' activities, particularly housing, would make them more fitted to approach the reconstruction and development which might then be appropriate. Unfortunately such a time of local government redevelopment cannot at present be easily foreseen, but that does not constitute a reason for a lack of preparation of the groundwork.

The present crisis in local government finance concerning radical retrenchment, 'rate-capping' and grant withdrawal penalties is as much philosophical as it is financial. Is the view likely to prevail that a system of local government having maximum independence of central government is a sound constitutional necessity? Much lip-service has been paid over the years by a variety of governments to the importance of sustaining a strong local democracy.

But are both local and central government prepared to pay the price involved? The price to local government must be, to a considerable degree, a recognition that overwhelming financial support from central government cannot be expected, if the local authorities wish to maintain a substantial degree of right to solve their own problems in their own way. If local government remains (or returns to a state of being) predominantly local, inequality of financial burdens and a lack of standardization will inevitably arise. In the present scene is the general public any longer prepared to accept these inequalities? The answer may well be that it is not. Is the national economy in a world context now such that central government can no longer attempt to control the nation's destiny unless it has a firm grip on the local economy? The price which central government must pay if local democracy is to survive is that it must not expect to take all important decisions out of local hands. The irony of the situation is that what is called local government is, to a substantial extent, the devolution of centrally determined policies on to a local administrative machine; what is principally being argued is how closely local government must follow the lines laid down both in direction and cost in these centrally determined policies.

The issue may be partly illustrated by consideration of the status of the PWLC. The PWLC has in recent years, under the pressures of a variety of motives, put itself on an efficient operational basis. Its attitude to the handling of debt is modern and its organization rationalized. What may be a moot-point is whether there is still any merit in the present formula by which the degree of aid in the provision of capital funds is determined, and the result of which falls only slightly short of full provision. Certainly, to make all local authority capital needs available (except for short loans) would not add much to the burden of the commission, and provided that access to the commission remained a free choice to the local authorities, this might be an unobjectionable simplification. The PWLC can certainly borrow more cheaply than the local authorities in the market, although the two bodies are not always tapping the same sources of funds, and as long as the PWLC rules retain their present flexibility what is to be lost if local authorities rely entirely on the commission and government borrowing? The doubt is simply that, in these circumstances, the local authorities might lose an element of independence which in the long run might be harmful in constitutional terms.

But where is the line to be drawn? The local authorities would probably not wish to be made wholly dependent on direct access to the market, although experience has shown that they could cope with this situation. Suppose the PWLC supplied only the funds required for housing finance. This might well remove a disruptive element from consolidated loans funds. Or suppose that local authorities should be able to obtain up to one-half of their needs from the PWLC and must compete in the market for the remainder. Though quite a subjective solution, this might do more for the good of local government in the long run than the present generous facility. This is not the place to argue the issue, but a similar rule-of-thumb policy in the degree of overall grant aid might also have constitutional advantages, as much central revenue aid overall is borne from the local rate. This is of course far from being a simple issue and whether the burden of need and the distribution of wealth in this country is now so erratic that such a system is not feasible might well be argued, apart from any question of the necessity for the firm central control by central government of the whole public sector expenditure.

Local government is almost where it was in the 1950s, when it was first compelled to obtain all its capital needs from the commission. This was followed by a short spell in which it could continue to obtain all its needs but was not under an obligation to do so. The position was changed in a precipitate manner in 1954, but whether the present lavish support of the commission will in due course be similarly withdrawn, and if so at short notice, must be a question in the minds of municipal treasurers. Local government is also at a point where the PWLC promise to stand as 'lender of last resort' may be at issue. Will the central government use the PWLC as part of its weaponry to bring into line authorities who will not willingly accept revenue restraint? The 'last resort' facility is not a matter of law, it is an offer made by the PWLC within its statutory terms, no doubt, with Treasury blessing, but not an obligation.

Within a period of not much more than five years there have been four developments all of which impose stricter control on local government – and this against the background of an earlier period of time, since the later 1930s, when in regular stages one service after another has been removed from the local sphere and put on a basis of direct central control. These four changes were: the overall control of capital expenditure and the introduction of annual cash limits; the introduction of rate penalties and 'rate-capping'; an enhanced system of audit which takes this subject well beyond the area of financial probity; and the provision of (almost all) capital moneys via the PWLC. Moreover, the first whispers are currently to be heard of an intention to lay down a form of accounts across the whole of the local authority operation to which all authorities would have to conform; the motive behind this is clearly the determination to facilitate the laying down of prescribed expenditure parameters. Prognostications about the future independence of local government must be gloomy; it is against this background that the generosity of the PWLC at this stage must be assessed.

As our historical recital has shown, the logical basis of amortization as applicable to local authority debt has at last been recognized. There is no longer any confusion of borrowing with loan sanction periods; the consolidated loans fund is seen as an interface between the two aspects of borrowing and its use reduces confusion to simplicity. Yet two criticisms may still be directed at the statutory provisions in this respect. The first is the curious way in which the CLF is made partly mandatory and partly optional for local authorities in England and Wales. A permissive power for local authorities to regulate the amortization of their debt through a consolidated loans fund would have been adequate. There is no way in which modern loan portfolios can be handled without loans pooling. *Per contra*, the second source of criticism is that the Scottish statutes not only require the operation of a CLF for all loans, but insist on spelling out the operational details within the statute, very much as the early stock regulations did for stock. As a satisfactory model scheme has been long agreed between the central and local authorities, and as the modifications which may be needed from time to time in a constantly changing market cannot be foreseen, scheme procedure rather than statutory pre-emptiveness seems to be an adequate way of coping with this not very complex problem. The protection of lenders can hardly be made the excuse in this case for the statutory specification of a CLF. These are not grave criticisms, but are indicative of an unnecessarily dominating attitude by Whitehall towards this important and now well-established device.

A somewhat more material comment may be applied to the form and duration of amortization. With the interface of the CLF, all annual provision for the repayment of advances by borrowing accounts to the CLF must be on an annual basis – in contrast to the repayment of loans to lenders where with the exception of substantial proportions of PWLC advances repayments are at maturity, as is preferred by modern investors. As has several times been indicated in this book, the EIP method of annual repayment is cheaper in interest costs over the life of the loan and has the further advantage that the reducing annual combination of principal and interest may be considered as balancing the increasing annual maintenance costs. The question is whether pressure should be brought on local authorities to adopt this system of repayment of advances in CLFs, and whether the PWLC should modify its present options by insisting on this system of repayment of their loans. On the whole, while the prudent course seems certainly to be that both of these steps should be encouraged, the balance probably lies in leaving discretion with the local authorities on the basis at least that the more they are trusted, the more they will take a responsible view.

A similar issue arises with loan sanction periods. Although lip-service is paid to the myth that loan sanction periods are broadly equated with the useful life of the asset, this can be seen to be a very rough-and-ready attempt at establishing a principle. Equipment apart (which is probably, in any event, best bought direct from revenue), the active life of most assets is considerably longer than the loan sanction period; if it is argued that the quality of services would be improved if assets were replaced at dates certainly no longer than sanction periods, the fact must be faced that the economy would not cope with a replacement programme on such a basis. The point has already been made that the nation's stock of houses simply cannot be replaced every sixty years, and the same applies to the life of schools. There are many hospitals in this country which are established in former Poor Law buildings well over a century old, and likely to have to last the greater part of another century whatever the urgency of changing design. The argument of life duration does not even begin to apply to land purchases where the period is without significance. This is not to say that loan sanction periods might therefore be lengthened; it means rather that the hypothetical link between sanction period and theoretical life should be abandoned, and a much less open-handed attitude taken to the propriety of transferring burdens to generations yet unborn. In retrospect there seems to have been prudence and a good deal of sound thinking in the early use of short loan sanction periods, particularly if as suggested earlier in this chapter, local government is no longer in a period of general expansion. Against the background of earlier suggestions for a more dynamic policy of 'pay-as-you-go', would there be merit in the use of 15/20 or 20/30 years as the modal basis for loan sanctions as against the present 40/60? The Whitehall approach seems to be inclined to long sanctions and long maturities. There seems to be an implication that funding – borrowing for long periods – has some special merit because borrowing is related to long-life assets; in fact greater merit can perhaps be seen in policies of not borrowing at all, or at least using modest loan sanction periods. There may well be a case to be made that an important element in responsible local government would be a determination not to relieve those who introduce schemes of the costs involved, at the expense of those who inherit them willingly or unwillingly.

There is some complacency in local government financial circles about the significance of the statutory requirement that amortisation provision must begin immediately capital expenditure has been incurred from borrowed money. This is certainly an important provision, but what is the real impact of this rule? Today a much-debated feature of national finance is what is referred to as the public sector borrowing requirement (PSBR). Government accounting is basically on a simple receipts and payments cash basis, and expenditures of a capital or revenue nature are not strictly segregated. Expressed in simple form, the total national budget require-ment is calculated irrespective of the nature of the expenditure. From this total is deducted the income which the government thinks proper to raise by taxes and other general means, and the shortfall of this income from the total projected expenditure is the PSBR. When the PSBR is a positive figure, there is an increase in the National Debt; if the PSBR is negative, then National Debt reduces. Whether the amount borrowed is for capital or revenue purposes, or both, is a consideration which does not arise. The problem of the desirability or feasibility of a proper sinking fund for the discharge of the National Debt goes back more than two centuries.

Whatever official steps are taken to create a sinking fund for debt repayment, if at the end of the year the total debt taking into account any funds in hand as a sinking fund is greater than the initial debt, what claim can there be for an effective sinking fund? The realities of this problem were clearly seen as long ago as 1810 by Dr Robert Hamilton of Aberdeen University, and argued in his book – 'An enquiry concerning the rise and progress, the redemption and present state, and the management of the National Debt of Great Britain'. In this he produced the cogent statement: 'The excess of revenue above expenditure is the only real sinking fund by which public debt can be discharged'.

There is a counterpart to this issue in local government. If local government debt is greater at the end of the year than at the beginning, how true is it to say that the statutory amortization provisions are other than illusory? However much is set aside to repay earlier debt, if total debt still increases, all that has happened in arithmetical terms is that debt on one asset has been switched to another. The underlying pattern is that debt has indeed been amortized, but as more debt has been undertaken of what significance is this amortization? Local government debt overall is certainly increasing from year to year, even if this is mainly for housing purposes. As debt increases the statutory rules require that the amount raised in annual revenue to pay off debt also increases (as well as the interest cost). Local authorities do maintain a strict demarcation between capital and revenue outlays, and what is finally borrowed as the local authority borrowing requirement (LABR) is certainly for capital purposes (subject to the reservation of temporary borrowing for revenue cash-flow purposes). Thus the LABR is also arrived at, as is the PSBR, by adding together the capital and revenue budgets and deducting the amounts raised in miscellaneous income and from grants and by the residual amount of rate levy. However, in local government the amount collected in this revenue is not only the annual running costs of the services, but must include an annual theoretical sum for the amortization of earlier capital expenditure. Leaving aside 'roll-over' borrowing merely for the replacement of maturing loans, the amount borrowed is the sum by which new capital expenditure exceeds the revenue contribution for debt redemption. Despite the iron rule that all debt must be counterbalanced by annual amortization provisions, at any one time there are no funds whatever in hand to meet outstanding debt, and if total debt does increase from year to year, there has been no effective sinking fund provision. There is no way in which the argument can be advanced that debt is being effectively discharged, if the debt at the end is greater than the debt at the beginning.

The following situations may be envisaged:

(1) A local authority which has capital expenditure in the year, but has no earlier debt outstanding. The LABR is the whole of the expenditure envisaged.
(2) A local authority in which capital expenditure for the year is less than the amount of amortization provided in the revenue budget on its

outstanding debt. The net LABR is nil; more old debt will be discharged than new debt incurred; and the net effect is that the new expenditure can be met from a portion of the revenue contributions intended for debt discharge, and that the surplus of amortization moneys constitutes a true 'sinking fund'.

(3) A local authority where the capital expenditure for the year exceeds the year's amortization provisions on existing debt. The LABR will be the excess of capital outlay over the revenue provision for amortization of previous debt; that is, some debt will be switched from one asset to another, and some new debt will be incurred. There can have been no true sinking fund provision in so far as total debt has increased.

(4) A local authority where the new capital outlay is approximately equal to the amount available in the year for amortization of old debt. Here the LABR is nil, but there is no effective sinking fund provision. Such debt as has been theoretically repaid by the annual amortization provision is counterbalanced by the new debt undertaken. The sinking fund provision has been exactly nullified.

(5) A local authority where there is no new capital expenditure in the year, but where there is existing debt for which annual amortization provision is required to be made. Here there is no LABR and a true and effective sinking fund operates.

The underlying reality is therefore that the local authority statutory amortization provisions are only effective in so far as they exceed the amount of new capital outlay during the year. Put in the simplest terms if new debt exceeds debt discharged, there can have been no amortization.[1]

These arguments are not intended to suggest that local authority amortization provisions are hallucinatory; the strength of the local authority position is twofold. Such borrowing (however short) as does take place is by definition for capital (long-term) purposes. However, the aggregation of debt is automatically restrained to the extent that while there is existing debt, notional amortization must be charged against revenue. As these sums are not used to meet current service operational expenditure, they are used to pay off old debt to counterbalance some or all of the new debt which would otherwise be undertaken.

However regularly, and by however much, new capital expenditure is incurred, there is automatic restriction in the accumulation of new debt because the law requires that old debt must be systematically written off. This may only involve the switching of debt from old to new assets, but this is a more prudent method than one in which all new capital expenditure is represented by an increase in aggregate debt. In other words, the local authority system is not a restriction of new expenditure of a capital nature, but is a restriction of the rate of aggregation of debt. The statutory amortization provision on old debt is simply a measure, or rule-of-thumb, by which a restraint is provided on the amount of new debt. These provisions, like those for receivership, are highly valued by institutional investors.

NOTE: CHAPTER 24

1 Inflation complicates but does not fundamentally change this argument. In periods of inflation lenders seek to compensate for the fact that they will eventually be repaid their capital in depreciated currency by seeking a higher nominal interest rate. Part of the interest payment effectively represents an early return of capital. As a result, amortization provisions understate the rate at which capital is being repaid. This is simply the point that inflation reduces the real value of debts. The line of argument on amortization remains valid in terms of the real, inflation-adjusted, level of debt.

Chapter 25

THE STANDARDIZATION OF LOCAL AUTHORITY BORROWING PRACTICES

> Entia non sunt multiplicanda praeter neces-
> sitatem: Entities ought not to be multiplied
> except from necessity – or – All unnecessary facts
> or constituents in the subject being analysed are
> to be eliminated: Occam's Razor – *c.* 1340
> (Brewer, *A Dictionary of Phrase and Fable*)

A standardized code of borrowing practice for local authorities – particularly if it embraced Scotland and Northern Ireland as well as England and Wales – would increase the understanding and hence the confidence of lenders involved in the financing of local authority capital expenditure. This concluding outline of the nature of a simple and efficient code of agreed rules for local authority borrowing is drawn from the examination of the historical evolution of the operation, with some modifications to meet modern market attitudes and with the suggested removal of certain anachronisms. These comments are in three parts: first, what may be called the 'infrastructure', the underlying principles which should guide the relationships between borrowers and lenders; secondly, the 'mechanics' of the operation; and thirdly, the appropriate form(s) of borrowing instrument required for those alternative methods of borrowing which have characteristic differences. These forms of borrowing instruments are not here referred to as 'securities', which is the term appropriate to the underlying financial guarantees.

Most of these rules are established and well understood; some are of ancient origin, others relatively recent:

(1) all local authority borrowings should rank equally;
(2) all should have the security of all the revenues and funds of the authority on which they should be charged indifferently, even though this is not expressed in writing;
(3) both repayment and interest should be a first charge on this security;
(4) a lender should not be obliged to satisfy himself that money is borrowed by statutory authority, nor that once borrowed it is properly applied;
(5) lenders should have access to a receiver through the courts in the event of specified default in interest or repayment, in addition to any other normal processes of law;

(6)   annual provision should be made for the amortization of debt within maximum periods laid down by the Secretary of State;

(7)   with the exception of a margin of revenue borrowing for cash-flow purposes, borrowing should only be undertaken to finance expenditure of a capital nature as approved by the Secretary of State.

Certain comments arise. That loan creditors should have priority over other creditors is a long-established principle in both the local authority and commercial worlds but the grounds for this practice are not abundantly clear. Justification based on expediency can be seen in the early days of local authority turnpike borrowing – that is, that unless assurances of this kind were given, the entrepreneurs would have been unable to borrow the relatively substantial sums involved – and this may still be the underlying justification. Certainly, the practice is now too well established to be altered. The provision for equal ranking, very different from commercial practice, is very significant for local authorities where a range of priorities seems quite inappropriate. There may have been a case at one time for priority based on date of issue, so that the existing priority of a lender was not watered down by further borrowings, but this was more or less impracticable in the light of the 'roll-over' practices of local authorities under which dated priorities might have caused considerable confusion. Another point which is not clear is why the security is now so specifically attached solely to the revenues of the authorities. This has always proved entirely satisfactory, but the addition of the words 'and properties' might seem more logical, particularly when revenues are attached to the operation of activities of a trading nature or to housing. An earlier example has been quoted in which the 'properties' attached to a turnpike trust formed part of the security as without access to these, lenders could hardly have collected the tolls. The Scottish provision is more positive than the English, 'the whole funds, rates and revenues of the authority', but the addition of the words 'and not otherwise' indicates a firm rejection of properties. The Northern Ireland Act alone makes specific reference to the security 'notwithstanding that it is not evidenced in writing'. This presumably applies to a bank overdraft, where a deed is not usually issued. This seems to be a point worth clarifying. The relatively recent introduction of the provision that lenders are not required to satisfy themselves about the propriety of borrowing was obviously again a matter of practicalities.

Despite the recognition of such a borrowing code, every encouragement should be given to local authorities to restrict the amount of debt passed on to future generations, by restriction of sanction periods, the use of the EIP method of amortization provision, finance of suitable and recurring items from revenue, and the development of capital funds and such supporting financial measures as repairs and renewals funds.

Also underlying the borrowing activity – but less matters of principle than those referred to above as 'infrastructure' – are the various mechanical details for borrowing and repayment, standardization of which creates confidence among lenders and avoids confusion and disputes. The most important feature in these mechanics is the need for the management of the borrowing and amortization through a consolidated loans fund, the addition of the word 'consolidated' being not essential, but desirable to emphasize that such a fund is of a truly overall character. On balance, there must be doubt as to whether the Scottish practice of including details of the CLF in the borrowing schedule of the Act is desirable. Preferably, as in the English system, a voluntary model scheme designed by municipal treasurers in co-operation with central government officials would give greater flexibility and responsiveness to change. Certainly, the English Act should embrace the concept that the essence of a consolidated loans fund is that it must cover all forms of borrowing, unless perhaps an authority is determined to finance all its borrowings from the PWLC on the basis of the full term of the loan sanction. Certainly, a CLF scheme should provide for 'scheduling' of specific loans which, though handled through the fund, may be dealt with outside the general averaging of the loans pool in appropriate cases – perhaps, for example, borrowing to on-lend in authorized cases, or for a trading activity. Such exceptions should be rare.

All local authority loans should be subject, without central direction, to such rates of interest as the borrowing authority is able to negotiate whether fixed or variable, or a combination of both. Local authorities should be free to borrow abroad and in non-sterling currencies, though a central government right to superimpose exchange control must be conceded. There should be no need for any local authority borrowing instrument to be sealed, and mechanically impressed signatures, if any signature is needed at all, should suffice. All loans should be registered (unless a bearer type is reintroduced) and there seems to be a case for making these registers open to inspection by any interested party. There should of course be no restriction on disposal or assignment, and a local authority should be able to make premature repayments and to incorporate 'stress' clauses. As has been shown, regulations are apt to provide that both entry in a register and the certificate should give evidence of title without explaining which takes precedence if there is a difference. While there seems to be greater logic in making the document which is put into the lender's hand the final proof of title, this could create problems if certificates were lost or stolen. It would thus appear that the entry in the register would have to take precedence. Naturally, in today's climate, registers should be acceptable in 'non-legible' form, so that the fullest use may be made of computer facilities. The local authority should be free to appoint different registrars for different purposes. Depending on the practice of the market, there seems to be no reason to deny a local authority the right to issue any appropriate document subject to discount or premium, but there is no doubt that fiscal considerations will require that the Treasury should retain a right to limit the degree of discounting which may be applied. Local authorities have not shown any interest in bearer documents for many years, and although the statutes give leave for this type of instrument, the Treasury have indicated that they do not intend to extend the field in this way. Nevertheless, the facility should at least continue to be available to accommodate new forms of borrowing which may be devised such as, for example, a local authority type of certificate of deposit as presently in widespread use in the commercial sector. The underlying thought behind this statement of facilities is that scope for the development of new forms of borrowing should be adequate to meet changes in market conditions and practices without further legislation.

For the many detailed points of day-to-day practice applicable to local authority loans agreed 'voluntary' codes, such as those for short and longer-term borrowing introduced by CIPFA, are necessary. On the question of maturities, however desirable freedom of choice to the local authorities, central government seems determined to control the volume of short borrowing (and experience indicates the necessity for this) and the average maturity period for longer-term borrowing. But for the sake of encouraging the independence of local government to a maximum degree there is much to be said for the use of voluntary codes for these purposes. Consequently, the control of short-term borrowing through the Control of Borrowing Order and the General Consent should be withdrawn, and a single voluntary code be evolved on the basis of that now operating for longer-term borrowing.

The appropriate forms of borrowing instruments will now be considered. However, at this point it may perhaps be made clear that there is no longer need for regulations for the issue of stocks and bonds and mortgages, and that operational details can safely be left to general market practice. While the basic provisions for borrowing are reasonably clear (though outmoded) in the statutes, there are many surrounding details imposed by various means, as already discussed. The present lull in the local authority borrowing market would be an appropriate time for a review of these and cancellation of all controls which are simply derived from earlier and less settled times and which are no longer essential. This is equally applicable to the forms of borrowing instruments.

Much the greater part of the essential underlying borrowing code is included in the present operative legislation, though in some instances in somewhat convoluted form. Scope still exists for the rationalization of the borrowing instrument and a clarification of purposes. The methods at present permitted by statute are: mortgage, bond (in two types), debentures, annuity certificates, stock, bills, temporary loans, overdraft, the Public Works Loan Commission (PWLC) and any other approved method. This book has shown how and when each of these processes was introduced. Other instruments, or at least other titles for similar instruments, have been discovered – principally the assignment and the indenture, and rarer forms such as a simple 'certificate', deed poll and variations of the form of annuities including the tontine. The bond – originally in the two forms of the penalty and the simple bond – continues in two variants, now both of the simple bond, the non-negotiable and the negotiable bond, for which distinctive marketing provisions have been made. The deposit receipt, a term also once in vogue, is seen to be simply a variant of the temporary loan receipt. The temporary loan receipt has also been shown to have a variant, according to peculiarity in the form of wording, as an 'agreement'. There is a general provision that with Treasury consent (which is at present withheld) appropriate instruments may be issued in bearer form.

These provisions will now be examined in two groups: those which though assignable are 'non-negotiable' in the sense that a market with daily quoted rates has not been created, and those which represent 'negotiable paper' and have daily quoted markets. Those in the second group are the bond in its negotiable form, the money bill and stock; the others form the first group. The fundamental point which must be reiterated is that all these forms of borrowing have the same security – namely, the revenues of the authority – and that all rank equally without priority of any kind. Such differences as there are relate to facilities for, or ease of, marketability.

Taking first the non-negotiable instruments, whatever they are called, the process which is taking place when they are issued is that the revenues of the authority are being assigned to the lenders as security for a loan at interest. An alternative form of words would be that the revenues are being mortgaged as security for a loan. Does this make every act of borrowing a 'mortgage'? This may well be so, but the point does not really seem to be of significance. For example, when stock is issued what in fact is happening, in effect if not in words, is that a lien or mortgage is placed on the revenues as security. 'Mortgaging' in this sense, like assigning, is an act which is applicable to any instrument, whatever it is called, which promises access to the revenues on default. When the local authority gives a bond, a binding promise, to repay at interest, the same act of mortgaging the future revenues is involved. What a lender needs from the authority is the acknowledgement of a debt (a debenture indeed) and a right of access to the revenues through a receiver on default. Thus the statement might fairly be made that any local authority acknowledgement of debt is a mortgage debenture in which the revenues are assigned as security. This equally can be expressed by saying that a local authority bond is an acknowledgement of debt, in which the authority binds itself to pay interest at stated intervals, and to repay the debt on a due date and meanwhile to mortgage the revenues as a surety for due performance; the whole, in so far as it acknowledges a debt, is a legal debenture. The question which remains is which of the several available terms is to be used for the sake of simplicity, uniformity and clarity as the name of the local authority loan acknowledgement.

The original simple term 'assignment' has long fallen into desuetude, being gradually replaced by the term 'mortgage'. A process is now underway in which the term bond is replacing that of mortgage, so that the time would now seem to be ripe for giving mortgage honourable discharge in place of the term 'bond', accepting that the security for the bond is a mortgaging or assigning of the revenues. The CIPFA annual debt statistics already make no distinction between bond and mortgage debt. If this step is conceded, the problem still remains that in current statutes a local authority may also issue debentures or annuity certificates under the Local Loans Act 1875.

A reading of the 1875 Act, along with the County Debentures Act 1873, leads to the conclusion that the term 'debenture' is simply used therein as an improvement or alternative to the term 'mortgage'. If this practice had been followed up, instead of being subverted by the Public Health Act 1875 provisions which clung to the mortgage, this might have been a rational development. Such a debenture might be expected to be repayable at maturity, but this is by no means clear as both Acts make confusing references to the need to repay some debentures each year. There is no demand at present for local authority loans repayable by instalments except from the PWLC, but there does not seem to be any valid reason why a present-day bond issued to a lender should necessarily be repaid at maturity if repayment by instalments were desired. Whether, if this were provided, such an instrument would need a different name is doubtful. Certainly, many early loans were repayable on either instalment method or at maturity. The same issues arise with the annuity certificate under the 1875 Act, still technically available to local authorities. These are not life or perpetual annuities, but term annuities, and seem to be no different from bonds repayable over a period of years, not at maturity but on an annuity, flat rate basis of a portion of capital and interest combined. The solution seems clearly to be that these two 1875 facilities, no longer in use, should be statutorily abandoned and local authorities left to borrow by bonds repayable at maturity or by either of the annuity methods, by agreement of the parties to the deal. Life and perpetual annuities may also be dismissed as having no future in local authority borrowing.

One other issue remains to be settled in regard to the non-negotiable borrowings of local authorities – the 'temporary' loan. Here the situation has so developed that a bond with an initial borrowing period of less than a year is no different from a bond for a year or more, except that any form of borrowing in which the interest is deemed to be other than 'annual' interest can be paid without deduction of tax. This fiscal requirement does not change the nature of the loan. In fact there are bonds for more than a year the interest on which is paid gross. Here the question is not of 'annual interest', but involves bonds of the non-negotiable type which are issued to banks as specific investments; similarly, overdraft interest is not taxed at source. By agreement with the Inland Revenue, the interest on these transactions is paid gross, and continues so if the bond is transferred from one bank to another. So the right of interest to be paid gross does not affect the designation or nature of the bond. Consequently, there is no need today for a separate instrument for loans of less than a year. A bond for six days or six months has all the attributes of a bond for six years, and all would be subject to the bond regulations, including receivership, a control which the present 'temporary loan receipt' escapes.

The English and Scottish Acts differ somewhat in their references to the purpose of a temporary borrowing. In England such a borrowing for capital purposes is 'pending the raising of a loan', whereas this is not categorically stated in the Scottish Act. Perhaps the two clauses are intended to mean the same, that a temporary loan is simply to tide over until a longer-term loan has been negotiated – but if so, this point, if once true, is no longer valid in a local authority striving to create a well-balanced 'book'. In the CLF loans initially for less than a year, and loans which were initially for longer periods but are now in their final year, are no different from loans which still have many years to run. The argument cannot even be advanced that the volume of loans for less than a year is subject to controls not applicable to longer loans. The truth is that the voluntary maturity code now in being establishes for longer-term loans controls which are not essentially different from the long-standing short-loan controls.

The 1972 Act list of methods by which a local authority may borrow includes 'an agreement entered into with the PWLC'. Since 1982 the PWLC no longer requires a written application for a loan and will accept a telephone application. The commission's own letter of notification of the loan is regarded as completing the agreement, the security being automatically and statutorily the revenues of the authority. There is no need to authorize the local authorities to borrow from the PWLC as this is part of the commission's own legislation. Borrowing from the commission is a source of funds and not a type of borrowing, so that whether this source needs mention in the local authority borrowing statute may be questionable. If a local authority document is required for PWLC loans, the bond would satisfy the need. This may be compared with the earlier system under which special forms of PWLC mortgage were required. The PWLC has certainly radically simplified the documentation as part of its recent modernizations.

The list of borrowing methods concludes by giving the Secretary of State and the Treasury power to approve other methods. That local authorities need statutory power to borrow, and to pledge the revenues in doing so, must be accepted. Whether this implies that the methods by which they may borrow need be specified is less certain, but this has been done from the earliest days: need this continue to be so? The restrictions imposed on borrowing by local authorities by negotiable instruments suggests that the current significance of Treasury approval of borrowing methods is in 'damping down' the volume of 'negotiable paper', the form of borrowing which competes most with the central government methods. But restrictions on bills, bonds and stock, or any other form of negotiable borrowing, could probably be achieved without the necessity of designating the methods which may be used, through the Control of Borrowing Order. The point is not perhaps an important one, but any modification which reduces the amount of central control through statutory detail and stimulates local enterprise is probably worthwhile.

The conclusion of this debate is therefore that in the area of non-negotiable loans the local authorities need only one instrument which is probably most conveniently to be called a 'bond'. This can be extremely simple as the example of the Chelmsford bond, reproduced as Figure 25.1, indicates. A final degree of rationalization would be to abandon the tradition that a bond is necessarily a document under seal, at least in its local authority context. Such a bond would have exactly the same function as the ancient mortgage. Why should these anachronisms be maintained when the pattern could be so easily simplified?[1]

CHELMSFORD BOROUGH COUNCIL
BOND CERTIFICATE

Certificate Issued   No. Z   )629

Amount of Bond   (£   )

Rate of Interest per Centum

Repayable on

This Bond is issued subject to the Conditions of issue set out overleaf. Interest is payable on 31st May and 30th November in each year and the first payment of interest will be on

EXAMINED
BY

Treasurer & Registrar
Civic Centre
Chelmsford
Essex CM1 1JE

SPECIMEN

REGISTERED BOND HOLDER(S)

Figure 25.1 *The 'Chelmsford' bond certificate. This elegant Chelmsford bond is prepared as a three-part document. The first part is issued to the lender; the second is the registrar's copy and forms the register; and the third is the borrower's office working copy. This distribution reflects precisely that of the three-part chirograph, described in the Introduction, and specified in the Statute concerning the Jews 1233 A.D. First thoughts were best.*

There remains now the consideration of the appropriate form(s) of instrument for local authority negotiable types of borrowing. The majority of central government borrowing is in this form, long borrowing being through government stocks ('gilts') issued under a variety of names, periods and interest rates (some even at variable rates), and normally at a discount, and short borrowings by Treasury bills issued weekly through the discount houses. Apart from its more general interest in keeping control of local debt, generally the central government is certainly concerned to restrict the volume of local authority debt in negotiable form. The manner in which the local authority bond developed a negotiable facility has already been described (see pp. 288-91). The amount of negotiable bond borrowing is restricted both by statutory and extra-statutory methods, including the imposition of a minimum period of one year. The popularity of this bond, which might otherwise be much greater than it is, has been constricted not only by control of the quantity which might be issued by each local authority, but by the Bank of England's refusal to accept this paper as 'overnight' collateral. Because it is negotiable, it normally costs the local authority less than when in non-negotiable form even for the same periods. Although it is simply a local authority bond for which 'same-day arrangements for transferability' have been made in the London market, it is also close in nature to stock, and shares the same regulations. However, to the market it is simply a local authority bond, in which it has a special interest because of its ready marketability. Thus the proposal above that local authorities should borrow non-negotiable money simply by the use of a bond would easily comprehend this further aspect of the bond's activities. Because the negotiable bond is usually referred to in the London market simply as the 'LAB', this might constitute a case for some other name for the non-negotiable borrowing instrument, but the use of the term for the bond in both its aspects does not seem to have caused any market misunderstandings.

The obvious point about the local authority money bill is that it should now be recognized as the negotiable form of the 'less-than-a-year' bond, the negotiable bond being at present excluded from this period. With so-called temporary borrowing, now an official and permanent part of the local authority 'book' and equally guaranteed by the revenues and accepted without question by the market, the case no longer holds, if it ever did, that the market will only accept the bill if it is seen to be in anticipation of revenue and thus 'self-liquidating'. When seen in its full perspective, there are simply no grounds for the argument that short borrowing of this kind is not suitable for longer-term capital expenditure. The objective of the local authority today is to achieve a balanced portfolio – a 'seamless robe' – in which the bill has a contributory part to play.

The questions which arise on analysis, assuming that an attachment to anticipation of revenue is now abandoned, are, first, whether if the restriction of the negotiable bond to a minimum period of one year – not laid down in the statute – could be abandoned, would the negotiable bond when issued for less than a year serve the purpose of the bill? There is little doubt that it could be made to do so, but on balance the bill is an instrument so well understood in the wholesale market that probably, once the fictitious attachment to revenue is dropped, the continuance of this somewhat specialized instrument (with an equally specialized market in the discount houses) should remain. The second question is whether a local authority certificate of deposit should be introduced which might support, or even replace, the bill. A broader definition of a borrowing instrument than that of the certificate of deposit would be hard to find; it occurs in the Finance Act 1968, chapter 44: 'Certificate of Deposit means a document relating to money, in any currency, which has been deposited with the issuer or some other person, being a document which recognises an obligation to pay a stated amount to bearer or to order, with or without interest, and being a document by the delivery of which, with or without endorsement, the right to receive the stated amount, with or without interest, is transferable.' Here again there is no doubt that a local authority certificate of deposit could readily be introduced, but the question would be, how would it effectively differ from a local authority bill or from a negotiable bond for less than a year? The thesis of this argument is that the borrowing instruments should be simplified, not merely multiplied, unless the multiplication has real significance.

What is fundamentally at issue is which would best constitute a local authority short-term borrowing instrument for capital purposes: the continued but wider use of the bill, a less-than-a-year negotiable bond, or the introduction of a local authority certificate of deposit? There are no doubt those who would favour the use of all these instruments on the grounds that access to different markets would be facilitated. The conclusion here is that the well-established money bill (a promissory note, if Scottish friends will) should continue as a capital borrowing instrument under such restrictions as to volume as the official sources insist is desirable. Even if the bill retains its nomenclature, what it is in effect is a short-term negotiable bond on which, for convenience, interest is paid by the discounting of the issue price. What stands out pre-eminently is that the differences between these various instruments are not of a fundamental character, but simply relate to minor variations of the ways in which they are issued or in which interest (with or without tax) is paid.

The mystical aspect of local authority stock has been substantially reduced in recent times by the development of the 'syndicated loan', which is simply a bond or mortgage for sums often quite as substantial as the proceeds a stock issue might produce. However, the negotiability of the syndicated loan is restricted in practice, so that there seem to be good grounds for the continued issue of stock in appropriate circumstances, once the PWLC relaxes its attractions.

In recapitulation, the methods of borrowing which local authorities appear to need are the bond, in its non-negotiable and its negotiable forms, bills and stock, plus the use of bank overdrafts in so far as the banks are still inclined to allow these, and access to the PWLC. How the volumes of each of these are to be controlled depends upon Treasury attitudes. In February 1982 the report appeared of a working party of the Treasury's Local Authority Borrowing Committee on the marketability of local authority debt; the recommendations were mainly concerned with slight increases in the control levels for issues of negotiable debt.

The strange anomaly has now been created that while the Treasury maintains a close control on the amount and purposes for which local authorities may borrow by the issue of negotiable paper, at the same time it has greatly extended access to the PWLC the funds of which are substantially based on negotiable government securities. Therefore, at present in a general sense nearly all local authority new borrowing, being through the PWLC, is based on negotiable instruments. The Treasury's original conviction of the importance of restricting local authority pressures on the market for negotiable investments is overridden by its own practices. If the Treasury is content to finance local borrowing in the market by the issue of negotiable paper, why cannot authorities do this for themselves without restraint? But without doubt the present convoluted borrowing provisions require a rethinking both as to objectives and methods. Where borrowing is required in response to cash-flow problems in anticipation of revenue – until now not a matter of any significance – there is no reason why the instruments available should not be equally applicable, even though such loans might perhaps not pass through the CLF. The outstanding conclusion must be that a rethinking of local authority borrowing methods is needed, with simplification and greater coherence in the light of the developments of the last twenty-five years.

NOTE: CHAPTER 25

1 Whitehall's reluctance to streamline the borrowing instruments has led to a somewhat comic situation. In 1978 I suggested, in *Money Services for Local Authorities*, a standard simple instrument to be called a 'local authority loan acknowledgement' (LALA), to avoid the ancient connotations of the bond. The Deputy Treasurer of South Kesteven District took up this suggestion. Any form of instrument not listed in the 1972 Act requires the approval of the Treasury. The Treasury was unable to approve the 'new instrument' because it did not differ from the bond. The South Kesteven Deputy Treasurer (Christopher Farmer) argued that if it was not different, it was the same and did not then require approval. The authority thereupon began to use this instrument both for bond and temporary loan purposes, accepting that the Bond Regulations were applicable. This instrument continues in use; a copy is reproduced as Figure 25.2.

SOUTH KESTEVEN DISTRICT COUNCIL

**Treasurer,
Guildhall, Grantham,
Lincs. NG31 6PZ.
Telephone (0476) 72457**

LOAN ACKNOWLEDGEMENT

South Kesteven District Council acknowledge the receipt of the loan specified in the Schedule below, on the terms stated therein. This document constitutes a security under the Local Government Act, 1972, Schedule 13, Paragraph 11; under this provision all money borrowed by a local authority is chargeable indifferently on all the revenues of the authority, and all securities rank equally without any priority. For the purposes of schedule 13, Para. 2(i), this document is recognised by the Department of the Environment as being a bond and is regulated as such.

The Schedule

Registered Lender(s): _____

Amount of Principal: _____
Date Received: _____
Rate of Interest: _____
Payment of Interest: _____
Additional Terms & Conditions: _____

_____
Treasurer

DISCHARGE: To be completed by lender on repayment of loan.

RECEIVED the above mentioned sum with all interest due thereon.

Date...............................   ....

Figure 25.2 *Local authority loan acknowledgement, South Kesteven District Council.*

EPILOGUE

The general conclusions which emerge from this historical review are of a somewhat melancholy character. The story which comes to light over two centuries or more is that of the lack of application of penetrating thinking to the objectives and procedures of local authority borrowing, and of incomprehensibly protracted delays in the adoption of improved procedures. True, the essential basic infrastructure applicable to borrowing has eventually been evolved but in a very piecemeal manner, and even now less than comprehensively. For a half-century to pass between the emergence of a new idea in this field and its general absorption into the system has been commonplace – for example, from the 1920s to the 1970s for the consolidated loans fund and the bond (both of which were canvassed long before the initial date), and almost a century from first to last for money bills, where the situation is still confused. Nor has the fundamental change in the nature of 'temporary' borrowing been recognized and incorporated into the system. The Public Works Loan Commission took over a century to reach its present state of excellence, most of its developments being of recent years. In the nineteenth century two attempts were made, in the Commissioners and Companies Clauses Acts and in the Local Loans Act, to bring in a comprehensive and rationalized code. The Clauses Acts can be seen to have influenced later thinking, but the Local Loans Act was a failure from the start and in conflict with the Public Health Act code of the same year. Yet Local Loans Act provisions still find a place in current legislation, where they are unused and probably not understood. Probably hundreds of local authority private Acts have been necessary to enable powers established by one authority to be taken up by another, in a haphazard fashion. In a particular reference to borrowing the Chelmsford Committee, reporting in 1933 on what needed to be done in the local government Act of that year, referred back to the Select Committee of the House of Commons which recommended in 1930 (HC 158) that 'a Public Bill should be introduced every five years to make general the provisions inserted in local Acts'. Yet the 1933 Act provided neither for bonds nor consolidated loans funds, already well established in local Acts. Whitehall seems to have preferred to provide 'model clauses' which implicitly assumed that each local authority should seek powers individually. This procrastinatory approach has not been simply a fault of central government. Local authorities, even when their parliamentary consultants persuaded them to apply for and obtain powers, have been slow in bringing these, once obtained, into effect; and many authorities simply repeated the powers obtained earlier by other authorities without re-examination or rethinking. The persistence of the mortgage today, many years after the availability of the simple bond, and

the confused thinking still apparent about temporary borrowing, are
indicative of this frame of mind.

Yet despite these reluctances and delays, that local authorities have
managed this important aspect of their finances with great success must be
granted. Local authorities have responded to all the challenges, though not
by any means always in ways approved by government. New markets have
been developed and complete public confidence in the integrity and
security of the local authorities has been established. No breakdowns in
the system have occurred, no authority has ever defaulted and the only
fraud of any significance in this area (the Hatry case in the 1930s) was
committed by an issuing house in the London market and not within any
local authority, nor did it impose any losses on the general public.

Is there a future for local authority borrowing? Because of PWLC
intervention, local authorities are at present in the market, in the main, for
money from overnight to up to three years, although the volume of
business in this area is restricted by the 'maturity' code. Certain longer-
term deals of large 'wholesale' sums are also being negotiated in special
cases. Beyond this, the bulk of borrowing is from the PWLC and likely to
remain so until at least 1986; what will then happen is a matter of
speculation. As described in this book, there has been an earlier episode in
which practically all local authority borrowing came from the PWLC, a
facility which was withdrawn at short notice at a time of what were then
thought to be high interest rates. The reasons for today's generous help
from the PWLC are much different from those which underlay the period
1945–55. Since then, apart from changes in government attitudes, there
have been vast changes in financial markets; money is increasingly
regarded as a 'commodity' and follows interest rates round the world with
great rapidity. The establishment of financial futures markets in the United
States, and more recently in this country, is the latest but only one of these
developments. Reference has not been made in this book to this futures
market but already, shortly before the PWLC made its recent changes,
methods were being devised in which the operations of the futures market
could be used to underwrite aspects of interest rate variations in the local
authority field in relation to stock issues. The reimposition of exchange
controls, if this proved to be necessary, and the trends in inflation could
also have a material effect on local authority markets. Attempts to abolish
the local rating system, or to modify its impact, perhaps by the separation
of one or more further services from local government – especially housing
– could also have a substantial effect on local authority borrowing. The
situation is very fluid.

Speculation therefore seems pointless. However, while the possibility
exists that there will be a return to and an upsurge of local authority
borrowing, the present lull seems to be an appropriate time for a review
and modernization of the present complex statutory provisions, preferably
in a new Local Authority Loans Act embracing the whole of the British
Isles. Hopefully this historical study of local authority borrowing will
provide a useful basis for such a review and rationalization.

SELECT BIBLIOGRAPHY

BOOKS ABOUT MAJOR STATUTES

Rating and Valuation Act 1925, by G. P. Warner Terry (London: Knight, 1927; 3rd edn).

Local Government Act 1929 including Poor Law Act 1930 and Public Assistance Order 1930, by A. M. Tristram Eve and F. A. Martineau (London: Knight, 1930).

Local Government Act 1933, by G. E. Hart (London: Butterworth, 1934).

Financial Provisions of the Local Government Acts 1933–1958, by M. W. Bowley (London: IMTA, 1962).

Local Government Act 1972, by C. Arnold Baker (London: Butterworth, 1973).

BOOKS ON LOCAL AUTHORITY FINANCE AND BORROWING

Loans and Borrowing Powers of Local Authorities, by J. H. Burton (London: Pitman, c. 1924).

Local Administration – Finance and Accounts, by A. Carson Roberts (London: Harrison, 1930; 2nd edn).

Local Authority Finance, Accounts and Auditing, by J. H. Burton (London: Gee, 1932).

Consolidated Loans Funds of Local Authorities, by J. M. Drummond and A. H. Marshall (London: Hodge, 1938).

Municipal Capital Finance, by A. B. Griffiths (London: Knight, 1936).

Local Authority Capital Finance, by W. S. Hardacre and N. D. B. Sage (London: Knight, 1965; 2nd edn, rev. and rewritten, N. D. B. Sage, 1977).

The Finance of Local Government, by N. P. Hepworth (London: Allen & Unwin, 1976; 3rd edn).

Loans of Local Authorities (England and Wales), by J. R. Johnson (London: Knight, 1925; 2nd edn).

Financial Management in Government, by A. H. Marshall (London: Allen & Unwin, 1974).

General Code of Practice for the Regulation of the Borrowing of Local Authorities in England, Scotland and Wales (the 'Maturity' Code) (issued jointly by the Associations of Local Authorities, 1977).

'MARKET' PUBLICATIONS

Money Services for Local Authorities, by Sir H. Page (London: Butler Till Ltd, 1978, and Supplement 1981).

The London Discount Market (London: Gerard and National Discount Co. Ltd, 1981; 3rd edn).

The Bill on London (London: Gillett Bros Discount Co. Ltd, 1964; 3rd edn).

TREASURERS' INSTITUTE PUBLICATIONS

Pooling of Local Authority Loans, by W. W. Ayling and J. A. Neale (1960).
Capital Accounts of Local Authorities, by M. F. Stonefrost (1970).
Capital Finance and Borrowing of Local Authorities, by J. M. Rogers (1971).
Local Authority Borrowing, by Group Research (chairman, N. Doodson) (1972; rev. edn).
Capital Budgeting, by Group Research (1977).
Financial Information Service. Vol. 6, Capital Expenditure and Finance, by Group Research (constantly updated).
Monthly Journal: originally *Financial Circular*, later *Local Government Finance*, currently *Public Finance and Accountancy*.
Annual Conference Papers and Reports.
Students Lecture series; approx. 1910–50.
Financial Clauses in Local Acts, 1933 with supplements to 1950.
Local Authority Borrowing: Loans Fund Model Scheme, 1974. (Recommended Procedures – Temporary and Longer-Term Borrowing, 1978.)

GOVERNMENT PUBLICATIONS OF DIRECT INTEREST

Select Committee on the Repayment of Loans, 1902.
Select Committee on the Application of Sinking Funds in the Exercise of Borrowing Powers, 1909.
Interim Report of the Local Government and Public Health Consolidation Committee (Chelmsford Committee) (Cmnd 4272), 1933.
Committee on the Working of the Monetary System (chairman, Rt Hon. the Lord Radcliffe) (Cmnd 827), 1959.
The Control of Public Expenditure (Plowden Committee) (Cmnd 1432), 1961.
Local Authority Borrowing, White Paper on Control of Short Borrowing (Cmnd 2162), 1963.
Local Government Finance (Layfield Committee) (Cmnd 6453), 1976.
Local Government Finance (Cmnd 6813), 1977.
Local Government Finance in Scotland, Discussion Green Paper (Cmnd 6811), 1977.

GENERAL HISTORY

History of the Poor, by Thomas Ruggles, 1794.
History of the National Debt, by J. J. Grellier (London, 1810).
Decline and Fall of the English System of Finance, by Thomas Paine (London, 1810).
The Management of the National Debt of Great Britain, by Robert Hamilton (London, 1814).
An Account of the Public Funds and a History of the National Debt and Sinking Fund, by William Fairman (London: John Richardson, 1795; updated to 1824, B. Cohen, 1824).
History of the English Poor Law, by Sir George Nicholls (London, 1854; updated to 1898 and subsequently to 1968).
History of Local Rates in England, by Professor Edwin Connan (London: Longmans, Green, 1902).

History of Local Government in England, by Josef Redlich and F. W. Hirst (London: Macmillan, 1903; repr. and updated, Brian Keith-Lucas, 1970; 2nd edn).

English Local Government, The Story of the King's Highway, The Poor Law, Parish and County, The Borough, by Sidney and Beatrice Webb (London: Longmans, Green, 1906–13).

Municipal Origins, F. H. Spencer (London: Constable, 1911).

The London County Council from Within, by Sir Harry Haward (London: Chapman & Hall, 1932).

History of Local Government in Manchester, by A. Redford (London: Longman, 1939).

The Incorporation of Boroughs, by Martin Weinbaum (Manchester: Manchester University Press, 1937).

The Growth and Reform of English Local Government (Key Documents), ed. W. Thornhill (London: Weidenfeld & Nicolson).

Local Government Areas 1834–1945, by V. D. Lipman (Oxford: Blackwell, 1949).

British Banks and Banking – a Pictorial History, by R. M. Fitzmaurice (London: Bradford Barton, 1975).

The National Debt, by E. L. Hargreaves (London: Cass, 1930; reprinted 1966).

A History of Local Government, by K. B. Smellie (London: Allen & Unwin, 1968; 4th edn).

A Century of Municipal Progress, ed. by H. J. Laski, W. I. Jennings and W. A. Robson (London: Allen & Unwin, 1935) esp. Chapter by E. Halévy 'Before 1835'.

English Local Administration in the Middle Ages, by Helen M. Jewell (Newton Abbot: David & Charles, 1972).

The Treasury 1660–1870, by Henry Roseveare (London: Allen & Unwin, 1973).

The Sheriff – the Man and his Office, by Irene Gladwin (London: Gollancz, 1974).

The Workhouse, by Norman Longmate (London: Temple Smith, 1974).

The Turnpike Road System in England 1663–1840, by William Albert (Cambridge: Cambridge University Press, 1972).

Pauper Palaces, by Anne Digby (London: Routledge & Kegan Paul, 1978).

The Un-Reformed Local Government System, by Brian Keith-Lucas (London: Croom Helm, 1980).

ADDENDUM

Tontine-Tables or Calculations respecting the Loan of £265,000 on which are to be granted Life Annuities of £6 per cent with benefit of Survivorship, by J. Y. Mathematician (Dublin, 1774).

Legal and Useful Information to purchasers of . . . annuities, mortgages, tontines, by Revd Dr Trusler (London, 1790).

The Tontine: Fact and Fiction, by R. M. Jennings and A. P. Trout (London: Harvard: Kress Library, Harvard University Graduate School of Business Administration, 1974).

A City Council from Within: Manchester, by E. D. Simon (London: Longmans, Green, 1926).

A Century of City Government: Manchester 1838–1938, by Shena D. Simon (London: Allen & Unwin, 1938).

Local Government Finance in a Unitary State, by C. D. Foster, R. A. Jackman and M. Perlman (London: Allen & Unwin, 1980).

CITATION REFERENCES OF STATUTES

Statutes in the text are here given in chronological order with the appropriate citation references. This consists of the regnal year and chapter number until 1962. Thereafter the chapter number within the calendar year was adopted by Parliament. The citation references derive from *Chronological Table of the Statutes 1235–1979* and *Index to Local & Personal Acts 1801–1947*, both published by the Statutory Publications Office. An additional source was *Numbered List of Original Acts 1497–1902* in the House of Lords Records Office. It should be noted that other sources, indeed the Acts themselves, may occasionally indicate an alternative reference.

Year	Reference	Short Title
1233	17 Hen. III	Statute concerning the Jews
1285	13 Edw. I	Statute of Winchester
1350	23 Edw. III	Act against Vagabonds and Beggars
1361	34 Edw. III, c. 1	Justices of the Peace Act
	34 Edw. III, c. 5	Weights & Measures Act
	34 Edw. III, c. 6	Measures Act
1362	36 Edw. III, c. 12	Quarter Sessions Act
1530	22 Hen. VIII, c. 5	Statute of Bridges
	22 Hen. VIII, c. 12	Vagabonds Act
1531	23 Hen. VIII, c. 2	Gaols Act
	23 Hen. VIII, c. 5	Statute of Sewers
1536	27 Hen. VIII, c. 25	Vagabonds Act
1545	37 Hen. VIII, c. 9	Act against Usury
1547	1 Edw. VI, c. 3	Vagabonds, etc. Act
1549	3 & 4 Edw. VI, c. 16	Vagabonds Act
1551	5 & 6 Edw. VI, c. 2	Poor Act
1552	5 & 6 Edw. VI, c. 20	Usury Act
1555	2 & 3 Phil. & M., c. 8	Highways Act
1562	5 Eliz. I, c. 3	Poor Act
	5 Eliz. I, c. 13	Highways Act
1571	13 Eliz. I, c. 8	Usury Act
	13 Eliz. I, c. 18	River Lee (new cut) Act
	13 Eliz. I, c. 24	Ipswich Improvement Act
1572	14 Eliz. I, c. 5	Vagabonds, etc. Act
1575	18 Eliz. I, c. 3	Poor Act
1580	23 Eliz. I, c. 11	Cardiff Bridge Act
	23 Eliz. I, c. 12	Paving Streets in London Act
1597	39 Eliz. I, c. 3	Poor Act
	39 Eliz. I, c. 23	Newport & Carleon Bridges Act
1601	41 Eliz. I, c. 2	Poor Relief Act
1603	1 Jac. I, c. 31	Plague Act
1609	7 Jac. I, c. 4	Vagabonds Act
1623	21 Jac. I, c. 17	Usury Act
1647	17 XII 1647	Commonwealth Ordinance for London Poor

Year	Reference	Short Title
1649	7 V 1649	Commonwealth Ordinance for London Poor
1651	8 VIII 1651	'An Act prohibiting any person to take above six pounds per loan of one hundred pounds by the year'
1654		Commonwealth Ordinances relating to Highways Commonwealth Ordinance for the appointment of Commissioners of Sewers
1660	12 Car. II, c. 13	Usury Act
1662	14 Car. II, c. 2	Streets (London & Westminster) Act
	14 Car. II, c. 6	Highways Act
	14 Car. II, c. 12	Poor Relief Act
	14 Car. II, c. 27	Dover Harbour Repairs Act
1663	15 Car. II, c. 1	Road Repair (Herts, Cambs & Hunts) Act – Wades-Mill
1664	16 & 17 Car. II, c. 10	Highways, Hertford Act
1670	22 Car. II, c. 2	Yarmouth Haven & Piers Repairs Act
	22 Car. II, c. 12	Bridges Act
1685	1 Jac. II, c. 16	Great Yarmouth Haven, etc. (Duties) Act
1691	3 W. & M., c. 12	Highways, etc. Act
1692	4 W. & M., c. 9	Highways, Herts Act
1694	5 & 6 W. & M., c. 10	Orphans Relief (London) Act
1695	7 & 8 Will. III, c. 9	Roads, London to Harwich, Act
	7 & 8 Will. III, c. 14	Act relating to Rivers Wye and Lugg
	7 & 8 Will. III, c. 32 (private)	Bristol Poor Law
1696	8 & 9 Will. III, c. 16	Highways Act
	8 & 9 Will. III, c. 29	Bridlington Piers, Yorks Act
1697	9 Will. III, c. 12	Bridgewater, Somerset (Repairs, etc.) Act
	9 Will. III, c. 18	Gloucester Roads Act
	9 Will. III, c. 19	Navigation, Colchester to Wivenhoe Act
	9 & 10 Will. III, c. 33 (private)	Exeter Poor Law
	9 & 10 Will. III, c. 34 (private)	Hereford Poor Law
1699	11 & 12 Will. III, c. 19	Gaols Act
1700	12 & 13 Will. III, c. 9	Minehead Harbour Act
1702	1 Anne, c. 13	Whitby Piers Act
	1 Anne, Statute 2, c. 11	River Cham, Cambridge Act
1705	4 & 5 Anne, c. 5	Parton Harbour, Cumberland Act
1706	6 Anne, c. 4	Bedfordshire & Bucks Roads Act
	6 Anne, c. 13	Bedfordshire Highways Act
	6 Anne, c. 14	Hertfordshire Highways Act
1707	6 Anne, c. 42	Bath Highways, Streets, etc. Act
	6 Anne, c. 58	Mischiefs from Fire Act
1708	7 Anne, c. 17	Mischiefs by Fire Act
1709	8 Anne, c. 8	Liverpool Docks Act
1710	9 Anne, c. 10	Public Stock of Devonshire Act
1711	10 Anne, c. 6 (private)	Norwich Poor Law
1713	13 Anne, c. 15	Usury Act
	13 Anne, c. 32 (private)	Bristol, Poor Relief Act
1715	1 Geo. I, Statute 2, c. 52	Highways Act
1718	5 Geo. I, c. 31	Colne River, Essex, Navigation Act
1722	9 Geo. I, c. 7	Poor Relief Act – Knatchbull's Act
1725	12 Geo. I, c. 15	Norwich Norfolk, Improvement Act

Year Reference	Short Title
1727 1 Geo. II, Statute 2, c. 20	Canterbury Poor Relief Act
1735 9 Geo. II, c. 12	Maidstone Gaol, Kent (Expenses) Act
1738 12 Geo. II, c. 29	County Rates Act
1739 13 Geo. II, c. 30	River Colne, Essex, Navigation Act
1747 21 Geo. II, c. 21	Bury St Edmunds (Poor Relief) Act
1751 25 Geo. II, c. 23	St Margaret & St John, Westminster (Poor Relief, etc.) Act
1753 26 Geo. II, c. 97	St George's Hanover Square, Westminster (Poor Relief) Act
26 Geo. II, c. 99	Chichester Poor Relief Act
1756 29 Geo. II, c. 79	Carlford, Suffolk: Poor Relief Act
1759 33 Geo. II, c. 57	Maidstone to Cranbrook Road Act
1762 2 Geo. III, c. 21	London Streets Act
2 Geo. III, c. 44	Lancaster Roads Act
2 Geo. III, c. 45	Chester (Poor Relief, etc.) Act
2 Geo. III, c. 58	St James Westminster (Poor Relief, etc.) Act
1764 4 Geo. III, c. 89	Mutford & Lothingland, Suffolk (Poor Relief) Act
1765 5 Geo. III, c. 97	Wilford, etc. Suffolk; Poor Relief Act
5 Geo. III, c. 100	Chester, Lancaster & Yorks, Roads Acts
1766 6 Geo. III, c. 26	London Paving, Cleansing & Lighting Act
7 Geo. III, c. 42	Highways Act
1768 8 Geo. III, c. 21	Paving, etc. of London Act
8 Geo. III, c. 33	St Leonards, Shoreditch, Streets Act
1769 9 Geo. III, c. 10	Streets, New Windsor (Berks) Act
9 Geo. III, c. 13	Streets, St Martin's Le Grand, Westminster Act
9 Geo. III, c. 20	Shire Halls, etc. Act
9 Geo. III, c. 21	Gainsborough Improvement Act
9 Geo. III, c. 22	St Botolph Aldgate: Improvement Act
9 Geo. III, c. 23	St Bartholomew the Great, London (Improvement) Act
9 Geo. III, c. 32	Stroud & Rochester: Improvement Act
1771 11 Geo. III, c. 14	Oxford Poor Relief Act
11 Geo. III, c. 22	Westminster: Streets Act
11 Geo. III, c. 29	City of London Sewerage Act
11 Geo. III, c. 43	Isle of Wight, Poor Relief Act
11 Geo. III, c. 54	London: Streets Act
1772 12 Geo. III, c. 38	Christchurch Middlesex Paving, etc. Act
12 Geo. III, c. 68	St Sepulchre, Middlesex Poor Act
1773 13 Geo. III, c. 16	Act to enable the rebuilding of the Shire Hall at Exeter, Devon
13 Geo. III, c. 61	Kingston upon Thames: Streets Act
13 Geo. III, c. 78	Highways Act
1774 14 Geo. III, c. 30	Stepney: Streets Act
14 Geo. III, c. 38	Hereford: Streets Act
14 Geo. III, c. 55	St Stephen, Bristol
1775 15 Geo. III, c. 13	E. & W. Flegg Poor Relief Act
15 Geo. III, c. 21	St Marylebone Poor Relief Act
15 Geo. III, c. 23	Clerkenwell Poor Relief Act
15 Geo. III, c. 25	Hertford Prison Act
1776 16 Geo. III, c. 9	Forehoe Poor Relief Act

Year	Reference	Short Title
1776	16 Geo. III, c. 53	Isle of Wight Guardians Act
1777	17 Geo. III, c. 26	Grants of Life Annuities Act
1778	18 Geo. III, c. 7	Wigton Roads Act
	18 Geo. III, c. 17	Bodmin Gaol Act
	18 Geo. III, c. 35	Stow Poor Law
1781	21 Geo. III, c. 72	Plymouth Poor Relief Act
1782	22 Geo. III, c. 56	St Lukes Middlesex (Poor Relief, etc.) Act
	22 Geo. III, c. 83	Relief of the Poor Act – Gilbert's Act
1783	23 Geo. III, c. 20	Shrewsbury Guildhall Act
	23 Geo. III, c. 54	Birmingham Poor Relief Act
	23 Geo. III, c. 55	Kingston upon Hull, Improvement Act
1784	24 Geo. III, Statute 2, c. 5	Sheffield Market Place Act
	24 Geo. III, Statute 2, c. 54	Gaols Act
1785	25 Geo. III, c. 10	Gloucester Gaol Act
	25 Geo. III, c. 27	Tunstead & Happing, Norfolk Poor Relief Act
	25 Geo. III, c. 41	Richmond Surrey (Poor Relief, etc.) Act
	25 Geo. III, c. 85	Reading: Streets Act
	25 Geo. III, c. 93	New Sarum Gaol Improvement Act
1787	27 Geo. III, c. 61	Grantham Town Hall Act
1788	28 Geo. III, c. 60	Christchurch Middlesex Improvement Act
	28 Geo. III, c. 64	Cambridge Improvement Act
1790	30 Geo. III, c. 81	Manchester: Poor Relief Act
1791	31 Geo. III, c. 78	Ellesmere Poor Relief Act
1793	33 Geo. III, c. 31	Liverpool Note Issue Act
1795	36 Geo. III, c. 10	Poor Relief Act
1800	39 & 40 Geo. III, c. lxxiv	Bolton Turnpike
1800	41 Geo. III, c. 15	Census Act
1802	42 Geo. III, c. 74	Loans for Erection of Workhouses Act
1803	43 Geo. III, c. xlvii	Chester Amendment
	43 Geo. III, c. 59	Bridges Act – Lord Ellenborough's Act
	43 Geo. III, c. 110	Loans for Erection of Workhouses Act
1808	48 Geo. III, c. 96	Lunatic Paupers or Criminals Act
1811	51 Geo. III, c. xlviii	Tiverton Turnpike
	51 Geo. III, c. cii	Plymouth Corporation Act 1811
1812	52 Geo. III, c. lxxxii	Chatham to Canterbury Turnpike
1815	55 Geo. III, c. 51	County Rates Act
1817	57 Geo. III, c. 34	Public Works Loan Act
	57 Geo. III, c. lviii	Manchester, Blackfriars Bridge over Irwell
1819	59 Geo. III, c. 12	Poor Relief Act
1820	1 Geo. IV, c. xxviii	Stockport to Warrington Turnpike
1823	4 Geo. IV, c. 64	Gaols, etc. Act
1825	6 Geo. IV, c. 40	Mortgages of County Rates Act
1826	7 Geo. IV, c. 63	County Buildings Act
1828	9 Geo. IV, c. 40	County Lunatic Asylums Act
	10 Geo. IV, c. xcvii	Cheshire Police
1834	4 & 5 Will. IV, c. 76	Poor Law Amendment Act
1835	5 & 6 Will. IV, c. 38	Prisons Act
	5 & 6 Will. IV, c. 50	Highways Act
	5 & 6 Will. IV, c. 76	Municipal Corporations Act
1836	6 & 7 Will. IV, c. 86	Births & Deaths Registration Act
	6 & 7 Will. IV, c. 107	Poor Relief (Loans) Act
1837	7 Will. IV & 1 Vict., c. 24	County Buildings Act

Year	Reference	Short Title
1837	7 Will. IV & 1 Vict., c. 81	Municipal Rates Act
1838	1 & 2 Vict., c. 25	Poor Relief (Loans) Act
	1 & 2 Vict., c. 55	Debt of City of Edinburgh, etc. Act
1839	2 & 3 Vict., c. 93	County Police Act
1840	3 & 4 Vict., c. 29	Vaccination Act
	3 & 4 Vict., c. 88	County Police Act
1841	4 & 5 Vict., c. 45	Sewers Act
	4 & 5 Vict., c. 49	County Bridges Act
1842	5 & 6 Vict., c. 9	Advances for Public Works Act
	5 & 6 Vict., c. 98	Prisons Act
	5 & 6 Vict., c. 109	Parish Constables Act
1844	7 & 8 Vict., c. lvi	Coventry Waterworks Act
	7 & 8 Vict., c. 101	Poor Law Amendment Act
1845	8 & 9 Vict., c. 16	Companies Clauses Consolidation Act
	8 & 9 Vict., c. 18	Land Clauses Consolidation Act
	8 & 9 Vict., c. 43	Museums Act
	8 & 9 Vict., c. 126	Lunatics Act
1846	9 & 10 Vict., c. 74	Baths & Washhouses Act
	9 & 10 Vict., c. 96	Nuisances Removal, etc. Act
1847	10 & 11 Vict., c. 16	Commissioners Clauses Act
	10 & 11 Vict., c. 34	Towns Improvement Clauses Act
	10 & 11 Vict., c. 65	Cemeteries Clauses Act
1848	11 & 12 Vict., c. 39	Prisons Act
	11 & 12 Vict., c. 63	Public Health Act
	11 & 12 Vict., c. 112	Metropolitan Commissioners of Sewers Act
	11 & 12 Vict., c. xli	Huddersfield Improvement Act
1850	13 & 14 Vict., c. 52	Metropolitan Interments Act
	13 & 14 Vict., c. 57	Vestries Act
	13 & 14 Vict., c. 64	Bridges Act
	13 & 14 Vict., c. 65	Public Libraries & Museums Act
1851	14 & 15 Vict., c. 34	Lodging Houses Act
	14 & 15 Vict., c. 105	Poor Law Amendment Act
1852	15 & 16 Vict., c. 85	Metropolitan Interments (Amendment) Act
1853	16 & 17 Vict., c. 40	Public Works Loans Act
	16 & 17 Vict., c. 134	Burial Act
1854	17 & 18 Vict., c. 87	Burial Act
	17 & 18 Vict., c. 90	Usury Laws Repeal Act
1855	18 & 19 Vict., c. 70	Public Libraries Act
	18 & 19 Vict., c. 120	Metropolis Management Act
	18 & 19 Vict., c. 128	Burial Act
1856	19 & 20 Vict., c. 2	Metropolitan Police Act
	19 & 20 Vict., c. 69	County & Borough Police Act
1857	20 & 21 Vict., c. 81	Burial Act
1858	21 & 22 Vict., c. 97	Public Health Act
	21 & 22 Vict., c. 98	Local Government Act
1860	23 & 24 Vict., c. 15	Municipal Corporations Mortgages Act
	23 & 24 Vict., c. 64	Burial Act
	23 & 24 Vict., c. cxlviii	Swansea Local Board of Health Waterworks Act
1861	24 & 25 Vict., c. 61	Local Government Act 1858 (Amendment) Act
1862	25 & 26 Vict., c. 61	Highways Act
	25 & 26 Vict., c. 105	Highland Roads & Bridges Act

Year	Reference	Short Title
1863	26 & 27 Vict., c. 28	Stock Certificates Act (also referred to as National Debt Act)
	26 & 27 Vict., c. 61	Highways Act
	26 & 27 Vict., c. 70	Public Works Act
1864	27 & 28 Vict., c. 104	Public Works (Manufacturing Districts) Act
1865	28 & 29 Vict., c. 78	Mortgage Debenture Act
1866	29 & 30 Vict., c. 28	Labouring Classes Dwelling Houses Act
	29 & 30 Vict., c. 90	Sanitary Act
1867	30 & 31 Vict., c. 106	Poor Law Amendment Act
	30 & 31 Vict., c. 113	Sewage Utilization Act
1869	32 & 33 Vict., c. 45	Union Loans Act
	32 & 33 Vict., c. 100	Sanitary Loans Act
	32 & 33 Vict., c. 102	Metropolitan Board of Works (Loans) Act
1870	33 & 34 Vict., c. 20	Mortgage Debenture (Amendment) Act
	33 & 34 Vict., c. 71	National Debt Act
	33 & 34 Vict., c. 75	Elementary Education Act
	33 & 34 Vict., c. 78	Tramways Act
1871	34 & 35 Vict., c. 11	Poor Law Loans Act
	34 & 35 Vict., c. 27	Debenture Stock Act
	34 & 35 Vict., c. 47	Metropolitan Board of Works (Loans) Act
	34 & 35 Vict., c. 70	Local Government Board Act
	34 & 35 Vict., c. 71	Public Libraries Act 1855 Amendment Act
	34 & 35 Vict., c. xl	Batley Corporation Waterworks Act
1872	35 & 36 Vict., c. 2	Poor Law Loans Act
	35 & 36 Vict., c. 7	County Buildings (Loans) Act
	35 & 36 Vict., c. 79	Public Health Act
	35 & 36 Vict., c. ii	Bristol Waterworks Act
	35 & 36 Vict., c. xv	Swansea Local Board of Health Act
	35 & 36 Vict., c. xxxi	Manchester Corporation Waterworks & Improvement Act
	35 & 36 Vict., c. lxxviii	Bolton Corporation Act
1873	36 & 37 Vict., c. 35	County Debentures Act
	36 & 37 Vict., c. 86	Elementary Education Act
1875	38 & 39 Vict., c. 55	Public Health Act
	38 & 39 Vict., c. 65	Metropolitan Board of Works (Loans) Act
	38 & 39 Vict., c. 83	Local Loans Act
	38 & 39 Vict., c. 89	Public Works Loans Act
	38 & 39 Vict., c. clxi	Manchester Corporation Act
1877	40 & 41 Vict., c. 52	Metropolitan Board of Works (Money) Act
	40 & 41 Vict., c. clxxviii	Leeds Corporation Act
1879	42 & 43 Vict., c. 6	District Auditors Act
1880	43 & 44 Vict., c. lxxvii	Lancaster Corporation Act
1881	44 & 45 Vict., c. 48	Metropolitan Board of Works (Money) Act
1882	45 & 46 Vict., c. 50	Municipal Corporations Act
	45 & 46 Vict., c. 56	Electric Lighting Act
1883	46 & 47 Vict., c. cvi	Glasgow Corporation Loans Act
1884	47 & 48 Vict., c. 50	Metropolitan Board of Works (Money) Act
	47 & 48 Vict., c. cxxxi	Coventry Corporation (Gas Purchase) Act

Year	Reference	Short Title
1885	48 & 49 Vict., c. 30	Local Loans Sinking Funds Act
1886	49 & 50 Vict., c. 51	Poor Law Loans & Relief (Scotland) Act
	50 Vict., c. xvii	Manchester Confirmation Order
1887	50 & 51 Vict., c. 16	National Debt & Local Loans Act
1888	51 & 52 Vict., c. 41	Local Government Act
1889	52 & 53 Vict., c. 50	Local Government (Scotland) Act
	52 & 53 Vict., c. 56	Poor Law Act
	52 & 53 Vict., c. 61	London Council (Money) Act
1890	53 & 54 Vict., c. 5	Lunacy Act
	53 & 54 Vict., c. 16	Working Classes Dwellings Act
	53 & 54 Vict., c. 59	Public Health Acts Amendment Act
1891	54 & 55 Vict., c. 34	Local Authorities Loans (Scotland) Act
	54 & 55 Vict., c. 39	Stamp Act
	54 & 55 Vict., c. 65	Lunacy Act
	54 & 55 Vict., c. ccvii	Manchester Corporation Act
1892	55 & 56 Vict., c. 53	Public Libraries Act
	55 & 56 Vict., c. 57	Private Street Works Act
	55 & 56 Vict., c. clxxiii	Birmingham Waterworks Act
1893	56 & 57 Vict., c. 8	Local Authorities Loans (Scotland) Act
	56 & 57 Vict., c. 55	Metropolis Management (Plumstead & Hackney) Act
	56 & 57 Vict., c. 68	Isolation Hospitals Act
1894	56 & 57 Vict., c. 73	Local Government Act (also referred to as Parish Councils Act)
	57 & 58 Vict., c. 57	Diseases of Animals Act
	57 & 58 Vict., c. lvi	Edinburgh Corporation Stock Act
	57 & 58 Vict., c. clx	Liverpool Corporation Loans Act
1896	59 & 60 Vict., c. cxcix	Glasgow Corporation (General Powers) Act
	59 & 60 Vict., c. ccxiv	London County Council (Money) Act
1897	60 & 61 Vict., c. 24	Finance Act
	60 & 61 Vict., c. 29	Poor Law Act
	60 & 61 Vict., c. 40	Local Government (Joint Committees) Act
	60 & 61 Vict., c. xxxii	Edinburgh Corporation Act
	60 & 61 Vict., c. cxxxiii	City of London Sewers Act
	60 & 61 Vict., c. ccxviii	Leicester Corporation Act
	60 & 61 Vict., c. ccxx	London County Council (Money) Act
1898	61 & 62 Vict., c. cclviii	St Helens Corporation Act
1899	62 & 63 Vict., c. 9	Finance Act
	62 & 63 Vict., c. 44	Small Dwellings Acquisition Act
	62 & 63 Vict., c. lxxi	Edinburgh Corporation Act
	62 & 63 Vict., c. clxxxviii	Manchester Corporation Act
	62 & 63 Vict., c. cclxiii	Leeds Corporation Act
1901	1 Edw. VII, c. cxciii	Manchester Corporation Act
	1 Edw. VII, c. cclv	Leeds Corporation (General Powers) Act
1902	2 Edw. VII, c. 42	Education Act
	2 Edw. VII, c. clxxxv	Glasgow Corporation (Gas, etc.) Order Confirmation Act
1903	3 Edw. VII, c. 10	Education (Provision of Working Balances) Act
1907	7 Edw. VII, c. 43	Education (Administrative Provisions) Act
1908	8 Edw. VII, c. 6	Public Health Act
	8 Edw. VII, c. 36	Small Holdings & Allotments Act

Year	Reference	Short Title
1908	8 Edw. VII, c. 67	Children Act
1909	9 Edw. VII, c. 38	County Councils Mortgages Act
	9 Edw. VII, c. 44	Housing, Town Planning, etc. Act
1912	2 & 3 Geo. V, c. cv	London County Council (Finance Consolidation) Act
1913	3 & 4 Geo. V, c. 28	Mental Deficiency Act
	3 & 4 Geo. V, c. xliii	Leeds Corporation Act
1914	4 & 5 Geo. V, c. cxlvi	Manchester Corporation Act
1916	6 & 7 Geo. V, c. 47	Municipal Savings Banks (War Loan Investment) Act
	6 & 7 Geo. V, c. 69	Public Authorities & Bodies (Loans) Act
1919	9 & 10 Geo. V, c. 99	Housing (Additional Powers) Act
	9 & 10 Geo. V, c. liii	Leeds Corporation Act
1920	10 & 11 Geo. V, c. 57	Unemployment (Relief Works) Act
1921	11 & 12 Geo. V, c. 51	Education Act
	11 & 12 Geo. V, c. 67	Local Authorities (Financial Provisions) Act
1922	12 & 13 Geo. V, c. lxiv	Swansea Corporation Act
1923	13 & 14 Geo. V, c. xvi	Macclesfield Corporation Act
1924	14 & 15 Geo. V, c. lxxxix	Leeds Corporation Act
	14 & 15 Geo. V, c. xcv	Manchester Corporation Act
1925	15 & 16 Geo. V, c. 14	Housing Act
	15 & 16 Geo. V, c. 71	Public Health Act
	15 & 16 Geo. V, c. 90	Rating & Valuation Act
1926	16 & 17 Geo. V, c. lxvi	Dundee Corporation Act
1927	17 & 18 Geo. V, c. 14	Poor Law Act
	17 & 18 Geo. V, c. xc	Coventry Corporation Act
1928	18 & 19 Geo. V, c. lxxxvii	Sheffield Corporation Act
	19 & 20 Geo. V, c. 17	Local Government Act
1929	20 & 21 Geo. V, c. xxi	Hendon UDC Act
1930	20 & 21 Geo. V, c. 17	Poor Law Act
1932	22 & 23 Geo. V, c. xc	Wolverhampton Corporation Act
1933	23 & 24 Geo. V, c. 51	Local Government Act
1934	24 & 25 Geo. V, c. xcvii	Manchester Corporation Act
1945	8 & 9 Geo. VI, c. 18	Local Authorities Loans Act
	8 & 9 Geo. VI, c. x	Reigate Corporation Act
1946	9 & 10 Geo. VI, c. 58	Borrowing (Control & Guarantees) Act
1947	10 & 11 Geo. VI, c. 43	Local Government (Scotland) Act
1950	14 Geo. VI, c. xl	Doncaster Corporation Act
	14 & 15 Geo. VI, c. 1	Expiring Laws Continuation Act
1953	1 & 2 Eliz. II, c. 26	Local Government (Miscellaneous Provisions) Act
1954	2 & 3 Eliz. II, c. xlvi	Orpington UDC Act
1957	5 & 6 Eliz. II, c. 56	Housing Act
	5 & 6 Eliz. II, c. xxxvii	East Ham Act
1958	6 & 7 Eliz. II, c. 55	Local Government Act
	6 & 7 Eliz. II, c. l	Wallasey
	7 Eliz. II, ss. 2, c. vi	Kent County Council Act
1959	7 & 8 Eliz. II, c. xxxiii	Reading
1960	8 & 9 Eliz. II, c. lii	Oldham Corporation Act
1961	9 & 10 Eliz. II, c. v	Cardiff Corporation Act
	9 & 10 Eliz. II, c. xlv	Devon County Council
1962	10 & 11 Eliz. II, c. xiv	Liverpool Corporation Act

Year	Reference	Short Title
1962	10 & 11 Eliz. II, c. xxx	Manchester Corporation Act
1963	c. 25	Finance Act
	c. 33	London Government Act
	c. 46	Local Government (Financial Provisions) Act
1964	c. 9	Public Works Loans Act
1965	c. 63	Public Works Loans Act
1967	c. 9	General Rate Act
	c. 54	Finance Act
	c. xl	Manchester Corporation Act
1968	c. 13	National Loans Act
1969	c. 32	Finance Act
1970	c. li	Manchester Corporation Act
1972	c. 9 (NI)	Local Government Act (Northern Ireland)
	c. 70	Local Government Act
1973	c. 65	Local Government (Scotland) Act
1975	c. 30	Local Government (Scotland) Act
	c. 77	Community Land Act
1976	c. 57	Local Government (Miscellaneous Provisions) Act
1980	c. 65	Local Government Planning & Land Act
1982	c. 32	Local Government Finance Act

Index

amortization of debt 7, 8, 330, 365–6
  and consolidated loans funds 338, 339–47
  and government controls on capital
    expenditure 346–51
  and life annuities 332–3
  annuity method 33, 346, 358
  development of provision for 333–9
  equal instalments of principal method 11,
    333, 345, 363
  periods 331
  see also repayment arrangements
annuities 146, 148
  default 83
  deferred 224
  fixed-term 222–3
  for gaol provision 103–4
  for Poor Law purposes 78, 81, 82–3, 84,
    88
  Metropolitan 141–2
  perpetual 223–4, 373
  problems of definition 11, 222
  see also life annuities
annuity certificate 148, 216, 373
Association of Municipal Corporations 287,
  289
Avon 25

Bank of England 14, 58
  and approval of negotiable bonds 291–3
  and 'bearer' bills 266, 273–4
  and restrictions on local authority bills
    271–2, 275
  controls on borrowing 193
banks
  and local authority borrowing 161
  and syndicated loans 203–4
  foreign 178
  see also overdrafts
Bentham, J. 8
'bill' 261
  see also money bill
bill of exchange 10, 11, 264
block grants 162, 164, 166
Boards of Guardians 22, 111
  abolition 164–5
  and burial facilities 127
  and public health services 131
Bolton
  and early mortgaging 217, 220
  housing bonds 284

bonds 257
  as a borrowing technique 11, 13, 80–1,
    159, 162, 185–6, 258, 285–7, 294–6,
    372, 375, 380
  definitions 278–9
  development of 289–91, 293–4
  early forms of 280–2
  'Gilbert's' 214
  'housing' 163, 282–5
  'Manchester' nationalised 287–9
  restrictions on 184, 287, 288–9
  see also negotiable bonds
borough 17, 90, 111, 115
  administrative changes 21, 29–30, 152
  'charter' 4, 28, 114, 330
  early organisation of borrowing 90–7,
    138, 152–3
  origins of 28–9
  rate 115, 116
  see also county boroughs
borrowing
  and Treasury 'General Consent' 184–5,
    292
  and the turnpike trusts 37, 38, 49, 50–2,
    59–60, 61–4
  by harbour authorities 67–8
  by inland waterways authorities 65, 66–7
  by Poor Law incorporations 73–5, 76–85,
    331–2
  early statutes 53–4, 102–6, 331, 358
  justifications for 7, 329–30, 357–8
  restrictions 176–8, 183, 193, 200–1, 303,
    330
  see also foreign borrowing; revenue
    borrowing; temporary borrowing
borrowing practices 356–7
  and consolidated loans funds 370
  and Gilbert's Act 86–7, 112–13
  and local Acts 9–10
  and Treasury approval 374
  code 116–19, 368–9
  growth of 137–45, 158–66, 169–75,
    190–1, 193–5
  in boroughs 29, 90–7, 152–3
  in counties 98–107
  minimum borrowing period 308
  voluntary code 201–2, 371
borrowing techniques 170, 191, 288, 371
  historical development 12–14
  in early local authority systems 120–45

and administrative buildings 153
and borrowing restrictions 176, 177–8, 182, 303
and education services 302
and housing services 128, 302, 303
and loans pools 343
and local authority capital finance 310–12, 361–2
and public health services 135, 136, 301–2
and temporary borrowing 162
Commissioners 310
early loans 300–2
expansion of borrowing facilities 204–5, 304, 313, 378, 381
historical background 298–9, 302–3
interest rates 309–10
'last resort' loans 304–5, 362
long-term loans incentives 305–7
repayment methods 307–9

quarter sessions 21

railway companies 5
'rapes' 24
rate-capping 330, 362
rates
adequacy of levy 163
and borough finance 115, 116
and capital funds 316, 319–20
and county finance 98–9, 100–2
as security 171
collection 27
levy for bridge maintenance 40–1, 98
levy for road maintenance 60–1
see also capital purpose rate; poor rate
rating systems 16, 17
early 98–9, 330
restructuring 163, 166
Reading
and short-term borrowing 180
receivership provisions 193
and borrowing defaults 118, 123, 133, 149
in Scotland 174–5
in stock regulations 250
Redcliffe-Maud, Lord 22
redemption 9
registration
and compilation of statistics 112, 225
Repairs and Renewal Funds 185, 193
repayment arrangements 157, 171, 194, 222, 334–5, 345
and extension of maturity periods 202
and Local Loans Act 149–50
and Poor Law borrowing 333–4
and Public Works Loan Commission 182,

300, 306, 307–8, 335
comparative costs 345–6
premature 302–3
revenue 170
and creation of capital assets 320–3
and mortgaging 209, 210, 211–12
as security 369, 372
'revenue' borrowing 159, 161
and money bills 261, 263, 270–1
limiting 164
temporary 177, 256
revenue expenditure 355
reductions 200, 313
'riding' 24
river navigation 5
road maintenance
and borrowing 37, 47–8, 54
and turnpike trusts 38–9, 49–52, 100
early statutes 43–5, 52
early rates 44, 45, 46–7
tolls 53–5, 56–7, 58–9, 60–1
roads
as function of the parish 27, 28
early administration 129–30
early system of 37–9
toll- 46, 60
see also turnpike trusts
'roll-over' 8, 118, 132, 369
Royal Commission on Local Government 22
Royal Sanitary Commission 135
rural district councils 17

St Helens
sinking fund for mortgage loans 157, 339
sanitary authorities 131
savings banks 159
School Boards 30, 113, 136, 160
Scotland
administrative and borrowing code 174–5
county councils 154
development of borrowing provisions 192–3
early rates for road maintenance 47
limits on temporary borrowing 181, 183
loans funds provision 343, 344
reorganisation of local government structure 190
security for borrowing 369
stock issue 250–2
see also Edinburgh; Glasgow
security
and early Public Works Loan Commission loans 300
and local authority borrowing 159, 170–1, 192, 369
and 'temporary' borrowing 173, 256–7
problems of terminology 12, 52, 63, 117

Select Committee Reports
  local authority loans 157
  sinking funds 157
sewers rate 120–1
Sheffield
  controls on bill issues 274
  land fund 316
sheriff 4
  origin of term 18
shire 17, 20
  origin of term 18
  see also county
Short Loan & Mortgage Company Ltd 178
short-term borrowing, see temporary
    borrowing
short-term deposit 179
'sinking fund' 94, 104, 118–19, 123, 132–3,
    137, 150, 350
  and debt repayment 365
  and mortgage repayments 173–4
  reuse for new capital purposes 157, 339,
    343
stamp duty
  and borrowing 112, 187
  and deposit receipts 255, 256
  and money bills 267–8
  problems 187–9
statutes
  chronological listing 385–93
  on local government administration 33
stock 11, 54, 243
  'consolidated' 140–1, 142–3
  debenture 143, 147–8
  origin of term 241–2
  registration 244, 250
  Regulations 171, 248–50
  restrictions 184
Stock Exchange 139, 241, 243
  and negotiable bonds 291–2, 293
stock issue
  as a financial technique 139–40, 242–3,
    252–3
  early local government arrangements
    244–9
  in Scotland 250–2
  marketability 243–4
Sussex 24
Swansea
  and debenture stock issue 143

tallies 12, 241
tap-stocks 139, 243
taxation
  and money bills 265
  and temporary loans 373
  'local' 69
'temporary' borrowing 161, 163–4, 172–3,

176–7, 182, 192, 200–1, 254–7, 260,
    275, 304, 374, 380
  definition 179
  IMTA recommended procedures 258–9
  on open market 178
  restrictions on 181–2, 184, 186, 371
  ultra-short 177, 178–9, 180–1, 373
  see also temporary loan receipts
temporary loan receipts 218, 257–60
  and stamp duty 188–9, 257
  mortgages as security 257
'tithings' 24
toll-road system, see turnpike trusts
tolls
  for harbour maintenance 65–6
  for road maintenance 53–5, 56–7, 58–9,
    60–1
  market 74
  'mortgaging' 21, 212–13
  on bridges and piers 43, 65
Tonti, L. 232
tontines 80, 96–7
  for Poor Law borrowing 82, 84, 235–7
  private 231
  public 231–2, 232–4
  use in local government 234–9
transfers
  and duty 187–8
Treasury 14
  and development of bonds 186
  and local authority foreign currency
    borrowing 325–7
  and problems of short-term borrowing
    180–1
  and Public Works Loan Commission 302,
    312, 378
  and restrictions on local authority
    borrowing 177, 183, 193, 262, 275,
    303, 374, 378
  bills 261–2, 275
  controls on capital investments 196
  controls on local authority bonds 292–3
  controls on local authority capital bills
    270–1, 274–7
  'General Consent' for borrowing 184–5,
    292
Turnpike Acts 10, 50, 58–60
  and borrowing code 51, 60, 61–4, 331
  and early mortgaging 211–12, 213
turnpike roads 38, 46, 49–51
  and early mortgaging 211–12
turnpike trusts 4–5, 28, 38, 46, 49, 57, 58
  and financial system 51–2
  and Public Works Loan Commission
    loans 301
  and toll roads 50–1, 58–9, 60
  as 'local authorities' 49–50, 120